주한미군지위협정(SOFA)

서명 및 발효 11

주한미군지위협정(SOFA)

서명 및 발효 11

| 머리말

미국은 오래전부터 우리나라 외교에 있어서 가장 긴밀하고 실질적인 우호·협력관계를 맺어 온 나라다. 6·25전쟁 정전 협정이 체결된 후 북한의 재침을 막기 위한 대책으로서 1953년 11월 한미 상호방위조약이 체결되었다. 이는 미군이 한국에 주둔하는 법적 근거였고, 그렇게 주둔하게 된 미군의 시설, 구역, 사업, 용역, 출입국, 통관과 관세, 재판권 등 포괄적인 법적 지위를 규정하는 것이 바로 주한미군지위협정(SOFA)이다. 그러나 이와 관련한 협상은 계속된 난항을 겪으며 한미 상호방위조약이 체결로부터 10년이 훌쩍 넘은 1967년이 돼서야 정식 발효에 이를 수 있었다. 그럼에도 당시 미군 범죄에 대한 한국의 재판권은 심한 제약을 받았으며, 1980년대 후반 민주화 운동과 함께 미군 범죄 문제가 사회적 이슈로 떠오르자 협정을 개정해야 한다는 목소리가 커지게 되었다. 이에 1991년 2월 주한미군지위협정 1차 개정이 진행되었고, 이후에도 여러 사건이 발생하며 2001년 4월 2차 개정이 진행되어 현재에 이르고 있다.

본 총서는 외교부에서 작성하여 최근 공개한 주한미군지위협정(SOFA) 관련 자료를 담고 있다. 1953년 한미 상호방위조약 체결 이후부터 1967년 발효가 이뤄지기까지의 자료와 더불어, 이후 한미 합동위원회을 비롯해 민·형사재판권, 시설, 노무, 교통 등 각 분과위원회의 회의록과 운영 자료, 한국인 고용인 문제와 관련한 자료, 기타 관련 분쟁 자료 등을 포함해 총 42권으로 구성되었다. 전체 분량은 약 2만 2천여 쪽에 이른다.

2024년 3월
한국학술정보(주)

| 일러두기

· 본 총서에 실린 자료는 2022년 4월과 2023년 4월에 각각 공개한 외교문서 4,827권, 76만 여 쪽 가운데 일부를 발췌한 것이다.

· 각 권의 제목과 순서는 공개된 원본을 최대한 반영하였으나, 주제에 따라 일부는 적절히 변경하였다.

· 원본 자료는 A4 판형에 맞게 축소하거나 원본 비율을 유지한 채 A4 페이지 안에 삽입 하였다. 또한 현재 시점에선 공개되지 않아 '공란'이란 표기만 있는 페이지 역시 그대로 실었다.

· 외교부가 공개한 문서 각 권의 첫 페이지에는 '정리 보존 문서 목록'이란 이름으로 기록물 종류, 일자, 명칭, 간단한 내용 등의 정보가 수록되어 있으며, 이를 기준으로 0001번부터 번호가 매겨져 있다. 이는 삭제하지 않고 총서에 그대로 수록하였다.

· 보고서 내용에 관한 더 자세한 정보가 필요하다면, 외교부가 온라인상에 제공하는 『대한 민국 외교사료요약집』 1991년과 1992년 자료를 참조할 수 있다.

| 차례

정/리/보/존/문/서/목/록

기록물종류	문서-일반공문서철	등록번호	927 / 9600	등록일자	2006-07-27
분류번호	741.12	국가코드	US	주제	

문서철명	한.미국 간의 상호방위조약 제4조에 의한 시설과 구역 및 한국에서의 미국군대의 지위에 관한 협정 (SOFA) 전59권. 1966.7.9 서울에서 서명 : 1967.2.9 발효 (조약 232호) *원본

생산과	미주과/조약과	생산년도	1952 - 1967	보존기간	영구

당당과(그룹)	조약	조약 ·	서가번호	--

참조분류	

권차명	V.29 실무교섭회의. 제73-76차, 1965.4월

내용목차	1. 제73차 회의. 4.20 (p.2~57)
	2. 제74차 회의. 4.23 (p.58~129)
	3. 제75차 회의. 4.28 (p.130~166)
	4. 제76차 회의. 4.30 (p.167~249)
	
	* 일지 :
	1953.8.7 이승만 대통령-Dulles 미국 국무장관 공동성명
	                    - 상호방위조약 발효 후 군대지위협정 교섭 약속
	1954.12.2 정부, 주한 UN군의 관세업무협정 체결 제의
	1955.1월, 5월 미국, 제의 거절
	1955.4.28 정부, 군대지위협정 제의 (한국측 초안 제시)
	1957.9.10 Hurter 미국 국무차관 방한 시 각서 수교 (한국측 제의 수락 요구)
	1957.11.13, 26 정부, 개별 협정의 단계적 체결 제의
	1958.9.18 Dawling 주한미국대사, 형사재판관할권 협정 제외 조건으로 행정협정 체결 의사 전달
	1960.3.10 정부, 토지, 시설협정의 우선적 체결 강력 요구
	1961.4.10 장면 국무총리-McConaughy 주한미국대사 공동성명으로 교섭 개시 합의
	1961.4.15, 4.25 제1, 2차 한.미국 교섭회의 (서울)
	1962.3.12 정부, 교섭 재개 촉구 공한 송부
	1962.5.14 Burger 주한미국대사, 최규하 장관 면담 시 형사재판관할권 문제 제기 않는 조건으로
	                    교섭 재개 통고
	1962.9.6 한.미국 간 공동성명 발표 (9월 중 교섭 재개 합의)
	1962.9.20~ 제1-81차 실무 교섭회의 (서울)
	  1965.6.7
	1966.7.8 제82차 실무 교섭회의 (서울)
	1966.7.9 서명
	1967.2.9 발효 (조약 232호)

마/이/크/로/필/름/사/항

촬영연도	*롤 번호	화일 번호	후레임 번호	보관함 번호
2006-11-23	I-06-0069	06	1-249	

0001

1. 제73차 회의, 4.20

0002

SOFA NEGOTIATION

Agenda for the 73rd Session

10:30 April 20, 1965

1. Continuation of Discussions on:

   a. Labor Article

2. Other Business

3. Agenda and Date of the Next Meeting

4. Press Release

한·미국 간의 상호방위조약 제4조에 의한 시설과 구역 및 한국에서의 미국군대의 지위에 관한 협정(SOFA)
전59권. 1966.7.9 서울에서 서명 : 1967.2.9 발효(조약 232호) (V.29 실무교섭회의, 제73-76차, 1965.4월)

LABOR ARTICLE

(Draft Representation at 73rd Session)

1. With regard to the invited contractors, the Korean negotiators are ~~hesitant~~ *reluctant* to ~~an inclusion~~ *include* in the Article of the contractors, for we believe the contractors are apparently different from those military personnel. We are now elaborating ~~to formulate~~ the procedures under which the U.S. armed forces can deviate from the labor laws and regulations of the Republic of Korea. This sort of deviation derives from legal status, under international law, of the U.S. armed forces ~~a branch of the U.S. Government which deserves such rights as a sovereign state.~~ We fully concede to this, and, therefore, we have agreed to recognize immunities of the U.S. Government under international law, as shown in the Agreed Minute #1 of Korean draft. However, the private firms ~~with~~ whatever roles they play and with whomever contracts are made, could not be considered ~~tantamount to~~ government organs and could *not have* ~~not withhold~~ the same immunities and rights enjoyed by a state under international law. It is, therefore, our ~~established~~ view that the rights and obligations of private firms in connection with their employees shall be governed in a different *way* ~~manner~~; that is, to be subject to the legislation of the state where they *operate* ~~work~~. The Paragraph 1 of the Contractors Article ~~which we have already agreed upon~~ *was made upon our agreement* ~~stipulates to this effect~~. Nevertheless, we would reconsider the U.S. proposal upon receipt of a detailed information on categories and roles of invited contractors and of their Korean employees.

2. As regards the objection raised by the U.S. side at the previous session concerning the nationality of employees, the Korean negotiators would like to make it clear that it was not our intention ~~of that phrase~~ to cover those

6-1

0004

civilian components of the U.S. nationality. Therefore, the
Korean negotiators now amend the phrase to meet the U.S.
position, as follows:

"Such civilian personnel (other than members of the
civilian component) shall be natinnals of the Republic of
Korea.

3. Turning to the Paragraph 3 regarding the U.S.
phrase "to the extent not inconsistent with the provisions
of this article," the Korean side now accepts the inclusion
of the U.S. phrase in the paragraph 3.

As regards the phrase "military requirements of the
U.S. Armed Forces," the Korean side could not accept the
U.S. proposal and formula by which any deviation from conforming
with the Korean labor legislation could come under post-
review at the Joint Committee. In this respect, the U.S.
side predicted the contingent circumstances in which cases
there would be no time to have mutual discussions. However,
the Korean side does not understand the U.S. conception with
respect to the deviation from conditions of employment.
In our view, the conditions of employment such as wages,
work hours, leave days, dispute settlement procedures, etc.
could and should, be consolidated in advance of any circumstance. In the case of emergency such as hostilities or war,
the necessity of deviation from the Korean labor legislation
might arise according to the gravity of the situation. We
think this sort of deviation at the time of emergency should
be the object of mutual deliberation on the Agreement as a whole.
Therefore, it is the firm belief of the Korean negotiators
that our formula, as appeared in Para. 3 and Agreed Minute
#4, are well conceived to cover any situation we may normally
encounter. Why should we not cooperate in advance?

0005

4. With regard to resolution of employee grievances, provided for in Paragraph 4 of the Korean draft, the Korean negotiators accept the U.S. version.

As for ~~the~~ Paragraph 4(a) of U.S. draft concerning the right to strike, the Korean side is unable to accept the U.S. formula to restrain all Korean employees from exercising the right to strike, *on the grounds* ~~in light of the fact~~ that the Korean public officials (according to Article 29 of the Constitution) and civilian employees of the Korean armed forces are inhibited to do so. It is obvious that inasmuch as the Korean employees of U.S. armed forces are *(Para 2)* not the Korean public officials, the Article 29 of the Constitution cannot be applied. Among the public officials, there are so many government employees who could exercise the right to strike pursuant to Article 27 of the Public Officials Service Decree. As to the civilian employees of the Korean armed forces, no provisions are designed to prohibit the strike by them, except the civilian components of the armed forces in accordance with Article 30(b) of the Personnel Management Law of Armed Forces Civilian Components. ~~We would like to inquire whether there is any Korean employee~~ /Inasmuch as the Korean employees are not civilian components, ~~who is treated as civilian components,~~ we are unable to ask them to act, or be treated, as civilian component.

According to the statement of U.S. negotiators, the Korean employee signed the so-called "affidavit", and the Labor Unions pledged in 1961, in effect, not to engage in strikes. The Korean Government cannot take such measures as reasonable and legal, according to the spirit laid down in the relevant Korean labor legislation, e.g. Article 39 of Labor Union Law. Moreover, we are doubtful whether such measures taken against the interests of the employees have

6-3

0006 ~~0007~~

been possibly and effectively enforced in the past.

For the consideration of U.S. side, we would like to
~~keep in mind the fact~~ that according to the Korean legal
system, ~~the right to strike is granted to~~ every employee *who
is not granted to strike is denied even one right to be*
~~unless he is precluded from~~ organizing or being a member
of ~~collective~~ union. The relevant Korean laws and regulations
stipulate the prohibit of collective actions by certain
officials in the Government posts including members of civilian
component. In other words, inasmuch as there is labor union,
there is the right to strike. Therefore, we could not
understand the U.S. proposition that while recognizing
the existence of labor unions, the right to strike should be
exterminated.

We consider the right to strike would not be hinderance
to U.St.armed forces *who are* faithful and good employers. We recall
that the U.S. negotiators pledged to be good employers in
relation with their Korean employees on many occasions.
We, and the Korean employees, are well aware that the right
to strike is one of the fundamental rights of workers,
which they have gained through long history of hardships
and they have been enjoying up to date. In summary, the
Korean negotiators are not in a position to ~~ask them to~~ *deny*
~~sacrifice such a right and to concede any proposition to~~
~~deprive them of such a fundamental right in any manner.~~
Therefore, we earnestly ~~ask~~ *request* again the U.S. side ~~for~~ *to*
~~accepting~~ *accept* the Korean formula.

annihilate
*to ~~deny~~ the fundamental rights of workers simply
because they are employed by the U.S armed
forces.*

한·미국 간의 상호방위조약 제4조에 의한 시설과 구역 및 한국에서의 미국군대의 지위에 관한 협정(SOFA)
전59권. 1966.7.9 서울에서 서명 : 1967.2.9 발효(조약 232호) (V.29 실무교섭회의, 제73-76차, 1965.4월)   13

5. Turning to the representation made at 73rd session, the U.S. negotiators ~~discussed on topics of~~ *expressed their views on* the availability of USFK Korean employees at the time of emergency and the right of USFK to terminate employment.

With regard to the availability of Korean employees, both sides had fully taken their views and explained their positions. Therefore, we would not repeat them again, but we would like to add here one again our assurances to the U.S. side that the Korean employees essential for the U.S. force will be available in an emergency to continue their works if the agreement on the list, including the number, types, and skills of employees is made through mutual consultation. The word "may be deferred" is absolutely based on the wordings in the provisions of relevant Korean laws. ~~The~~ *agreed* ~~essential Korean employees will be available to USFK without let or hinderance.~~ As we stated at the previous session, you ~~are~~ *can* rest assured that the Korean skilled employees essential in emergency *, if so agreed, made* will be available *without let or hinderance, if it is so* ~~to the fullest extent through mutual cooperation.~~ *Without ~~claims~~ impediments.*

6. As for the right of USFK to terminate Korean employees, the Korean side would like to point out that any employer may terminate employment with justifiable reason under the relevant Korean labor legislation. May I draw your attention to ~~the~~ Paragraph 2 of the Article which stipulates that "the employers may .... administer their personnel". We understand the word "administer" refers to all personnel management process from recruitment to seperation of employment, as was explained by Mr. Reed at 65th session. We take this phrase for granted that USFK has the right to terminate employment of their personnel. You are not precluded to exercise your right to terminate your employees under any provisions of this article and of Korean laws if it is done with justifiable *reason* ~~cause~~

0008

For example, whenever you are ~~going to reduce in~~ *about to reduce* ~~force a~~ certain member of employees owing to the budgetary deduction, ~~you have a reason. In this case,~~ why won't you refer this matter to the Joint Committee for consultation. As is clearly stated in ~~para 1~~ *Minute #4* the ~~Agreement~~, the Korean side will give due consideration to such requirements *for y* ~~you~~ have justifiable cause. It has been the established ~~tradition~~ *practice* that whenever you were to reduce ~~in force~~ the employees, you have referred the matter to the relevant Korean authorities. ~~Why won't you continue to have amicable cooperation between us until after the Agreement is made.~~

For this reason, we think you have no difficulty to terminate employment with justifiable reason under normal condition, and with mutual consultation under abnormal condition such as ~~in case of reduction in force or of emergency~~ *in time of emergency or inevitable reduction of employees*. We believe this formula precribed in the Korean draft will fully meet, ~~at any time, satisfaction of~~ such *US* requirements ~~as U.S. side has been seeking~~. Therefore, we proposed to delete from the Article the second sentence of Agreed Minute #2 of U.S. draft, which would ~~make overlaping~~ *overlap* the agreed provisions of Para. 2.

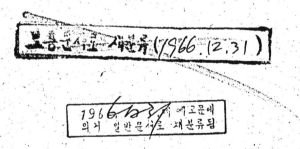

한·미국 간의 상호방위조약 제4조에 의한 시설과 구역 및 한국에서의 미국군대의 지위에 관한 협정(SOFA)
전59권. 1966.7.9 서울에서 서명 : 1967.2.9 발효(조약 232호) (V.29 실무교섭회의, 제73-76차, 1965.4월)   15

LABOR ARTICLE

(Draft Representation at 73rd Session)

1965.4.2

1. With regard to the invited contractors, the Korean negotiators are reluctant to include in the Article of the contractors, for we believe the contractors are apparently different from those military personnel. We are now elaborating the procedures under which the U.S. armed forces can deviate from the labor laws and regulations of the Republic of Korea. This sort of deviation derives from legal status of the U.S. armed forces under international law. Therefore, we have agreed to recognize immunities of the U.S. Government under international law, as shown in the Agreed Minute #1 of Korean draft. However, the private firms, whatever roles they play and with whomever contracts are made, could not be considered government organs and could not have the same immunities and rights enjoyed by a state *organ* under international law. It is, therefore, our view that the rights and obligations of private firms in connection with their employees shall be governed in a different way; that is, to be subject to the legislation of the state where they operate. Paragraph 1 of the Contractors Article was made upon our agreement. Nevertheless, we would reconsider the U.S. proposal *more in detail and would take our views* ~~upon receipt of a detailed~~ *at a later meeting. We ask you further* information on categories and roles of invited contractors and of their Korean employees.

2. As regards the objection raised by the U.S. side at the previous session concerning the nationality of employees, the Korean negotiators would like to make it clear that it was not our intention to cover those civilian components of the U.S. nationality in that phrase.

0010

Therefore, the Korean negotiators now amend the phrase to
meet the U.S. position, as follows:

"Such civilian personnel (other than members of the
civilian component) shall be nationals of the Republic of
Korea.

3. Turning to Paragraph 3 regarding the U.S. phrase
"to the extent not inconsistent with the provisions of this
article," the Korean side accepts the inclusion of the U.S.
phrase in paragraph 3.

As regards the phrase "military requirements of the
U.S. Armed Forces," the Korean side could not accept the
U.S. proposal and formula by which any deviation from
conforming with the Korean labor legislation could come
under post-review at the Joint Committee. In this respect,
the U.S. side predicted the contingent circumstances in
which cases there would be no time to have mutual discussions.
However, the Korean side does not understand the U.S. conception with respect to the deviation from conditions of
employment. In our view, the conditions of employment such
as wages, work hours, leave days, dispute settlement
procedures, etc., could and should, be consolidated in advance
of any circumstance. In the case of emergency such as
hostilities or war, the necessity of deviation from the
Korean labor legislation might arise according to the gravity
of the situation. We think this sort of deviation at the
time of emergency should be the object of mutual deliberation.
Therefore, it is the firm belief of the Korean negotiators
that our formula, as appeared in Para 3 and Agreed Minute
#4, are well conceived to cover any situation we may normally
encounter. Why should we not cooperate in advance?

0011

4. With regard to resolution of employee grievances, provided for in Paragraph 4 of the Korean draft, the Korean negotiators accept the U.S. version.

As for Paragraph 4(a) of U.S. draft concerning the right to strike, the Korean side is unable to accept the U.S. formula to restrain all Korean employees from exercising the right to strike, on the grounds that the Korean public officials (according to Article 29 of the Constitution) and civilian employees of the Korean armed forces are inhibited to do so. It is obvious that inasmuch as the Korean employees of U.S. armed forces are not the Korean public officials, the Para. 2 of Article 29 of the Constitution cannot be applied. Among the public officials, there are so many government employees who could exercise the right to strike pursuant to Article 27 of the Public Officials Service Decree. As to the civilian employees of the Korean armed forces, no provisions are designed to prohibit the strike by them, except the civilian components of the armed forces in accordance with Article 30(b) of the Personnel Management Law of Armed Forces Civilian Components. Inasmuch as the Korean employees are not civilian components, we are unable to ask them to act, or be treated, as civilian component.

According to the statement of U.S. negotiators, the Korean employee signed the so-called "affidavit", and the Labor Unions pledged in 1961, in effect, not to engage in strikes. The Korean Government cannot take such measures as reasonable and legal, according to the spirit laid down in the relevant Korean labor legislation, e.g. Article 39 of Labor Union Law. Moreover, we are doubtful whether such measures taken against the interests of the employees have been possibly and effectively enforced in the past.

0012

We consider the right to strike would not be hinderance to U.S. armed forces who are faithful and good employers. We recall that the U.S. negotiators pledged to be good employers in relation with their Korean employees on many occasions. We, and the Korean employees, are well aware that the right to strike is one of the fundamental rights of workers, which they have gained through long history of hardships and they have been enjoying up to date. In summary, the Korean negotiators are not in a position to annihilate the fundamental rights of workers simply because they are employed by the U.S. armed forces. Therefore, we earnestly request again the U.S. side to accept the Korean formula.

5. Turning to the representation made at 73rd session, the U.S. negotiators expressed their views on the availability of USFK Korean employees at the time of emergency and the right of USFK to terminate employment.

With regard to the availability of Korean employees, both sides had fully taken their views and explained their positions. Therefore, we would not repeat them again, but we would like to add here once again our assurances to the U.S. side that the Korean employees essential for the U.S. force will be available in an emergency to continue their works if the agreement on the list, including the number, types, and skills of employees is made through mutual consultation. The word "may be deferred" is absolutely based on the wordings in the provisions of relevant Korean laws. As we stated at the previous session, you can rest assured that the Korean skilled employees essential in emergency, if so agreed, will be made available without impediments.

한·미국 간의 상호방위조약 제4조에 의한 시설과 구역 및 한국에서의 미국군대의 지위에 관한 협정(SOFA)
전59권. 1966.7.9 서울에서 서명 : 1967.2.9 발효(조약 232호) (V.29 실무교섭회의, 제73-76차, 1965.4월)   19

6. As for the right of USFK to terminate Korean employees, the Korean side would like to point out that any employer may terminate employment with justifiable reason under the relevant Korean labor legislation. May I draw your attention to Paragraph 2 of the Article which stipulates that "the employers may ... administer their personnel.' We understand the word "administer" refers to all personnel management process from recruitment to seperation of employment, as was explained by Mr. Reed at 65th session. We take this phrase for granted that USFK has the right to terminate employment of their personnel. You are not precluded to exercise your right to terminate your employees under any provisions of this article and of Korean laws if it is done with justifiable reason.

For example, whenever you are about to reduce in force certain member of employees owing to the budgetary deduction, why won't you refer this matter to the Joint Committee for consultation. As is clearly stated in the Agreed Minute #4, the Korean side will give due consideration to such requirements you have justifiable cause. It has been the established practice that when you were to reduce in force the employees, you have referred the matter to the relevant Korean authorities.

For this reason, we think you have no difficulty to terminate employment with justifiable reason under normal condition, and with mutual consultation under abnormal condition such as in time of emergency and inevitable reduction of employees. We believe this formula precribed in the Korean draft will fully meet the such U.S. requirements. Therefore, we proposed to delete from the Article the second sentence of Agreed Minute #2 of U.S. draft, which would overlap the agreed provisions of Para. 2.

0014

Provisions of Laws and Relations referred to in the paper

1. Article 29, Constitution

   (1) Workers shall have the right of independent associa-
       tion, collective bargaining and collective action
       for the purpose of improving their working conditions.

   (2) The right of association, collective bargaining,
       and collective action shall not be accorded to the
       workers who are public officials except for those
       authorized by the provisions of law.

2. Article 66, Public Officials Law

   Public officials shall not engage in labor movements
   or any other collective action than in accomplishment
   of public service, except those who are engaging actually
   in labor works to be otherwise authorized by the
   Presidential Decree.

3. Article 27, Public Officials Service Decree (No. 1604,
   Jan. 8, 1964, as amended)

   Public officials engaging actually in labor works
   mentioned in the Article 66 of the Law refers to those
   serving at such working places of organizations as
   provided for in the annexed list, except those who are
   in charge of general affairs, personnel, supplies,
   accounting, confidential matters, and supervisory
   service of workers.

   Annex

   1. Ministry of Transportation

   2. Ministry of Communications

   3. Office of Monopoly

   4. National Medical Centre.

2018   0015

4. Article 30(b), Personnel Management Law of Armed Forces Civilian Components

Members of Armed Forces Civilian Components shall not engage in labor movements or any other collective action.

5. Article 39, Labor Union Law

An employer shall not commit an act falling under the category of any of the following items (hereinafter to as "unjust act of labor").

1. An act dismissing a laborer or an act discriminating against a laborer on the ground that the laborer has joined or tried to join a labor union, or has attempted to organize a labor union, or has done a justifiable act for the operation of a labor union;

2. An act fixing a condition for employment that a laborer does not join, or withdraws from, a specific labor union, or an act fixing a condition for employment that the laborer become a member of a specific labor union. However, the provision of this item shall not be applied to the conclusion of a collective agreement which makes it a condition for employment that the laborer become a member of a labor union, in case the labor union represents two thirds or more of the laborers engaged in the workshop.

3. An act rejecting or neglecting, without justifiable reasons, conclusion of a collective agreement or any other collective negotiations with the representative of a labor union or with the person entrusted by a labor union.

4. An act controlling, or interfering with the laborers in the formation or operation of a labor union, and an act subsidizing the expenses for operation of a labor union. However, it shall be justifiable that

0016

the employer allow the laborer to conduct negotiations or bargaining with the employer during the labor hours, and that the employer donate welfare funds or fund for prevention of relief from economic troubles and other disasters, or that the employer offer an office building on the minimum scale for the labor union.

5. An act dismissing a laborer or an act discriminating against disadvantages to a laborer on the ground that the laborer has joined a collective action which is justifiable, that the laborer has reported or made a testimony to the Labor Committee that the employer violate the provision of this article, or that the laborer has presented the evidence of violation to the administrative office.

0017

3. 勞務調達

順	項目	美國案	韓國案	解決方案
1.	勞務調達條項의 適用 項의 適用 範圍 (1) 雇傭主 (2) 雇用人	(1) 美國軍隊 非戰鬪出稼商 軍契約者 (2) 美軍屬이 아닌 雇傭人 韓國防務師団(KSC)와 但 韓國防務 家事使用人을 除外.	(1) 美國軍隊, 非戰鬪出稼商 (2) 美国国籍을 가진 民間人	(1) 美國軍隊非戰鬪出稼商 軍契約者 (2) 美軍屬이 아닌 韓國国籍을 가진 民間人
2.	勞動條件의 適用範囲	本條項의 規定과 美國軍의 軍事上 必要에 相反되지 않는 限 勞動法 慣例와 慣例를 遵守	別途合意되지 않는 限 勞動令을 遵守, 但 軍事上 必要로 韓國法을 遵守하기 못할 때 軍補에 合同委員會에서 合意	本條項의 規定에 相反되지 않거나 別途合意되지 않는 限 勞動令을 遵守 단, 但, 美軍이 軍事上 必要로 韓國法을 遵守하기 못할 時 合同委員會에서 合意

項目	美國案	韓國案	解決方案
3. 罷業權의 行使	韓國軍雇傭人과 同一하게 罷業權을 行使 (罷業이 不可能)	韓國法令에 依한 罷業權을 承認	(1) 合同委員會에서 罷業行使를 禁止할 計者를 際外하고 罷業行使 (2) 上記案이 反諮되지 않을 境遇 間接採備制度를 再採果
4. 雇傭人의 兵役義務	美軍業務遂行에 不可缺한 技術者에 對하니 名單을 提出하며 兵役義務를 實際하여야 한다.	事前에 要求하면 美軍業務遂行에 不可缺한 技術者에 對하여 兵役義務를 延期할 수 있다.	美軍業務遂行에 不可缺한 技術者에 對한 計 事前에 要求하면 軍前에 兵役義務를 延期한다
5. 紛爭解決節次	紛爭解決期間中 正常業務를 遂行하는 行務不評	紛爭解決期間中 爭動斤이 附된 날로부터 定草하여 爭議	(1) 紛爭解決期間中 合同委員會의 同附된 날로부터 定草하며 爭議는 第12條

題目	美國案	解決方案
	法 第14條에 規定된 冷却期間中 正常業務를 行하는 行爲 不許	이 規定되어 冷却期間中 正常業務를 行하는 行爲를 不許 (2) 上記 3의 /案이 妥結되지 않을때에는 韓國政府에 依하여 解決될 것을 提案

~53~

STATUS OF FORCES NEGOTIATIONS:
SUBJECT:
PLACE:
DATE:
PARTICIPANTS:

73rd Meeting
Labor Article
Ministry of Foreign Affairs
April 20, 1965

Republic of Korea

CHANG Sang-mun
HO Sung-chung
KIM Ki-cho
HWANG Yong-chae
PAK Won-chol
YI Kun-pal (Interpreter)

United States

Philip C. Habib
Brig. Gen. Carroll H. Dunn, USA
Col. Allan G. Pixton, USA
Capt. George Hagerman, USN
Col. Kenneth C. Crawford, USA
Robert A. Kinney
Benjamin A. Fleck
Jack Friedman
Maj. Alton Harvey, USA
David Y. C. Lee (Interpreter)

Ogden Reed (Observer)
G. W. Flowers (Observer)

1. Mr. Habib opened the meeting by introducing two new members of the US negotiating team: Colonel Allan G. Pixton, replacing Colonel Smigelow, and Captain George Hagerman, replacing Captain Wayne. Mr. Chang welcomed Colonel Pixton and Captain Hagerman to the negotiations on behalf of the Korean negotiators.

2. T king up the Labor Article, Mr. Habib tabled a revised draft of the entire article. He stated that the US negotiators were tabling this draft, in a spirit of compromise, in order to reach early full agreement on this article. As revised, the US draft would provide continued fair and equitable treatment for Korean employees of the US armed forces, as well as sound and just procedures for the resolution of labor grievances and disputes. Mr. Habib said he would discuss the changes in the draft on a paragraph by paragraph basis. The principal revisions related to Paragraphs 3, 4, 5 and their Agreed Minutes.

3. Paragraph 1 and related Agreed Minute #1 - In Paragraph 1, Mr. Habib said, the word "paramilitary" had been added to differentiate clearly the paramilitary Korean Service Corps from the direct hire employees of the US armed forces covered by this article. The US armed forces plan to discuss the status of the Korean Service
/Corps,

CONFIDENTIAL

Corps, which is commanded by ROK Army officers on active duty and in reserve (and which has operated outside ROK labor laws and courts) directly with authorities in the Ministry of National Defense. In order to expedite agreement regarding the language relative to domestic servants, the US negotiators had deleted the second sentence of the previous draft of Agreed Minute #1, subject to an understanding that the present situation with regard to domestics employed by individual members of the US armed forces and civilian component shall continue. As the Korean negotiators were aware, Mr. Habib continued, individual members of the United States armed forces, civilian component, and dependents hire and pay domestic servants directly, subject only to USFK security and health checks and general guidance. Applicable Korean laws would govern employment of such domestics.

4. Paragraph 2 - Mr. Habib noted that the US and Korean negotiators are in agreement regarding Paragraph 2, except for minor differences of wording. The US negotiators concurred in the Korean proposal to substitute the word "such" for the word "available" in the second sentence, subject to Korean understanding that we cannot furnish information not available to us as part of our normal operating procedure. The US negotiators foresee no problems in supplying the information desired by the Korean authorities, as indicated in Paragraph 20 of the Agreed Joint Summary of the 46th negotiating meeting.

5. Paragraph 3 and related Agreed Minute #5 - Mr. Habib stated that the US negotiators believe that they are in essential agreement with the Korean negotiators regarding Paragraph 3, except for possible differences in interpretations of the phrase "military requirements". In order to be responsive to the Korean desire for review and consideration by the Joint Committee of situations in which the US armed forces cannot conform to the ROK labor legislation because of military requirements, the US negotiators were tabling a new Agreed Minute #5. The US negotiators believe, Mr. Habib continued, that the US armed forces only rarely, if ever, will not be able to conform to ROK labor legislation applicable under this Article, except in emergency situations. The new Agreed Minute #5 would provide that when the US armed forces cannot conform to ROK labor legislation on account of military requirements, the matter shall be reported, in advance whenever possible, to the Joint Committee for its consideration and review. The US negotiators believe that the Agreed Minute demonstrates the good faith of the US armed forces, in pledging to conform to the ROK labor laws, customs, and practices, to the extent not inconsistent with the provisions of this article, and to agree to this type of Joint Committee consideration of possible situations in which military requirements may be at variance with ROK labor legislation. In this regard, the ROK negotiators had mentioned the possibility that in an emergency the provisions of the Labor Article might be suspended. The US negotiators believe that the new US language is the best way to take care of unforeseeable situations in which military necessity may require non-conformance to ROK labor legislation.

/6. Paragraph 4

6. **Paragraph 4** - Mr. Habib stated that the US negotiators were tabling a new Paragraph 4 which sets forth clearly the positive US commitments to be a good employer, pursuing enlightened policies and procedures relating to employer-employee relationships. Subparagraph (a) would provide that employers will maintain procedures designed to assure the just and timely resolution of employee grievances. Subparagraph (b) would provide the employees the right to organize and join a union. Under its terms, membership or non-membership in such groups would not be a factor in employment or in other actions affecting employees. Subparagraph (c) would assure recognized unions the right of consultation with US military authorities. Such labor-management consultations are currently an established part of the US armed forces' relations with the recognized union.

7. Subparagraph (d) of Paragraph 4, Mr. Habib continued, incorporates much of the previously tabled Agreed Minute #5, setting forth procedures for settling labor disputes which cannot be settled by use of established USFK procedures. These procedures closely parallel the previously-tabled Korean proposals, and provide that disputes which cannot be settled by use of USFK procedures shall be referred to the ROK Office of Labor Affairs for conciliation. If a dispute cannot be settled by the Office of Labor Affairs, it would be referred to the Joint Committee, which might refer it to a Labor Sub-Committee or to a specially designated committee or take it under consideration directly. The Joint Committee would be the final arbiter of any such labor disputes. The US and Korean negotiators were in agreement that its decisions shall be binding upon employers, employees, and the union.

8. As stated in subparagraph (e) of Paragraph 4, Mr. Habib continued, the US negotiators firmly maintain that a Korean working for the US armed forces in the joint US-ROK defense effort shall be subject to the same legal provisions concerning strikes and other work stoppages as an employee in a comparable position in the employment of the armed forces of the Republic of Korea. Both categories of Korean employees of our two governments are working directly in the defense of their country. The US negotiators believe firmly in the principle that our employees must be subject to the same ROK legal provisions with regard to strikes or work stoppages as comparable employees working for the ROK armed forces. This is a basic and unchanging US position, which is related directly to the effectiveness of the US armed forces in the defense of the Republic of Korea.

9. **Paragraph 5** - Mr. Habib pointed out that Paragraph 5 of both drafts deals with the important topic of the availability of essential Korean employees of the US armed forces for their assigned defense tasks in time of emergency. The newly-tabled Paragraph 5 of the US draft had been patterned after the language of the Korean draft tabled at the 69th negotiating session. It is almost identical with the Korean Paragraph 5 except for the use of the word "shall" instead of "may" in subparagraph

/(b). The

CONFIDENTIAL

한·미국 간의 상호방위조약 제4조에 의한 시설과 구역 및 한국에서의 미국군대의 지위에 관한 협정(SOFA)
전59권. 1966.7.9 서울에서 서명 : 1967.2.9 발효(조약 232호) (V.29 실무교섭회의, 제73-76차, 1965.4월)   29

(b). The use of the word "shall" would assure US and Korean defense planners that in time of emergency, essential employees of the US armed forces in Korea would be available to continue to perform their essential roles during the emergency. USFK requirements for Korean manpower, Mr. Habib continued, are very small in comparison to Korean manpower availabilities. On the other hand, the role of the US forces in a war emergency in the Republic of Korea would be of an extremely important and probably decisive nature. Their essential civilian employees are basic to the effectiveness of the US armed forces. Therefore, the US negotiators wished to emphasize that deferment of essential USFK personnel in advance must be provided for. This vital matter cannot be left to consideration and decision in time of emergency. There would be a great deal of paper work in listing and processing essential employees who would be deferred. This work must be accomplished to our mutual satisfaction before the emergency arises, if implementation is to be effective. The US negotiators believe that the details can be worked out in consultation between the US armed forces and officials of the Ministry of National Defense in advance, to the mutual satisfaction of both parties.

10. Mr. Habib noted that the Agreed Minutes in the new US draft had been renumbered so that they now appear in the same order as the paragraphs to which they refer.

11. Mr. Habib stated that the revised US draft was the result of many hours of discussion of this Article by both sides over the past 15 months. The US negotiators urged early acceptance of the revised draft by the Korean negotiators. The US negotiators believe that it fully protects the legitimate rights and interests of Korean employees of the US armed forces and, at the same time, is consistent with joint US-ROK defense requirements.

12. Mr. Chang replied that the Korean negotiators appreciated the compromising spirit in which the US negotiators had presented their revised draft in the hope for full agreement as soon as possible. The Korean negotiators would carefully consider the US draft and respond in a few days. However, the Korean negotiators believed that considerable differences still existed between the positions of the two sides. They wished, therefore, to make some preliminary comments to indicate the basic Korean position.

13. With regard to Paragraph 1, Mr. Chang said the Korean negotiators still wished to settle the question of the Korean Service Corps outside the framework of the SOFA negotiations, since the US negotiators had insisted that the KSC is a semi-military or paramilitary organization, while the Korean negotiators had maintained otherwise and agreement on the question was not foreseeable.

/14. With

CONFIDENTIAL

14. With regard to subparagraphs (a), (b), and (c) of Paragraph 4, Mr. Chang recalled that the US negotiators had stated that the US armed forces will conform to ROK labor laws to the maximum extent possible. The Korean negotiators believe, therefore, that the detailed provisions set forth in these subparagraphs were unnecessary. However, they had no objection if the US negotiators felt it necessary to include them, subject to agreement on the other outstanding problems of the Labor Article.

15. Regarding Paragraph 4(e), which had to do with the right to strike, Mr. Chang said the Korean negotiators believed that if they accepted the US language, the Government of the Republic of Korea would be obliged to enact a law prohibiting the employees of the US armed forces from resorting to strikes. The Korean negotiators doubted that the language of the US draft was in accordance with ROK labor legislation.

16. Regarding Paragraph 5(b), Mr. Chang noted two main points. First, employees shall be deferred on the request of the US armed forces. Secondly, a list of essential employees is to be furnished in advance. The US proposal did not appear to provide for the mutual satisfaction desired by the Korean negotiators. If they accepted the US language, the ROK authorities would have to defer everyone whose name appeared on the list furnished in advance. They believed that the ROK authorities should have discretion, in consultation with the US armed forces, to decide who would be deferred.

17. Mr. Habib pointed out that what the Korean negotiators wanted was implied in the US language. The US negotiators believed that there would be mutual satisfaction, since there must be agreement on the attainment of essential skills by the employees whose names would appear on the list furnished by the US armed forces. The Joint Committee would be the mechanism for attaining mutual satisfaction. If the Korean authorities questioned that any person named on the list had actually attained the required skills, they could raise the question in the Joint Committee.

18. Mr. Chang said the Korean negotiators still felt that the language regarding this question could be more specific. He said they would propose such language.

19. Mr. Chang noted that the US negotiators had modified the language of Agreed Minute #5, by providing for notification "in advance whenever possible". The phrase "whenever possible" should be omitted, however, since the Korean negotiators believed that it would always be possible to report in advance. Furthermore, if the US armed forces found that they could not conform to the ROK labor laws, they should always refer the matter to the Joint Committee in advance.

20. Mr. Habib replied that if it is always possible to report in advance, then the Korean position was met by the US language and no problem existed. The US armed forces did not intend this provision to be a means of avoiding conformity to the Korean labor laws. They did believe, however, that in times of emergency it might not always be possible to notify the Joint Committee in advance of non-conformity. There had to be some qualifying phrase; otherwise the provision would be unreasonable. Mr. Chang

CONFIDENTIAL

21. Mr. Chang said he wished to close his preliminary remarks by stating that the Korean negotiators noted and appreciated the sincerity of the US negotiators in submitting their revised draft.

22. Mr. Habib said that he wished to reply briefly to Mr. Chang's comments regarding Paragraph 4(e). The US negotiators wished to reiterate that neither the US armed forces nor the ROK armed forces are ordinary employers. The phraseology of the revised US draft of this subparagraph had been carefully chosen from the standpoint of the Korean requirements as well as those of the US armed forces. The language is not unreasonable, given the unusual nature of the employers. Neither employer is an ordinary business enterprise. They are not in business to make money but to defend the Republic of Korea.

23. Regarding Paragraph 1, Mr. Habib pointed out that in revising the language, the US negotiators had done exactly what the Korean negotiators had desired - they had excluded members of the Korean Service Corps from the definition of employees and, therefore, from the coverage provided by this article. It appeared that both sides were substantially in agreement regarding this issue.

24. It was agreed that the Korean negotiators would call the next meeting as soon as they were prepared to comment in detail on the US draft.

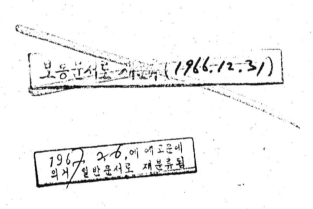

보통문서로재분류 (1966.12.31)

1967. 2.6, 에 예고문에
의거 일반문서로 재분류됨

Revised Korean Draft of Labor Procurement Article
(The underlined parts are modifications)

1. In this Article the expression

 (a) "employer" refers to the United States Armed Forces (including non-appropriated fund activities) and the persons referred to in the first paragraph of Article ___ .

 (b) "employee" refers to any civilian personnel of nationals of the Republic of Korea (other than a member of the civilian component of the United States armed forces) employed by an employer, ~~except a domestic employed by an individual member of the United States armed forces, civilian component or dependent thereof.~~

2. The employers may recruit, employ and administer their personnel. Recruitment services of the Government of the Republic of Korea shall be utilized to the maximum extent practicable. In case employers accomplish direct recruitment of employees, the United States armed forces shall provide such relevant information as may be required for labor administration to the Office of Labor Affairs of the Republic of Korea.

3. To the extent not inconsistent with the provisions of this Article or except as amy otherwise be mutually agreed, the conditions of employment and work, such as those relating to wages and supplementary payments, the conditions for the protection and welfare of employees, compensations, and the rights of employees, concerning labor relations shall conform with those laid down by the legislation of the Republic of Korea.

4. (a) An employee shall have the right to strike under the relevant provisions of Korean labor legislation, except such employees as are prohibited ~~who is~~ otherwise ~~inhibited~~ to exercise the right to strike by the Joint Committee.

 (b) Employers will ~~shall~~ maintain procedures designed to assure the just and timely resolution of employee grievances.

0027

5. (a) Should the Republic of Korea adopt measures allocating labor, the United States Armed Forces shall be accorded allocation privileges no less favorable than those enjoyed by the Armed Forces of the Republic of Korea.

(b) In the event of a national emergency such as war, hostilities, or other imminent situations, the employees who have acquired skills essential to the mission of the United States Armed Forces will, upon request of the United States Armed Forces, be deferred from Republic of Korea military service or other compulsory services. The United States Armed Forces shall in advance furnish to the Republic of Korea lists of those employees deemed essential.

6. Members of the civilian component shall not be subject to Korean laws or regulations with respect to their terms and conditions of employment.

AGREED MINUTES

1. The Undertaking of the United States to conform to the labor legislation of the Republic of Korea does not imply any waiver by the United States Government of its immunities under international law.

2. Employers shall withhold from the pay of their employees, and pay over to the Government of the Republic of Korea, withholdings required by the imcome tax legislation of the Republic of Korea.

3. It is understood that the Government of the Republic of Korea shall be reimbursed for direct costs incurred in providing assistance pursuant to Paragraph 2.

4. In case where it is impossible for the employers to conform, on account of the military requirements of the United States Armed Forces, with the Korean labor legislation under the provisions of Paragraph 3, the matter shall be referred to the Joint Committee for mutual agreement. The Republic of Korea will give due consideration to the military requirements of the United States Armed Forces.

0028

5. With regard to any dispute between the employers and any employees or labor unions which cannot be settled through the use of existing procedures of the United States Armed Forces, settlement shall be accomplished in the following manner:

(a) The dispute shall be referred to the Office of Labor Affairs of the Republic of Korea for conciliation.

(b) In the event that the dispute is not settled by the procedures described in (a) above, the dispute shall be referred to a special committee designated by the Joint Committee for further conciliation efforts.

(c) In the event that the dispute is not settled by the procedures outlined above, the Joint Committee will resolve the dispute. The decisions of the Joint Committee shall be binding.

(d) Neither employee organizations nor employees shall engage in any practices disruptive of normal work requirements unless the cooling-off period set forth in Article 14 of the Korean Labor Dispute Law has elapsed after the dispute is referred to the ~~Office of Labor Affairs~~ Joint Committee mentioned in (b) ~~(a)~~ above.

(e) Failure of any employee organization or employee to abide by the decision of the Joint Committee on any dispute, or engaging in practices disruptive of normal work requirements in violation of the provisions of Paragraph (d) above, shall be considered cause for the depriviation of the rights and protection accorded by the relevant laws of the Republic of Korea.

한·미국 간의 상호방위조약 제4조에 의한 시설과 구역 및 한국에서의 미국군대의 지위에 관한 협정(SOFA)
전59권. 1966.7.9 서울에서 서명 : 1967.2.9 발효(조약 232호) (V.29 실무교섭회의, 제73-76차, 1965.4월) 35

Labor Article

(Underlining indicates changes from U.S. draft of the Labor
Article tabled on December 23, 1964)

1. In this Article the expression:

    (a) "employer" refers to the United States Armed Forces (including
nonappropriated fund activities) and the persons referred to in the first paragraph of Article (   ).

    (b) "employee" refers to any civilian (other than a member of the
civilian component) employed by an employer, except (1) a member of the
paramilitary Korean Service Corps and (2) a domestic employed by an individual
member of the United States Armed Forces, civilian component or dependent
thereof.

2. Employers may recruit, employ and administer their personnel.
Recruitment services of the Government of the Republic of Korea will be
utilized ~~insofar as is~~ *to the maximum extent* practicable. In case employers accomplish direct
recruitment of employees, employers will provide such relevant
information as may be required for labor administration to the *Office of*
Labor Affairs of the Republic of Korea.

3. To the extent not inconsistent with the provisions of this
except as may otherwise be mutually agreed,
article or the military requirements of the United States Armed Forces,
the conditions of employment, compensation, and labor-management
practices established by the United States Armed Forces for their
employees will conform with the labor *legistlation of RoK* ~~laws, customs and practices of the~~
~~Republic of Korea.~~

4. (a) Employers will maintain procedures designed to assure
the just and timely resolution of employee grievances.

0030

(L-1)

(b) An employee may voluntarily organize and join a union or other employee group whose objectives are not inimical to the interests of the United States. Membership or non-membership in such groups shall not be a factor in employment or other actions affecting employees.

(c) Unions or other employee groups recognized by the armed forces of the United States, pursuant to sub-paragraph (b) above, will be accorded the right of consultation with appropriate authorities of the United States armed forces.

(d) Any dispute between employers and employees or any recognized employee organization, which cannot be settled through the use of procedures of the United States armed forces, shall be settled as follows:

   (1) The dispute shall be referred to the Office of Labor Affairs, Ministry of Health and Social Affairs, Republic of Korea for conciliation.

   (2) In the event that the dispute is not settled by the procedure described in (1) above, the matter will be referred to the Joint Committee, which may refer the matter to the Labor Sub-Committee or to a specially-designated committee, for further fact-finding, review, and conciliation efforts.

   (3) In the event that the dispute is not settled by the procedures outlined above, the Joint Committee will resolve the dispute. The decisions of the Joint Committee shall be binding.

   (4) Failure of any recognized employee organization or employee to bide by the decision of the Joint Committee on any dispute,

L-2   0031

or engaging in practices disruptive of normal work requirements during settlement procedures, shall be considered just cause for the withdrawal of recognition of that organization and the discharge of that employee.

(e) An employee shall be subject to the same legal provisions concerning strikes and other work stoppages as an employee in a comparable position in the employment of the armed forces of the Republic of Korea.

5. (a) Should the Republic of Korea adopt measures allocating labor, the United States Armed Forces shall be accorded allocation privileges no less favorable than those enjoyed by the Armed Forces of the Republic of Korea.

(b) In the event of a national emergency, such as war, hostilities, or situations where war or hostilities may be imminent, employees who have acquired skills essential to the mission of the United States Armed Forces shall, upon request of the United States Armed Forces, be deferred from Republic of Korea military service or other compulsory service. The United States Armed Forces shall furnish in advance to the Republic of Korea lists of those employees deemed essential. (e)

6. Members of the civilian component shall not be subject to Korean laws or regulations with respect to their terms and condition of employment.

3

AGREED MINUTES

1. The Republic of Korea will make available, at designated induction points, qualified personnel for Korean Service Corps units in numbers sufficient to meet the requirements of United States Armed Forces.

2. It is understood that the Government of the Republic of Korea shall be reimbursed for direct costs incurred in providing assistance requested pursuant to paragraph 2.

3. The undertaking of the United States Government to conform to Korean labor laws, customs, and practices, does not imply any waiver by the United States Government of its immunities under international law. The United States Government may terminate employment at any time the continuation of such employment is inconsistent with the military requirements of the United States Armed Forces.

4. Employers will withhold from the pay of their employees, and pay over to the Government of the Republic of Korea withholdings required by the income tax legislation of the Republic of Korea.

5. When employers cannot conform with provisions of labor legislation of the Government of the Republic of Korea applicable under this Article on account of the military requirements of the United States Armed Forces, the matter shall be reported in advance whenever possible, to the Joint Committee for its consideration and review.

0033

기 안 지

기 안 자	미주과 이근팔	전화번호		공 보	필 요	불필요

	과장	국장	차관	장관		
	(서명)	(서명)	(서명)	(서명)		
	10/4	10/6				

협 조 자 서 명					보 존 한 년	
기 안 년월일	1965. 4. 26.	시 행 년월일		통제관 (도장)	정 서	기 장
분류기호 문서번호	외구미 722.2 —					
경 유 수 신 참 조	대 통 령 참조: 비서실장 국무총리 참조: 비서실장 사본: 보건사회부장관		발 신	1965. 4. 27 이무부		
제 목	제 73 차 주둔군지위협정 체결 교섭실무자회의 결과 보고					

　　　　1965 년 4 월 20 일 상오 10 시 30 분 부터 동 11 시 30 분
까지 외무부 제 1 회의실에서 개최된 제 73 차 주둔군지위협정
체결 교섭실무자회의에서 토의된 노무조항에 관한 내용을 별첨과
같이 보고합니다.

　　　유 첨: 제 73 차 주둔군지위협정 체결 교섭실무자회의 결과

　　　　　　　보고서 1부. 끝.

보통문서　(7100-1R-2)

공통서식 1—2 (갑)　　　　　　　　　　　　　　　　　0034　(16절지)

기 안 지

기 안 자	미주과 이근팔	전화 번호		공 보	필 요	불필요
	과 장	국 장	차 관	장 관		

협 조 서 자 명			보 존 년 한	
기 안 년 월 일	1965. 4. 26.	시 행 년월일	통 제 관	정 서 기 장
분 류 기 호 문 서 번 호	의구미 722.2 —			
경 유 수 신 참 조	보건사회부장관 노동청장	발신	장 관 9/1-3	
제 목	제 73 차 주둔군지위협정 체결 교섭실무자회의 개최			

1965 년 4 월 20 일 상오 10 시 30 분 부터 동 11 시 30 분

까지 외무부제 1 회의실에서 개최된 제 73 차 주둔군지위협정

체결 교섭실무자회의에서 토의된 노무조항에 관한 내용을 별첨과

같이 알리오니 참고하시기 바랍니다.

유 첨: 제 73 차 주둔군지위협정 체결 교섭실무자회의 결과

보고서 1 부. 끝.

공통서식 1—2 (갑)   0035   (16절지)

한·미국 간의 상호방위조약 제4조에 의한 시설과 구역 및 한국에서의 미국군대의 지위에 관한 협정(SOFA)
전59권. 1966.7.9 서울에서 서명 : 1967.2.9 발효(조약 232호) (V.29 실무교섭회의, 제73-76차, 1965.4월)   41

제 73 차
한·미간 주둔군지위협정 체결 고섭실무자회의
보 고 서

1. 일 시: 1965 년 4 월 20 일 상오 10 시 30 분 부터 동 11 시 30 분 까지.

2. 장 소: 외무부 제 1 회의실

3. 토의사항:

노 무 조 항

가. 미측은 고용주로서의 미국군당국은 한국군과 같이 공동방위를 그 사명
으로 하고 있음으로 영리를 목적으로 하는 일반기업체인 고용주와 상이
함을 강조하고 다음과 같이 미측 입장을 주장하였다.

(1) K.S.C.문제는 협정의 테두리 밖에서 논의하기로 하되 한국국방부의
현역 및 예비역장교의 지휘하에 있는 K.S.C. 는 그 성격이
"준군사적" 이며 따라서 미군에 고용된 일반노무자와 구별되어야
한다.

(2) 미군은 미군의 군사상의 필요성과 상반되지 않는 한도내에서 만
한국의 노동관계 법령과 관습을 준수할 것이며 예측할 수 없는
군사상의 필요성으로 말미아마 한국의 법령과 관습을 준수할 수 없을
때에는 미군당국은 가능한 한 사전에 합동위원회에 보고하여 재심과
협의를 할 것이다.

(3) 미군노무자는 그 목적이 미국의 이익에 해롭지 않은 한 노동조합이나
또는 기타 노무자단체를 조직할 수도 있고 또한 이에 가입할 수
있으며 미군당국이 인정하는 노동조합 또는 기타 노무자의 단체는
미군당국과 협의할 수 있는 권리가 부여될 것이며. 파업권과 작업중단
문제에 관하여서는 한국군에 고용된 그와 동등한 지위에 있는
노무자에게 적용되는 것과 같은 법령이 미군노무자에게도 적용되어야
한다.

나. 우리측은 이와 같은 미측 주장에 대하여 우리측의 입장을 우선 다음과
같이 밝히고 자세한 것은 검토후 다음기회에 답변할 것이라고 말
하였다.

0036

65-5-18

65-5-1 (2)

맹믈 112-6(2)

한·미국 간의 상호방위조약 제4조에 의한 시설과 구역 및 한국에서의 미국군대의 지위에 관한 협정(SOFA)
전59권. 1966.7.9 서울에서 서명 : 1967.2.9 발효(조약 232호) (V.29 실무교섭회의, 제73-76차, 1965.4월) 43

(1) 우리측이 K.S.C.는 미군에 고용된 일반노무자와 동등하게 취급되어야 한다는 입장인데 반하여 미측은 K.S.C. 가 준군사적인 성격을 띠고 있다고 주장하여 양측이 상반된 입장을 취하고 있는 이상 이문제에 대한 합의에 도달하기만 곤란할 것임으로 협정 밖에서 해결하는 것이 좋을 것이다.

(2) 미군이 군사상의 필요성에 의하여 한국의 노동관계법령을 준수할 수 없을 경우에는 반듯이 사전에 합동위원회에 보고하여 합의를 보아야 하며 미측 주장대로 "가능한 한" 사전에 보고 하는 것으로 하여서는 아니된다.

(3) 우리측이 노무자의 파업권에 관한 미측 제안을 수락한다면 노무자들은 사실상 파업을 할 수 없게 되는바 한국군에 고용된 노무자가 파업을 할 수 없는 것은 그들의 지위 때문이 아니라 그들의 군속이라는 신분에 기인한 것이며 미군노무자와 신분이 동일할 수는 없는 것이다.

4. 기타 사항

가. 차기 회의일자: 1965 년 4 월 23 일 상오 10 시.　　끝.

0038

65 - 5 - 7/2)

명은 112-6(2)

0039

STATUS OF FORCES NEGOTIATIONS: 73rd Meeting

SUBJECT: ~~£xxixxxxx~~ Labor Article

PLACE: Ministry of Foreign Affairs

DATE: April 20, 1965

PARTICIPANTS:

Republic of Korea	United States
CHANG Sang-mun	Philip C. Habib
HO Sung-chung ⟨ Maj. LEE	Brig. General Carroll H. Dunn, USA
KIM Ki-cho	✓ Colonel Allan G. Pixton, USA
HWANG Yong-chae	✓ Captain George Hagerman, USN
PAK Won-chol	Colonel Kenneth C. Crawford, USA
YI Kun-pal (Interpreter)	Robert A. Kinney
	Benjamin A. Fleck
	(Jack Friedman)
	Major Alton Harvey, USA
	David Y. C. Lee (Interpreter)
	Ogden Reed (Observer)
	G. W. Flowers (Observer)

1. Mr. Habib opened the meeting by introducing two new members of the U.S. negotiating team: Colonel Allan G. Pixton, replacing Colonel Smigelow, and Captain George Hagerman, replacing Captain Wayne. Mr. Chang welcomed Colonel Pixton and Captain Hagerman to the negotiations on behalf of the Korean negotiators.

2. Taking up the Labor Article, Mr. Habib ~~introduced and discussed the following subjects~~ tabled a revised draft of the entire article. He stated that the U.S. negotiators were tabling this draft, in a spirit of compromise, in order to reach early full agreement on this article. As revised, the U.S. draft ~~provided~~ (would provide) continued fair and equitable treat-ment for Korean employees of the U.S. armed forces, as well as sound and just procedures for the resolution of labor grievances and disputes. Mr. Habib said he would discuss the changes in the draft on a paragraph by paragraph basis. The principal revisions related to Paragraphs 3, 4, 5 and their Agreed Minutes.

3. Paragraph 1 and related Agreed Minute #1 - In Paragraph 1, Mr. Habib said, the word "paramilitary" had been added to differentiate clearly the paramilitary Korean Service Corps from the direct hire employees of the U.S. armed forces covered by this article. The U.S. armed forces plan to discuss the status of the Korean Service Corps, which is commanded by ROK Army officers on active duty and in reserve (and which has operated outside ROK labor laws and courts) directly with ~~the~~ authorities in the Ministry of National Defense. In order to expedite agreement regarding the language relative to domestic servants, the U.S. negotiators had deleted the second sentence of the previous ~~text~~ draft of Agreed Minute #1, subject to an understanding that the present situation with regard to domestics employed by individual members of the U.S. armed forces and civilian component shall continue. As the Korean negotiators were aware, Mr. Habib continued, individual members of the United States armed forces, civilian component, and dependents hire and pay domestic servants directly, subject only to USFK security and health checks and general guidance. Applicable Korean laws would govern employment of such domestics.

0041

4. **Paragraph 2** - Mr. Habib noted that the U.S. and Korean negotiators ~~were~~ are in agreement regarding Paragraph 2, except for minor differences of wording. The U.S. negotiators concurred in the Korean proposal to substitute the word "such" for the word "available" in the second sentence, subject to Korean understanding that we cannot furnish ~~in~~formation not available to us as part of our normal operating procedure. ~~We~~ [The U.S. negotiators] foresee no problems in supplying the information desired by the Korean authorities, as indicated in Paragraph 20 of the Agreed Joint Summary of the 46th negotiating meeting.

5. **Paragraph 3 and related Agreed Minute #5** - Mr. Habib stated that the U.S. ~~ne~~gotiators believe that they are in essential agreement with the Korean negotiators regarding Paragraph 3, except for possible differences in interpretations of the phrase "military requirements". In order to be responsive to the Korean desire for review and consideration by the Joint Committee of situations in which the U.S. armed forces cannot conform to the ROK labor legislation because of military requirements, the U.S. negotiators were tabling a new Agreed Minute #5. The U.S. negotiators believe, Mr. Habib continued, that the U.S. armed forces only rarely, if ever, will not be able to conform ~~to~~ to ~~the~~ ROK labor legislation applicable under this Article, except in emergency situations. The new Agreed Minute #5 ~~would~~ would provide that when the U.S. armed forces cannot conform ~~with~~ [to] ROK labor legislation on account of military requirements, the matter shall be reported, in advance whenever possible, to the Joint Committee for its consideration ~~and~~ review. The U.S. negotiators believe that the Agreed Minute demonstrates the good faith of the U.S. armed forces, in pledging to conform ~~with~~ [to] the ROK labor laws, customs, and practices, to the extent not inconsistent with the provisions of this article, and to agree to this type of Joint Committee consideration of possible situations in which military requirements may be at variance with ROK labor legislation. In this regard, the ROK negotiators had mentioned the possibility that in an emergency the provisions of the Labor Article might be suspended. The U.S. negotiators believe that the new U.S. language is the best way to take care of ~~unforeseeable situations~~ in which military necessity may require non-conformance to ROK ~~labor legislation~~.

0042

6. Paragraph 4 - Mr. Habib stated that the U.S. negotiators were tabling a new Paragraph 4 which sets forth clearly the positive U.S. commitments to be a good ~~employer~~ employer, pursuing enlightened policies and procedures relating to employer-employee relationships. Subparagraph (a) would provide that employers will maintain procedures designed to assure the just and timely resolution of employee grievances. Subparagraph (b) would provide the employees the right to organize and join a union. Under its terms, membership or non-membership in such groups would not be a factor in employment or in other actions affecting employees. Subparagraph (c) would assure recognized unions the right of consultation with U.S. military authorities. Such labor-management consultations are currently an established part of the U.S. armed forces' relations with the recognized union.

7. Subparagraph (d) of Paragraph 4, Mr. Habib continued, incorporates much of the previously tabled Agreed Minute #5, setting forth procedures for settling labor disputes which cannot be settled by use of established USFK procedures. These procedures closely parallel the previously-tabled Korean proposals, and provide that disputes which cannot be settled by use of USFK procedures shall be referred to the ROK Office of Labor Affairs for conciliation. If a dispute cannot be settled by the Office of Labor Affairs, it ~~will then~~ would be referred to the Joint Committee, which might refer it to a Labor Sub-Committee or to a specially designated committee or take it under consideration directly. The Joint Committee would be the final arbiter of any such labor disputes. ~~~~ The U.S. and Korean negotiators were in agreement that its decisions shall be binding upon employers, employees, and the union.

8. As stated in subparagraph (e) of Paragraph 4, Mr. Habib continued, the U.S. negotiators firmly maintain that a Korean working for the U.S. armed forces in the joint U.S.-ROK defense effort shall be subject to the same legal provisions concerning strikes and other work stoppages as an employee in a comparable position in the employment of the armed forces of the Republic of Korea. Both categories of Korean employees of our two governments are working ~~directly in the defense~~ defense of their country. The U.S.

0043

negotiators believe firmly in the principle that our employees must be subject to the same ROK legal provisions with regard to strikes or work stoppages as comparable employees working for the ROK armed forces. This ▬ is a basic and unchanging U.S. position, which is related directly to the effectiveness of the U.S. armed forces in the defense of the Republic of Korea.

9. <u>Paragraph 5</u> - Mr. Habib pointed out that Paragraph 5 of both drafts deals with the important topic of the availability of essential Korean employees of the U.S. armed forces for their assigned defense tasks in time of emergency. The newly-tabled Paragraph 5 of the U.S. draft had been patterned after the language of the Korean draft tabled at the 69th negotiating session, It is almost identical with the Korean Paragraph 5 except for the use of the word "shall" instead of "may" in subparagraph (b). The use of the word "shall" would assure U.S. and Korean defense planners that in time of emergency, essential employees of the U.S. armed forces in Korea would be available to continue to perform their essential roles during the emergency. USFK requirements for Korean manpower, Mr. Habib continued, are very small in comparison to Korean manpower availabilities. On the other hand, the role of the U.S. forces in a war emergency in the Republic of Korea would be of an extremely important and probably decisive nature. Their essential civilian ▬▬▬▬▬▬ employees are basic to the ef- the U.S. negotiators wished to fectiveness of the U.S. armed forces. Therefore, ▬emphasize that ▬▬▬▬. deferment of essential USFK personnel in advance must be provided for. This vital matter cannot be left to consideration and decision in time of emergency. There ▬ would be a great deal of paper work in listing and processing essential employees who would be deferred. This work must be accomplished to our mutual satisfaction before the emergency arises, if implementation is to be effective. The U.S. negotiators believe that the details can be worked out in consultation between ▬▬▬ the U.S. armed forces and officials of the Ministry of National Defense in advance, to the mutual satisfaction of both parties.

0044

10. Mr. Habib noted that the ~~revised agreed minutes were~~ Agreed Minutes in the new U.S. draft had been renumbered so that they now appear in the same order as the paragraphs to which they refer.

11. Mr. Habib stated that the revised U.S. draft was the result of many hours discussion of this Article by both sides over the past 15 months. The U.S. negotiators urged early acceptance of the revised draft by the Korean negotiators. The U.S. negotiators believe that it fully protects the legitimate rights and interests of Korean employees of the U.S. armed forces and, at the same time, is consistent with ~~Jint~~ U.S.-ROK defense requirements.

12. Mr. Chang replied that the Korean negotiators appreciated the compromising spirit in which the U.S. negotiators had presented their revised draft in the hope for full agreement as soon as possible. The Korean negotiators would carefully consider the U.S. draft and respond in a few days. However, the Korean negotiators believed that considerable differences ~~~~ still existed between the positions of the two ~~ties~~. They wished, therefore, to make some preliminary comments to indicate the basic ~~Ko~~ position.~~~~

13. With regard to Paragraph 1, Mr. Chang said the Korean negotiators still wished to ~~settle~~ ~~raise~~ the question of the Korean Service Corps outside the framework of the ПИГА negotiations, since ~~they believe~~ U.S. side *had* insisted that the KSC ~~to be~~ a (semi-military or) paramilitary organization, *while the Korean side had maintained otherwise, and agreement on the question was not foreseeable.*

14. With regard to Subparagraphs (a), (b), and (c) of Paragraph 4, Mr. Chang recalled that the U.S. negotiators had stated that the U.S. armed forces will conform to ROK labor laws to the maximum extent possible. The Korean negotiators believe, therefore, that the detailed provisions set forth in ~~these~~ these subparagraphs were unnecessary. However, they had no objection if the U.S. negotiators felt it necessary to include them, *subject to agreement on the other ~~points of~~ out-standing problems of the labor article.*

15. Regarding Paragraph 4(e), which had to do with the right to strike, Mr. Chang

0045

said the Korean negotiators believed that if they accepted the U.S. language, the Government of the Republic of Korea would be obliged to enact a law prohibiting the employees of the U.S. armed forces from resorting to strikes. The Korean negotiators doubted that the language of the U.S. draft was in accordance with ROK labor legislation. ~~They believed that the phrase "comparable position" should read "comparable status", since denial of the right to strike was based on a person's status as a member of the civilian component, rather than on the position he occupied.~~

16. Regarding Paragraph 5(b), Mr. Chang noted two main points. First, employees shall be deferred on the request of the U.S. armed forces. Secondly, a list of essential employees is to be furnished in advance. The U.S. proposal did not appear to provide for the mutual satisfaction desired by the Korean negotiators. If they accepted the U.S. language, the ROK authorities would have to defer everyone whose name appeared on the list furnished in advance. They believed that the ROK authorities should have discretion, in consultation with the U.S. armed forces, to decide who would be deferred.

17. Mr. Habib pointed out that what the Korean negotiators wanted was implied in the U.S. language. The U.S. negotiators believed that there would be mutual satisfaction, since there must be agreement on the attainment of essential skills by the employees whose names would appear on the list furnished by the U.S. armed forces. The Joint Committee would be the mechanism for attaining mutual satisfaction. If the Korean authorities questioned that any person named on the list had actually attained the required skills, they could raise the question in the Joint Committee.

18. Mr. Chang said the Korean negotiators still felt that the language regarding this question could be more specific. He said they would propose such language.

19. Mr. Chang noted that the U.S. negotiators had modified the language of Agreed Minute #5, by providing for notification "in advance whenever possible". The

0046

phrase "whenever possible" should be omitted, however, since the Korean negotiators believed that it would always be possible to report in advance. Furthermore, if the U.S. armed forces found that they could not conform to the ROK labor laws, they should always ~~refer~~ refer the matter to the Joint Committee in advance.

20. Mr. Habib replied that if it is always possible to report in advance, then the Korean position was met by the U.S. language and no problem existed. The U.S. armed forces did not intend this provision to be a means of avoiding conformity to the Korean labor laws. They did believe, however, that in times of emergency it might not always be possible to notify the Joint Committee in advance of non-conformity. There had to be some qualifying phrase; otherwise the provision would be unreasonable.

21. Mr. Chang said he wished to close his preliminary remarks by stating that the Korean negotiators noted and appreciated the sincerity of the U.S. negotiators in submitting their revised draft.

22. Mr. Habib said that he wished to reply briefly to Mr. Chang's comments regarding Paragraph 4(e). The U.S. negotiators wished to reiterate that neither the U.S. armed forces nor the ROK armed forces are ordinary employers. The phraseology of the revised U.S. draft of this subparagraph had been carefully chosen from the standpoint of the Korean requirements as well as those of the U.S. armed forces. The language is not unreasonable, given the unusual nature of the employers. Neither employer is an ordinary business enterprise. They are not in business to make money but to defend the Republic of Korea.

23. Regarding Paragraph 1, Mr. Habib pointed out that in revising the language, the U.S. negotiators had done exactly what the Korean negotiators had desired - they had ~~omitted~~ the Korean Service Corps from the provided by this SOFA. It appeared that both sides were substantially in agreement regarding this issue.

0047

23. It was agreed that the would call the next meeting

as soon as they were prepared to comment in detail on the U.S. draft.

0048

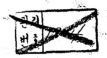

1. Time and Place: 10:30-11:30 A.M., April 20, 1965 at the Foreign Ministry's Conference Room (No.1)

2. Attendants:

ROK Side:

Mr. Chang, Sang Moon	Director European and American Affairs Bureau
Mr. Huh, Sung Joon	Director Labor Administration Bureau Office of Labor Affairs
Maj. Lee, Kye Hoon	Military Affairs Section Ministry of National Defense
Mr. Kim, Kee Joe	3rd Secretary Ministry of Foreign Affairs
Mr. Lee, Keun Pal (Rapporteur and Interpreter)	3rd Secretary Ministry of Foreign Affairs
Mr. Hwang, Young Jae	3rd Secretary Ministry of Foreign Affairs
Mr. Park, Won Chul	3rd Secretary Ministry of Foreign Affairs

U.S. Side:

Mr. Philip C. Habib	Counselor American Embassy
Brig. Gen. Carroll H. Dunn	Deputy Chief of Staff 8th U.S. Army
Col. Allan G. Pixton	Deputy Chief of Staff 8th U.S. Army
Capt. George Hagerman	Assistant Chief of Staff USN/K
Col. Kenneth C. Crawford	Staff Judge Advocate 8th U.S. Army
Mr. Benjamin A. Fleck	First Secretary American Embassy
Mr. Robert A. Kinney	J-5 8th U.S. Army
Mr. Jack Friedman	Second Secretary American Embassy
Maj. Alton H. Harvey	Staff Judge Advocate's Office 8th U.S. Army

0049

Mr. David Y.C. Lee	Second Secretary
(Interpreter)	American Embassy
Mr. Ogden C. Reed	Civilian Personnel Director
	8th U.S. Army
Mr. G. W. Flowers	Observer

1. Mr. Habib opened the meeting by introducing two new members of the U.S. negotiating team: Colonel Allan G. Pixton, replacing Colonel Smigelow, and Captain George Hagerman, replacing Captain Wayne. Mr. Chang welcomed Colonel Pixton and Captain Hagerman to the negotiations on behalf of the Korean negotiators.

2. Taking up the Labor Article, Mr. Habib tabled a revised draft of the entire article. He stated that the U.S. negotiators were tabling this draft, in a spirit of compromise, in order to reach early full agreement on this article. As revised, the U.S. draft would provide continued fair and equitable treatment for Korean employees of the U.S. armed forces, as well as sound and just procedures for the resolution of labor grievances and disputes. Mr. Habib said he would discuss the changes in the draft on a paragraph by paragraph basis. The principal revisions related to Paragraphs 3,4,5 and their Agreed Minutes.

3. <u>Paragraph 1 and related Agreed Minute #1</u> - In Paragraph 1, Mr. Habib said, the word "paramilitary" had been added to differentiate clearly the paramilitary Korean Service Corps from the direct hire employees of the U.S. armed forces covered by this article. The U.S. armed forces plan to discuss the status of the Korean Service Corps, which is commanded by ROK Army officers on active duty and in reserve (and which has operated outside ROK labor laws and courts) directly with authorities in the Ministry

0050

of National Defense. In order to expedite agreement regarding
the language relative to domestic servants, the U.S. negotiators had deleted the second sentence of the previous draft
of Agreed Minute #1, subject to an understanding that the
present situation with regard to domestics employed by
individual members of the U.S. armed forces and civilian
component shall continue. As the Korean negotiators were
aware, Mr. Habib continued, individual members of the
United States armed forces, civilian component, and dependents
hire and pay domestic servants directly, subject only to USFK
security and health checks and general guidance. Applicable
Korean laws would govern employment of such domestics.

4. <u>Paragraph 2</u> - Mr. Habib noted that the U.S. and
Korean negotiators are in agreement regarding Paragraph 2,
except for minor differences of wording. The U.S. negotiators
concurred in the Korean proposal to substitute the word
"such" for the word "available" in the second sentence,
subject to Korean understanding that we cannot furnish
information not available to us as part of our normal
operating procedure. The U.S. negotiators foresee no problems
in supplying the information desired by the Korean authorities,
as indicated in Paragraph 20 of the Agreed Joint Summary
of the 46th negotiating meeting.

5. <u>Paragraph 3 and related Agreed Minute #5</u> - Mr. Habib
stated that the U.S. negotiators believe that they are in
essential agreement with the Korean negotiators regarding
Paragraph 3, except for possible differences in interpretations
of the phrase "military requirements". In order to be
responsive to the Korean desire for review and consideration
by the Joint Committee of situations in which the U.S.
armed forces cannot conform to the ROK Labor legislation

because of military requirements, the U.S. negotiators
were tabling a new Agreed Minute #5. The U.S. negotiators
believe, Mr. Habib continued, that the U.S. armed forces only
rarely, if ever, will not be able to conform to ROK labor
legislation applicable under this Article, except in emergency
situations. The new Agreed Minute #5 would provide that when
the U.S. armed forces cannot conform to ROK labor legislation
on account of military requirements, the matter shall
be reported, in advance whenever possible, to the Joint
Committee for its consideration and review. The U.S.
negotiators believe that the Agreed Minute demonstrates the
good faith of the U.S. armed forces, in pledging to conform
to the ROK labor laws, customs, and practices, to the
extent not inconsistent with the provisions of this article,
and to agree to this type of Joint Committee consideration
of possible situations in which military requirements may
be at variance with ROK labor legislation. In this regard,
the ROK negotiators had mentioned the possibility that in
an emergency the provisions of the Labor Article might be
suspended. The U.S. negotiators believe that the new U.S.
language is the best way to take care of unforeseeable
situations in which military necessity may require non-
conformance to ROK labor legislation.

    6. <u>Paragraph 4</u> - Mr. Habib stated that the U.S.
negotiators were tabling a new Paragraph 4 which sets forth
clearly the positive U.S. commitments to be a good employer,
pursuing enlightened policies and procedures relating to employer-
employee relationships. Sub-paragraph (a) would provide
that employers will maintain procedures designed to assure the
just and timely resolution of employee grievances. Subparagraph
(b) would provide the employees the right to organize and
join a union. Under its terms, membership or non-membership
in such groups would not be a factor in employment or other actions affecting employees.

Subparagraph (c) would assure recognized unions the right of consultation with U.S. military authorities. Such labor-management consultations are currently an established part of the U.S. armed forces' relations with the recognized union.

7.   Subparagraph (d) of Paragraph 4, Mr. Habib continued, incorporates much of the previously tabled Agreed Minute #5, setting forth procedures for settling labor disputes which cannot be settled by use of established USFK procedures. These procedures closely parallel the previously-tabled Korean proposals, and provide the disputes which cannot be settled by use of USFK procedures shall be referred to the ROK Office of Labor Affairs for conciliation. If a dispute cannot be settled by the Office of Labor Affairs, it would be referred to the Joint Committee, which might refer it to a Labor Sub-Committee or to a specially designated committee or take it under consideration directly. The Joint Committee would be the final arbiter of any such labor disputes. The U.S. and Korean negotiators were in agreement that its decisions shall be binding upon employers, employees, and the union.

8.   As stated in subparagraph (e) of Paragraph 4, Mr. Habib continued, the U.S. negotiators firmly maintain

0053

that a Korean working for the U.S. armed forces in the joint
U.S.-ROK defense effort shall be subject to the same legal
provisions concerning strikes and other work stoppages
as an employee in a comparable position in the employment
of the armed forces of the Republic of Korea. Both categories
of Korean employees of our two governments are working
directly in the defense of their country. The U.S.
negotiators believe firmly in the principle that our
employees must be subject to the same ROK legal provisions
with regard to strikes or work stoppages as comparable employees
working for the ROK armed forces. This is a basic and
unchanging U.S. position, which is related directly to the
effectiveness of the U.S. armed forces in the defense of
the Republic of Korea.

    9. <u>Paragraph 5</u> - Mr. Habib pointed out that
Paragraph 5 of both drafts deals with the important topic of
the availability of essential Korean employees of the U.S.
armed forces for their assigned defense tasks in time of
emergency. The newly-tabled Paragraph 5 of the U.S. draft
had been patterned after the language of the Korean draft
tabled at the 69th negotiating session. It is almost
identical with the Korean Paragraph 5 except for the use
of the word "shall" instead of "may" in subparagraph (b).
The use of the word "shall would assure U.S. and Korean
defense planners that in time of emergency, essential
employees of the U.S. armed forces in Korea would be available
to continue to perform their essential roles during the
emergency. USFK requirements for Korean manpower, Mr. Habib
continued, are very small in comparison to Korean manpower
availabilities. On the other hand, the role of the U.S.
forces in a war emergency in the Republic of Korea would be

0054

of an extremely important and probably decisive nature.
Their essential civilian employees are basic to the
effectiveness of the U.S. armed forces. Therefore, the U.S.
negotiators wished to emphasize that deferment of essential
USFK personnel in advance must be provided for. This vital
matter cannot be left to consideration and decision in
time of emergency. There would be a great deal of paper
work in listing and processing essential employees who
would be deferred. This work must be accomplished to our
mutual satisfaction before the emergency arises, if
implementation is to be effective. The U.S. negotiators
believe that the details can be worked out in consultation
between the U.S. armed forces and officials of the Ministry
of National Defense in advance, to the mutual satisfaction
of both parties.

10. Mr. Habib noted that the Agreed Minutes in the new
U.S. draft had been renumbered so that they now appear
in the same order as the paragraphs to which they refer.

11. Mr. Habib stated that the revised U.S. draft was
the result of many hours of discussion of this Article by
both sides over the past 15 months. The U.S. negotiators
urged early accpetance of the revised draft by the Korean
negotiators. The U.S. negotiators believe that it fully
protects the legitimate rights and interests of Korean
employees of the U.S. armed forces and, at the same time,
is consistent with joint U.S.-ROK defense requirements.

12. Mr. Chang replied that the Korean negotiators
appreciated the compromising spirit in which the U.S.
negotiators had presented their revised draft in the
hope for full agreement as soon as possible. The Korean
negotiators would carefully consider the U.S. draft and
respond in a few days. However, the Korean negotiators

0055

believed that considerable differences still existed between the positions of the two sides. They wished, therefore, to make some preliminary comments to indicate the basic Korean position.

13. With regard to Paragraph 1, Mr. Chang said the Korean negotiators still wished to settle the question of the Korean Service Corps outside the framework of the SOFA negotiations, since U.S. side had insited that the KSC is a semi-military or paramilitary organization, while the Korean side had maintained otherwise, and agreement on the question was not foreseeable.

14. With regard to subparagraphs (a), (b), and (c) of Paragraph 4, Mr. Chang recalled that the U.S. negotiators had stated that the U.S. armed forces will conform to ROK labor laws to the maximum extent possible. The Korean negotiators believe, therefore, that the detailed provisions set forth in these subparagraphs were unnecessary. However, they had no objection if the U.S. negotiators felt it necessary to include them, subject to agreement on the other outstanding problems of the Labor Article.

15. Regarding Paragraph 4(e), which had to do with the right to strike, Mr. Chang said the Korean negotiators believed that if they accepted the U.S. language, the Government of the Republic of Korea would be obliged to enact a law prohibiting the employees of the U.S. armed forces from resorting to strikes. The Korean negotiators doubted that the language of the U.S. draft was in accordance with ROK labor legislation."

16. Regarding Paragraph 5(b), Mr. Chang noted two main points. First, employees shall be deferred on the

0056

request of the U.S. armed forces. Secondly, a list of essential employees is to be furnished in advance. The U.S. proposal did not appear to provide for the mutual satisfaction desired by the Korean negotiators. If they accepted the U.S. language, the ROK authorities would have to defer everyone whose name appeared on the list furnished in advance. They believed that the ROK authorities should have discretion, in consultation with the U.S. armed forces, to decide who would be deferred.

17. Mr. Habib pointed out that what the Korean negotiators wanted was implied in the U.S. language. The U.S. negotiators believed that there would be mutual satisfaction, since there must be agreement on the attainment of essential skills by the employees whose names would appear on the list furnished by the U.S. armed forces. The Joint Committee would be the mechanism for attaining mutual satisfaction. If the Korean authorities questioned that any person named on the list had actually attained the required skills, they could raise the question in the Joint Committee.

18. Mr. Chang said the Korean negotiators still felt that the language regarding this question could be more specific. He said they would propose such language.

19. Mr. Chang noted that the U.S. negotiators had modified the language of Agreed Minute #5, by providing for notification "in advance whenever possible." The phrase "whenever possible" should be omitted, however, since the Korean negotiators believed that it would always be possible to report in advance. Furthermore, if the U.S. armed forces found that they could not conform to the ROK labor laws, they

한·미국 간의 상호방위조약 제4조에 의한 시설과 구역 및 한국에서의 미국군대의 지위에 관한 협정(SOFA)
전59권. 1966.7.9 서울에서 서명 : 1967.2.9 발효(조약 232호) (V.29 실무교섭회의, 제73-76차, 1965.4월)

should always refer the matter to the Joint Committee in advance.

20. Mr. Habib replied that if it is always possible to report in advance, then the Korean position was met by the U.S. language and no problem existed. The U.S. armed forces did not intend this provision to be a means of avoiding conformity to the Korean labor laws. They did believe, however, that in times of emergency it might not always be possible to notify the Joint Committee in advance of non-conformity. There had to be some qualifying phrase; otherwise the provision would be unreasonable.

21. Mr. Chang said he wished to close his preliminary remarks by stating that the Korean negotiators noted and appreciated the sincerity of the U.S. negotiators in submitting their revised draft.

22. Mr. Habib said that he wished to reply briefly to Mr. Chang's comments regarding Paragraph 4(e). The U.S. negotiators wished to reiterate that neither the U.S. armed forces nor the ROK armed forces are ordinary employers. The phraseology of the revised U.S. draft of this subparagraph had been carefully chosen from the standpoint of the Korean requirements as well as those of the U.S. armed forces. The language is not unreasonable, given the unusual nature of the employers. Neither employer is an ordinary business enterprise. They are not in business to make money but to defend the Republic of Korea.

23. Regarding Paragraph 1, Mr. Habib pointed out that in revising the language, the U.S. negotiators had done exactly what the Korean negotiators had desired - they had excluded members of the Korean Service Corps from the definition of employees and, therefore, from the coverage provided by this article. It appeared that both sides were substantially in agreement regarding this issue.

0058

24. It was agreed that the Korean negotiators would call the next meeting as soon as they were prepared to comment in detail on the U.S. draft.

한·미국 간의 상호방위조약 제4조에 의한 시설과 구역 및 한국에서의 미국군대의 지위에 관한 협정(SOFA)
전59권. 1966.7.9 서울에서 서명 : 1967.2.9 발효(조약 232호) (V.29 실무교섭회의, 제73-76차, 1965.4월)

2. 제74차 회의, 4.23

0060

기 안 용 지

자체통제		기안처	미주과 이근팔	전화번호	근거서류접수일자

과장	국장	차관	장관		

관계관 서명

기안년월일	1965. 4. 22.	시행년월일		보존년한		정서	기장

분류기호	의구미 722. 2	전체 통제		종결			

경유수신참조	대통령 참조: 비서실장	발신	장 관
	국무총리 참조: 비서실장		

제 목 한·미간 주둔군지위협정 체결 교섭에 관한 미측 입장

　　　　우리측이 1965 년 2월 12일 개최된 제 70 차주둔군지위협정

체결 교섭 실무자회의 석상에서 제시한 형사재판관할권조항에

관한 대안을 검토하여 오던 미측이 그들의 수정안을 차기

회의 개최 시 제안함에 앞서 미측교섭실무자단의 수석대표인

주한미국대사관의 Habib 참사관은 우리측 실무자단의 수석대표인

구미국장을, 그리고 Brown 주한미대사는 외무부장관을

2월 19일과 동 21일 각각 방문하고 협정 체결 교섭에 관한

미국정부의 태도를 별첨과 같이 시사한바 있음으로 이를 보고

합니다.

　　　　유 첨: 한·미간 주둔군지위협정 체결 교섭에 관한 미측 입장. 끝

승인서식 1-1-3　　(11-00900-03)　　　　　(195mm×265mm16절지)

0061

1. 제 목: 한·미간 주둔군지위협정 체결 교섭에 관한 미측 입장

2. 참석자: 한국측: 이동원외무부장관, 장상문구미국장

　　　　　미국측: Brown 주한미국대사, Habib 참사관 및 Fleck 1등서기관.

3. 담화 내용:

(1) 한·미간 주둔군지위협정 체결 교섭 미국측실무자단의 수석대표인 Habib 참사관은 4월 19일 장상문구미국장을, 그리고 Brown 주한미국대사는 4월 21일 이동원외무부장관을 각각 방문하고 우리측이 지난 2월 12일 개최된 제70차 주둔군지위협정 체결 교섭실무자회의 시 제시한 형사재판관할권에 관한 대안에 언급하여 미국정부는 그간 세밀한 검토를 마친 바 있음으로 4월 23일 개최되는 실무자회의를 통하여 새로운 대안을 우리측에 수교할 것이라고 말하였음.

(2) 미측이 금번 제안할 형사재판관할권조항의 가장 중요한 문제인 한국당국의 제1차관할권의 포기에 관한 미측의 입장은 대체적으로 서독보충협정의 포기조항의 내용과 같은 것이 될 것이라고 말하였음.

(3) 우리측은 이에 대하여 한국측으로서는 접수국에 관할권 포기 여부에 관한 재량권을 인정하지 아니하는 서독협정의 형태는 국회나 또는 국민이 도저히 용납할 수 없는 것이기 때문에 수락할 수 없다고 답변하였던바 미측은 금번 제안은 미측의 최종적인 제안이며 한국측이 이를 수락하지 않는다면 형사재판관할권조항의 타결은 물론 주둔군지위 협정 전반에 걸친 일괄적 조기타결은 한국정부의 요망에도 불구하고 당분간 난망일 것이라는 미국정부의 입장을 피력하였음.

(4) 미측은 또한 노무문제에도 언급하여 양측의 의견이 대립되고 있는 미군에 고용된 노무자의 파업권은 미군의 군사상의 필요성에 비추어 인정할 수 없다고 부언하였음.

4. 형사재판관할권 포기조항에 관한 한·미양측의 입장 및 서독보충협정

(1) 한국측 입장

(가) 대한민국당국은 미군당국이 요청하면 대한민국당국이

관할권을 행사함이 특히 중요하다고 결정하는 경우를 제외하고

0062

제 1 차관할권을 미군당국에 포기한다.

(나) 대한민국이 관할권을 행사함이 특히 중요하다고 결정하는
사건의 범주에 해당하는 경우는 다음 범죄를 포함한다:

(ㄱ) 대한민국의 안전에 관한 범죄, (ㄴ) 사람을 죽이거나
또는 치사케한 범죄, (ㄷ) 강간죄, (ㅌ) 강도죄, (ㅁ)한미
양국중 어느 당국이 특히 중요하다고 인정하는 범죄,

(ㅂ) 상기 각범죄의 미수 또는 공법.

(2) 미국측 입장

(가) 대한민국당국은 미국당국에 제 1차관할권을 포기하여야하며

(나) 미국당국과 협의후 대한민국의 안전에 관한 범죄, 강간죄,
및 고의적 살인죄에 관한 특정사건에 있어서 특수한 사정을
이유로 대한민국이 관할권을 행사함이 극히 중요하다는
의견을 가질 때에는 그 의견을 미국당국에 통고하여 포기를
철회할 수 있다.

(3) 독일보충협정

(가) 독일국은 파견국이 요청하면 독일국에 부여된 제 1 차
관할권을 파견국을 위하여 포기하여야 한다.

(나) 독일국은 특정사건에 있어서 특수한 사정을 이유로 독일의
사법행정의 중대한 이익을 위하여 독일이 관할권을 행사함이
불가피하다는 의견을 가진 경우에는 관계파견당국에 통고하여
포기를 철회할 수 있다.

(다) 특정사건의 상세한 조사 결과에 따를 것을 조건으로 독일의
사법행정상의 중대한 이익을 위하여 특히 다음과 같은 경우
독일의 관할권 행사가 불가피한 것으로 할 수 있다.

(ㄱ) 연방고등법원이 제 1심 및 최종심에 관여할 권한을
가진 범죄 또는 검찰총장이 연방고등법원에서 소추할 수
있는 범죄.

(ㄴ) 사람을 죽이거나 치사케한 범죄, (ㄷ) 강간죄,

(ㄷ) 강도죄, (ㅁ) 상기 각범죄의 미수 및 공법.

0063

5. 당부 의견

(1) 1962 년 9 월 20 일 교섭이 재개된 이래 2 년 반이라는 세월이 경과하였으며 형사재판관할권조항의 초안이 교환된지도 이미 1 년 2 개월여가 되었는바 그간 우리측 실무자단은 동 조항이 우방 미국의 군대의 접수국으로서의 우리 나라의 주권이 존중되어야 한다는 원칙 밑에서 해결되어야 한다고 주장하여왔음.

(2) 특히 형사재판관할권조항의 핵심인 관할권의 포기조항을 위요하고 양국간의 의견이 대립되고 있는바 우리측은 모든 미군관계 범죄를 무조건 한국법정에서 재판하려는 의도는 없으나 원칙적으로 한국당국이 특히 중요하다고 인정하는 사건에 대하여 재판권을 행사할 수 있는 길이 보장되어야 한다는 입장을 견지하고 있음.

(3) 그러나 미측은 금번 서독보충협정의 포기조항과 유사한 내용의 대안을 최종안으로 제출할 것이라는바 미국인 패전국인 일본측 일본국과도 관대한 협정을 체결하였음에도 불구하고 우리에게는 미·일협정의 형태는 고사하고 독일보충협정과 같은 불평등한 형태의 수락을 종용하고 있는 실정인바 동 협정은 대등한 입장에서 접수국의 주권을 존중하는 것이 아니며 따라서 독일국이 원하는 때에 재 재판권을 행사할 수 있는 보장이 없다 할 수 있음.

(4) 우리가 협정의 조기타결을 위주로 한 나머지 이와 같은 불평등한 형태의 협정을 체결하게 된다면 국회나 또는 국민에게 우리 나라의 주권행사가 침해된 듯한 인상을 줄 염려가 있을 뿐만 아니라 미군에게 배타적인 재판권행사를 허용하고 있는 대전협정을 지양하려는 우리측 본래의 목적인 실리를 거둘수 없을 것임.

(5) 따라서 우리측은 미측이 말한바와 같이 우리측의 입장을 참작하지 않고 서독협정과 같은 대안을 제시한다면 협정 자체의 체결시기가 다소 지연되는 한이 있더라도 이를 수락하지 않고 좀 더 유리한 협정의 체결을 위하여 교섭을 계속함이 가할 것으로 판단됨.

재무(1966.10.31)

0064

형사재판권조항

1. 형사재판권 조항 개요

1. 금번 우리나라가 미국과 주둔군 지위협정을 체결함으로서 과거 대전 협정하에서 주한 미군이 배타적 재판권을 행사하여 왔던 상태를 지양하고 본 형사재판권 조항에 의거 한·미 양국이 접수국 또는 파견국으로서 국가 상호 존중의 원칙하에서 재판권을 행사하게 되었다.

2. 즉 나토협정, 미·일 협정을 포함한 각국 협정의 선례에 따라 미합중국은 공무 집행중 범죄 또는 미국 군대 내부의 범죄에 대하여 제1차적 재판권을 가지며 대한민국은 기타의 모든 범죄에 대하여 제1차적 재판권을 행사하게 되었다.

3. 또한 대한민국은 서독 보충협정의 포기조항의 형태를 받아들여 대한민국이 가지는 제1차적 권리를 원칙적으로 미국에 포기하되 이러한 포기는 개개의 사건이 발생하였을 경우 대한민국의 사법상의 이익으로 말미암아 대한민국 법정에서 재판하는 것이 필요하다고 결정하는 경우에는 대한민국이 권리포기를 철회할수 있는 권리를 가지는 것을 조건으로 하였으며 권리 포기의 철회를 둘러싸고 한·미 양국간에 의견 차이가 있을 때에도 대한민국이 최종적인 결정권을 확보하게 되었다는 사실을 잊어서는 아니될 것이다.

4. 그밖에도 본 조항은 대한민국의 법정에서 재판을 받는 미군 관계자의 권리를 규정하고 있는데 이러한 권리는 한국 헌법과 관계법들이 보장하고 있는 권리는 물론 합중국 헌법과 소송제도에서 미국 시민에게 보장된 기본권을 비롯하여 합중국 정부 대표를 모든 소송절차에 참여 시킬수 있는 권리를 포함하고 있다. 또한 대한민국의 안건에 관한 범죄를 행한 자는 대한민국이 구금하며 기타 재판건 피의자는 합중국군 당국이 구금하는 것으로 되었다.

- 1 -

0065

5. 이와 같이 우리나라가 제 1 차 재판권의 포기를 비롯하여 피의자
의 신병구금, 수사상의 협조 등 여러면에서 독일 보충협정의 명세
를 받아드리게 되었는데 이것은 우리나라가 독일국의 경우와 같이
국토 양단으로 인하여 공산군과 대치하고 있기 때문에 국토 방위
를 위하여서는 많은 외국 군대의 주둔을 필요로 한다는 공통점이
크게 작용하였다고 말할수 있다.

11. 중요 문제별 내용

본 조항에 규정된 중요 규정의 내용을 문제별로 고찰하여 보면 다음과
같다.
1. 재판권 행사에 대한 예외
우리나라의 재판권 행사는 계엄령 선포의 경우 및 한국의 협약의
범죄에 관하여 다음과 같은 예외적 규정을 두었다.
가. 계엄령 선포와 재판권 행사
우리나라가 계엄령을 선포하였을 때에는 그 선포지구 내에서는
형사 재판권 조항의 효력이 정지되며 그 지역내에서 계엄령
이 해제될때 가지 미군 당국이 전속적 재판권을 행사한다.
(1) 계엄령은 전시, 사변등 국가 비상사태시에 선포되며
체포, 구금, 수색 및 재판등 소송절차 전반에 걸쳐 국민의

- 5 -

0066

자유와 권리를 제한하게 됨으로 이번때에는 미군당국이 전속적인 재판권을 행사하는 것으로 규정하였다.

(2) 각국 협정에 이떠한 선례는 없지만 미국이 협정을 맺고 있는 각국에는 계엄령 제도가 없거나 또는 제도 자체는 있어도 실지 선포할 임이 없다는 사실을 고려하여 이를 성문화한 것이다.

나. 한국 영역외 범죄

우리나라의 재판권은 미군인, 군속 및 그들의 가족이 우리나라 영역외에서 범한 범죄에는 미치지 아니한다.

(1) 각국 협정에 선례가 없으나 실지운영상 접수국이 이떠한 사건을 취급할 여가 없다 한다.

(2) 또한 우리나라 밖위를 위하여 주둔하는 미군이 국외에서 우리형법 제 5 조에 구정된 중요한 범죄를 범한 자들 구성원 군속 또는 그들의 가족으로 종군 시킬되도 만무할 것임으로 이떠한 경우에는 우리나라의 재판권이 미치지 아니하는 것으로 하였다.

2. 전속적 재판권의 포기 요청

우리나라가 가지는 전속적 재판권을 특정 사건에 있어서 미군 당국이 합동 위원회에서 포기할 것을 요청하면 한국 당국은 호의적 고려를 할 것을 구정하고 있다.

(1) 비록 미국 법령에 처벌구정은 없다 알지라도 미국 군대의 행정적, 또는 징계적 제재로서도 충분히 그 목적을 달성할수 있는 경미한 범죄의 경우를 예상하여 법적 근거를 마련한데 불과하다.

(2) 요청이 있을때 호의적 고려를 하고 안하고는 한국 당국의 재량에 달려 있으며 국가 안위에 권한 중요 범죄는 비록 요청을 할 경우에도 포기할 수 없음은 당연하다.

3. 공무 집행중 범죄

미군 당국은 미군인, 또는 군속이 인정한 공무를 집행하는 동안 작위 또는 부작위로 인하여 범죄를 범하였을 경우 제 1 차적 재판권을 행사한다.

0067

- 3 -

(1) 공무 집행중명서 발행권차

미국 군인. 또는 군속이 공무 집행중 행위로 인한 범죄로 말미아마
우리나라 수사당국에 의하여 입건 되었을 때에는 미국 군대의 관계당국
이 그 혐의받은 범죄가 공무 수행중 행한 행위에 기인한 것이라는
중명서를 발행하게 되어 있으며 이와 같은 중명서는 그 사건에 대한
재판권 행사 당국을 결정하기 위한 충분한 증거가 된다.

(2) 한국 당국의 이의 제기와 재검토

미군당국이 발행한 중명서의 내용에 대한 반증이 있을 때에는 한국
검찰 총장은 이의를 제기할수 있으며 이때에는 한국 정부관계당국과
주한 미국 외교사절은 반드시 재검토하여여 한다.

(3) 국제적 선례

미•일 협정 제 17조 합의 의사록 제 3 (가) (2)항, 서독 보충협정
제 18 조, 웨스트 인디즈 협정 제 9조 11항등은 각국이 파견군의
지휘관 또는 관계당국이 공무 집행중명서를 발행하는 것으로 되어 있으며
기타 나토 협정의 당사국인 영국, 불란서, 이태리, 또이기등 각국도
또한 동일하다.

(4) 공무의 정의

(ㄱ) 어떤 범죄가 공무 집행중 행하여진 것이라고 증명하는 권한이 있을
지라도 공무라는 것이 무엇인가를 명확히 규정할 필요가 있다.
그래서 본 협정에서는 "공무라는 것은 미국 군대 군인, 군속이 공무
를 집행하는 기간중 행한 모든 행위를 포함하는 것이 아니다라는
점을 명백히 하는 동시에 그 개인이 집행하고 있는 공무의 기능
으로서 행할 것이 요구되는 행위에만 적용된다고 한정하였다.

(ㄴ) 이와같이 공무의 내용을 한정한 국제적 선례는 어느나라 협정
에서도 찾아볼수 없다. 이 규정은 심지 운영상 공무 집행
중 범죄 여부를 결정하기 위한 판단의 표준이 될 것이다.

4. 우리나라의 제 1 적격 재판권의 포기

우리나라 협정은 독일 보충협정에 구정된 포기제도를 제택하여 우리나라가

0068

- 4 -

행사하기로 되어 있는 제1차적 재판권을 일단 미국을 위하여 일괄적으로 포기한후 개개 사건이 발생하였을 때에 우리나라가 재판권을 행사하는 것이 중요하다고 인정할 때에는 포기하였던 제1차적 재판권을 철회하여 재판할수 있는 것으로 하였다.

가. 포기제도의 내용

(1) 우방 미국의 군대가 우리나라의 요청에 따라 이땅에 주둔하여 우리나라 군대와 더불어 공동으로 국토를 방위함에 있어서 항시 임전태세를 갖추어야 한다는 그들의 군사상의 특수 사명을 고려하여 서독의 경우와 같은 포기제도를 채택하게 된 것이다.

(2) 그러나 우리나라의 안전에 관한 범죄, 살인에 관한 범죄, 강간, 강도죄를 비롯하여 우리나라가 재판하는 것이 중요하다고 인정할 때에는 포기하였던 재판권을 철회하여 재판할수 있다.

(3) 또한 우리나라가 포기를 철회하였을 경우에 한·미 양국간의 의견차가 있을 때에도 우리나라가 재판권을 행사하기로 결정할때에는 그러한 결정은 최종적이며 확정적인 것으로 된 점은 독일 보충협정에서는 볼수 없는 우리한 규정인 것이다.

나. 각국의 선례

(1) 나토협정, 미·일 협정, 희랍협정, 네덜란드 협정, 서독 보충협정등 각국 협정은 조문상의 표현 차이에도 불구하고 심지 운영에 있어서는 이들 각국들은 바같이 미군관기 용범죄 건수의 80% 내지 100%에 달하는 많은 사건을 포기하고 있는 것이 실정이다.

(2) 우리나라도 한·미 양국간의 특별한 우호관계와 국제사회의 일원이라는 점에서 이와 같은 각국의 일반적인 선례에 따라야 할 것은 너무도 당연한 일이다.

5. 피의자의 재판 전 구금

우리나라가 재판권을 가지는 사건에 관련된 미군인, 군속 또는 가족이 체포되었을 때에는 피의자에 대한 모든 재판 절차가 다 끝나고 법원의

0069

판결이 확정될때 까지 미군당국이 피의자를 구금한다.

그러나 한국의 안전에 관한 범죄를 행한 피의자는 한국 당국이 구금한다.

(1) 각국의 협정의 선례를 보면 접수국이나 또는 파견군 당국이 범인을 체포하였을 때에는 일반적으로 파견군 당국이 구금하게 되어 있다. 본 항의 규정과같은 선례는 독일 보충협정 제22조에서 볼수 있으며 희랍협정 제3조, 네델란드 협정, 니카라구아 협정 9조 4항등 모든 재판 절차가 끝날때 까지 파견군당국이 피의자를 구금 하게 되어 있다.

(2) 그러나 우리나라 당국이 수사나 재판을 할수 있게 하기 위하여 미군당국은 모든 적절한 편의를 제공하여야 함은 물론, 증거의 인멸, 또는 범인의 도주 등을 방지하기 위하여 필요한 조치를 취하게 되어 있다.

6. 형의 집행

미국당국이 한국 법원이 언도한 자유형을 복역중에 있는 미군의·군속 또는 그들의 가족의 구금을 인도하여 달라고 요청할때에는 한국 당국이 이러한 미국 당국의 요청에 대하여 호의적인 고려를 할 것을 규정하고 있다.

(1) 이와 같은 규정은 미국 군대의 특수한 군사상의 사명과 또한 우리나라 구금시설의 현실이 구미 선진국가의 구금 시설의 수준에 도달되지 못하고 있는 점등을 고려에 넣어 특수한 경우 미측 요청이 있을 것을 고려한 것이다.

(2) 그러나 이 규정은 어디까지나 호의적인 고려를 할 것을 규정하고 있는데 불과한 것이며 개개의 경우 미국 당국의 요구를 받아 드리고 안드리고는 전여 한국 당국의 결정에 달려 있는 것이다.

(3) 한국 당국이 미국 당국의 요청을 받아들여 수형자의 구금을 미국당국에 인도하였을 때에는 미국 당국은 잔여 형기를 미국의 구금 시설에서 계속 집행하여야 하며

(4) 이러한 때에는 미국 당국은 수형자의 복역 동향에 관한 정보를 정규적으로 한국 당국에 제공하여야 할 뿐며며 한국 정부 대표는 수시로 이들의 복역 상황을 시찰 확인할 권리를 가진다.

7. 피의자 또는 피고인의 권리

제 9 항은 우리나라 재판권에 복하는 피의자 또는 피고인이 소송절차에 있어서 향유하는 권리를 열거하고 있다.

(1) 이와 같은 권리들은 우리나라 헌법과 관계 국내법이 피의자 또는 피의자의 이익을 위하여 보장하고 있는 여러권리를 재확인 한 것인 뿐만 아니다

(2) 기타 각국의 친례 또는 미국 헌법이 미국 시민에게 인정한 기본권 들을 구정한 것이다.

- 7 -

Claims Article

Proposed Changes in Korean Draft

<1965. 4. 23>

1. **Paragraph 2(a)**

   Delete "and located in the Republic of Korea"

2. **Paragraph 2(f)**

   "Each party waives its claim in any such case up to the amount of 1,400 United States dollars or its equivalent in Korean currency at the rate of exchange provided for in the Agreed Minute to Article ___ at the time the claim is filed."

3. **Paragraph 5(e)(i)**

   "Where the United States alone is responsible, the amount awarded or adjudged shall be distributed in the proportion of 25 percent chargeable to the Republic of Korea and 75 percent chargeable to the United States."

4. **Paragraph 5(e)(iii)**

   "Every half year, a statement of the sums paid by the Republic of Korea in the course of the half-yearly period in respect of every case regarding which the liability, amount, and proposed distribution on a percentage basis has been approved by the United States shall be sent to the appropriate authorities of the United States, together with a request for reimbursement. Such reimbursement shall be made in won within the shortest possible time."

5. **Paragraph 5(f)**

   Change "excluding" to "including".

6. **Paragraph 9(b)**

   "In the case of any private movable property, excluding that in use by the United States armed forces, which is subject to compulsory execution under Korean law, and is within the facilities and areas in use by the United States armed forces, the United States authorities shall, upon the request of the Korean courts, render all assistance within their power to see that such property is turned over to the Korean authorities."

0072

7. Paragraph 9(c)

"The authorities of the United States and the Republic of Korea shall cooperate in the procurement of evidence for a fair disposition of claims under this Article."

8. Paragraph 12   (new)

"For the purposes of this Article, members of the Korean Augmentation to the United States Army (KATUSA) shall be considered as members of the United States armed forces, and members of the Korean Service Corps (KSC) shall be considered as employees of the armed forces of the Republic of Korea."

9. Paragraph 13   (new)

"The provisions of this Article shall not apply to any claims which arose before the entry into force of this Agreement."

10. Proposed Agreed Minute

Tabled separately

11. In order to make this article conform to the rest of the Agreement:

a. Substitute "armed forces" for "armed services"

b. Substitute "performance of his official duties" for "execution of his official duties"

c. Substitute "for official purposes" for "in the execution of its official duty"

d. Substitute "counter claims" for "counter measures"

wherever appropriate.

한·미국 간의 상호방위조약 제4조에 의한 시설과 구역 및 한국에서의 미국군대의 지위에 관한 협정(SOFA) 전59권. 1966.7.9 서울에서 서명 : 1967.2.9 발효(조약 232호) (V.29 실무교섭회의, 제73-76차, 1965.4월)   79

12. Paragraph 9(a)

The United States shall not claim immunity from the jurisdiction of the courts of the Republic of Korea for members or employees of the United States armed forces in respect of the civil jurisdiction of the courts of the Republic of Korea except in respect of proceedings for the enforcement of any judgment given against them in the Republic of Korea in a matter arising from the performance of their official duties or except after payment in full satisfaction of a claim.

Agreed Minute

A. Unless otherwise provided,

1. The provisions of paragraphs five, six, seven and eight of this article will become effective six months from the date of entry into force of this agreement as to claims arising from incidents in the Seoul Special City area.

2. The provisions of paragraphs five, six, seven and eight will be progressively extended to other areas of Korea as determined and defined by the Joint Committee.

B. Until such time as the provisions of paragraphs five, six, seven and eight become effective in any given area

1. The United States shall process and settle claims (other than contractual claims) arising out of the acts or omissions of members or employees of the United States armed forces done in the performance of official duty or out of any other act, omission or occurence for which the United States armed forces are legally responsible, which cause damage in the Republic of Korea to parties other than the two governments;

2. The United States shall entertain other non-contractual claims against members or employees of the armed forces and may offer an ex gratia payment in such cases and in such amount as is determined by the appropriate United States authorities; and

3. Each party shall have the right to determine whether a member or employee of its armed forces was engaged in the performance of official duties and whether property owned by it was being used by its armed forces for official purposes.

C. For the purposes of subparagraph 2(d), subparagraph 5(e) shall be effective throughout Korea from the date of entry into force of this agreement.

0075

*#/23, 65
74th Session
U.S. proposal*

Re Paragraph 3(b)

At request of the United States, shall

1. The Government of the Republic of Korea waives in favor of the United States the primary right granted to the Korean authorities under sub-paragraph (b) of Paragraph 3 of this Article in cases of concurrent jurisdiction, in accordance with Paragraphs 2, 3, 4, 5, 6, and 7 of this Minute.

2. Subject to any particular arrangements which may be made under Paragraph 7 of this Minute, the military authorities of the United States shall notify the competent Korean authorities of individual cases falling under the waiver provided in Paragraph 1 of this Minute.

3. Where the competent Korean authorities hold the view that, by reason of special circumstances in a specific case, major interests of Korean administration of justice make imperative the exercise of Korean jurisdiction, they may recall the waiver granted under Paragraph 1 of this minute by a statement to the competent military authorities of the United States within a period of twenty-one days after receipt of the notification envisaged in Paragraph 2 of this Minute or any shorter period which may be provided in arrangements made under Paragraph 7 of this Minute. The Korean authorities may also submit the statement prior to receipt of such notification.

0076

(a) Subject to a careful examination of each specific case and to the results of such examination, major interests of Korean administration of justice within the meaning of Paragraph 3 above (may) make imperative the exercise of Korean jurisdiction, in particular, in the following cases:

(i) Security offenses against the Republic of Korea;

(ii) Offenses causing (the death of a human being) robbery, and (rape) except where the offenses are directed against a member of the United States Armed Forces or the civilian component, or a dependent; and

(iii) Attempts to commit such offenses or participation therein.

(b) In respect of the offenses referred to in Subparagraph (a) of this Paragraph, the authorities concerned shall proceed in particularly close cooperation from the beginning of the preliminary investigation in order to provide the mutual assistance envisaged in Paragraph 6 of this Article.

한·미국 간의 상호방위조약 제4조에 의한 시설과 구역 및 한국에서의 미국군대의 지위에 관한 협정(SOFA)
전59권. 1966.7.9 서울에서 서명 : 1967.2.9 발효(조약 232호) (V.29 실무교섭회의, 제73-76차, 1965.4월)

4. If, pursuant to Paragraph 3 of this Minute, the competent Korean authorities have recalled the waiver in a specific case and in such case an understanding cannot be reached in discussions between the authorities concerned, the Government of the United States may make representations to the Government of the Republic of Korea (through diplomatic channels.) (The Government of the Republic of Korea, giving due consideration to the interests of Korean administration of justice and to the interests of the Government of the United States, shall resolve the disagreement in the exercise of its authority in the field of foreign affairs.

5. With the consent of the competent Korean authorities, the military authorities of the United States may transfer to the Korean courts or authorities for investigation, trial and decision, particular criminal cases in which jurisdiction rests with the United States.

With the consent of the military authorities of the United States, the competent Korean authorities may transfer to the military authorities of the United States for investigation, trial and decision, particular criminal cases in which jurisdiction rests with the Republic of Korea.

6. (a) Where a member of the United States Armed Forces or civilian component, or a dependent, is arraigned before a court of the United States, for an offense committed in the Republic of Korea against Korean interests, the trial shall be held within the Republic of Korea.

(i) Except where the law of the United States requires otherwise, or

(ii) Except where, in cases of military exigency or in the interests of justice, the military authorities of the United States intend to hold the trial outside the Republic of Korea. In this event they shall afford the Korean authorities timely opportunity to comment on such intention and shall give due consideration to any comments the latter may make.

(b) Where the trial is held outside of the Republic of Korea the military authorities of the United States shall inform the Korean authorities of the place and date of the trial. A Korean representative shall be entitled to be present at the trial, except where his presence is incompatible with the rules of the court of the United States or with the security requirements of the United States, which

한·미국 간의 상호방위조약 제4조에 의한 시설과 구역 및 한국에서의 미국군대의 지위에 관한 협정(SOFA)
전59권. 1966.7.9 서울에서 서명 : 1967.2.9 발효(조약 232호) (V.29 실무교섭회의, 제73-76차, 1965.4월)　85

are not at the same time the security requirements of the Republic of Korea. The authorities of the United States shall inform the Korean authorities of the judgment and the final outcome of the proceedings.

7. In the implementation of the provisions of this Article and this agreed minute, and to facilitate the expeditious disposal of offenses of minor importance, arrangements may be made between the military authorities of the United States and the competent Korean authorities. These arrangements may also extend to dispensing with notification and to the period of time referred to in Paragraph 3 of this Minute, within which the waiver may be recalled.

CONFIDENTIAL

5. (a) The authorities of the United States and the authorities of the Republic of Korea shall assist each other in the arrest of members of the United States armed forces, the civilian component, or their dependents in the territory of the Republic of Korea and in handing them over to the authority which is to have custody in accordance with the following provisions.

(b) The authorities of the Republic of Korea shall notify promptly the authorities of the United States of the arrest of any member of the United States armed forces, or civilian component, or a dependent. The military authorities of the United States shall promptly notify the authorities of the Republic of Korea of the arrest of a member of the United States armed forces, the civilian component, or a dependent in any case in which the Republic of Korea has the primary right to exercise jurisdiction.

(c) The custody of an accused member of the United States armed forces or civilian component, or of a dependent, over whom the Republic of Korea is to exercise jurisdiction shall, if he is in the hands of the United States, remain with the United States pending the conclusion of all judicial proceedings and until custody is requested by the authorities of the Republic of Korea. If he is in the hands of the Republic of Korea, he shall be promptly handed over to the authorities of the United States and remain in their custody pending completion of all judicial proceedings and until custody is requested by the authorities of the Republic of Korea. When an accused has been in the custody of the military authorities of the United States, they shall give sympathetic consideration to any request for the transfer of custody which may be made by the authorities of the Republic of Korea in specific cases. The United States authorities will make any such accused available to the authorities of the

CONFIDENTIAL   0081

Republic of Korea upon their request for purposes of investigation and trial. The authorities of the Republic of Korea shall give sympathetic consideration to a request from the authorities of the United States for assistance in maintaining custody of an accused member of the United States armed forces, the civilian component, or a dependent.

(d) In respect of offenses solely against the security of the Republic of Korea provided in Paragraph 2(c), an accused shall be in the custody of the authorities of the Republic of Korea. (Subject US-ROK agreement on two understandings.)

The Republic of Korea, recognizing that it is the primary responsibility of the United States authorities to maintain good order and discipline where persons subject to United States law are concerned, waives its primary right to exercise jurisdiction under paragraph 3b. In accordance therewith, the United States authorities shall notify the authorities of the Republic of Korea of their intention to exercise jurisdiction in such cases through the Joint Committee. When the authorities of the Republic of Korea, after consultation with United States authorities, are of the opinion that, by reason of special circumstances in a specific case involving an offense against the security of the Republic of Korea, or of forcible rape, or of a malicious killing, the exercise of Korean jurisdiction is of vital importance to the Republic of Korea in that case, they will notify the United States authorities of that opinion within fifteen days after receipt of notification that the United States intends to exercise jurisdiction. The United States shall not have the right to exercise jurisdiction within those fifteen days. If any question arises concerning who is to exercise jurisdiction the United States diplomatic mission will be afforded an opportunity to confer with the proper authorities of the Republic of Korea before a final determination of this matter is made.

Trials of cases in which the authorities of the Republic of Korea waive the primary right to exercise jurisdiction, and trials of cases involving offenses described in para 3(a)(ii) committed against the state or nationals of the Republic of Korea will be held within a reasonable distance from the place where the offenses are alleged to have taken place unless other arrangements are mutually agreed upon. Representatives of the Republic of Korea may be present at such trials.

In the implementation of the provisions of Article   and this Minute, and to facilitate the expeditious disposal of offenses, arrangements may be made between the authorities of the United States and the Republic of Korea to dispense with notification.

Agreed Minute Re Paragraph 3(a)

2. Where a member of the United States armed forces or
civilian component is charged with an offense, a certificate issued
by competent authorities of the United States forces stating that the
alleged offense, if committed by him, arose out of an act or omission
done in the performance of official duty shall be sufficient evidence of
the fact for the purpose of determining primary jurisdiction.

In those exceptional cases where the chief prosecutor for
the Republic of Korea considers that there is proof contrary to a
certificate of official duty, it may be made the subject of review
through discussions between appropriate officials of the Government
of the Republic of Korea and the diplomatic mission of the United States
in Korea.

0085

CONFIDENTIAL
CLASSIFIED

한·미국 간의 상호방위조약 제4조에 의한 시설과 구역 및 한국에서의 미국군대의 지위에 관한 협정(SOFA)
전59권. 1966.7.9 서울에서 서명 : 1967.2.9 발효(조약 232호) (V.29 실무교섭회의, 제73-76차, 1965.4월)   91

1. The United States may contract for any materials, supplies, equipment and services (including construction work) to be furnished or undertaken in the Republic of Korea for purposes of, or authorized by, this Agreement, without restriction as to choice of contractor, supplier or person who provides such services. Such materials, supplies, equipment and services may, upon agreement between the appropriate authorities of the two Governments, also be procured through the Government of the Republic of Korea.

0086

2. No Korean tax shall be imposed on sales of merchandise or services by such organizations, except as provided in paragraph 1 (b) of this article. Purchases within the Republic of Korea of merchandise and supplies by such organizations shall be subject to the Korean taxes to which other purchasers of such merchandise and supplies are subject unless otherwise agreed between the two Governments.

0087

CONFIDENTIAL

Agreed Minute

7. It is understood that the duty free treatment provided in paragraph 2 shall apply to materials, supplies, and equipment imported for sale through commissaries and non-appropriated fund organizations, under such regulations as the United States armed forces may promulgate, to those individuals and organizations referred to in Article_____ and its Agreed Minute.

CONFIDENTIAL

0088

94 주한미군지위협정(SOFA) 서명 및 발효 11

CONFIDENTIAL

PROPOSED STATEMENT FOR JOINT AGREED SUMMARY

The ROK and U.S. negotiators agree that nothing in the Status of Forces Agreement in any way prevents the appropriate authorities of either the Republic of Korea or the U.S. from raising any appropriate matter at any time with each other. The U.S. negotiators recognize the desire of the ROK authorities to discuss the disposal of MPC's under custody of the ROK Government. However, both the ROK and U.S. negotiators have agreed to remove from the SOFA text any reference to the question of compensation for MPC's held by unauthorized persons. This agreement does not prejudice the position of either party in connection with discussion of this question through other channels.

CONFIDENTIAL

0089

CONFIDENTIAL

"If the US authorities determine that there would be significant advantage for US-ROK mutual defense to utilize one or more third-country corporations as USFK-invited contractor, the authorities of the Government of the Republic of Korea shall give sympathetic consideration to a US request to extend the benefits of this agreement to such non-US corporations. "

CONFIDENTIAL

0090

CONFIDENTIAL

"If the US authorities determine that there would be significant advantage for US-ROK mutual defense to utilize one or more third-country corporations as USFK-invited contractor, the authorities of the Government of the Republic of Korea shall give sympathetic consideration to a US request to extend the benefits of this agreement to such non-US corporations. "

CONFIDENTIAL

0090

96 주한미군지위협정(SOFA) 서명 및 발효 11

기 안 지

기 안 자	미주과 이근팔	전 화 번 호		공 보		필 요	불필요
	과 장	국 장	차 관	장 관			
협 조 자 서 명						보 존 년 한	
기 안 년 월 일	1965. 4. 24.	시 행 년월일		통제관	검열 1965.0.3 통제관	정 서	기 장
분류기호 문서번호	외구미 722.2 —						발송
경 유 수 신 참 조	대 통 령 참조: 비서실장 국 무 총 리 참조: 비서실장 사본: 법무부장관			발신		No.928-1~2 1965. 4. 30 외 무 부	
제 목	제 74 차 주둔군지위협정 체결 교섭실무자회의 결과 보고						

　　　　1965 년 4 월 23 일 상오 10 시부터 동 11 시까지 외무부

제 1 회의실에서 개최된 제 74 차 주둔군지위협정 체결 교섭실무자

회의에서 토의된 형사재판관할권에 관한 내용을 별첨과 같이

보고합니다.

　　유 첨: 1. 제 74 차 주둔군지위협정 체결 교섭실무자회의 결과

　　　　　　　　보고서 1부.

　　　　　2. 한·미간 주둔군지위협정 체결 교섭자료(형사재판

　　　　　　　관할권의 포기 및 피의자의 재판전 신병구금

　　　　　　　조항에 관한 미측 제안) 1부. 끝.

기 안 지

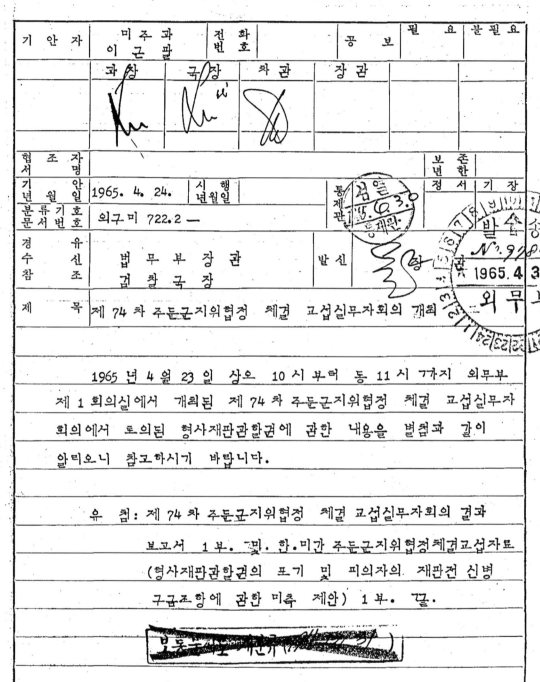

기 안 자	미 주 과 이 근 팔	전 화 번 호		공 보	필 요	불필요
	과 장	국 장	차 관	장 관		

협 조 서 자 명				보 존 년 한	
기 안 년 월 일	1965. 4. 24.	시 행 년월일		정 서	기 장
분류기호 문서번호	외구미 722.2 —				
경 수 참 조	유신조 법 무 부 장 관 검 찰 국 장		발 신		
제 목	제 74 차 주둔군지위협정 체결 교섭실무자회의 개최				

      1965 년 4 월 23 일 상오 10 시 부터 동 11 시 7까지 외무부

제 1 회의실에서 개최된 제 74 차 주둔군지위협정 체결 교섭실무자

회의에서 토의된 형사재판관할권에 관한 내용을 별첨과 같이

알리오니 참고하시기 바랍니다.

    유 첨: 제 74 차 주둔군지위협정 체결 교섭실무자회의 결과

        보고서 1 부. 및 한.미간 주둔군지위협정체결교섭자료

        (형사재판관할권의 포기 및 피의자의 재판전 신병

        구금조항에 관한 미측 제안) 1 부. 끝.

공통서식 1—2 (갑)　　　　　　　　　　　　　0092 (16절지)

제 74 차
한.미간 주둔군지위협정 체결 교섭실무자회의
보 고 서

1. 일 시: 1965 년 4 월 23 일 상오 10 시 부터 동 11 시 까지.

2. 장 소: 외무부 제 1 회의실

3. 토의사항:

형사재판관할권

우리측이 1965 년 2 월 12 일 개최된 제 70 차 한.미간 주둔군지위협정 체결 교섭 실무자회의 석상에서 수교한 형사재판관할권조항에 관한 제안에 대하여 미측은 그중 재판관할권을 행사하는 제 1 차적권리의 포기, 재판전 피의자의 신병구금, 및 공무집행중 범죄등 가장 중요한 문제에 관하여 다음과 같은 새로운 수정안을 제시하면서 금번 미측 제안은 미측으로서는 가장 중요하며 최종적인 제안이라고 강조하고 우리측이 수락할 것을 촉구 한바 있다.

가. 제 1 차관할권의 포기

(1) 한국당국이 재판권을 행사함이 특히 중요하다고 결정하는 경우를 제외하고 제 1 차적관할권을 미국당국에 포기한다는 것이 우리측 입장인데 반하여 미측은 서독의 관할권의 포기에 관한 조항과 같은 수정안을 제시하였다.

(2) 미측은 동 제안에서 한국정부는 재판관할권이 경합한 경우에는 한국당국에 부여된 제 1 차적관할권을 미국당국에 포기하고 한국당국이 특정사건에 있어서 특수한 사정을 이유로 한국의 사법상의 중대한 이익을 위하여 재판권을 행사함이 불가피하다는 의견을 가질 경우에는 미군당국에 통고하여 권리포기를 철회할 수 있으며,

(3) 특히 대한민국의 안전에 관한 범죄, 사람을 죽음에 이르게 한 범죄, 강간죄, 및 강도죄와 이들 각범죄의 미수 및 공범의 경우 한국당국이 한국의 사법상의 중대한 이익을 위하여 한국 당국이 재판관할권을 행사함이 불가피하게 할 수 있는 것으로 하여 한국이 포기한 재판권을 철회할 수 있게 하였다.

0093

0094

(4) 한국당국이 특정사건에 있어서 권리포기를 철회한 경우 한·미간에 양해가 성립되지 않을 때에는 미국정부는 외교경로를 통하여 한국정부에 한국정부에 이의를 제기할 수 있으며 한국정부는 양국의 이의을 충분히 고려한 후 의견차의를 해결하여야 한다.

나. 재판전 피의자의 신병 구금

재판전 피의자의 신병 구금에 관하여서는 원칙적으로 모든 사법절차가 끝나고 한국당국이 요구할 때 가지 미국당국이 피의자의 신병을 구금하되,

(1) 대한민국의 안건에 대한 범죄에 관한 피의자의 신병은 구금사정의 적당여부에 관한 한·미간의 합의와 한국의 구금시설이 미국 수준으로 보아 적당할 것을 조건으로 하여 한국당국의 구금 하에 두기로 하였으며,

(2) 또한 한국당국이 특정사건에 있어서 피의자의 신병구금의 인도를 요구하면 미국당국은 이 요구에 대하여 호의적인 고려를 하여야 하는 것으로 하여

한국당국이 특정사건에 있어서 기필 피의자의 신병을 구금코져 할 때에 구금할 수 있는 길이 마련됨으로서 사실상 한·미간의 입장이 접근하였다.

다. 공무집행중 범죄

미측은 공무집행중 범죄문제에 관한 양측의 입장이 거의 합의에 도달하였음을 지적하고 다음과 같은 몇 가지 점에 대한 미측 입장을 피력하였다.

(1) 공무집행중명서의 발행권자에 관하여 우리측이 미군법무관이 발행할 것을 제의하였음에 대하여 미측은 미측 종태 주장대로 "미국군대의 권한있는 당국"으로 할 것을 조건으로 우리측이 원하는 바에 따라 "증명서는 반듯이 미군법무관의 권고를 받은 후에만 발행한다"는 양해사항을 기록에 남길 것을 제의하였으며,

(2) 미측이 발행한 증명서에 관하여 반증이 있다고 사려할 때 이의를 제기할 수 있는 한국기관을 우리측은 "대한민국지방검찰청검사장"으로 할 것을 제안하였는데 대하여 미측은 한국당국이 반증이 있다고 사려하여 이의를 제기하면 미측과 외교교섭을 0095되는

한·미국 간의 상호방위조약 제4조에 의한 시설과 구역 및 한국에서의 미국군대의 지위에 관한 협정(SOFA)
전59권. 1966.7.9 서울에서 서명 : 1967.2.9 발효(조약 232호) (V.29 실무교섭회의, 제73-76차, 1965.4월)   101

65-5-8

마 ㅌ 112-5(

0096

것임으로 지방검찰청검사장으로서는 적당하지 않으며 "대한민국 검찰총장"이어야 한다고 지적하였다.

(3) 공무집행의 정의에 관하여 우리측은 미국동군이 1956년도에 예하부대에 지시한 정의를 일부 수정하여 합의의사록으로 제안 하였음에 반하여 미측은 미국동군의 정의대로 양해사항으로 채택할 것을 주장하였다.

(4) 우리측이 대한민국당국이 공무집행증명서에 대한 반증이 있다고 사려하는 예외적인 경우에는 공무집행증명서는 대한민국관계당국과 주한외교사절간의 협의를 통한 재심의 대상이 "되어야 한다" (shall)라고 제의한데 대하여 미측은 그런 경우에 재심의 대상이 "될 수 있다" (may)라고 하는 것이 좋으며 이의 제기 여부에 관한 재량권은 한국당국에 있는 것이라고 말하였다.

(5) 미국측이 "공무집행증명서는 수정에 합의되지 않는 한 확정적 이다" 라는 양해사항을 기록에 남길 것을 제의한데 대하여 우리측은 이를 원칙적으로 수락하되 "미국당국은 대한민국의 지방검찰청검사장이 제기하는 이의에 대하여 정당한 고려를 하여야 한다"라는 것을 추가 기록할 것을 제의한바 있는데 미측은 한국당국이 제기하는 이의에 대하여 증명서 발행에 관한 합의의사록의 규정에 따라 미국당국이 고려를 할 것이라고 말하고 한국측의 요구를 명확하게 하기 위하여 다음과 같이 미측양해사항을 수정할 것을 제안하였다.

　　　"공무집행증명서는 합의의사록 3(a)(ii)에 규정된 절차에 따라 수정에 합의되지 않는 한 확정적이다".

4. 당부 의견

1964년 2월 14일 개최된 제 42차심무자회의에서 형사재판관할권에 관한 초안이 교환된 이래 한.미양측은 1년 2개월 이상 교섭을 계속하여 온 결과 금번 미측이 서독보충협정의 프기조항의 내용과 대동소이한 수정안을 제시하고 우리측이 수락할 것을 촉구하고 있는바 미측제안 수락여부에 따른 장단점을 검토하여 보면 다음과 같다.

0097

한·미국 간의 상호방위조약 제4조에 의한 시설과 구역 및 한국에서의 미국군대의 지위에 관한 협정(SOFA)
전59권. 1966.7.9 서울에서 서명 : 1967.2.9 발효(조약 232호) (V.29 실무교섭회의, 제73-76차, 1965.4월) 103

'05-5-8   미문112·5

0098

가. 장 점

(1) 우리 정부의 주둔군지위협정 체결 교섭의 주된 목적이 6.25 동란이란 긴급사태 하에서 우방미국 군대에 배타적인 재판관할권의 행사를 허용하게 된 소위 대전협정을 지양함으로서 주권국가로서 미국군대에 대한 재판관할권을 회복하려는데 있는 만큼 금번 미측 제안이 우리측이 주장하여 온 입장과는 거리가 있긴 하지만 이를 수락함으로서 재판권이 전여 박탈된 현상태를 극복할수 있으며,

또한 한국당국이 미측 요구에 따라 한국당국에 부여된 재판관할권을 미국당국에 일단 포기하는 경우에도 개개 특정사건이 발생하였을 때에 한국당국이 사법상 중대한 이익을 위하여 재판권을 행사코저 할 때에 그렇게 할 수 있는 결정권이 보장되어 있다.

(2) 우리 정부는 한.미간에 체결될 협정이 미.일협정이나 또는 NATO 협정의 형태로 해결되기를 바라왔지만 미측이 지적하고 있는 바와 같이 우리 나라가 미군이 주둔하고 있는 기타 국가의 경우와 달라서 사실상 휴전상태 하에 있으며 많은 미군이 공산재침을 막기 위하여 주둔하여 임전태세를 가추어야 할 실정이며 정부로서도 미국군대의 계속적인 주둔과 장기적인 경제원조를 요구하지 않을 수 없는 특수성에 비추어 우리 나라에 유리한 입장 만을 추구할 수 없는 처지에 있다.

(3) 금번 Brown 주한미국대사는 새로운 제안을 제시함에 앞서 4월 21일 외무부장관을 방문하고 이번 미측제안은 미국정부의 최종적 제안이며 만약에 한국정부가 이를 수락하지 않을 경우에는 협정의 조기타결은 불가능할 것이라고 미국정부의 태도를 밝힌바 있으며 본회의 석상에서도 미측은 이번 제안이 미측의 중대한 양보이며 또한 최종적 제안임을 강조한바 있음에 비추어 정부가 금번 미측제안을 수락하지 않을 경우 협정전반의 타결이 상당히 지연될 것으로 사려된다.

0000

미 문11265

0100

나. 단 점

    (1) 한·일회담이 최종적인 단계에 도달한 이 지음 국민의
        관심이 정부나 국회에 집중되고 있는 만큼 우리 정부가
        인접국가이며 패전국이던 일본국이 수년전에 미국과
        체결한 협정에 비하여 체제상 거리가 있는 협정을
        체결하게 되면 국민감정을 자극할 우려가 있다.

    (2) 우리 나라 뿐만 아니라 중국이나 비율빈국에서도 미주둔군
        지위협정의 체결 또는 개정을 위한 교섭이 진행되고
        있는바 우리가 입수한 정보에 의하면 이들 각국도 미·일
        협정과 같은 형태를 목표로 하여 교섭을 추진중이라 하며
        만약에 한국이 중국이나 비율빈국 보다 앞서 미측 제안을
        수락하게 되면 이들 각국도 불원간 한·미간협정과 유사한
        내용의 협정을 수락하지 않을 수 없는 결과가 될 것이다.

5. 기타 사항:
    가. 차기 회의 일자: 1965 년 4 월 28 일 하오 3 시 30 분. 끝.

한·미국 간의 상호방위조약 제4조에 의한 시설과 구역 및 한국에서의 미국군대의 지위에 관한 협정(SOFA)
전59권. 1966.7.9 서울에서 서명 : 1967.2.9 발효(조약 232호) (V.29 실무교섭회의, 제73-76차, 1965.4월) 107

65 - 5 - A (±)   미국문 1125(5)

0102

STATUS OF FORCES NEGOTIATIONS: 74th Meeting

SUBJECT: Criminal Jurisdiction Article

PLACE: Ministry of Foreign Affairs

DATE: April 23, 1965

PARTICIPANTS:

Republic of Korea   United States

CHANG Sang-mun   Philip C. Habib
YUN Wun-yong   Brig. Gen. Carroll H. Dunn, USA
YI Nam-ki   Colonel Allan G. Pixton, USA
Major YI Ke-hun, ROKA   Captain George Hagerman, USN
KIM Ki-cho   Colonel Kenneth C. Crawford, USA
HWANG Yong-chae   Robert A. Kinney
PAK Won-chol   Benjamin A. Fleck
XxIx   Jack Friedman
YI Kun-pal   (Interpreter)   Major Alton Harvey, USA
                                        David Y.C. Lee,(Interpreter)

0103

1. Mr. Habib opened the meeting by stating that the U.S. negotiators wished to speak at this meeting on the subjects of waiver of jurisdiction, pre-trial custody, and duty certificate. In order to expedite the negotiations and enable the two governments to reach full agreement on the Status of Forces Agreement, he said, the U.S. Government was now prepared to make a major and final concession on the waiver issue by offering what is generally called the German NATO waiver formula. This is the heart of the final U.S. position on the Criminal Jurisdiction Article. Noting that the U.S. and Korean negotiators are in essential agreement regarding paragraphs 3 and 4, Mr. Habib said that the U.S. negotiators wished to table at this time a new Agreed Minute Re Paragraph 3(b) to replace the previous Agreed Minute Re Paragraph 3 of the U.S. draft. The draft of the Agreed Minute was tabled.

2. With regard to the waiver issue, Mr. Habib continued, the U.S. negotiators have proceeded on the basis of the Korean conception that the Korean authorities will seek to exercise jurisdiction only when, by reason of special circumstances in a special case, major interests of the Korean administration of justice make imperative the exercise of Korean jurisdiction. The new U.S. waiver formula, he pointed out, is similar to this proposal, for in special circumstances in a specific case where major interests of Korean administration of justice make imperative the exercise of Korean jurisdiction the ROK Government can recall its waiver and exercise its jurisdiction.

3. Mr. Habib stated that the U.S. negotiators were offering this formula because the Korean negotiators had clearly indicated the intention of the Korean authorities to exercise restraint. In the light of these repeated assurances, the U.S. negotiators do not expect the ROK Government to seek frequent recall of waiver. On the contrary, they expect that restraint in recall of waiver will be exercised in all cases, except where special circumstances of fundamental interest apply. This is not, Mr. Habib continued, an unusual expectation. For example, the U.S. negotiators would like to present the following German waiver statistics which point up the host country's restraint in recalling waivers under this formula. The following tabula-

0104

tion, he pointed out, presents the percentage of U.S. servicemen subject to German jurisdiction for the latest reporting period, the 12-month period from December 1, 1963 to November 30, 1964, by various categories of offenses:

Cases of Murder	50 % tried by Germany
Rape	4 %
Manslaughter	10 %
Robbery	26%%
Burglary	0 %
Arson	0 %
Assault	0%%
Forgery	0 %
Economic Control Laws	0 %
Disorderly Conduct	0 %

Mr. Habib stated that these statistics shows that the Federal Republic of Germany has exercised its right of recall of waiver in only a small percentage of cases. The U.S. negotiators are reassured by the ROK negotiators' emphasis in the Agreed Joint Summary that, if given the right of jurisdiction, they would show great restraint in exercising jurisdiction over U.S. servicemen.

4. The U.S. negotiators believe, Mr. Habib said, that this new U.S. Agreed Minute provides a sound basis for early conclusion of the negotiations. The new language on waiver of jurisdiction is fully consistent with the ROK Government's desire for a clearcut exposition of its right to exercise jurisdiction over U.S. servicement. This waiver formula meets the needs of both the host state and the sending state. It reserves to the Republic of Korea the right to exercise jurisdiction in cases where it believes exercise of jurisdiction is imperative. At the same time, the formula defers to the needs of the sending state for necessary control and disciplinary authority over its armed forces. The U.S. negotiators believe that this formula should be a positive factor in promoting friendly U.S.-ROK relations. After the Korean

0105

negotiators had had an opportunity to study this proposal in detail, Mr. Habib said, the U.S. negotiators would be glad to provide any further desired explanations.

5. Turning to the subject of pre-trial custody, Mr. Habib declared that the proposals made by the Korean negotiators at the 70th negotiating meeting had brought the two sides closer to agreement on this portion of the Criminal Jurisdiction Article. In response to those proposals, the U.S. negotiators now wished to table a revised Paragraph 5 which is responsive to the Korean views. ~~expressed~~ They hoped that this revised draft will result in full agreement on this question.

6. Mr. Habib noted that the subparagraph (c) proposed by the Korean negotiators, which provides that the U.S. military authorities will promptly notify the Korean authorities of the arrest of personnel of the U.S. armed forces in any case in which the Republic of Korea has primary jurisdiction, had been incorporated verbatim as an additional sentence in subparagraph (b) of the U.S. draft. The Korean negotiators had pointed out that the first sentence of Paragraph 5(b) stipulates the obligation of the Korean authorities to notify the U.S. military authorities of the arrest of U.S. personnel. They believed, therefore, that ~~consequently~~ there should be a reciprocal obligation on the part of the U.S. authorities. ~~accordingly~~ The U.S. negotiators agreed with this position and had incorporated the proposed Korean language into the U.S. draft.

7. Mr. Habib noted that the Korean negotiators had urged several times that language be included in the Article which would provide for sympathetic consideration by the U.S. military authorities of requests by the Korean authorities for transfer of custody in specific cases. The U.S. negotiators ~~concurred in~~ now accepted this proposals and had added a new sentence to provide the language desired by the Korean negotiators, an additional sentence was now included in subparagraph (c) of the U.S. draft. This sentence provides that the U.S. military authorities will give sympathetic consideration to any request for transfer of custody which may be made by the Korean authorities in specific cases. Mr. Habib noted that the last two sentences of subparagraph

0106

(c) are also similar to the last two sentences of subparagraph (f) of the Korean draft, tabled at the 70th negotiating meeting.

8. Mr. Habib said that the U.S. negotiators were prepared to incorporate *verbatim* subparagraph (e) of the Korean draft as subparagraph (d) in the U.S. draft, provided that the Korean negotiators would accept the two understandings tabled by the U.S. negotiators at the 58th meeting. These *proposed* understandings were as follows:

a. There must be mutual U.S.-ROK agreement as to the circumstances in which such custody is appropriate;

b. Korean confinement facilities must be adequate by U.S. standards.

Noting that the U.S. armed forces *are* in Korea to help protect and preserve the security of the Republic, Mr. Habib stated that the U.S. negotiators had the obligation to protect the legitimate rights of American military personnel. Therefore, there should be mutual agreement as to the circumstances in which such custody is appropriate. It is obvious, he continued, that before this subparagraph can be effective, there must be agreement between the two sides. Otherwise, the subparagraph has no meaning.

9. Mr. Habib then took up the question of duty certificates. On this subject, he noted, the two sides are not far apart. The U.S. negotiators were proposing several changes in the U.S. position which should expedite full agreement on Paragraph 3 and *the* Agreed Minute Re Paragraph 3. (a)

10. The Korean negotiators had tabled language at the 70th meeting, Mr. Habib recalled, which provided that the duty certificate should be issued by a Staff Judge Advocate. The U.S. negotiators agreed that a Staff Judge Advocate would usually be in the best position to avoid legal problems which could follow errors in issuing duty certificates. However, such an officer, regardless of his *technical* qualifications, is not in a position of command and does not have command responsibilities. In order to be responsive to the Korean viewpoint and to assure the Korean negotiators that the

0107

Staff Judge Advocate will be consulted with regard to duty certificates, the U.S. negotiators wished to make a proposal. If the Korean negotiators would accept the provision in the U.S. draft that the duty certificate will be issued by "competent authorities" of the U.S. armed forces, the U.S. negotiators will agree to the inclusion of the following understanding in the Agreed Joint Summary:

"A duty certificate will be issued only upon the advice of a Staff Judge Advocate."

11. Mr. Habib stated that the U.S. negotiators were puzzled by the substitution in the Korean draft of the phrase "Chief District Prosecutor" for the previously used phrase "Chief Prosecutor". The U.S. negotiators agreed that the district prosecutors undoubtedly would make recommendations to the Chief Prosecutor. However, the U.S. negotiators believed that it would be quite improper for the District Prosecutors to initiate discussions directly with U.S. diplomatic officials regarding duty certificates. This should be done only by the Chief Prosecutor in Seoul. The U.S. draft provides that the Chief Prosecutor may raise the issue with U.S. diplomatic officials when he considers that there is proof contrary to a duty certificate. Whether or not he does raise the issue is up to him. Therefore, the word "may" is preferable to the word "shall". The initiative would still lie with the ROK Government to raise the issue at the diplomatic level if it thought it necessary.

12. Mr. Habib recalled that the Korean negotiators, at the 70th negotiating session, had proposed the addition of a second sentence to the first of two understandings originally proposed by the U.S. negotiators regarding the issuance of duty certificates. Under the provisions of Agreed Minute #2 Re Paragraph 3(a) of the U.S. draft, the U.S. authorities will give consideration to any points raised by the ROK Chief-Prosecutor. To make this point clear in the [first] agreed understanding, the U.S. negotiators wished to propose modification of the under-standing by adding a phrase to the version originally suggested by them. The modified understanding would then read as 0108

U.S. authorities shall give due consideration to any objection which may be raised by the ~~~~ ~~~~ for the R.O.K.,

"a. The certificate will be conclusive unless modification is agreed upon under procedures outlined in Agreed Minute No. 2 Re Paragraph 3(a)."

13. Mr. Habib recalled that the Korean negotiators, at the 47th negotiating meeting, had stated that if the definition of official duty based on that contained in the U.S. Army, Far East, Circular of January 1956 ~~~~ were read into the ~~~~ Agreed Joint Summary, existing differences over the language of the Agreed Minute #2 Re Paragraph 3 (a) could be resolved on the basis of the U.S. draft. This definition of official duty, which clearly spells out that a substantial departure from the acts a person is required to perform in a particular duty usually will indicate an act outside of "official duty", was tabled at the 49th meeting. A modified version of this definition was tabled by the Korean negotiators at the 70th meeting as Agreed Minute #2 Re Paragraph 3(a)(ii). The U.S. negotiators remain willing to agree to the original Korean proposal, Mr. Habib continued, that the U.S. Army definition, as tabled at the 49th meeting, be incorporated into the Agreed Joint Summary when agreement is reached on the duty certificate issue.

14. Mr. Habib said that the U.S. negotiators were prepared to discuss a few additional issues in connection with the Criminal Jurisdiction Article but would reserve such discussion until a later meeting.

15. Mr. Chang ~~~~~~~~~ expressed the appreciation of the Korean negotiators for the tabling by the U.S. negotiators of ~~~~~~~~~~~ revisions of certain portions of the Criminal Jurisdiction Article. He said that Korean negotiators would carefully consider the proposed revisions and would respond at a later meeting.

16. It was agreed to hold the 75th meeting on April 27 to discuss the Labor Article and the 76th ~~~~~~~~~~~ April 28 to discuss ~~~~~ Criminal Jurisdiction Article.

0109

JOINT SUMMARY RECORD OF THE 74TH SESSION

1. Time and Place: 10:00 - 11:00 A.M., April 23, 1965 at
   the Foreign Ministry's Conference
   Room (No. 1)

2. Attendants:

ROK Side:

Mr. Chang, Sang Moon	Director European and American Affairs Bureau
Mr. Lee, Nam Ki	Chief America Section Ministry of Foreign Affairs
Mr. Hur, Hyong Koo	Chief Prosecutors Section Ministry of Justice
Maj. Lee Kye Hoon	Military Affairs Section Ministry of National Defense
Mr. Kim, Kee Joe	3rd Secretary Ministry of Foreign Affairs
Mr. Lee, Keun Pal (Rapporteur and Interpreter)	3rd Secretary Ministry of Foreign Affairs
Mr. Lee, Chung Bin	3rd Secretary Ministry of Foreign Affairs
Mr. Hwang, Young Jae	3rd Secretary Ministry of Foreign Affairs

U.S. Side:

Mr. Philip C. Habib	Counselor American Embassy
Mr. Brig. Gen. Caroll H. Dunn	Deputy Chief of Staff 8th U.S. Army
Col. Allan G. Pixton	Deputy Chief of Staff 8th U.S. Army
Capt. George Hagerman	Assistant Chief of Staff USN/K
Col. Kenneth C. Crawford	Staff Judge Advocate 8th U.S. Army
Mr. Benjamin A. Fleck	First Secretary American Embassy

0110

Mr. Robert A. Kinney	J-5 8th U.S. Army
Mr. Goodwin Shapiro	Second Secretary American Embassy
Maj. Alton H. Harvey	Staff Judge Advocate's Office 8th U.S. Army
Mr. David Y.C. Lee (Interpreter)	Second Secretary American Embassy

1. Mr. Habib opened the meeting by stating that the U.S. negotiators wished to speak at this meeting on the subjects of waiver of jurisdiction, pre-trial custody, and duty certificate. In order to expedite the negotiations and enable the two governments to reach full agreement on the Status of Forces Agreement, he said, the U.S. Government was now prepared to make a major and final concession on the waiver issue by offering what is generally called the German NATO waiver formula. This is the heart of the final U.S. position on the Criminal Jurisdiction Article. Noting that the U.S. and Korean negotiators are in essential agreement regarding paragraph 3 and 4, Mr. Habib said that the U.S. negotiators wished to table at this time a new Agreed Minute Re Paragraph 3(b) to replace the previous Agreed Minute Re Paragraph 3 of the U.S. draft. The draft of the Agreed Minute was tabled.

2. With regard to the waiver issue, Mr. Habib continued, the U.S. negotiators have proceeded on the basis of the Korean conception that the Korean authorities will seek to exercise jurisdiction only when, by reason of special circumstances in a special case, major interests of the Korean administration of justice make imperative the exercise of Korean jurisdiction. The new U.S. waiver

0111

formula, he pointed out, is similar to this proposal, for in special circumstances in a specific case where major interests of Korean administration of justice make imperative the exercise of Korean jurisdiction the ROK Government can recall its waiver and exercise its jurisdiction.

3. Mr. Habib stated that the U.S. negotiators were offering this formula because the Korean negotiators had clearly indicated the intention of the Korean authorities to exercise restraint. In the light of these repeated assurances, the U.S. negotiators do not expect the ROK Government to seek frequent recall of waiver. On the contrary, they expect that restraint in recall of waiver will be exercised in all cases, except where special circumstances of fundamental interest apply. This is not, Mr. Habib continued, an unusual expectation. For example, the U.S. negotiators would like to present the following German waiver statistics which point up the host country's restraint in recalling waivers under this formula. The following tabulation, he pointed out, presents the percentage of U.S. servicemen subject to German jurisdiction for the latest reporting period, the 12-month period from December 1, 1963 to November 30, 1964, by various categories of offenses:

Cases of Murder	50% tried by Germany
Rape	4%
Manslaughter	10%
Robbery	0.6%
Burglary	0%
Arson	0%
Assault	0%
Forgery	0%
Economic Control Laws	0%
Disorderly Conduct	0%

0112

Mr. Habib stated that these statistics show that the
Federal Republic of Germany has exercised its right of
recall of waiver in only a small percentage of cases.
The U.S. negotiators are reassured by the ROK negotiators'
emphasis in the Agreed Joint Summary that, if given the
right of jurisdiction, they would show great restraint
in exercising jurisdiction over U.S. servicemen.

4. The U.S. negotiators believe, Mr. Habib said, that
this new U.S. Agreed Minute provides a sound basis for early
conclusion of the negotiations. The new language on waiver
of jurisdiction is fully consistent with the ROK Government's
desire for a clearcut exposition of its right to exercise
jurisdiction over U.S. servicemen. This waiver formula
meets the needs of both the host state and the sending
state. It reserves to the Republic of Korea the right to
exercise jurisdiction in cases where it believes exercise
of jurisdiction is imperative. At the same time, the formula
defers to the needs of the sending state for necessary control
and disciplinary authority over its armed forces. The
U.S. negotiators believe that this formula should be a
positive factor in promoting friendly U.S.-ROK relations.
After the Korean negotiators had had an opportunity to study
this proposal in detail, Mr. Habib said, the U.S. negotiators
would be glad to provide any further desired explanations.

5. Turning to the subject of pre-trial custody,
Mr. Habib declared that the proposals made by the Korean
negotiators at the 70th negotiating meeting had brought the
two sides closer to agreement on this portion of the Criminal
Jurisdiction Article. In response to those proposals, the
U.S. negotiators now wished to table a revised Paragraph 5
which is responsive to the Korean views. They hoped that
this revised draft will result in full agreement on this
question.

0113

6. Mr. Habib noted that the subparagraph (c) proposed by the Korean negotiators, which provides that the U.S. military authorities will promptly notify the Korean authorities of the arrest of personnel of the U.S. armed forces in any case in which the Republic of Korea has primary jurisdiction, had been incorporated verbatim as an additional sentence in subparagraph (b) of the U.S. draft. The Korean negotiators had pointed out that the first sentence of Paragraph 5(b) stipulates the obligation of the Korean authorities to notify the U.S. military authorities of the arrest of U.S. personnel. They believed, therefore, that there should be a reciprocal obligation on the part of the U.S. authorities. The U.S. negotiators agreed with this position and had incorporated the proposed Korean language into the U.S. draft.

7. Mr. Habib noted that the Korean negotiators had urged several times that language be included in the Article which would provide for sympathetic consideration by the U.S. military authorities of requests by the Korean authorities for transfer of custody in specific cases. The U.S. negotiators now accepted this proposals to provide the language desired by the Korean negotiators, and an additional sentence was now included in subparagraph (c) of the U.S. draft. This sentence provides that the U.S. military authorities will give sympathetic consideration to any request for transfer of custody which may be made by the Korean authorities in specific cases. Mr. Habib noted that the last two sentences of subparagraph (c) are also similar to the last two sentences of subparagraph (b) of the Korean draft, tabled at the 70th negotiating meeting.

0114

8. Mr. Habib said that the U.S. negotiators were prepared
to incorporate verbatim subparagraph (e) of the Korean draft
as subparagraph (d) in the U.S. draft, provided that the
Korean negotiators would accept the two understandings
tabled by the U.S. negotiators at the 58th meeting. These
proposed understandings were as follows:

    a. There must be mutual U.S.-ROK agreement as to
the circumstances in which such custody is appropriate;

    b. Korean confinement facilities must be adequate
by U.S. standards.

Noting that the U.S. armed forces are in Korea to help
protect and preserve the security of the Republic, Mr. Habib
stated that the U.S. negotiators had the obligation to protect
the legitimate rights of American military personnel.
Therefore, there should be mutual agreement as to the
circumstances in which such custody is appropriate. It is
obvious, he continued, that before this subparagraph can be
effective, there must be agreement between the two sides.
Otherwise, the subparagraph has no meaning.

9. Mr. Habib then took up the question of duty
certificates. On this subject, he noted, the two sides are
not far apart. The U.S. negotiators were proposing
several changes in the U.S. position which should expedite
full agreement on Paragraph 3 and the Agreed Minute Re
Paragraph 3(a).

10. The Korean negotiators had tabled language at the
70th meeting, Mr. Habib recalled, which provided that the
duty certificate should be issued by a Staff Judge Advocate.
The U.S. negotiators agreed that a Staff Judge Advocate
would usually be in the best position to avoid legal

0115

problems which could follow errors in issuing duty
certificates. However, such an officer, regardless of his
technical qualifications, is not in a position of command
and does not have command responsibilities. In order to
be responsive to the Korean viewpoint and to assure the
Korean negotiators that the Staff Judge Advocate will be
consulted with regard to duty certificates, the U.S.
negotiators wished to make a proposal. If the Korean
negotiators would accept the provision in the U.S. draft
that the duty certificate will be issued by "competent authorities" of the U.S. armed forces, the U.S. negotiators will
agree to the inclusion of the following understanding in
the Agreed Joint Summary:

"A duty certificate will be issued only upon the
advice of a Staff Judge Advocate."

11. Mr. Habib stated that the U.S. negotiators were
puzzled by the substitution in the Korean draft of the
phrase "Chief District Prosecutor" for the previously
used phrase "Chief Prosecutor". The U.S. negotiators
agreed that the district prosecutors undoubtedly would make
recommendations to the Chief Prosecutor. However, the
U.S. negotiators believed that it would be quite improper
for the District Prosecutors to initiate discussions directly
with U.S. diplomatic officials regarding duty certificates.
This should be done only by the Chief Prosecutor in Seoul.
The U.S. draft provides that the Chief Prosecutor may raise
the issue with U.S. diplomatic officials when he considers
that there is proof contrary to a duty certificate. Whether
or not he does raise the issue is up to him. Therefore,
the word "may" is preferable to the word "shall". The

0116

initiative would still lie with the ROK Government to raise the issue at the diplomatic level if it thought it necessary.

12. Mr. Habib recalled that the Korean negotiators, at the 70th negotiating session, had proposed the addition of a second sentence to the first of two understandings originally proposed by the U.S. negotiators regarding the issuance of duty certificates. Under the provisions of Agreed Minute #2 Re Paragraph 3(a) of the U.S. draft, the U.S. authorities will give consideration to any points raised by the ROK Chief Prosecutor. To make this point clear in the first agreed understanding, the U.S. negotiators wished to propose modification of the understanding by adding a phrase to the version originally suggested by them. The modified understanding would then read as follows:

"a. The certificate will be conclusive unless modification is agreed upon under procedures outlined in Agreed Minute No.2 Re Paragraph 3(a)."

13. Mr. Habib recalled that the Korean negotiators, at the 47th negotiating meeting, had stated that if the definition of official duty based on that contained in the U.S. Army, Far East, Circular of January 1956 were read into the Agreed Joint Summary, existing differences over the language of the Agreed Minute #2 Re Paragraph 3(a) could be resolved on the basis of the U.S. draft. This definition of official duty, which clearly spells out that a substantial departure from the acts a person is required to perform in a particular duty usually will indicate an act outside of "official duty", was tabled at the 49th meeting. A modified version of this definition was tabled by the Korean negotiators at the 70th meeting as Agreed Minute #2 Re Paragraph 3(a)(ii).

0117

The U.S. negotiators remain willing to agree to the original Korean proposal, Mr. Habib continued, that the U.S. Army definition, as tabled at the 49th meeting, be incorporated into the Agreed Joint Summary when agreement is reached on the duty certificate issue.

14. Mr. Habib said that the U.S. negotiators were prepared to discuss a few additional issues in connection with the Criminal Jurisdiction Article but would reserve such discussion until a later meeting.

15. Mr. Chang expressed the appreciation of the Korean negotiators for the tabling by the U.S. negotiators of revisions of certain portions of the Criminal Jurisdiction Article. He said that Korean negotiators would carefully consider the proposed revisions and would respond at a later meeting.

16. It was agreed to hold the 75th meeting on April 27 to discuss the Labor Article and the 76th meeting on April 28 to discuss the Criminal Jurisdiction Article.

0118

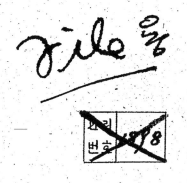

韓美間駐屯軍地位協定締結交渉資料

〔刑事裁判管轄權의抛棄 및 被疑者의 裁判 前 身柄拘禁條項에 關한 美側提案〕

1965 年 4 月

外 務 部

0119

I. 裁判管轄權의 抛棄

合意議事錄 第3 (b) 項

第 1 項 大韓民國政府는 裁判管轄林이 競合한 境遇에는
本條 第3項의 (b) 細項에 依하여 大韓民國當局
에 賦與된 第一次的 權利를 本合意議事錄 第2,
3, 4, 5, 6, 및 7項에 따라 合衆國을 爲하
여 抛棄한다.

第 2 項 本合意議事錄 第7項에 依하여 締結될수 있는
特別한 約定에 따라 合衆國 軍当局은 本合意議
事錄 第1項에 規定한 權利抛棄에 該当하는 個
別的事件을 大韓民國関係当局에 通告하여야 한다.

第 3 項 大韓民國関係当局이 特定事件에 있어서 特殊한

事情을 理由로하여 大韓民国의 司法上의 重大한 利益이 大韓民国의 裁判管轄權의 行事를 不可避하게 한다는 意見을 가질 境遇에는 本合意議事錄 第2項에 規定한 通告를 받은 날로부터 21日以內에 또는 第7項에 의거하여 締結되는 約定上의 그보다 短期間內에 合衆国의 関係軍当局에 通告를 함으로서 本合意議事錄 第1項에 規定한 權利抛棄를 撤回할 수 있다.

大韓民国当局은 또한 이러한 通告를 받기에 앞서 通告書를 提出할수도 있다.

(a) 個々 特定事件의 愼重한 檢討와 이러한 檢討의 結果에 따를것을 條件으로, 特히 다음과 같은 事件에 있어서 上記第3項의 趣旨內에서

~2~

0121

大韓民国의 司法上의 重大한 利益이 大韓民国
의 裁判管轄权 行使를 不可避하게 할수있는
것으로 한다.

(i) 大韓民国의 安全에 関한 犯罪

(ii) 사람을 죽음에 이르게한 犯罪, 强盜罪,
및 强姦罪, 但 그犯罪가 合衆国 軍隊의 構成
員, 軍屬, 또는 家族에 対하여 行하여진 境
遇는 除外한다. 및

(iii) 上記 各 犯罪의 未遂 또는 共犯

(라) 本項의 (a)細項에서 規定한 犯罪에 関하여
関係当局은 本條 第6項에 規定된 相互間의
助力을 提供하기 爲하여 予備授査의 着手時부
터 特히 緊密한 協力을 하여야 한다

~3~

0122

第 4 項 本合意議事錄 第3項에따라 大韓民國関係当局이
特定事件에 対한 権利拋棄를 撤回하고 이러한
事件에 있어서 関係当局間의 討議에 있어서 諒
解가 이루어지지 않을 때에는 合衆国政府는 外
交経路를 通하여 大韓民国政府에 異議를 提起할
수 있다。

大韓民国政府는 大韓民國의 司法上의 利益과
合衆国의 利益을 充分히 考慮하여 外交分野에
있어서의 그의 権限을 行使하여 意見差異를 解
決하여야 한다。

第 5 項 合衆国 軍当局은 大韓民国関係当局의 同意를
얻어 捜査. 裁判 및 決定을 위하여 合衆国에
裁判管轄権이 있는 特定刑事事件을 大韓民国法院

~4~

한·미국 간의 상호방위조약 제4조에 의한 시설과 구역 및 한국에서의 미국군대의 지위에 관한 협정(SOFA)
전59권. 1966.7.9 서울에서 서명 : 1967.2.9 발효(조약 232호) (V.29 실무교섭회의, 제73-76차, 1965.4월)   129

이나 当局에 移送할 수 있다.

大韓民國関係当局은 合衆國 軍当局의 同意를
얻어 搜査, 裁判 및 決定을 위하여 大韓民國에
裁判管轄权이 있는 特定刑事事件을 合衆國 軍当
局에 移送할 수 있다.

第6項 (a)° 合衆國軍隊의 構成員, 軍属 또는 家族이 大
韓民國內에서 大韓民國의 利益에 反하여 犯하
여진 犯罪때문에 合衆國法院에 訴追되었을 境
遇에는 그 裁判은 大韓民國內에서 行하여야 한
다.

(i) 但. 合衆國의 法律이 달리 要求하는境遇
또는

(ii) 軍事上 緊急事態의 境遇 또는 司法上의

~5~

0124

利益을 爲한 境遇에 合衆国軍当局이 大韓民
国外에서 裁判을 行할 意図가 있는 境遇는
除外한다. 이러한 境遇에 있어서 合衆国軍当
局은 大韓民国当局에 그러한 意図에 対한
意見을 陳述할수 있는 機会를 適時에 賦與하
여야 하며 大韓民国当局이 陳述하는 意見에
対하여 充分한 考慮를 하여야 한다.

(b) 裁判이 大韓民国外에서 行하여질 境遇에는
合衆国軍当局은 大韓民国当局에 裁判의 場所와
日字를 通告하여야 한다. 1名의 大韓民国代
表는 그裁判에 参席할 権利를 가진다.
但 그代表의 参席이 合衆国의 法院規則과 両
立되지 않거나 또는 合衆国의 安全上의 必要

~6~

0125

性으로서 同時에 大韓民国의 安全上의 必要性
이 아닌 그러한 合衆国의 安全上의 必要性과
兩立되지 않을 境遇는 除外한다. 合衆国当局
은 訴訟의 判決과 最終的 結果를 大韓民国当
局에 通告하여야 한다.

第 7 項 本條 및 本合意議事錄의 規定을 履行함에 있
어서나 輕微한 犯罪의 迅速한 處理를 위하여
合衆国軍当局과 大韓民国関係当局間에 約定이 締
結될수 있다.

同 約定은 또한 通告없이하는 處理와 本合意
議事錄 第3項에 言及된 権利拋棄가 撤回될수있
는 期間에도 미칠수 있다.

~7~

Ⅱ. 裁判前 被疑者의 身柄拘禁

本條 第5項

(a) 合衆国 当局 및 大韓民国当局은 大韓民国 領域內에서 合衆国 軍隊의 構成員, 軍屬 또는 그들의 家族을 逮捕함에 있어서, 그리고 다음 規定에 따라 身柄을 拘禁할 当局에 引渡함에 있어서, 相互助力하여야 한다.

(b) 大韓民国当局은 合衆国当局에 合衆国軍隊의 構成員 軍屬 또는 家族의 逮捕를 即時 通告하여야 한다. 合衆国軍当局은 大韓民国当局에 大韓民國이 裁判管轄 権을 行使하는 第一次的 権利를 갖는 事件에 있어서 合衆国軍隊의 構成員, 軍屬 또는 家族의 逮捕를

~8~

0127

即時通告하여야 한다.

(C) 大韓民國이 裁判管轄权을 行使할 合衆国軍隊의 構成員.軍屬 또는 家族인 被疑者의 身柄拘禁은 그者가 合衆國의 手中에 있다면 모든 訴訟節次가 終結되고 그리고 大韓民國當局이 身柄拘禁을 要求할때가지 合衆國이 이를 行한다.

그者가 大韓民国 手中에 있다면 即時 合衆国当局에 引渡되어야 하며 모든 訴訟節次가 終結되고 그리고 大韓民国当局이 身柄拘禁을 要求할때까지 合衆国当局의 身柄拘禁下에 두어야 한다. 被疑者가 合衆國軍当局의 拘禁下에 있을境遇에 있어서 合衆國軍当局은 特定事件에 있어서 大韓民国当局이 行한 身柄拘禁引渡 要求에 对하여 好意的 考慮를 하여야

~9~

0128

한다. 合衆國当局은 大韓民國当局의 要求를 받으면
大韓民国当局으로 하여금 被疑者에 対한 捜査와 裁
判을 可能케 한다. 合衆国当局이 合衆国軍隊의 構
成員, 軍屬 또는 家族의 身柄拘禁을 継續함에 있어
서 同当局으로부터의 助力을 要求하면, 大韓民国当局
은 이 要求에 対하여 好意的 考慮를 하여야 한다

(d) 第2(c)項에 規定된바, 全的으로 大韓民国의 安全에
対한 犯罪에 関하여 被疑者의 身柄은 大韓民国当局
의 拘禁下에 두어야 한다 (그個의 諒解事項에
対한 韓美間의 合意를 條件으로 함)

~10~

I. Waiver of Primary Right to exercise Jurisdiction

Re Paragraph 3(b)

1. The Government of the Republic of Korea waives in favor of the United States the primary right granted to the Korean authorities under sub-paragraph (b) of Paragraph 3 of this Article in cases of concurrent jurisdiction, in accordance with Paragraph 2, 3, 4, 5, 6, and 7 of this Minute.

2. Subject to any particular arrangements which may be made under Paragraph 7 of this Minute, the military authorities of the United States shall notify the competent Korean authorities of individual cases falling under the waiver provided in Paragraph 1 of this Minute.

3. Where the competent Korean authorities hold the view that, by reason of special circumstances in a specific case, major interests of Korean administration of justice make imperative the exercise of Korean jurisdiction, they may recall the waiver granted under Paragraph 1 of this minute by a statement to the competent military authorities of the United States within a period of twenty-one days after receipt of the notification envisaged in Paragraph 2 of this

0130

Minute or any shorter period which may be provided in arrangements made under Paragraph 7 of this Minute. The Korean authorities may also submit the statement prior to receipt of such notification.

(a) Subject to a careful examination of each specific case and to the results of such examination, major interests of Korean administration of justice within the meaning of Paragraph 3 above may make imperative the exercise of Korean jurisdiction, in particular, in the following cases:

(i) Security offenses against the Republic of Korea;

(ii) Offenses causing the death of a human being, robbery, and rape, except where the offenses are directed against a member of the United States Armed Forces or the civilian component, or a dependent; and

(iii) Attempts to commit such offenses or participation therein.

(b) In respect of the offenses referred to in Subparagraph (a) of this Paragraph, the authorities concerned shall proceed in particularly close cooperation from the beginning of the preliminary investigation in order to

~2~

0131

provide the mutual assistance envisaged in Paragraph 6 of this Article.

4. If, pursuant to Paragraph 3 of this Minute, the competent Korean authorities have recalled the waiver in a specific case and in such case an understanding cannot be reached in discussions between the authorities concerned, the Government of the United States may make representations to the Government of the Republic of Korea through diplomatic channels. The Government of the Republic of Korea, giving due consideration to the interests of Korean administration of justice and to the interests of the Government of the United States, shall resolve the disagreement in the exercise of its authority in the field of foreign affairs.

5. With the consent of the competent Korean authorities, the military authorities of the United States may transfer to the Korean courts or authorities for investigation, trial and decision, particular criminal cases in which jurisdiction rests with the United States.

With the consent of the military authorities of the United States, the competent Korean authorities may transfer to the military authorities of the United States for investigation, trial and decision, particular criminal cases in which jurisdiction rests with the Republic of Korea.

~/3~

0132

6.　(a) Where a member of the United States Armed Forces
or civilian component, or a dependent, is arraigned before
a court of the United States, for an offense committed in
the Republic of Korea against Korean interests, the trial
shall be held within the Republic of Korea.

　　　　　　(i) Except where the law of the United States
　　　　　　　　requires otherwise, or

　　　　　　(ii) Except where, in cases of military exigency
　　　　　　　　or in the interests of justice, the military
　　　　　　　　authorities of the United States intend to
　　　　　　　　hold the trial outside the Republic of
　　　　　　　　Korea. In this event they shall afford
　　　　　　　　the Korean authorities timely opportunity
　　　　　　　　to comment on such intention and shall give
　　　　　　　　due consideration to any comments the
　　　　　　　　latter may make.

　　　　(b) Where the trial is held outside of the Republic
of Korea the military authorities of the United States
shall inform the Korean authorities of the place and date
of the trial. A Korean representative shall be entitled
to be present at the trial, except where his presence is
incompatible with the rules of the court of the United
States or with the security requirements of the United

~14~

0133

States, which are not at the same time the security requirements of the Republic of Korea. The authorities of the
United States shall inform the Korean authorities of the
judgment and the final outcome of the proceedings.

    7. In the implementation of the provisions of this
Article and this agreed minute, and to facilitate the
expeditious disposal of offenses of minor importance,
arrangements may be made between the military authorities
of the United States and the competent Korean authorities.
These arrangements may also extend to dispensing with
notification and to the period of time referred to in
Paragraph 3 of this Minute, within which the waiver may be
recalled.

~15~

0134

II. Pre-trial Custody

Revised U.S. Draft of Paragraph 5

5. (a) The authorities of the United States and the authorities of the Republic of Korea shall assist each other in the arrest of members of the United States armed forces, the civilian component, or their dependents in the territory of the Republic of Korea and in handing them over to the authority which is to have custody in accordance with the following provisions.

(b) The authorities of the Republic of Korea shall notify promptly the authorities of the United States of the arrest of any member of the United States armed forces, or civilian component, or a dependent. The military authorities of the United States shall promptly notify the authorities of the Republic of Korea of the arrest of a member of the United States armed forces, the civilian component, or a dependent in any case in which the Republic of Korea has the primary right to exercise jurisdiction.

(c) The custody of an accused member of the United States armed forces or civilian component, or of a dependent, over whom the Republic of Korea is to exercise jurisdiction shall, if he is in the hands of the United States, remain with the United States pending the conclusion of all judicial

~16~

0135

proceedings and until custody is requested by the authorities of the Republic of Korea. If he is in the hands of the Republic of Korea, he shall be promptly handed over to the authorities of the United States and remain in their custody pending completion of all judicial proceedings and until custody is requested by the authorities of the Republic of Korea. When an accused has been in the custody of the military authorities of the United States, they shall give sympathetic consideration to any request for the transfer of custody which may be made by the authorities of the Republic of Korea in specific cases. The United States authorities will make any such accused available to the authorities of the Republic of Korea upon their request for purposes of investigation and trial. The authorities of the Republic of Korea shall give sympathetic consideration to a request from the authorities of the United States for assistance in maintaining custody of an accused member of the United States armed forces, the civilian component, or a dependent.

(d) In respect of offenses solely against the security of the Republic of Korea provided in Paragraph 2(c), an accused shall be in the custody of the authorities of the Republic of Korea. (Subject US-ROK agreement on two understandings.)

~17~

3. 제75차 회의, 4.28

0137

4/27　　　　實務者會議(改善局長室)

관리번호 3097

早期招請의 制限(合同委合意設定)

1. 許局長 說明
　李課長 ─ 早期招請者(生活各 規制) 用數

　安全局長　人員制限
　　　例 遊離職業

3. 張局長: 約 40元 退金
　　　앞으로 들어올 召集은 合意에서 승인
　　　現在 申請 있기의 不可能
　　　　　　　　　　　　　　　　　 韓口要案
　　　　　　　　　　　　　　　　　　　　고용

━━━━━━━━━━━━━━━━━━━━━━━

Ⅲ　고용인
安局長　KSC 뿐 용인이니다　우고용인이 그目
　　　더더 용事하고 용용이 있으며도
　　　그런 現在을 하지 않는다

　口防部 ─ 한국 員 안의 원복 곤란
　芳安局長 KSC 下�하기가 곤란

　張局長 ─ 한국정부가 我務가 있다
　　　　口防토案의 責任 ─ 我影 에서온다
　安局長 ─ 德용을 용利 있다
　　　自擇을 모집(自由勞動者)
　　　一般的으로 모집을 해끔
　許局長 ─ 3民制 動員 不可能
　　　了 ─

0138

安全源泉 ─ 194X年 戰時動員法則하に
戰時目的下에서 勞動

口方部 ─ 人事, 等需 ─ 民者고용인

7-2

0139

한·미국 간의 상호방위조약 제4조에 의한 시설과 구역 및 한국에서의 미국군대의 지위에 관한 협정(SOFA)
전59권. 1966.7.9 서울에서 서명 : 1967.2.9 발효(조약 232호) (V.29 실무교섭회의, 제73-76차, 1965.4월) 145

3. 勞務調達

題 目	韓 國 側 案	美 國 側 案	解 決 方 案
1. 勞務條項의 適所經理			
(1) 雇傭主	美國軍(非戦出機関을含)	美國軍(非戦出機関을含) 契約者	(1) 美國側의 案을 受諾 *경3억2고수 ... 3억人*
(2) 雇傭人	韓國國籍을 가진民間人	美軍屬이 아니며 雇傭人 KSC 및 軍隊使用人除外 (準軍隊)	(2) (KSC와 軍事雇傭人을 例外로 함) 韓國國籍을 有한 (美軍屬이아닌) 者에限 *한22.12분 10勝*
2. 雇傭行政	(1) 雇備主는 雇傭人을 募集採所, 行政을 可能한 最大限度로 韓國政府의 募集機関을 利用한다.	(1) 雇備主는 雇傭人을 募集, 採用 行政判事 可能한限 韓國政府機関을 利用한다.	(1) 韓國側 例)達主張

題　目	韓　國　側	美　國　側	解　決　方　案
3. 勞動條件의 適用範圍	(2) 直接雇傭時 美國은 그 內容을 韓國法令 勞動	(2) 直接雇傭時는 勞動斤에 通報	案(例)參照
	(1) 閣議合意되지 않는限 韓國法令을 遵守	本條規定과 美軍의 軍事上必要에 相反되지 않는限 韓國勞動法·慣·價例를 遵守	(1)本規定과 ... 軍事上 ... 않는限 ... 別途合意 ... (2) 合意된 事項에 ...
	(2) 遵守하지 못할時는 合同委에서 事前에 合意		
4. 紛爭行爲와 工解決節次	(1) 雇用人 不平을 正當히 解決하여야 한다	(1) 雇用人 不平을 正當히 그 適期에 ... 解決된 請願을 세운다	
	美(韓國法依據)	(2) 雇用은 美國利益에 相反되지 않는限 組合을 組織加入할수있다	

한·미국 간의 상호방위조약 제4조에 의한 시설과 구역 및 한국에서의 미국군대의 지위에 관한 협정(SOFA)
전59권. 1966.7.9 서울에서 서명 : 1967.2.9 발효(조약 232호) (V.29 실무교섭회의, 제73-76차, 1965.4월) 147

0142

題目	韓國側案	美國側案	解決方案	끗
	(2) 仲裁로 解決되지 않는 紛 爭은 다음 方法으로 解決한다. (ㄱ) 勞動方 에 回附, 調整 (ㄴ) 合同委가 指示한 特別委에 回附 調整 (ㄷ) 合同委에 回附 決審 (ㄹ) 前記決定 不服時 人給爭解決進行 中 勞動方에 回附된날부터 韓國 勞動爭議法 14條에 規	(3) 美軍이 承認한 前記組合은 協 議城을 가진다. (4) 仲裁后 訴爭 解決되지 않는 紛爭은 다음 節次로 解決한다. (ㄱ) 勞動方 에 回附 調整 (ㄴ) 合同委員會(勞動分委) 或은 特委에 回附 調整, 調整 (ㄷ) 合同委에 回附 決審 (ㄹ) 前記決定 不服時 或은 紛爭 節次進行中 正常業務防害行爲 는 勞組의 解体와 雇用人解	(3) 案中의 協議城 採 (4) 우리(案) 基本으로 (ㅁ) (ㄴ)案 削除(案 에)	OK

exercise of the right

except in case (where) ~~~~ it is limited by the Joint Com.

~~~~

provided that the J.C. may ~~determine~~ limit the exercise of the right ~~to~~ by.

An Employee shall have the right concerning strike,
J.C. may, however, limit the exercise of the right ~~to~~ by

0143

ㄱ-6

題目	韓 國 側	美 國 側	解	示
	罷業된 冷却期間 內 正常業務에 對한 活動法을 ~ 行爲는 軍國家에 依한 授權에 뿐임	屆의 原因이 된다.	요망됨	
無	(5) 韓國法令이 依한 罷業權 認定 (韓國法令에 依한 罷業權 認定)	(5) 韓國軍屬編入과 同一하게 罷業과 業務停止에 關한 法的規制를 받는다	(合同委에서 別途 定한 者를 除外하고는 罷業權認定으로 한다.)	
5. 非常措置		軍事上 必要로 韓國法 遵守不能時 可能한 返限 事前에 合同委에 報告基礎		
(1) 技術者의 戰時勤務	(1) 戰時軍 國家非常時 美軍業務	(1) 戰時軍 國家非常時 美軍業務 技術者에		
	美軍業務에 對하 技術者에 對하	이 不可缺한 技術者에 對하		

題目	韓 國 側 案	美 國 側 案	解 決 方 案
	이 事前에 要求하면 兵役義務를 延期하여야 한다.	이 事前에 要求하면 兵役義務를 延期할 수 있다.	에서 合意될때 兵役義務를 延期 한다.
6. KSC 및 家事使用人	無 (除外)	KSC人員의 充當	~~該條項은 安保 軍이 必要하다는 뜻이 강하여서 韓國이 強力히 反對한것임.~~
7. 國際法上의 免除	韓國이 韓國法令 遵守를 免除할 不物案	(1) 美國이 韓國送達中은 國際法의 免除를 受物案 (2) 美軍은 平時로 軍事上 必要로는 主權을 保有	(1) 同 — (2) 本條款은 外交上의 理由는 削除.(外務當局) × ~~(22 노마나 me)~~

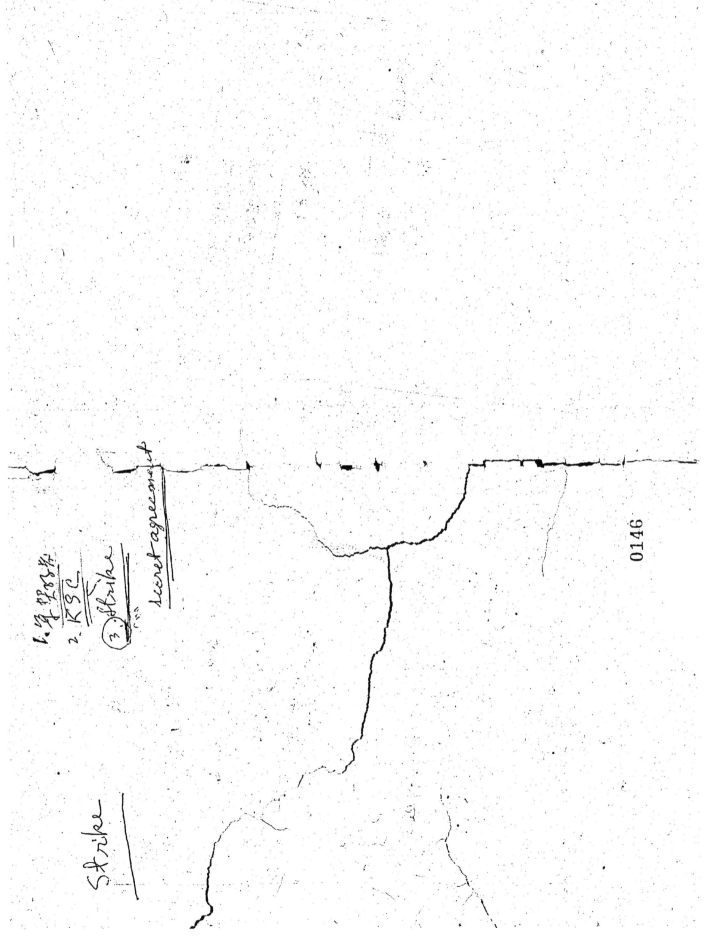

SOFA NEGOTIATION

Agenda for the 75th Session

15:30 April 23, 19

1. Continuation of Discussions on:
   a. Labor Article (*Karea*)
   b. Criminal Jurisdiction Article.
2. Other Business
3. Agenda and Date of the Next Meeting
4. Press Release

0147

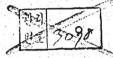

presented at
75th session
April 28, 1965

LABOR ARTICLE

(Underlining indicates modifications from Korean
draft of the Labor Article tabled at 69th session)

1.   In this Article the expression:

(a) "employer" refers to the United States Armed Forces (including non-appropriated fund activities).

(b) "employee" refers to any civilian (other than a member of the civilian component of the United States Armed Forces) employed by an employer. Such civilian personnel shall be nationals of the Republic of Korea.

2.   Employers may recruit, employ and administer their personnel. Recruitment services of the Government of the Republic of Korea shall be utilized to the maximum extent practicable. In case employers accomplish direct recruitment of employees, The United States Armed Forces shall provide such relevant information as may be required for labor administration to the Office of Labor Affairs of the Republic of Korea.

3.   To the extent not inconsistent with the provisions of this Article or except as may otherwise be mutually agreed, the conditions of employment and work, such as those relating to wages and supplementary payments, the conditions for the protection and welfare of employees, compensations, and the rights of employees, concerning labor relations shall conform with those laid down by the labor legislation of the Republic of Korea.

4.   (a) With regard to any dispute between employers and any employees or labor unions which cannot be settled through the use of existing procedures of the United States Armed Forces, settlement shall be accomplished in the following manner:

8 -1

0148

(1) The dispute shall be referred to the Office of Labor Affairs of the Republic of Korea for conciliation.

(2) In the event that the dispute is not settled by the procedures described in (1) above, the dispute shall be referred to a special committee designated by the Joint Committee for further conciliation efforts.

(3) In the event that the dispute is not settled by the procedures outlined above, the Joint Committee will resolve the dispute. The decisions of the Joint Committee shall be binding.

(4) Neither employee organizations nor employees shall engage in any practices disruptive of normal work requirements unless the cooling-off period set forth in Article 14 of the Korean Labor Dispute Law has elapsed after the dispute is referred to the specially-designated committee mentioned in (2) above.

(5) Failure of any employee organization or employee to abide by the decision of the Joint Committee on any dispute, or engaging in practices disruptive of normal work requirements in violation of the provisions laid down in (4) above, shall be considered cause for the depriviation of the rights and protection accorded by the relevant labor legislation of the Republic of Korea.

(b) The right concerning strike shall be accorded to employees except those whose exercise of the right is prohibited by the Joint Committee.

8-2

0149

5.   In the event of a national emergency, such as war, hostilities or situations where war or hostilities is imminent, the application of this Article shall be limited in accordance with the emergency measures taken by the Government of the Republic of Korea, and, in addition, the following arrangements will be made:

(a) Should the Government of the Republic of Korea adopt measures allocating labor, the United States Armed Forces shall be accorded allocation privileges no less favorable than those enjoyed by the Armed Forces of the Republic of Korea.

(b) Employees who have acquired skills essential to the mission of the United States Armed Forces will, upon request of the United States Armed Forces and through mutual agreement, be deferred from Republic of Korea military service or other compulsory services. The United States Armed Forces shall in advance furnish to the Government of the Republic of Korea lists of those employees deemed necessary.

6.   Members of the civilian component of the United States Armed Forces shall not be subject to Korean laws or regulations with respect to their terms and conditions of employment.

AGREED MINUTES

1.   The undertaking of the United States to conform to the labor legislation of the Republic of Korea does not imply any waiver by the United States Government of its immunities under international law.

2.   It is understood that the Government of the Republic of Korea shall be reimbursed for direct costs incurred in providing assistance pursuant to Paragraph 2.

8-3

0150

3.   Employers will withhold from the pay of their employees, and pay over to the Government of the Republic of Korea withholdings required by the income tax legislation of the Republic of Korea.

4.   In case where it is impossible for employers to conform to the labor legislations of the Republic of Korea applicable under Paragraph 3 on account of the military requirements of the United States Armed Forces, the matter shall be referred, in advance, to the Joint Committee for mutual agreement. The Government of the Republic of Korea will give due consideration to the military requirements of the United States Armed Forces.

8-4

0151

LABOR ARTICLE

presented at 75th Session
April 28, 1965

1. The Korean negotiators, as promised at the 73rd session, have carefully considered the U.S. draft on Labor Article. Now, the Korean side would like to table new Korean revised draft of the entire Article. The underlining indicates modifications from the Korean draft tabled at the 69th session. For convenience, I would like to discuss mainly the substantial changes in the draft on a paragraph by paragraph basis.

2. **Para. 1**

As for definition of "employer", we accept the U.S. formula, except the invited contractors for whom the Korean side still maintains former position to exclude from this Article to the effect that the invited contractors should be subject to Korean laws in respect of local employment relations.

As for the employee, the Korean side similarly modified the clause (b) taking into account of the U.S. suggestion i.e., civilian component of the United States Armed Forces. With regard to the KSC and a domestic, the Korean side maintains previous positions that the word should not appear in the Paragraph. As for the domestic, it is unnecessary to mention here in the Paragraph, because the domestic is not covered by our Korean labor legislation (e.g., Article 10 of the Labor Standard Law.) As for the Korean Service Corps, the Korean negotiators still believe they should be treated as employees applicable under this Article. For, they are recruited from free labor market as manual laborers serving for the U.S. Army ever since September 1955.

As for Agreed Minute #1 of U.S. draft, Korean side considers that such provisions are already covered in Para. 2 and therefore the Korean Government will make available, as has

8-5

0152

done, upon the request of U.S. armed forces, Korean personnel not only for the Korean Service Corps but for any employment, insofar as possible, to meet the requirements of the U.S. armed forces.

3. Para. 3 and Agreed Minute #4

The Korean side has made modifications on some wording in Para. 3 to meet the U.S. satisfaction which are self-explanatory. Also, some changes of wording are effected in Agreed Minute #4, but we maintain it is reasonable that any deviation from our law shall be referred to the Joint Committee in advance for mutual agreement. In this regard, it is recalled that the U.S. side kept in mind the deviation from our law at the time of emergency, for which the Korean side has drafted new Para. 5. Our explanation on this new proposal will be made later. We foresee no difficulty on the part of U.S. side in referring, in advance, any matter of deviation from our law to the Joint Committee for mutual agreement.

4. Para. 4

The Korean side now propose to delete the U.S. version of sub-para. (a) regarding the resolution of employee grievances, for such provisions are fully described in our legislation. And, the Korean negotiators could not accept the U.S. version of sub-paras. (b) and (c) of U.S. draft, on the ground that the employee's rights of union organization and consultation are to a satisfactory extent provided for in our labor legislation and that, in a sense, any formula of recognising the organization of labor unions are against the spirit of the labor legislation.

As for the settlement of dispute, we have made significant concession to the effect that the cooling-off period shall be reckoned on after the dispute is referred to the second

8-6

0153

stage, i.e., the specially-designated committee, which implies
many more days' prolongation of the prohibition of disruptive
practices by the employees. This formula would satisfy the
U.S. desire.

With respect to the right to strike, we have drawn out
new formula, as are shown in (b) of Korean draft, which
provides that right concerning strike shall be accorded
to employees except those whose exercise of the right is
prohibited by the Joint Committee. There have been great
many deliberations on this right to strike and now we propose
to conclude this by our draft under which the Joint Committee
will resolve the matter. It is understood that the U.S.
side has held the position that the certain employees shall
not exercise the right to strike. Now, we agree there would
be some employees in the U.S. Armed Forces, who should not
exercise the right to strike. Therefore, we propose that
the classification of such persons shall be made at the Joint
Committee.

5. Para. 5

Taking into account of the worries of U.S. negotiators
concerning the deviation from our law at the time of emergency,
the Korean side has introduced a new paragraph providing that
the application of the Labor Article may be suspended, partly
or in all in accordance with the extent promulgated in the
emergency measures taken, by the Government of the Republic
of Korea. We believe this formula will relieve the U.S.
worries and the U.S. side would accept Para. 3 and Agreed
Minute #4 of Korean draft without any objection.

We have no problem with regard of sub para. (a). As,
for the sub-para. (b), we have inserted the wording "through
mutual agreement" so as to clarify the points we reached an
agreement at the previous session.

8-7

0154

6. Finally, I would like to comment on the second sentence of Agreed Minute #3 of U.S. draft. The U.S. side held the view that nowhere in the Article is provided for the right to terminate of employees by the employers. May I draw your attention to the first sentence of Paragraph 2, which reads: "Employers may recruit, employ and administer their personnel." We understand the word "administer" indicates the stages of personnel administration from hire to fire, as were explained by U.S. negotiators at the 65th session (October 23, 1964). The U.S. side has the right to terminate employment under Para. 2 and in that case, under Para. 3, there should be justifiable reasons. If the U.S. side insists the inclusion of this phrase, there should be many more rights of employers to be included in the Article in respect of personnel administration. Therefore, we maintain that such clause is unnecessary.

8-8

기 안 지

기안자	미주과 이근팔	전 화 번 호		공 보		필 요	불필요

	과 장	국 장	차 관	장 관		

협 조 서	자 명					보 존 년 한	
기 안 년 월 일	1965. 5. 8.	시 행 년월일		통제관	5.10	정 서 기 장	
분류기호 문서번호	외구미 722.2 —						

경 수
유 신
참 조 : 대통령 참조: 비서실장
국무총리 참조: 비서실장 발신
사본: 법무부장관 참조: 검찰국장
사본: 보건사회부장관, 참조: 노동청장   장 관

제 목 제 75 차 주둔군지위협정 체결 교섭실무자회의 결과 보고

　　　1965 년 4 월 28 일 하오 3 시 30 분 부터 동 4 시 30 분 까지

외무부 제 1 회의실에서 개최된 제 75 차 주둔군지위협정 체결

교섭실무자회의에서 토의된 형사재판관할권 및 노무조항에

관한 내용을 별첨과 같이 보고합니다.

　　유 첨: 제 75 차 주둔군지위협정체결 교섭실무자회의 결과

　　　　　보고서 1 부. 끝.

0156

기 안 지

기 안 자	미주과 이근팔	전 화 번 호		공 보	필 요	불필요

	과 장	국 장	차 관	장 관		
		김		/		

협 조 서	자 명					보 존 년 한	
기 안 년 월 일	1965. 5. 8.	시 행 년월일		통 제 관	5.10	정 서 기 장
분 류 기 호 문 서 번 호	외구미 722.2 —					
경 수 참	유 신 조	법무부장관 참조:검찰국장 보건사회부장관 참조:노동청장		발 신	장 관	
제 목	제 75 차 주둔군지위협정 체결 교섭실무자회의 개최					

1965년 4월 28일 하오 3시 30분 부터 등 4시 30분 까지

외무부 제 1 회의실에서 개최된 제 75 차 주둔군지위협정 체결 교섭

실무자회의에서 토의된 형사재판관할권 및 노무조항에 관한

내용을 별첨과 같이 알립니다.

유 첨: 제 75 차 주둔군지위협정 체결 교섭실무자회의 결과

보고서 1 부. 끝.

한·미국 간의 상호방위조약 제4조에 의한 시설과 구역 및 한국에서의 미국군대의 지위에 관한 협정(SOFA)
전59권. 1966.7.9 서울에서 서명 : 1967.2.9 발효(조약 232호) (V.29 실무교섭회의, 제73-76차, 1965.4월)   163

제 75 차
한.미간 주둔군지위협정 체결 교섭 실무자회의
보 고 서

1. 일 시: 1965 년 4 월 28 일 하오 3:30 분 부터 4:30 까지.

2. 장 소: 외무부 제 1 회의실

3. 토의사항:

가. 노무조달

　　　미측이 제 73 차 회의에서 제시한 수정안에 대하여 우리측은
다음과 같은 우리측 입장을 제시하였다:

(1) 군계약자는 한국의 노동관계 법령을 준수하여야함으로 고용주의
정의로 부터 제외되어야 한다.

(2) 미측이 "준군사적"이라고 주장하고 있는 K.S.C. 는 1955 년 이태
미군이 자유모집에 의하여 채용하고 있음으로 일반 미군노무자와
같이 본조항의 노무자의 정의에 규정되어야 한다.

(3) 노사간의 분쟁이 조정을 위하여 한국노동청에 회부될 때 부터
냉각기간이 개시되는 것으로 하였던 우리측 입장을 일부 수정하여
분쟁이 조정을 위하여 특별위원회에 회부된 날 부터 시작하는 것
으로 하여 분쟁이 해결될 수 있는 기간에 여유를 두었다.

(4) 미측이 미군관계 노무자에게 사실상 파업권을 인정하지 않으려는데
대하여 우리측은 미측의 주장을 참작하여 " 파업에 관한 권리는
권리 행사가 합동위원회에서 금지된 자를 제외한 노무자에게 부여
하여야한다" 라고 제안하여 미군노무자중 파업권을 행사할 수 있는
자와 행사할 수 없는 자의 범위를 합동위원회에서 결정할 것을
제의하였다.

(5) 우리측은 전쟁 또는 적대행위등 국가적 비상사태의 경우
미군이 군사상의 필요성을 이유로 한국의 노동관계 법령을 준수할
수 없다는 미측 주장을 참작하여 그러한 경우 한국정부가 정하는
바에 따라 본조항의 전부 또는 일부의 효력이 정지될 수 있는
것으로 하였다.

0158

0159

나. 형사재판관할권

　　　미측이 제74차회의 석상에서 제시한 형사재판관할권의 포기 및
공무집행중 범죄에 관한 제안에 대하여 우리측은 다음과 같은 몇
가지 문제점에 관한 미측 입장을 확인한 바 있다.

　(1) 우리측은 미측이 제74차회의에서 제안한 포기조항에서 "한국의
　　　사법상의 중대한 이익이 한국의 관할권 행사를 불가피하게 할
　　　때에 한국당국이 포기를 철회할 수 있는 것으로 하였는바 동 제안이
　　　우리측의 종전 제안에서 주장하여 온 "대한민국이 관할권을 행사함이
　　　특히 중요"하다고 결정하는 취지와 동일한 것인지를 질의한데 대하여
　　　미측은 양측이 의도한바는 동일한 것으로 본다. 그러나 미측안이
　　　한국당국에 특정사건에 있어서 포기를 철회할 수 있는 권리를 부여
　　　하였지만 포기를 철회할수 있는 사정에 관하여 양국간의 협의가
　　　있어야 하며 또한 한국당국은 포기철회권을 행사함에 있어서
　　　신중을 기하여야 한다고 설명하였다.

　(2) 우리측은 한국측이 사법상의 중대한 이익을 위하여 한국당국이
　　　관할권을 행사함이 불가피할 때에는 비록 미국당국과의 협의에서
　　　양해가 성립되지 아니하여도 포기를 철회할 수 있는지의 여부와
　　　그 철회의 효과가 자동적인지에 대하여 문의하였던바 미측은
　　　포기의 철회여부에 관한 재량권은 한국당국에 있지만 포기의
　　　효과는 자동적이 아니며 양측의 협의가 있어야 한다라고 말하였으며,

　(3) 미측 제안에 규정된 바 한국당국이 포기를 철회할 수 있는 범죄의
　　　종류는 한정적인가 또는 예시적인가라는 우리측 질문에 대하여
　　　미측은 동 규정이 한정적이 아니라 예시적이며 따라서 한국당국이
　　　"사법상의 중대한 이익을 위하여 한국당국이 관할권을 행사함이
　　　불가피하다"고 인정할 때에는 예시된 범죄 이외의 경우에도
　　　재판권을 행사할 수 있다고 설명하였다.

　(4) 공무집행중 범죄에 관하여 미측은 "미군의 권한있는 당국"이
　　　공무집행증명서를 발급하는 것으로 하였는바 우리측은 그 범주에
　　　해당하는 미군기관은 무엇이며 미국군대의 중대단위의 지휘관도

0160

65 - 5 - 9

미문 112-4

0161

포함될 수 있는 것인가를 문의한데 대하여 미측은 공무집행증명서는 반듯이 미군법무관의 의견을 들은 후에만 발행할 것이며 발행권자는 지휘권이 있는 장교가 되어야 한다. 현재 주한미국에 배속되고 있는 법무관의 수는 5 명밖에 않되며 법무관이 있는 최하미군단위는 사단임으로 공무집행증명서를 발행할 수 있는 최하기관은 "준장급" 이 될 것이라고 해명하였다.

4. 기타 사항:

차기 회의 일자: 1965 년 4 월 30 일 2 시 30 분. 끝

STATUS OF FORCES NEGOTIATIONS: 75th Meeting

SUBJECTS: 1. Labor Article
                                      2. Criminal Jurisdiction Article

PLACE: Ministry of Foreign Affairs

DATE: April 28, 1965

PARTICIPANTS:

Republic of Korea   United States

CHANG Sang-mun   Philip C. Habib
HO Sung-chung   Brig. General Carroll H. Dunn, USA
YI Nam-ki   Col. Allan G. Pixton, USA
Major YI Ke-hun, ROKA   Captain George Hagerman, USN
KIM Ki-cho   Col. Kenneth C. Crawford, USA
HWANG Yong-chae   Frank R. LaMacchia
PAK Won-chol   Benjamin A. Fleck
YI Kun-pal (Interpreter)   Robert A. Kinney
                                      Goodwin Shapiro
                                      Major Alton Harvey, USA
                                      David Y.C. Lee (Interpreter)

                                      Ogden Reed (Observer)
                                      G.W. Flowers (Observer)

0164

CONFIDENTIAL

Labor Article

1. Mr. Chang opened the meeting by stating that the Korean negotiators, as they had promised at the 73rd negotiating session, had carefully considered the revised draft of the Labor Article tabled by the U.S. negotiators at that meeting. They would now table a revised draft of the entire article, in which the underlining indicates modifications of the draft which they had tabled at the 69th session. Mr. Chang said he would discuss the new revised draft on a paragraph by paragraph basis.

2. Paragraph 1 - Mr. Chang said the Korean negotiators accepted the U.S. formula for defining an "employer", except as regards invited contractors. The Korean negotiators continued to maintain their position that invited contractors should be subject to Korean laws with regard to local employment relations and, therefore, they should be excluded from the provisions of this Article.

3. With regard to the definition of an "employee", Mr. Chang continued, the Korean negotiators similarly had modified the language of their draft, taking into account the U.S. suggestion of excluding members of the civilian component. They believed that it is unnecessary to mention domestics in this paragraph because domestics are not covered by Korean labor legislation (e.g. Article 10, Labor Standards Law). The Korean negotiators believed that members of the Korean Service Corps should be considered as employees coming under the provisions of this Article. KSC personnel have been recruited from the free labor market as manual laborers serving for the U.S. Army since September, 1955, said Mr. Chang.

4. Referring to Agreed Minute #1, Mr. Chang said that the Korean negotiators consider that its provisions are already covered in Paragraph 2 of the Article. Under the terms of Paragraph 2, the ROK Government, as it has done in the past, will make available, on the request of the U.S. armed forces, Korean personnel not only for the Korean Service Corps but also for any employment insofar as possible, to meet the requirements of the U.S. armed forces.

0165

5. <u>Paragraph 3 and Agreed Minute #4</u> - Mr. Chang said that the Korean negotiators had made some self-explanatory modifications of the language in Paragraph 3 to satisfy the needs of the U.S. negotiators. There had also been some changes in Agreed Minute #4. The Korean negotiators believe it is reasonable to provide that any deviation from Korean law shall be referred to the Joint Committee in advance for mutual agreement. In this regard, the Korean negotiators recalled that the U.S. negotiators had in mind deviation from Korean law during times of emergency. In order to cover such situations, the Korean negotiators had drafted a new Paragraph #5, which they would explain shortly. They did not foresee any difficulty on the part of the U.S. authorities in referring ~~xxxxxxxxxxxxx~~ in advance any ~~xxxxxxxx~~ deviation from Korean law to the Joint Committee for mutual agreement.

6. <u>Paragraph 4</u> - Mr. Chang said the Korean ~~xxx~~ revised draft had deleted ~~xxx~~ subparagraph (a) of the U.S. draft, regarding the resolution of employee grievances, for such provisions are fully described in Korean legislation. Also, the Korean negotiators could not accept the U.S. versions of subparagraphs (b) and (c) because the employees' rights of union organization and consultation are provided for to a satisfactory extent in Korean labor legislation. Also, in a sense, any formula of recognizing the organization of labor unions is against the spirit of Korean labor legislation.

7. Regarding the issue of settlement of disputes, Mr. Chang said that the Korean negotiators had made a significant concession by providing in subparagraph (a)(4) of Paragraph 4 that the cooling-off period shall begin after the dispute is referred to the second stage, i.e. the specially-designated committee. This implies, he continued, ~~xxxxxxxx~~ prolongation by many more days of the prohibition against disruptive practices by the employees. The Korean negotiators believed this formula would satisfy the U.S. desires.

8. Mr. Chang said the Korean negotiators had drawn up a new formula with regard to the right to strike. This was contained in subparagraph (b) of Paragraph 4, 0166

which would **provide** that the right to strike shall be accorded to employees except those whose exercise of this right is prohibited by the Joint Committee. There had been a great many deliberations on the right to strike and now the Korean negotiators were proposing to settle the matter by providing in their draft that the Joint Committee would resolve the question. (The U.S. negotiators had held the position that certain employees **should not** exercise the right to strike. The Korean negotiators agree that there would be some **employees** of the U.S. armed forces who should not exercise that right. Therefore, Mr. Chang said, the Korean negotiators were proposing that the Joint Committee designate such persons.)

9. <u>Paragraph 5</u> - Mr. Chang said that the Korean negotiators, taking into account the worries of the U.S. negotiators concerning deviation from Korean law during times of emergency, had introduced a new paragraph, which would provide that the application of the Labor Article may be suspended, in whole or in part, in accordance with the extent promulgated in the emergency measures taken by the Government of the Republic of Korea. The Korean negotiators believed that this formula would **relieve** the worries of the U.S. negotiators and that they would accept Paragraph 3 and Agreed Minute #4 of the Korean draft without any objection.

10. Mr. Chang said the Korean negotiators had no problems with regard to subparagraph (a) of Paragraph 5 of the U.S. draft. In subparagraph (b), the Korean negotiators had inserted the words "through mutual agreement" in order to clarify the points agreed upon at the previous meeting.

11. Mr. Chang said that the Korean negotiators' final comments were directed toward the second sentence of Agreed Minute #3 of the U.S. draft. The U.S. negotiators held the view that nowhere in the Article is there provision for the **right of** employers to terminate employment of employees. The Korean negotiators wished to call the attention of the U.S. negotiators to the first sentence of Paragraph 2, which reads: "Employers may **recruit**, **employ** and administer their personnel". The Korean negotiators

0167

understand that the word "administer" indicates the stages of personnel administration from hire to fire, as explained by the U.S. negotiators at the 65th meeting. The U.S. authorities would have the right to terminate employment under the provisions of Paragraph 2, when, under the provisions of Paragraph 3, there were justifiable reasons. If the U.S. negotiators insist on the inclusion of the second sentence of Agreed Minute #3, then many more rights of employers ⌊in the field of personnel administration⌋ should be specifically spelled out in the Article. For that reason, the Korean negotiators maintain that this provision is unnecessary.

12. Mr. Habib stated that the U.S. negotiators would reserve discussion of the revised Korean draft of the Labor Article until the next meeting.

Criminal Jurisdiction Article

13. Turning to the Criminal Jurisdiction Article, Mr. Chang stated that the draft tabled by the U.S. negotiators at the previous meeting, which included the so-called German NATO waiver formula, was being given the most careful consideration by the Korean negotiators and competent ROK authorities. The Korean negotiators, therefore, would respond to the U.S. negotiators' presentation at a later meeting. Meanwhile, the Korean negotiators wished to seek clarification of a few points with regard to the U.S. draft.

14. First, with regard to the provisions of Paragraphs 3 and 4, the Korean negotiators wished clarification of the phrase "major interests of Korean administration of justice make imperative the exercise of Korean jurisdiction". Specifically, they wished to know if this phrase had the same meaning as the phrase in the Korean draft that "it is of particular importance that jurisdiction be exercised by the authorities of the Republic of Korea".

15. The Korean negotiators would also like to know, Mr. Chang continued, whether, whenever the Korean authorities consider that in a specific case major interests of Korean administration of justice make imperative the exercise of Korean

0168

jurisdiction, that particular case can be recalled automatically, regardless of whether ~~xxxxxx~~ or not an understanding is reached between the Korean and American authorities. ~~In other words,~~ Does the initiative and discretion whether or not to recall waiver rest with the Korean authorities when they consider it to be necessary?

16. Mr. Habib replied that the answer to the second question was yes. The discretion whether or not to recall waiver would rest with the Korean authorities. However, he pointed out the language of the U.S. draft illustrates and is responsive to the statement of the Korean negotiators that *they would arrive in as many cases as* ~~the recall of waiver is not something~~ *their countries do under their very simple waiver provisions.* ~~to be taken lightly.~~ There is no automaticity involved in the process ~~xxx~~ provided for in the U.S. draft. The right of recall of waiver is granted to the Government of the Republic of Korea. However, discussion between the Korean authorities and the U.S. authorities is provided for. Moreover, the illustrative list of offenses is further intended to emphasize the restraint which the U.S. negotiators have been told that the Korean authorities would exercise. The list of offenses is illustrative; it is not intended to provide for automatic recall of waiver in every case involving an offense included in the list.

17. In response to the first question asked by the Korean negotiators, Mr. Habib said that the U.S. negotiators hoped that what the Korean negotiators had in mind when they drafted the phrase "it is of particular importance that jurisdiction be exercised" was the same as what the U.S. negotiators had in mind in proposing the phrase "major interests of Korean administration of justice make imperative the exercise of Korean jurisdiction". The U.S. negotiators believe, however, that the language in the U.S. draft was a more specific response to the Korean intent. The U.S. negotiators assumed that if the Korean authorities indicated a desire to exercise jurisdiction, there would be discussion, including consideration of why it was necessary to recall the waiver in that particular case. To put it another way, the right of recall is granted; the circumstances of recall can be the subject of discussion. The U.S. negotiators expect that the Korean authorities would use restraint in the recall of

0169

waivers which would be ~~consist~~ fully consistent with the spirit expressed by the Korean negotiators.

18. Mr. ~~Chang~~ Ho said the Korean negotiators wished to know whether the pro-visions of Paragraph 3(a) of the Agreed Minute Re Paragraph 3(b) ~~xxxxxxxxxx~~ would permit the Korean authorities to exercise jurisdiction over offenses other than those ~~xxxxxxxxx~~ enumerated in subparagraphs (i)(ii), and (iii) of Paragraph 3(a) of that Agreed Minute. Mr. Habib replied that the ~~xxxxxxxxxxxxxxxxxxxxxxxxxxxxxxxxx~~ ~~xxxxxxxxxxxxxxxxxxxxxxxxxxxxxxx~~ language of the U.S. draft would permit the Korean authorities to exercise jurisdiction over ~~cases~~ cases involving offenses not listed specifical-ly, provided the ~~xxxxxxxxx~~ Korean authorities could show that it was imperative that Korean jurisdiction be exercised. The words "in particular" in the U.S. draft did not mean "exclusively" and the list is intended to be illustrative, not definitive.

19. With regard to the U.S. proposal on duty certificates, Mr. ~~Chang~~ Ho asked the U.S. negotiators to ~~xxxxxxx~~ specify the categories of U.S. authorities who would —e included in the phrase "competent authorities of the U.S. armed forces". In parti-cular, they wished to know whether the phrase should be construed to include the commanding officer of a company-size unit. In reply, Colonel Crawford explained that the U.S. proposal envisaged ~~xxxxxx~~ that a Staff Judge Advocate would be consulted in ach case before a duty certificate was issued, but the certificate would be issued by an officer with command responsibility. Staff Judge Advocates have no command responsibility but they do have the legal expertise and experience needed to insure the legal soundness of actions taken by commanding officers. Since there are only five Staff Judge Advocates assigned to the U.S. armed forces in Korea and since the lowest-ranking one is assigned at the division level, issuance of duty certificates would take place at the division level or higher and the lowest-ranking competent authority issuing a duty certificate would be a Brigadier General.

20. It was agreed to hold the next meeting on April 30.

0170

JOINT SUMMARY RECORD OF THE 75TH SESSION

1. Time and Place: 3:30-4:30 P.M., April 28, 1965 at
the Foreign Ministry's Conference
Room (NO.1)

2. Attendance:

ROK Side:

Mr.	Chang, Sang Moon	Director European and American Affairs Bureau
Mr.	Huh, Sung Joon	Director Labor Administration Bureau Office of Labor Affairs
Mr.	Lee, Nam Ki	Chief America Section Ministry of Foreign Affairs
Maj.	Lee, Kye Hoon	Military Affairs Section Ministry of National Defense
Mr.	Kim, Kee Joe	3rd Secretary Ministry of Foreign Affairs
Mr.	Lee, Keun Pal (Interpreter)	3rd Secretary Ministry of Foreign Affairs
Mr.	Hwang, Young Jae	3rd Secretary Ministry of Foreign Affairs
Mr.	Park, Won Chul	3rd Secretary Ministry of Foreign Affairs

U.S. Side:

Mr.	Philip C. Habib	Counselor American Embassy
Brig. Gen.	Carroll H. Dunn	Deputy Chief of Staff 8th U.S. Army
Col.	Allan G. Pixton	Deputy Chief of Staff 8th U.S. Army
Capt.	George Hagerman	Assistant Chief of Staff USN/K
Col.	Kenneth C. Crawford	Staff Judge Advocate 8th U.S. Army
Mr.	Frank R. LaMacchia	First Secretary American Embassy
Mr.	Benjamin A. Fleck	First Secretary American Embassy
Mr.	Robert A. Kinney	J-5 8th U.S. Army
Mr.	Goodwin Shapiro	Second Secretary American Embassy
Maj.	Alton H. Harvey	Staff Judge Advocate's Office 8th U.S. Army
Mr.	David Y.C. Lee (Interpreter)	Second Secretary American Embassy
Mr.	Ogden C. Reed (Observer)	Civilian Personnel Director 8th U.S. Army
Mr.	G. W. Flowers (Observer)	8th U.S. Army

0171

Labor Article

1. Mr. Chang opened the meeting by stating that the
Korean negotiators, as they had promised at the 73rd
negotiating session, had carefully considered the revised
draft of the Labor Article tabled by the U.S. negotiators
at that meeting. They would now table a revised draft of
the entire article, in which the underlining indicates
modifications of the draft which they had tabled at the
69th session. Mr. Chang said he would discuss the new
revised draft on a paragraph by paragraph basis.

2. Paragraph 1 - Mr. Chang said the Korean
negotiators accepted the U.S. formula for defining an
"employer", except as regards invited contractors. The
Korean negotiators continued to maintain their position
that invited contractors should be subject to Korean laws
with regard to local employment relations and, therefore,
they should be excluded from the provisions of this Article.

3. With regard to the definition of an "employee",
Mr. Chang continued, the Korean negotiators similarly had
modified the language of their draft, taking into account
the U.S. suggestion of excluding members of the civilian
component. They believed that it is unnecessary to
mention domestics in this paragraph because domestics
are not covered by Korean labor legislation (e.g. Article 10,
Labor Standards Law). The Korean negotiators believed that
members of the Korean Service Corps should be considered
as employees coming under the provisions of this Article.
KSC personnel have been recruited from the free labor
market as manual laborers serving for the U.S. Army since
September, 1955, said Mr. Chang.

4. Referring to Agreed Minute #1, Mr. Chang said that
the Korean negotiators consider that its provisions are
already covered in Paragraph 2 of the Article. Under
the terms of Paragraph 2, the ROK Government, as it has done

0172

in the past, will make available, on the request of the
U.S. armed forces, Korean personnel not only for the
Korean Service Corps but also for any employment, insofar
as possible, to meet the requirements of the U.S. armed forces.

　　　5. <u>Paragraph 3 and Agreed Minute #4</u> - Mr. Chang
said that the Korean negotiators had made some self-explanatory
modifications of the language in Paragraph 3 to satisfy the
needs of the U.S. negotiators.　There had also been some
changes in Agreed Minute #4.　The Korean negotiators believe
it is reasonable to provide that any deviation from Korean
law shall be referred to the Joint Committee in advance for
mutual agreement.　In this regard, the Korean negotiators
recalled that the U.S. negotiators had in mind deviation
from Korean law during times of emergency.　In order to
cover such situations, the Korean negotiators had drafted
a new Paragraph #5, which　they would explain shortly.
They did not foresee any difficulty on the part of the
U.S. authorities in referring in advance any deviation
from Korean law to the Joint Committee for mutual agreement.

　　　6. <u>Paragraph 4</u>　- Mr. Chang said the Korean revised
draft had deleted subparagraph (a) of the U.S. draft,
regarding the resolution of employee grievances, for such
provisions are fully described in Korean legislation.
Also, the Korean negotiators could not accept the U.S.
versions of subparagraphs (b) and (c) because the employees'
rights of union organization and consultation are provided
for to a satisfactory extent in Korean labor legislation.
Also, in a sense, any formula of recognizing the organization
of labor unions is against the spirit of Korean labor legislation.

　　　7. Regarding the issue of settlement of disputes,
Mr. Chang said that the Korean negotiators had made a
significant concession by providing in subparagraph (a)(4)

0173

of Paragraph 4 that the cooling-off period shall begin
after the dispute is referred to the second stage, i.e.
the specially-designated committee. This implies, he
continued, prolongation by many more days of the prohibition
against disruptive practices by the employees. The Korean
negotiators believed this formula would satisfy the U.S. desires.

8. Mr. Chang said the Korean negotiators had drawn
up a new formula with regard to the right to strike.
This was contained in subparagraph (b) of Paragraph 4,
which would provide that the right to strike shall be accorded
to employees except those whose exercise of this right is
prohibited by the Joint Committee. There had been a
great many deliberations on the right to strike and now
the Korean negotiators were proposing to settle the matter
by providing in their draft that the Joint Committee
would resolve the question. (The U.S. negotiators had held the
position that certain employees should not exercise the right
to strike. The Korean negotiators agree that there would
be some employees of the U.S. armed forces who should not
exercise that right. Therefore, Mr. Chang said, the Korean
negotiators were proposing that the Joint Committee designate
such persons.)

9. Paragraph 5   - Mr. Chang said that the Korean
negotiators, taking into account the worries of the U.S.
negotiators concerning deviation from Korean law during
times of emergency, had introduced a new paragraph which
would provide that the application of the Labor Article
may be suspended, in whole or in part, in accordance with the
extent promulgated in the emergency measures taken by the
Government of the Republic of Korea. The Korean negotiators
believed that this formula would relieve the worries of the
U.S. negotiators and that they would accept Paragraph 3

0174

and Agreed Minute #4 of the Korean draft without any objection.

10. Mr. Chang said the Korean negotiators had no problems with regard to subparagraph (a) of Paragraph 5 of the U.S. draft. In subparagraph (b), the Korean negotiators had inserted the words "through mutual agreement" in order to clarify the points agreed upon at the previous meeting.

11. Mr. Chang said that the Korean negotiators' final comments were directed toward the second sentence of Agreed Minute #3 of the U.S. draft. The U.S. negotiators held the view that nowhere in the Article is there provision for the right of employers to terminate employment of employees. The Korean negotiators wished to call the attention of the U.S. negotiators to the first sentence of Paragraph 2, which reads: "Employers may recruit, employ and administer their personnel". The Korean negotiators understand that the word "administer" indicates the stages of personnel administration from hire to fire, as explained by the U.S. negotiators at the 65th meeting. The U.S. authorities would have the right to terminate employment under the provisions of Paragraph 2, when, under the provisions of Paragraph 3, there were justifiable reasons. If the U.S. negotiators insist on the inclusion of the second sentence of Agreed Minute #3, then many more rights of employers in the field of personnel administration should be specifically spelled out in the Article. For that reason, the Korean negotiators maintain that this provision is unnecessary.

12. Mr. Habib stated that the U.S. negotiators would reserve discussion of the revised Korean draft of the Labor Article until the next meeting.

0175

한·미국 간의 상호방위조약 제4조에 의한 시설과 구역 및 한국에서의 미국군대의 지위에 관한 협정(SOFA)
전59권. 1966.7.9 서울에서 서명 : 1967.2.9 발효(조약 232호) (V.29 실무교섭회의, 제73-76차, 1965.4월) 181

Criminal Jurisdiction Article

13. Turning to the Criminal Jurisdiction Article, Mr. Chang stated that the draft tabled by the U.S. negotiators at the previous meeting, which included the so-called German NATO waiver formula, was being given the most careful consideration by the Korean negotiators and competent ROK authorities. The Korean negotiators, therefore, would respond to the U.S. negotiators' presentation at a later meeting. Meanwhile, the Korean negotiators wished to seek clarification of a few points with regard to the U.S. draft.

14. First, with regard to the provisions of Paragraph 3 and 4, the Korean negotiators wished clarification of the phrase "major interests of Korean administration of justice make imperative the exercise of Korean jurisdiction". Specifically, they wished to know if this phrase had the same meaning as the phrase in the Korean draft that "it is of particular importance that jurisdiction be exercised by the authorities of the Republic of Korea".

15. The Korean negotiators would also like to know, Mr. Chang continued, whether, whenever the Korean authorities consider that in a specific case major interests of Korean administration of justice make imperative the exercise of Korean jurisdiction, that particular case can be recalled automatically, regardless of whether or not an understanding is reached between the Korean and American authorities. Does the initiative and discretion whether or not to recall waiver rest with the Korean authorities when they consider it to be necessary?

16. Mr. Habib replied that the answer to the second question was yes. The discretion whether or not to recall waiver would rest with the Korean authorities. However, he pointed out, the language of the U.S. draft illustrates and is responsive to the statement of the

0176

Korean negotiators that they would waive in as many cases as other countries do under their very simple waiver provisions. There is no automaticity involved in the process provided for in the U.S. draft. The right of recall of waiver is granted to the Government of the Republic of Korea. However, discussion between the Korean authorities and the U.S. authorities is provided for. Moreover, the illustrative list of offenses is further intended to emphasize the restraint which the U.S. negotiators have been told that the Korean authorities would exercise. The list of offenses is illustrative; it is not intended to provide for automatic recall of waiver in every case involving an offense included in the list.

17. In response to the first question asked by the Korean negotiators, Mr. Habib said that the U.S. negotiators hoped that what the Korean negotiators had in mind when they drafted the phrase "it is of particular importance that jurisdiction be exercised" was the same as what the U.S. negotiators had in mind in proposing the phrase "major interests of Korean administration of justice make imperative the exercise of Korean jurisdiction". The U.S. negotiators believe, however, that the language in the U.S. draft was a more specific response to the Korean intent. The U.S. negotiators assumed that if the Korean authorities indicated a desire to exercise jurisdiction, there would be discussion, including consideration of why it was necessary to recall the waiver in that particular case. To put it another way, the right of recall is granted; the circumstances of recall can be the subject of discussion. The U.S. negotiators expect that the Korean authorities would use restraint in the recall of waivers which would be fully consistent with the spirit expressed by the Korean negotiators.

0177

18. Mr. Ho said the Korean negotiators wished to know whether the provisions of Paragraph 3(a) of the Agreed Minute Re Paragraph 3(b) would permit the Korean authorities to exercise jurisdiction over offenses other than those enumerated in subparagraphs (i)(ii), and (iii) of Paragraph 3(a) of that Agreed Minute. Mr. Habib replied that the language of the U.S. draft would permit the Korean authorities to exercise jurisdiction over cases involving offenses not listed specifically, provided the Korean authorities could show that it was imperative that Korean jurisdiction be exercised. The words "in particular" in the U.S. draft did not mean "exclusively" and the list is intended to be illustrative, not definitive.

19. With regard to the U.S. proposal on duty certificates, Mr. Ho asked the U.S. negotiators to specify the categories of U.S. authorities who would be included in the phrase "competent authorities of the U.S. armed forces". In particular, they wished to know whether the phrase should be construed to include the commanding officer of a company -size unit. In reply, Colonel Crawford explained that the U.S. proposal envisaged that a Staff Judge Advocate would be consulted in each case before a duty certificate was issued, but the certificate would be issued by an officer with command responsibility. Staff Judge Advocates have no command responsibility but they do have the legal expertise and experience needed to insure the legal soundness of actions taken by commanding officers. Since there are only five Staff Judge Advocates assigned to the U.S. armed forces in Korea and since the lowest-ranking one is assigned at the division level, issuence of duty certificates would take place at the division level or higher and the lowest-ranking competent authority issuing a duty certificate would be Brigadier General.

20. It was agreed to hold the next meeting on April 30.

0178

4. 제76차 회의, 4.30

민사청구권 조항에 대한 검토자료

1. 한 · 미 초안 대조표 (해결방안 포함)
2. 교섭 경위
3. 대표적인 각국선례의 요약

1965. 4.

0180

청구권 조항중 주요분제에 대한

한·미양측 초안 대조표

한국측 초안	미국측 초안
1. 공무집행중에 일어나는 손해:	1. 공무집행중에 일어나는 손해:
가. 군대의 재산: (1항)	가. 군대의 재산: (1항)
나. 창후모건부재산: (2 항)	상호 포기
나. 기타 정부재산: (2항)	나. 기타정부재산: (2항)
(1) 상호합의에 의하여 선출하는 1인의 한국인 중재인을 통하여 해결.	(1) 피청구국의 국내법에 의하여 해결.
(2) 손해액은 양국정부가 분담.	(2) ₩1,400 이하의 손해 상호 포기.
(가) 미국책임 한국 15 퍼센트, 미국 85 "	
(나) 동시책임 한국 50 퍼센트 미국 50 "	
(다) 책임불명확 한국 50 퍼센트 미국 50 "	
(3) ₩800 이하의 손해상호 포기	
(4) 매 6 개월마다 원화로 청산	

해 결 방 안

제1안 한국안을 주장하되, "나토" 혹은 일본등의 선례에 따라
미국책임시의 분담율과 상호 청구포기금액의 한계에
있어 미국안을 수락.

제2안 미국안 수락.

0181

다. 제3자에 대한 손해: (5항)　　　　다. 제3자에 대한 손해: (5항)

(1) 한국군근이 손해를 가하　　　　(1) 미국법에 의하여 해결.
　　였을때에 적용하는 한국
　　법에 의하여 해결.

(2) 한국당국의 결정에 미국
　　당국이 불만이 있을때에는
　　한국당국은 이를 재심하며,
　　재심의 결과는 최종적이다
　　(합의의사록) 단, 재판의
　　결정은 재심불가.

(3) 한국은 모든 손해배상
　　청구를 해결하고 원화로
　　이를 지불.

(4) 한국이 지불한 청구사건에
　　대하여 미국측에 상세히
　　통보하며 양국정부가 분담
　　할 안을 제시.
　　2개월내에 회답이 없으면
　　상기 분담안은 수락된
　　것으로간주.

(5) 손해액은 양국정부가 분담-
　　(가) 미국책임
　　　　한국 15 퍼센트
　　　　미국 85 퍼센트

　　(나) 동시책임
　　　　한국 50 퍼센트
　　　　미국 50 　"

　　(다) 책임불명확
　　　　한국 50 퍼센트
　　　　미국 50 　"

(6) 매 6개월마다 원화로 청산-

(7) 미군구성원 및 고용원은
　　한국의 민사재판에 불복.

(8) 선박관계 손해는 적용하지
　　않음.

(9) 본항목은 협정발효 6개월후에
　　적용한다. (합의의사록)

0182

해 결 방 안

제1안 한국안을 주장하되, 분담율은 "나"항과 동일.

제2안 상기 제1안을 주장하되, 재심시 한국당국은 배상금을 미국 당국과 협의하여 결정.

제3안 ~~1.한국군이 손해를 가하였을 때에 적용하는 한국법에 준하여 해결.~~

2. 한국당국은 ^{재심시} 배상액을 미국당국과 상호합의하에 결정.

~~3.피해자가 한·미양당국이 결정한 배상금에 불만이 있을 때에는 1차에 한하여 재심.~~

4. 피해자가 민사소송을 제기할때에는, 한국정부는 미국 정부를 대신하여 피고가 되며, 미국당국과 긴밀한 협조.

5. 미군구성원 및 고용원은 한국민사재판에 불복.

6. 배상금은 미국당국이 지불.

2. 비공무중에 일어난 손해 (6항)	2. 비공무중에 일어난 손해 (5항)
(1) 한국당국이 사건을 조사 배상금을 사정하여 미국당국에 통고	(1) 미국정부는 미군 혹은 군속에 대한 기타 청구를 호의적인 고려를 하여 배상금을 지불
(2) 미국당국은 배상여부와 배상금을 결정하고, 피해자가 수락시 이를 지불.	(2) 피해자가 만족한 배상을 받지 않는한 한국의 민사소송제기권 보유 (6 (a) (ⅶ)항
(3) 피해자는 미국당국의 배상에 불만이 있을시 가해자를 상대로 한국의 민사재판.	

해 결 방 안

한국안을 계속 주장.

3. 공무집행 여부에 관한 분쟁해결. (9 (a)항)	3. 공무집행여부에 관한 분쟁해결. (6 (a)항)
미군구성원 및 고용원의 행위가 공무집행중에 행하여 졌는지의 여부와 차량사용의 허가유무에 관한 분쟁이 발생하였을 때에는 중재인이 결정.	각당사국은 그의 군대구성원 혹은 고용원의 공무집행여부와 재산이 공무를 위하여 사용중이였는가의 여부를 결정할 권한을 보유.

0183

해   결   방   안

미 국 안 을 수 락 .

4. 계 약 상 의 분 쟁 【 10 항)	4. 계 약 상 의 분 쟁
(1) 당 사 자 간 에 해 결 되 지 않 을 때 에 는 합 등 위 원 회 에 서 조 정 할 수 있 다 .	해 당 조 항 없 음 .
(2) 계 양 당 사 자 가 민 사 소 송 제 기 권을 보 유 시 이 를 침 해 하 지 않 는 다 .	

해   결   방   안

제1안 한 국 안 을 계 속 주 장

제2안 타 방 의 공 무 집 행 중 제 3 자 에 대 한 손 해 배 상 절 차 에 있 어 제 3 안 이 채 택 될 때 에 그 와 동 일 한 절 차 에 의 거 해 결 .

0184

1. Each Party waives all its claims against the other Party for damage to any property owned by it and used by its armed services, if such damage:

(a) was caused by a member or an employee of the armed services of the other Party, in execution of his official duties; or

(b) arose from the use of any vehicle, vessel or aircraft owned by the other Party and used by its armed services, provided either that the vehicle, vessel or aircraft causing the damage was being used in the execution of its official duty or that the damage was caused to property being so used.

claims for maritime salvage by one Party against the other Party shall be waived, provided that the vessel or cargo salved was owned by the other Party and being used by its armed services for official purposes.

2.(a) In the case of damage caused or arising as stated in paragraph 1 to other property owned by either Party and located in the Republic of Korea, the issue of liability of the other Party shall be determined and the amount of damage shall be

1. Each Party waives all its claims against the other Party for damage to any property owned by it and used by its armed forces, if such damage:

(a) was caused by a member or an employee of the armed forces of the other Party, in the performance of his official duties; or

(b) arose from the use of any vehicle, vessel or aircraft owned by the other Party and used by its armed forces, provided either that the vehicle, vessel or aircraft causing the damage was being used in the performance of its official duty or that the damage was caused to property being so used.

claims for maritime salvage by one Party against the other Party shall be waived, provided that the vessel or cargo salved was owned by the other Party and being used by its armed forces for official purposes.

2.(a) In the case of damage caused or arising as stated in paragraph 1 to other property owned by either Party, the issue of liability of the other Party shall be determined and the amount of damage shall be assessed, unless the two Governments agree

0185

otherwise, by a sole arbitrator selected in accordance with subparagraph (b) of this paragraph.

The arbitrator shall also decide any counter-claims arising out of the same incidents.

assessed, unless the two Governments agree otherwise, by a sole arbitrator selected in accordance with subparagraph (b) of this paragraph.
The arbitrator shall also decide any counter-measures arising out of the same incidents.

(b) The arbitrator referred to in subparagraph (a) above shall be selected by agreement between the two Governments from amongst the nationals of the Republic of Korea who hold or have held high judicial office.

(c) Any decision taken by the arbitrator shall be binding and conclusive upon the Parties.

(d) The amount of any compensation awarded by the arbitrator shall be distributed in accordance with the provisions of paragraph 5(e) (i), (ii) and (iii) of this Article.

(e) The compensation of the arbitrator shall be fixed by agreement between the two Governments and shall, together with the necessary expenses incidental to the performance of his duties, be defrayed in equal proportions by them.

(f) Each Party waives its claim in any such case up to the amount equivalent to 800 United Stated dollars or 104,000 won.

(f) Each party waives its claim in any such case up to the amount of 1,400 United States dollars or its equivalent in Korean currency

0186

at the rate of exchange provided for in the Agreed Minute to Article at the time the claim is filed.

In the case of considerable variation in the rate of exchange between these currencies the two Governments shall agree on the appropriate adjustments of these amounts.

3. For the purpose of paragraph 1 and 2 of this Article the expression "owned by a Party" in the case of a vessel includes a vessel on bare boat charter to that Party or requisitioned by it on bare boat terms or seized by it in prize (except to the extent that the risk of loss or liability is borne by some person other than such party).

4. Each Party waives all its claims against the other Party for injury or death suffered by any member of its armed services while such member was engaged in the performance of his official duties.

5. Claims (other than contractual claims and those to which paragraph 6 or 7/this Article of apply) arising out of acts or omissions of members or empoyees of the United States armed forces, including those employees who are nationals of or ordinarily resident in the Republic of

Korea, done in the performance
of official duty, or out of
any other act, omission or
occurence for which the United
States armed forces are legally
responsible, and causing damage
in the Republic of Korea to
third Parties, other than the
Government of the Republic of
Korea, shall be dealt with by
the Republic of Korea in accordance withe the following provisions:

(a) Claims shall be filed,
considered and settled or
adjudicated in accordance with
the laws and regulations of the
Republic of Korea with respect
to the claims arising from the
activities of its own armed
forces.

(b) The Republic of Korea may
settle any such claims, and payment
of the amount agreed upon or
determined by adjudication shall
be made by the Republic of
Korea in won.

(c) Such payment, whether
made pursuant to a settlement
or to adjudication of the case
by a competent tribunal of the
Republic of Korea, or the final
adjudication by such a tribunal
denying payment, shall be
binding and conclusive upon
the Parties.

(d) Every claim paid by the Republic of Korea shall be communicated to the appropriate United States authorities together with full particulars and a proposed distribution in conformity with subparagraph (e) (i) and (ii) below.

In default of a reply within two months, the proposed distribution shall be regarded as accepted.

(e) The cost incurred in satisfying claims pursuant to the preceding subparagraph and paragraph 2 of this Article shall be distributed between the Parties as follows:

(5)(e)(i) Where the United States alone is responsible, the amount awarded or adjudged shall be distributed in the proportion of 15 percent chargeable to the Republic of Korea and 85 percent chargeable to the United States.

(ii) Where the Republic of Korea and the United States are responsible for the damage, the amount awarded or adjudged shall be distributed equally between them. Where the damage was caused by the armed forces of the Republic of Korea and the United States and it is not possible to attribute it

(5)(e)(i) Where the United States alone is responsible, the amount awarded or adjudged shall be distributed in the proportion of 25 percent chargeable to the Republic of Korea and 75 percent chargeable to the United States.

(ii) Where the Republic of Korea and the United States are responsible for the damage, the amount awarded or adjudged shall be distributed equally between them. Where the damage was caused by the armed forces of the Republic of Korea and the United States and it is not possible to attribute it specifically to one or both of those armed services, the amount awarded or adjudged shall be distributed equally between the Republic of Korea and the United States.

(iii) Every half year, a statement of the sums paid by the Republic of Korea in the course of the half-yearly period in respect of every case regarding which the proposed distribution on a percentage basis has been accepted, shall be sent to the appropriate authorities of the United States, together with a request for reimbursement. Such reimbursement shall be made, in won, within the shortest possible time.

(f) Members or employees of the United States armed forces, excluding those employees who are nationals of or ordinarily resident in the Republic of Korea, shall not be subject to any proceedings for the enforcement of any judgement given against them in the Republic of Korea in a matter arising from the performance of their official duties.

(g) Except in so far as sub-paragraph (e) of this paragraph applies to claims covered by

---

specifically to one or both of those armed services, the amount awarded or adjudged shall be distributed equally between the Republic of Korea and the United States.

(iii) Every half year, a statement of the sums paid by the Republic of Korea in the course of the half-yearly period in respect of every case regarding which the liability, amount, and proposed distribution on a percentage basis has been approved by the United States shall be sent to the appropriate authorities of the United States, together with a request for reimbursement. Such reimbursement shall be made in won within the shortest possible time.

(f) Members or employees of the United States armed forces, including those employees who are nationals of or ordinarily resident in the Republic of Korea, shall not be subject to any proceedings for the enforcement of any judgement given against them in the Republic of Korea in a matter arising from the performance of their official duties.

[boxed, crossed out:]

(iii) Every half year, a statement of the sums paid by the Republic of Korea in the course of the half-yearly period in respect of every case regarding which the liability, amount, and proposed distribution on a percentage basis has been accepted by the United States shall be sent to the appropriate authorities of the United States, together with a request for reimbursement. Such reimbursement shall be made in won within the shortest possible time.

paragraph 2 of this Article, the provisions of this paragraph shall not apply to any claims arising out of or in connection with the navigation or operation of a ship or the loading, carriage, or discharge of a cargo, other than claims for death or personal injury to which paragraph 4 of this Article does not apply.

6. Claims against members or employees of the United States armed forces (except employees who are nationals of or ordinarily resident in the Republic of Korea) arising out of tortious acts or omissions in the Republic of Korea not done in the Performance of official duty shall be dealt with in the following manner:

(a) The authorities of the Republic of Korea shall consider the claim and assess compensation to the claimant in a fair and just manner, taking into account all the circumstances of the case, including the conduct of the injured persons, and shall prepare a report on the matter.

(b) The report shall be delivered to the appropriate United States authorities, who shall then decide without delay whether they will offer an ex gratia payment, and if so, of what amount.

(c) If an offer of ex gratia payment is made, and accepted by the claimant in full satisfaction of his claim, the United States authorities shall make the payment themselves and inform the authorities of the Republic of Korea of their decision and of the sums paid.

(d) Nothing in this paragraph shall affect the jurisdiction of the courts of the Republic of Korea to entertain an action against a member or an employee of the United States armed forces unless and until there has been payment in full satisfaction of the claim.

7. Claims arising out of the unauthorized use of any vehicle of the United States forces shall be dealt with in accordance with paragraph 6 of this Article, except in so far as the United States forces are legally responsible.

8. If a disput arises as to whether a tortious act or omission of a member or an employee of the United States armed forces was done in the performance of official duty or as to whether the use of any vehicle of the United States armed forces was unauthorized, the question shall be submitted to an arbitrator

0192

appointed in accordance with paragraph 2(b) of this Article, whose
decision on this point shall be
final and conclusive.

9. (a) The United States shall not
claim immunity from the jurisdiction
of the courts of the Republic of
Korea for members or employees of
the United States armed forces in
respect of the civil jurisdiction
of the courts of the Republic of
Korea except to the extent provided
in paragraph 5(f) of this Article.

(b) In case any private movable
property, excluding that in use by
the United States armed forces,
which is subject to compulsory
execution under the Korean law, is
within the facilities and areas in
use by the United States armed
forces, the United States authorities
shall, upon the request of the
courts of the Republic of Korea,
possess and turn over such property
to the authorities of the Republic
of Korea.

(c) The authorities of the
Republic of Korea and the United

9. (a) The United States shall not
claim immunity from the jurisdiction
of the courts of the Republic of
Korea for members or employees of
the United States armed forces in
respect of the civil jurisdiction
of the courts of the Republic of
Korea except in respect of proceedings for the enforcement of any
judgment given against them in
the Republic of Korea in a matter
arising from the performance of
their official duties or except
after payment in full satisfaction
of a claim.

(b) In the case of any private
movable property, excluding that
in use by the United States armed
forces, which is subject to
compulsory execution under Korean
law, and is within the facilities
and areas in use by the United
States armed forces, the United
States authorities shall, upon
the request of the Korean courts,
render all assistance within
their power to see that such
property is turned over to the
Korean authorities.

(c) The authorities of the United
States and the Republic of Korea shall

States shall cooperate in the procurement of evidence for a fair hearing and disposal of claims under this Article.

10. Disputes arising out of contracts concerning the procurement of materials, supplies, equipment, services by or for the United States armed forces, which are not resolved by the Parties to the contract concerned, may be submitted to the Joint Committee for conciliation, provided that the provisions of this paragraph shall not prejudice any right, which Parties to the contract may have, to file a civil suit.

11. Paragraph 2 and 5 of this Article shall apply only to claims arising incident to non-combat activities.

12. (Agreed Minute 3 in Korean draft)

cooperate in the procurement of evidence for a fair disposition of claims under this Article.

12. For the purposes of this Article, members of the Korean Augmentation to the United States Army (KATUSA) shall be considered as members of the United States armed forces, and members of the Korean Service Corps (KSC) shall be considered as employees of the armed forces of the Republic of Korea.

12. For the purpose of this Article, members of the Korean Augmentation to the United States Army (KATUSA) and members of the Korean Service Corps (KSC) shall be considered respectively as members and employees of the United States armed forces.

0194

13. The provisions of this Article shall not apply to any claims which arose before the entry into force of this agreement. Such claims shall be processed and settled by the authorities of the United States.

AGREED MINUTE

A. Unless otherwise provided, the provisions of paragraphs five, six, seven and eight of this article shall become effective six months from the date of entry into force of this agreement.

B. Until such time,
1.
2.
3.

---

13. (None in Korean draft)

The provisions of this Article shall not apply to any claims which arose before the entry into force of this agreement.

AGREED MINUTE

1. The amount to be paid to each claimant, under the provisions of paragraph 5(b) of this Article, except the cases being determined by adjudication, shall be communicated to the authorities of the United States before the payment is made.

In case any reply in favour of the decision is received from the U.S. side, or in default of a reply within one month of receipt of the communication envisaged above, the amount decided by the Korean Claims Authorities shall be regarded as agreed upon between the both Governments.

If, however, the authorities of the United States disagree to the amount decided by the Korean Claims Authorities and reply to this effect within the one-month period, the Korean Claims Authorities shall re-examine the case

AGREED MINUTE

1. The provisions of paragraphs five, six, seven and eight of this article will become effective six months from the date of entry into force of this agreement as to claims arising from incidents in the Seoul Special City area.

2. The provisions of paragraphs five, six, seven and eight will be progressively extended to other areas of Korea as determined and defined by the Joint Committee.

3. Until such time as the provisions of paragraphs five, six, seven and eight become effective in any given area.

1. The United States shall process and settle claims (other than contractual claims) arising

concerned. The amount decided as a result of the re-examination shall be final and conclusive. The Korean Claims Authorities shall notify the authorities of the United States of the result of re-examination as early as practicable.

The amount agreed upon between the both Governments or decided through the re-examination shall be paid to the claimant concerned without delay.

2. The provisions of paragraph 5 of this Article will become effective after six months from the date of entry into force of this Agreement. Until such time the United States agrees to pay just and reasonable compensation in settlement of civil claims (other than contractual claims) arising out of acts or omissions of members of the United States armed forces done in the performance of official duty or out of any other act, omission or occurrence for which the United States armed forces are legally responsible. In making such payments United States authorities would exercise the authority provided under United States laws relating to Foreign Claims and regulations issued thereunder. In settling claims which are

out of the acts or omissions of members of employees of the United States armed forces done in the performance of official duty or out of any other act, omission or occurence for which the United States armed forces are legally responsible, which cause damage in the Republic of Korea to parties other than the two governments,

2. The United States shall entertain other non-contractual claims against members or employees of the armed forces and may offer an ex gratia payment in such cases and in such amount as is determined by the appropriate United States authorities; and

3. Each party shall have the right to determine whether a member or employee of its armed forces was engaged in the performance of official duties and whether property owned by it was being used by its armed forces for official purposes.

C. For the purposes of sub-paragraph 2(d), subparagraph 5(e) shall be effective throughout Korea from the date of entry into force of this agreement.

C. For the purposes of sub-paragraph 2(d), subparagraph 5(e) shall be effective from the date of entry into force of this agreement.

0196

described as arising "..... out of any act, omission or occurrance for which the United States armed forces are legally responsible". United States authorities will take into consideration local law and practice.

3. For the purpose of paragraph 5 of this Article, members of the Korean Augmentation to the United States Army (KATUSA) and members of the Korean Service Corps (KSC) shall be considered respectively as members and employees of the United States armed forces.

Claims Article

Proposed Changes in Korean Draft

(1.) Paragraph 2(a)

Delete "and located in the Republic of Korea"

(2.) Paragraph 2(f)

"Each party waives its claim in any such case up to the amount of 1,400 United States dollars or its equivalent in Korean currency at the rate of exchange provided for in the Agreed Minute to Article ___ at the time the claim is filed."

(3.) Paragraph 5(e)(i)

"Where the United States alone is responsible, the amount awarded or adjudged shall be distributed in the proportion of 25 percent chargeable to the Republic of Korea and 75 percent chargeable to the United States."

(4.) Paragraph 5(e)(iii)

"Every half year, a statement of the sums paid by the Republic of Korea in the course of the half-yearly period in respect of every case regarding which the liability, amount, and proposed distribution on a percentage basis has been approved by the United States shall be sent to the appropriate authorities of the United States, together with a request for reimbursement. Such reimbursement shall be made in won within the shortest possible time."

(5.) Paragraph 5(f)

Change "excluding" to "including".

(6.) Paragraph 9(b)   u.s. 6(b)

"In the case of any private movable property, excluding that in use by the United States armed forces, which is subject to compulsory execution under Korean law, and is within the facilities and areas in use by the United States armed forces, the United States authorities shall, upon the request of the Korean courts, render all assistance within their power to see that such property is turned over to the Korean authorities."

0198

CONFIDENTIAL

-2-

7. **Paragraph 9(c)** U.S. 7.

"The authorities of the United States and the Republic of Korea shall cooperate in the procurement of evidence for a fair disposition of claims under this Article."

8. **Paragraph 12** (new) U.S. 10.

"For the purposes of this Article, members of the Korean Augmentation to the United States Army (KATUSA) shall be considered as members of the United States armed forces, and members of the Korean Service Corps (KSC) shall be considered as employees of the armed forces of the Republic of Korea."

9. **Paragraph 13** (new) U.S. 11.

"The provisions of this Article shall not apply to any claims which arose before the entry into force of this Agreement."

10. **Proposed Agreed Minute**

Tabled separately

11. In order to make this article conform to the rest of the Agreement:

a. Substitute "armed forces" for "armed services"

b. Substitute "performance of his official duties" for "execution of his official duties"

c. Substitute "for official purposes" for "in the execution of its official duty"

d. Substitute "counter claims" for "counter measures"

wherever appropriate.

0199

(12) Paragraph 9(a)

The United States shall not claim immunity from the jurisdiction of the courts of the Republic of Korea for members or employees of the United States armed forces in respect of the civil jurisdiction of the courts of the Republic of Korea except in respect of proceedings for the enforcement of any judgment given against them in the Republic of Korea in a matter arising from the performance of their official duties or except after payment in full satisfaction of a claim.

0200

CONFIDENTIAL

Agreed Minute

A. Unless otherwise provided,

   1. The provisions of paragraphs five, six, seven and eight of this article will become effective six months from the date of entry into force of this agreement as to claims arising from incidents in the Seoul Special City area.

   (20~25%) his claim

   2. The provisions of paragraphs five, six, seven and eight will be progressively extended to other areas of Korea as determined and defined by the Joint Committee.

B. Until such time as the provisions of paragraphs five, six, seven and eight become effective in any given area

   1. The United States shall process and settle claims (other than contractual claims) arising out of the acts or omissions of members or employees of the United States armed forces done in the performance of official duty or out of any other act, omission or occurence for which the United States armed forces are legally responsible, which cause damage in the Republic of Korea to parties other than the two governments;

   2. The United States shall entertain other non-contractual claims against members or employees of the armed forces and may offer an ex gratia payment in such cases, and in such amount as is determined by the appropriate United States authorities; and

   3. Each party shall have the right to determine whether a member or employee of its armed forces was engaged in the performance of official duties and whether property owned by it was being used by its armed forces for official purposes.

C. For the purposes of subparagraph 2(d), subparagraph 5(e) shall be effective throughout Korea from the date of entry into force of this agreement.

0201

CLAIMS ARTICLE

KOREAN POSITION	U. S. POSITION
1. Each party waives all its claims against the other party for damage to any property owned by it and used by its armed forces, if such damage:	1. (Same as Korean Draft)
(a) was caused by a member or an employee of the armed forces of the other party, in the performance of his official duties; or	
(b) arose from the use of any vehicle, vessel or aircraft owned by the other party and used by its armed forces, provided either that the vehicle, vessel or aircraft causing the damage was being used official ~~for~~ purposes or that the damage was caused to property being so used.	
claims for maritime salvage by one party against the other party shall be waived, provided that the vessel or cargo salved was owned by the other party and being used by its armed forces for official purposes.	
2. (a) In the case of damage caused or arising as stated in paragraph 1 to other property owned by either party, the issue of liability of the other party shall be determined and the amount of damage shall be assessed, unless the two Governments agree otherwise, by a sole arbitrator selected in accordance with subparagraph (b) of this paragraph.	2. (Same as Korean Draft)
The arbitrator shall also decide any counter-claims arising out of the same incidents.	
(b) The arbitrator referred to in subparagraph (a) above shall be selected by agreement between the two Governments from amongst the nationals of the Republic of Korea who hold or have held high judicial office.	

0202

KOREAN POSITION	U. S. POSITION

KOREAN POSITION

(c) Any decision taken by the arbitrator shall be binding and conclusive upon the parties.

(d) The amount of *any compen-* sation awarded by the arbitrator shall be distributed in accordance with the provisions of paragraph 5(e)(i),(ii) and (iii) of this Article.

(e) The compensation of the arbitrator shall be fixed by agreement between the two Governments and shall, together with the necessary expenses incidental to the performance of his duties, be defrayed in equal proportions by them.

(f) Each party waives its claim in any such case up to the amount of 1,400 United States dollars or its equivalent in Korean currency at the rate of exchange provided for in the Agreed Minute to Article_at the time the claim is filed.

3.
For the purpose of paragraph 1 and 2 of this Article the expression "owned by a party" in the case of a vessel includes a vessel on bare boat charter to that party or requisitioned by it on bare boat terms or seized by it in prize (except to the extent that the risk of loss or liability is borne by some person other than such party).

4.
Each Party waives all its claims against the other Party for injury or death suffered by any member of its armed forces while such member was engaged in the performance of his official duties.

5.
Claims (other than contractual claims and those to which paragraph 6 or 7 of this Article

apply) arising out of acts or omissions of members or empoyees of the United States armed forces, including those employees who are nationals of or ordinarily resident in the Republic of

U. S. POSITION

3.
(Same as Korean Draft)

4.
(Same as Korean Draft)

5.
(Same as Korean Draft except Subparagraphs (e)(i) and(iii) below.)

0203

Korea, done in the performance
of official duty, or out of
any other act, omission or
occurence for which the United
States armed forces are legally
responsible, and causing damage
in the Republic of Korea to
third parties, other than the
Government of the Republic of
Korea, shall be dealt with by
the Republic of Korea in accordance with the following provisions:

(a) Claims shall be filed,
considered and settled or
adjudicated in accordance with
the laws and regulations of the
Republic of Korea with respect
to the claims arising from the
activities of its own armed
forces.

(b) The Republic of Korea may
settle any such claims, and payment
of the amount agreed upon or
determined by adjudication shall
be made by the Republic of
Korea in won.

(c) Such payment, whether
made pursuant to a settlement
or to adjudication of the case
by a competent tribunal of the
Republic of Korea, or the final
adjudication by such a tribunal
denying payment, shall be
binding and conclusive upon
the parties.

(d) Every claim paid by the
Republic of Korea shall be
communicated to the appropriate
United States authorities
together with full particulars
and a proposed distribution in
conformity with subparagraph
(e) (i) and (ii) below.
In default of a reply within
two months, the proposed
distribution shall be regarded
as accepted.

(e) The cost incurred in
satisfying claims pursuant to the
preceding subparagraph and paragraph 2 of this Article shall be
distributed between the parties
as follows:

0204

KOREAN POSITION	U. S. POSITION
(5)(e)(i) Where the United States alone is responsible, the amount awarded or adjudged shall be distributed in the proportion of 15 percent chargeable to the Republic of Korea and 85 percent chargeable to the United States.	(5)(e)(i) Where the United States alone is responsible, the amount awarded or adjudged shall be distributed in the proportion of 25 percent chargeable to the Republic of Korea and 75 percent chargeable to the United States.
(ii) Where the Republic of Korea and the United States are responsible for the damage, the amount awarded or adjudged shall be distributed equally between them. Where the damage was caused by the armed forces of the Republic of Korea and the United States and it is not possible to attribute it specifically to one or both of those armed forces, the amount awarded or adjudged shall be distributed equally between the Republic of Korea and the United States.	(ii) Where the Republic of Korea and the United States are responsible for the damage, the amount awarded or adjudged shall be distributed equally between them. Where the damage was caused by the armed forces of the Republic of Korea and the United States and it is not possible to attribute it specifically to one or both of those armed forces, the amount awarded or adjudged shall be distributed equally between the Republic of Korea and the United States.
(iii) Every half year, a statement of the sums paid by the Republic of Korea in the course of the half-yearly period in respect of every case regarding which the proposed distribution on a percentage basis has been accepted, shall be sent to the appropriate authorities of the United States, together with a request for reimbursement. Such reimbursement shall be made, in won, within the shortest possible time. (See also Ageed Minute)	(iii) Every half year, a statement of the sums paid by the Republic of Korea in the course of the half-yearly period in respect of every case regarding which the liability, amount, and proposed distribution on a percentage basis has been approved by the United States shall be sent to the appropriate authorities of the United States, together with a request for reimbursement. Such reimbursement shall be made in won within the shortest possible time.
(f) Members or employees of the United States armed forces, including those employees who are nationals of or ordinarily resident in the Republic of Korea, shall not be subject to any proceedings for the enforement of any judgement given against them in the Republic of Korea in a matter arising from the performance of their official duties.	
(g) Except in so far as sub-paragraph (e) of this paragraph applies to claims covered by paragraph 2 of this Article, the provisions of this paragraph shall not apply to any claims arising out of or in connection with the navigation or operation of a ship or the loading, carriage, or discharge of a cargo, other than claims for death or personal injury to which paragraph 4 of this Article does not apply.	

한·미국 간의 상호방위조약 제4조에 의한 시설과 구역 및 한국에서의 미국군대의 지위에 관한 협정(SOFA) 전59권. 1966.7.9 서울에서 서명 : 1967.2.9 발효(조약 232호) (V.29 실무교섭회의, 제73-76차, 1965.4월) 211

6. Claims against members or
employees of the United States
armed forces (except employees
who are nationals of or ordinarily
resident in the Republic of Korea)
arising out of tortious acts or
omissions in the Republic of Korea
not done in the performance of
official duty shall be dealt with
in the following manner:

   (a) The authorities of the
Republic of Korea shall consider
the claim and assess compensation to
the claimant in a fair and just
manner, taking into account all the
circumstances of the case, including
the conduct of the injured persons,
and shall prepare a report on the
matter.

   (b) The report shall be
delivered to the appropriate
United States authorities, who
shall then decide without delay
whether they will offer an
ex gratia payment, and if so, of
what amount.

   (c) If an offer of ex gratia
payment is made, and accepted
by the claimant in full satisfaction of his claim, the United
States authorities shall make
the payment themselves and inform
the authorities of the Republic
of Korea of their decision and
of the sums paid.

   (d) Nothing in this paragraph
shall affect the jurisdiction of
the courts of the Republic of
Korea to entertain an action
against a member or an employee
of the United States armed forces
unless and until there has been
payment in full satisfaction of
the claim.

7. Claims arising out of the
unauthorized use of any vehicle
of the United States forces shall
be dealt with in accordance with
paragraph 6 of this Article,
except in so far as the United
States forces are legally responsible.

6.   (Same as Korean Draft)

7.   (Same as Korean Draft)

0206

KOREAN POSITION	U. S. POSITION
8. If a disput arises as to whether a tortious act or omission of a member or an employee of the United States armed forces was done in the performance of official duty or as to whether the use of any vehicle of the United States armed forces was unauthorized, the question shall be submitted to an arbitrator appointed in accordance with paragraph 2(b) of this Article, whose decision on this point shall be final and conclusive.	8. (Same as Korean Draft)
9. (a) The United States shall not claim immunity from the jurisdiction of the courts of the Republic of Korea for members or employees of the United States armed forces in respect of the civil jurisdiction of the courts of the Republic of Korea except in respect of proceedings for the enforcement of any judgment given against them in the Republic of Korea in a matter arising from the performance of their official duties or except after payment in full satisfaction of a claim.	9. (Same as Korean Draft)
(b) In the case of any private movable property, excluding that in use by the United States armed forces, which is subject to compulsory execution under Korean law, and is within the facilities and areas in use by the United States armed forces, the United States authorities shall, upon the request of the Korean courts, render all assistance within their power to see that such property is turned over to the Korean authorities.	
(c) The authorities of the United States and the Republic of Korea shall cooperate in the procurement of evidence for a fair disposition of claims under this Article.	
10. Disputes arising out of contracts concerning the procurement of materials, supplies, equipment, services by or for the United States armed forces, which are not resolved by the parties to the contract concerned, may be submitted to the Joint Committee for conciliation, provided that the provisions of	10. (Same as Korean Draft)

0207

this paragraph shall not pre-judice any right, which parties to the contract may have, to file a civil suit.	
11. Paragraph 2 and 5 of this Article shall apply only to claims arising incident to non-combat activities.	11. (Same as Korean Draft)
(Para 5 of) 12. For the purpose of this Article, members of the Korean Augmentation to the United States Army (KATUSA) and members of the Korean Service Corps (KSC) shall be considered respectively as members and employees of the United States armed forces.	12. For the purposes of this Article, members of the Korean Augmentation to the United States Army (KATUSA) shall be considered as members of the United States armed forces, and members of the Korean Service Corps (KSC) shall be considered as employees of the armed forces of the Republic of Korea.
13. The provisions of this Article shall not apply to any claims which arose before the entry into force of this Agreement. Such claims shall be processed and settled by the authorities of the United States.	13. The provisions of this Article shall not apply to any claims which arose before the entry into force of this Agreement.

AGREED MINUTE   AGREED MINUTE

1. Regarding the claims falling under the provisions of para-graph five of this Article, the authorities of the Republic of Korea and the United States shall seek mutual agreement as to the liability for damages and compen-sation to be awarded prior to the settlement by the authorities of the Republic of Korea, However, any adjudication of the case by a competent court of the Republic of Korea as a result of a suit which may be instituted by the claimant shall be binding and con-clusive upon the Parties of this Agreement.	1. (None in U.S. Draft)
2. (a) Unless otherwise provided, (1) The provisions of para-graphs five, six, seven and eight of this article will become effec-tive six months from the date of entry into force of this agreement as to claims arising from incidents in the Seoul Special City area.	2. (Same as Korean Draft except Subparagraph (2) below)

0208

(Cont'd)   AGREED MINUTE   (Cont'd)   AGREED MINUTE

    (2) As to claims arising from incidents in the other areas of the Republic of Korea, the provisions of paragraphs five, six, seven and eight of this Article will become effective twelve months from the date of entry into force of this Agreement. However, in case the authorities of the Republic of Korea are not prepared to assume the responsibility provided for in the preceding paragraphs within the twelve-month period, the authorities of the Republic of Korea may notify additional period required for the preparation to the Joint Committee for extention of the responsibility of the United States.

    (2) The provisions of paragraphs five, six, seven and eight will be progressively extended to other areas of Korea as determined and defined by the Joint Committee.

    (b) Until such time as the provisions of paragraphs five, six, seven and eight become effective in any given area,

    (b) (Same as Korean Draft)

    (1) The United States shall process and settle claims (other than contractual claims) arising out of the acts or omissions of members or employees of the United States armed forces done in the performance of official duty or out of any other act, omisstion or occurence for which the United States armed forces are legally responsible, which cause damage in the Republic of Korea to parties other than the two Governments;

    (2) The United States shall entertain other non-contractual claims against members or employees of the armed forces and may offer an ex gratia payment in such cases and in such amount as is determined by the appropriate United States authorities; and

    (3) Each party shall have the right to determine whether a member or employee of its armed forces was engaged in the performance of official duties and whether property owned by it was being used by its armed forces for official purposes.

    (c) For the pruposes of subparagraph 2(d), subparagraph 5 (e) shall be effective throughout Korea from the date of entry into force of this Agreement.

    (c) (Same as Korean Draft)

0209

1. Each Party waives all its claims against the other Party for damage to any property owned by it and used by its ①(forces) armed services, if such damage —

(a) was caused by a member or an employee of the armed services of the ②(armed forces) other Party, in execution of his official duties; or

(b) arose from the use of any vehicle, vessel or aircraft owned by the other Party and used by its armed services, provided either that the vehicle, vessel or aircraft causing ③(in official) the damage was being used in the execution of its official duty or that the damage was caused to property being so [used].

Claims for maritime salvage by one Party against the other party shall be waived, provided that the vessel or cargo salved was owned by the other Party and being used by its armed services for official purposes.

2. (a) In the case of damage caused or arising as stated in paragraph 1 to ⑤ property owned by either Party and located in the Republic of Korea, the issue of liability of the other Party shall be determined and the amount of damage shall be assessed, unless the two Governments agree otherwise, by a sole arbitrator selected in accordance with subparagraph (b) of this paragraph

ARTICLE

1. Each Party waives all its claims against the other Party for damage to any property owned by it and used by its land, sea or air armed forces, if such damage:

(a) was caused by a member or an employee of the armed forces of the other Party in the performance of his official duties; or

(b) arose from the use of any vehicle, vessel or aircraft owned by the other Party and used by its armed forces, provided either that the vehicle, vessel or aircraft causing the damage was being used for official purposes, or that the damage was caused to property being so used.

Claims by one Party against the other Party for maritime salvage shall be waived provided that the vessel or cargo salvaged was owned by a Party and being used by its armed forces for official purposes.

2. In the case of damage caused or arising as stated in paragraph 1 to other property owned by a Party:

(a) each Party waives its claim up to the amount of $1400 or its equivalent in Korean currency at the rate of exchange provided for in the Agreed Minute to Article ___ at the time the claim is filed.

0210

(b) Claims in excess of the

The arbitrator shall also decide any counter-measures arising out of the same incidents.

(b) The arbitrator referred to in subparagraph (a) above shall be selected by agreement between the two Governments from amongst the nationals of the Republic of Korea who hold or have held high judicial office.

(c) Any decision taken by the arbitrator shall be binding and conclusive upon the Parties.

(d) The amount of any compensation awarded by the arbitrator shall be distributed in accordance with the provisions of paragraph 5(e) (i), (ii) and (iii) of this Article.

(e) The compensation of the arbitrator shall be fixed by agreement between the two Governments and shall, together with the necessary expenses incidental to the performance of his duties, be defrayed in equal proportions by them.

(f) Each Party waives its claim in any such case up to the amount equivalent to 300 United States dollars or 81,000 won. In the case of considerable variation in the rate of exchange between these currencies the two Governments shall agree on the appropriate adjustments of these amounts.

amount stated in subparagraph (a) shall be settled by the Party against which the claim is made in accordance with its domestic law.

한·미국 간의 상호방위조약 제4조에 의한 시설과 구역 및 한국에서의 미국군대의 지위에 관한 협정(SOFA) 전59권. 1966.7.9 서울에서 서명 : 1967.2.9 발효(조약 232호) (V.29 실무교섭회의, 제73-76차, 1965.4월) **217**

3. For the purpose of paragraph 1 and 2 of this Article the expression "owned by a Party" in the case of a vessel includes a vessel on bare boat charter to that Party or requisitioned by it on bare boat terms or seized by it in prize (except to the extent that the risk of loss or liability is borne by some person other than such Party).

4. Each Party waives all its claims against the other Party for injury or death suffered by any member of its armed services while such member was engaged in the performance of his official duties.

5. Claims (other than contractual claims and those to which paragraphs 6 or 7 of this Article apply) arising out of acts or omissions of members or employees of the United States armed forces, including those employees who are nationals of or ordinarily resident in the Republic of Korea, done in the performance of official duty, or out of any other act, omission or occurrence for which the United States armed forces are legally responsible, and causing damage in the Republic of Korea to third parties, other than the Government of the Republic of Korea, shall be dealt with by the Republic of Korea in accordance with the following provisions:

(a) claims shall be fi

3. For the purpose of paragraph 1 and 2 of this Article, the expression "owned by a Party" in the case of a vessel includes a vessel on bare boat charter to that Party or requisitioned by it on bare boat charter terms or seized by it in prize (except to the extent that the risk of loss or liability is borne by some other person than such Party).

4. Each Party waives all its claims against the other Party for injury or death suffered by any member of its armed forces while such member was engaged in the performance of his official duties.

5. Claims (other than contractual claims) arising out of acts or omissions of members or employees of the United States armed forces done in the performance of official duty, or out of any other act, omission or occurrence for which the United States armed forces are legally responsible, and causing damage in the Republic of Korea to third parties other than the two Governments shall be processed and settled in accordance with the applicable provisions of United States law. The United States Government shall entertain other non-contractual claims against members of the United States armed forces or of the civilian component and may offer an ex gratia payment in such cases and in such

0212

…llered and settled or adjudicated in accordance with the laws and regulations of the Republic of Korea with respect to the claims arising from the activities of its own armed forces.

amount as is determined by the appropriate United States authorities.

(b) The Republic of Korea may settle any such claims, and payment of the amount agreed upon or determined by adjudication shall be made by the Republic of Korea in won.

(c) Such payment, whether made pursuant to a settlement or to adjudication of the case by a competent tribunal of the Republic of Korea, or the final adjudication by such a tribunal denying payment, shall be binding and conclusive upon the Parties.

(d) Every claim paid by the Republic of Korea shall be communicated to the appropriate United States authorities together with full particulars and a proposed distribution in conformity with subparagraph (c) (i) and (ii) below.

In default of a reply within two months, the proposed distribution shall be regarded as accepted.

(e) The cost incurred in satisfying claims pursuant to the preceding subparagraph and paragraph 5 of this Article shall be distributed between the Parties as follows:

0213

(i) Where the United States alone is responsible, the amount awarded or adjudged shall be distributed in the proportion of (15) per cent chargeable to the Republic of Korea and (85) per cent chargeable to the United States.

(ii) Where the Republic of Korea and the United States are responsible for the damage, the amount awarded or adjudged shall be distributed equally between them. Where the damage was caused by the armed forces of the Republic of Korea and the United States and it is not possible to attribute it specifically to one or both of those armed services, the amount awarded or adjudged shall be distributed equally between the Republic of Korea and the United States.

(iii) Every half-year, a statement of the sums paid by the Republic of Korea in the course of the half-yearly period in respect of every case regarding which the proposed distribution on a percentage basis has been accepted, shall be sent to the appropriate authorities of the United States, together with a request for reimbursement. Such reimbursement shall be made, in won, within the shortest possible time.

(f) Members or employees of the United States armed forces, including those employees who are nationals of or ordinarily resident in the Republic of Korea, shall not be subject to any proceedings for the enforcement of any judgement given against them in the Republic of Korea in a matter arising from the performance of their official duties.

(g) Except in so far as subparagraph (e) of this paragraph applies to claims covered by paragraph 2 of this article, the provisions of this paragraph shall not apply to any claims arising out of or in connection with the navigation or operation of a ship or the loading, carriage, or discharge of a cargo, other than claims for death or personal injury to which paragraph 4 of this Article does not apply.

6. Claims against members or 미경한 no problem employees of the United States armed forces (except employees who are nationals of, or ordinarily resident in the Republic of Korea) arising out of tortious acts or omissions in the Republic of Korea not done in the performance of official duty shall be dealt with in the following manner:

(a) The authorities of the Republic of Korea shall consider the claim and assess compensation to the claimant in a fair and just manner,

한·미국 간의 상호방위조약 제4조에 의한 시설과 구역 및 한국에서의 미국군대의 지위에 관한 협정(SOFA)
전59권. 1966.7.9 서울에서 서명 : 1967.2.9 발효(조약 232호) (V.29 실무교섭회의, 제73-76차, 1965.4월) 221

taking into account all the circumstances
of the case, including the conduct of
the injured persons, and shall prepare a
report on the matter.

(b) The report shall be delivered
to the appropriate United States authorities, who shall then decide without delay
whether they will offer an ex gratia
payment, and if so, of what amount.

(c) If an offer of ex gratia payment is made, and accepted by the clai-
ant in full satisfaction of his claim, the
United States authorities shall make
the payment themselves and inform the
authorities of the Republic of Korea
of their decision and of the sum paid.

(d) Nothing in this paragraph
shall affect the jurisdiction of the
courts of the Republic of Korea to
entertain an action against a member or
an employee of the United States armed
forces unless and until there has been
payment in full satisfaction of the
claim.

7. Claims arising out of the unauthorized use of any vehicle of the
United States forces shall be dealt
with in accordance with paragraph 6 of
this Article, except in so far as the
United States forces are legally responsible.

8. If a dispute arises as to   9. For the purposes of this
whether a tortious act or omission of   Article, each Party shall have the right

a member or an employee of the United States armed forces was done in the performance of official duty or not to whether the use of any vehicle of the United States armed forces was unauthorized, the question shall be submitted to an arbitrator appointed in accordance with paragraph 2(b) of this Article, whose decision on this point shall be final and conclusive.

9. (a) The United States shall not claim immunity from the jurisdiction of the courts of the Republic of Korea for members or employees of the United States armed forces in respect of the civil jurisdiction of the courts of the Republic of Korea except to the extent provided in paragraph 5(f) of this Article.

(b) In case any private movable property, excluding that in use by the United States Armed forces, which is subject ot compulsory execution under the Korean law, is within the facilities and areas in use by the United States armed forces, the United States authorities shall, upon the request of the courts of the Republic of Korea, possess and turn over such property to the authorities of the Republic of Korea.

to determine whether a member or employee of its armed forces was engaged in the performance of official duties and whether property owned by it was being used by its armed forces for official purposes.

6. (a) A member or employee of the United States armed forces shall not be afforded immunity from the jurisdiction of the civil courts of Korea except: (1) in a matter arising out of acts or omissions done in the performance of official duty; or (2) in respect to any claim where there has been payment in full satisfaction of the claimant.

(b) In the case of any private movable property, excluding that in use by the United States armed forces, which is subject to compulsory execution under Korean law, and is within the facilities and areas in use by the United States armed forces, the United States authorities shall, upon the request of the Korean courts, render all assistance within their power to see that such property is turned over to the Korean authorities.

한·미국 간의 상호방위조약 제4조에 의한 시설과 구역 및 한국에서의 미국군대의 지위에 관한 협정(SOFA) 전59권. 1966.7.9 서울에서 서명 : 1967.2.9 발효(조약 232호) (V.29 실무교섭회의, 제73-76차, 1965.4월) 223

(c) The authorities of the Republic of Korea and the United States shall cooperate in the procurement of evidence for a fair hearing and disposal of claims under this Article.

10. Disputes arising out of contracts concerning the procurement of materials, supplies, equipment, services (by) or (for) the United States armed forces, which are not resolved by the Parties to the contract concerned, may be submitted to the Joint Committee for conciliation, provided that the provisions of this paragraph shall not prejudice any right, which Parties to the contract may have, to file a civil suit.

11. Paragraphs 2 and 5 of this Article shall apply only to claims arising incident to non-combat activities.

12.

(13)

(14) 13.

7. The authorities of the United States and Korea shall cooperate in the procurement of evidence for a fair disposition of claims under this Article.

8. Paragraphs 2 and 5 of this Article shall apply only to claims arising incident to noncombat activities.

10. For the purposes of this Article, members of the Korean augmentation to the United States Army (KATUSA) shall be considered as members of the United States armed forces, and members of the Korean Service Corps (KSC) shall be considered as employees of the armed forces of the Republic of Korea.

11. The provisions of this Article shall not apply to any claims which arose before the entry into force of this agreement.

0218

민사청구권 조항에 대한 실무자회의 경위

1963 년 8 월 8 일 제 28 차 회의에서 한·미 양측의 초안을 교환한 이래,

1. 29 차회의 (63. 8. 22)

우리측 초안의 장점을 설명하고 동초안을 기초로 하여 토의를 진행할것을 제안한데 대하여 미국측은 한국측이 제안한 제도는 여러가지 복잡한 문제를 내포하고 있을 뿐만 아니라 한국군에는 현재 적합한 손해배상 지불제도가 없으므로 적당하지 않음을 지적하고 주한 미군소청사무소장으로 하여금 그들의 제도를 설명케 하였음.

2. 30 차회의 (63. 9. 5)

우리측은 29 차 회의시의 미국측 주장에 대하여 한국군의 손해배상지불제도로서 국가배상 법에 의한 국가 배상제도가 이미 마련되어 효율적으로 운영되고 있음을 지적하고 동제도에 대하여 상세히 설명한바 있으며, 한·미 양측은 손해배상문제에 관한 한·미 전문가들이 비공식적으로 토의를 계속하기로 합의하였음.

3. 비공식 접촉

1963 년 9월부터 1964 년 4 월까지에 걸쳐 한국측을 대표하여 법무부와 미국측을 대표하여 미 8군 법무참모 부의 실무자들은 각각 상대방의 손해배상제도의 운영실태를 직접 시찰한바 있으며, 미국측 실무자들은·

(가) 공무집행중 제3자에 미친 손해에 대한 ~~상약~~ 책임한계 및 배상금액은 한미양측이 사전에 합의 하여 결정하며 동 배상금의 75 퍼센트이상을 미국당국은 부담하지 않고,

(나) 상기 공무집행중 제3자에 미친 손해배상 해결규정은 협정발효후 한국당국이 배상업무를 수행할수 있는 준비가 된후 합동위원회의 합의에 의거 그효력을 갖도록 하며,

(다) "카츄사"는 미군구성원으로 간주하며 KSC 는 한국군 고용원으로 간주한다,

라는 내용에 한국측이 합의한다면 미국측이 한국안을 수락할 용의가 있음을 시사하였음.

4. 51차회의 (64.5.5)

상기 비공식 접촉을 통한 미국측 태도를 참작 하여 한국측은 요지 아래와 같은 합의의사록을 제안 하였음.

(가) 한국당국이 결정한 공무집행중 제3자에 미친 손해에 대한 배상액에 대하여 미국당국은 재심을 요청 할수 있다.

(나) 공무집행중 제3자에 미친 손해에 대한 배상 지불업무는 협정발효 6개월후부터 효력을 갖는다.

(다) "카츄사"와 KSC 는 각각 미군의 구성원 및 고용원으로 간주한다.

5. 61차회의 (64.8.14)

미국측은 상기 51차회의시에 한국측이 제안한 합의의사록은 수락할수 없음을 주장하고 29차회의시 그들의 입장을 되풀이 하였음.

6. 62차회의 (64.8.28)

한국측은 국가배상제도의 효율성을 재차설명 함으로서 미국측이 주장하는 제도상의 난관은 없을 것임을 역설하는 동시, 주한미군소청제도의 결함을 지적함.

7. 63차회의 (64.9.11)

미국측은 주한미군소청제도가 합리적인 제도로서 효율적으로 운영되고 있다고 계속 주장하였으며, 한국측은 이를 반박하는 동시 한국제도의 합리성 효율성을 강조 하였음.

0220

8. 66차 회의 (64. 11. 24.)

한국측은 미국측이 특히 관심을 갖고있는 공무
집행중 제3차에 미친 손해배상문제를 중심으로 한국이
제안한 제도가 현행 주한미군소청제도 보다 훨씬 합리적
이며 효율적인 것임을 지적하므로서 한국측 안을 토대로
하여 토의를 진행할 것을 재차 촉구하였으며, 이에 대하여
미국측은 단지 한국측의 입장을 이해하고 있음을 시사
하였음.

9. 72차 회의 (65. 3. 3.)

66차 회의시의 한국의 입장을 재강조하고 조속
한 회답을 요구함.

보통문서로 재분류(1966. 12. 31)

한·미국 간의 상호방위조약 제4조에 의한 시설과 구역 및 한국에서의 미국군대의 지위에 관한 협정(SOFA)
전59권. 1966.7.9 서울에서 서명 : 1967.2.9 발효(조약 232호) (V.29 실무교섭회의, 제73-76차, 1965.4월) 227

<u>각 국 의 협 정 예</u>

1. <u>NATO (1953), Australia (1963) 및 일 본 (1960)</u>
한국초안과 실제적으로 다른점이 거의 없으나,
(1) 이들 3개협정은 모두 정부재산 청구의 무기한계가
$1,400 (한국안 800 이하) 이하이며, 양국정부의
분담율이 접수국 25 퍼센트, 파견국 75 퍼센트 (한국안
접수국 15퍼센트, 파견국 85 퍼센트) 로 되여 있다
(2) NATO 및 Australia 협정에는 우리초안 10 항의
계약상의 분쟁해결절차가 규정되여 있지 않다
(3) Australia 협정에는 미군의 차량 및 군계약자들을
Australia 법규에 의거 보험에 가입하게 되었
으며, 따라서 차량에 의한 손해는 보험제도에
의하여 해결하게 되여 있음.

2. <u>독일보충협정 (1963)</u>
독일의 경우에 있어서는 "나토"협정 8조를 원칙적
으로 적용하되 1963년발효한 "보충협정 "에 의거 아래와
같은 요지의 보충 및 예외규정이 마련되었다
(1) <u>독일정부의 청구권 포기 (보충협정 2항 , 3(가) 항</u>
<u>및 합의의사록 4,5 및 6항)</u>
가. 정상적인 통행에서 일어나는 공공도로, 고량
수로 및 기타 공공교통시설의 손해
나. 점령비, 위임 혹은 지원비로 건설 혹은 구입한
재산으로서 파견국이 사용중에 일어난 손해
다. 파견국이 사용하는 독일연방재산의 손해 및
독일연방이 그주 (Shares) 를 소유하는 법인의
재산으로서 파견국에게 무료로 배타적인 사용을
인정한 재산의 손해 (단, 고의 및 중대한
과실과 수선 및 정비책임의 불이행으로 일어난
손해는 제외)

0222

(2) 파견국의 청구권 포기 (보충협정 5항 및 합의
    의사록 6항)

　가. 독일연방 군인 및 군속의 공무수행 혹은 선박,
    차량 및 항공기의 운행으로 일어나는 파견국
    정부재산의 손해 (단, 고의 및 중대한 과실
    제외)

(3) 철도, 우편 및 도로에 대한 특례 (보충협정 3(나)항)

　가. "나토" 협정 8조 2 (f)항 (공무중 +1,400 아하의
    정부재산 손해청구 포기)의 규정은 독일연방
    철도, 연방우편 및 연방도로의 손해에는 적용
    하지 않는다.

(4) 주 (Land) 정부 재산에 대한 특례 (보충협정 4항
    및 합의의사록 7항)

　가. 독일연방은 협정발효전에 일어난 주정부 (Land)
    가 소유하는 재산의 손해에 대한 파견국의
    배상책임을 해제한다.

　나. 보충협정 발효시와 재산반환시에 재산상태를
    조사하여 손해배상 청구문제를 해결한다.

(5) 파견국 군대의 대내적인 손해 (보충협정 6항)

　가. "나토" 협정 8조 5항 (공무중 제3자에 대한 손해)
    과 보충협정의 규정은 파견국의 군인 및 군속
    상호간의 손해 혹은 파견국 당국이 법적으로
    책임이 있는 파견국 군인 및 군속에 대한
    손해에는 적용하지 않는다.

(6) 파견국군대의 접수국 법규적용의 면제문제 (보충협정
    8항)

　가. 손해배상책임은 파견국의 군인 및 군속이 독일
    의 제반법규의 적용을 받지 않는다는 이유로
    면제되지 않는다. 단, 독일군대가 자국내에서
    향유하는 면제특권과 동일한 한도내에서 손해
    배상책임을 갖는다.

0223

(7) 과실상쇄(보충협정 9 (가) 항)

공무집행중 제3자에 손해를 가하거나 혹은 법적
으로 제3자에 대한 손해에 책임이 있는 경우로서, 동
제3자가 파견국측에도 손해를 가하여 그배상책임이 있을
때에는 제3자의 손해배상청구에 대하여 파견국의 손해
배상 청구를 상쇄한다.

(8) 파견국을 위한 접수국의 손해배상청구 (보충협정 9
(나) 항)

독일연방은 파견국과 사전합의 혹은 요청에 의거,
독일영토내의 거주자가 가한 파견국에 대한 손해를 위하여
배상청구를 한다. 단, 계약상의 손해에는 적용되지 않으며,
통상적인 행정비의 범위를 초과하는 경비지출은 파견국이
부담한다.

(9) 파견국이 사용하는 사유시설 및 동산 (보충협정 10 항)

1955년 5월 5일 이전에 군인 혹은 군속이 배타적
으로 사용하기 시작하여 현행협정이 발효한 후에 반환한
기타 시설 혹은 동산 (독일 연방 및 각주의 소유재산을
제외)의 손해에 대한 배상은 독일연방과 파견국이 균등
하게 분담한다.

(10) 공무집행여부에 관한 증명문제(보충협정 11 항)

가. 파견국은 손해의 책임을 정할수 없는 경우를
제외하고는 "나토"협정 8조 8항에서 취급된
문제에 관한 증명서를 제공하여야 하며, 독일
당국 혹은 독일법정이 상기 증명서에 대한
반증이 있다고 고려할 때에는 독일당국의 요청에
의하여 파견국은 그 증명서를 재검토한다.
나. 상기 증명서에 관한 의견의 차이를 양측의
고외관계 당국간의 협상으로 해결할수 없을
때에는 "나토"협정 8조 8항의 절차에 따라
해결한다.

0224

다. 독일당국이나 혹은 법정은 상기증명서 혹은
중재인의 결정과 부합되게 손해배상 청구에
관한 결정을 내려야 한다.

(11) 파견국의 직접 원상회복에 관한 특례(보충협정
합의의사록 2항)

가. (1) 독일연방 철도와 우편에 속하는 재산을
제외한 공공도로 및 기타 독일연방의 재산
이 기동연습이나 기타의 훈련으로 인하여
손해를 입은 경우로서 보충협정에 의거
배상을 지불할 성질의 사건인 때에, 파견국
군대는 배상금을 지불하는 대신 그들자신이
그 손해에 대한 원상회복을 시킬수 있다.

(2) 파견국 군대가 공공도로의 손괴에 대한
원상회복을 스스로 시키려 할때에는 권위
있는 독일당국과 협의하여야 하며, 만약
독일당국이 상당히 기술적인 건설이라든가
혹은 교통정리상의 이유로 직접적인 원상
회복을 반대할때에는 파견국은 이를 하여서는
안된다.

나. 상기 (가) 항 이외의 경우, 파견국 군대가 직접
피해자와의 합의하에 손해에 대한 원상회복을
하는 것을 금하지 않는다.

다. 상기 (가) 및 (나) 항의 경우, 피해자는 그의 견해로
보아 손해가 충분히 혹은 적합히 원상회복이
되지 않았을 때에는 그의 합리적인 손해배상을
주장하는 것을 금하지 않는다.

(12) 규정의 적용한계(보충협정 12항, 합의의사록 1항 및
8항)

가 "나토" 협정 8조와 보충협정의 규정은 보충협정
이 발효후 그 원인이 발생하였거나 혹은 발생한
것으로 생각되는 손해에 적용한다.

0225

나. 협정 발효전에 발생하였거나 혹은 발생한 것으로
　보이는 손해에 대하여는 협정발효전까지 적용
　하던 규정에 의거 취급되어야 한다.
다. 보충협정 41조는 계약 혹은 준계약 관계에서
　일어나는 손해에 관한 배상청구에는 적용하지
　않는다.
라. 미국적십자 및 Maryland 대학은 보충협정
　41조 7항의 목적을 위하여 군대의 일부로서
　규력되거나 혹은 취급되지 않으며, 손해배상
　청구에 대한 해결에 있어서는 독일관할권으로
　부터 면제되지 않는다.

(13) 기타 합의사항 (보충협정 13항, 합의의사록 3 및 9항)
　가. 손해배상 청구의 해결을 위한 파견국 당국과
　　독일당국간의 절차를 조정하기 위하여 행정적인
　　협정을 체결하여야 한다.
　나. 보충협정 41조 13항의 행정적인 합의사항에는
　　"나토"협정 8조에 포함된 절차와 상이한
　　합의도 포함될수 있다.
　다. 손해배상 업무가 신속히 처리될수 있도록
　　"나토"협정 8조와 보충협정 41조에 의한 손해
　　배상 청구를 할수있는 합리적인 기간을 설정
　　하여야 한다. 이런목적을 위하여 독일연방은
　　적합한 입법조치를 하여야 한다.

(14) 계약상의 분쟁해결
　　한국측 초안 제10항에서 취급된 계약상의 분쟁
해결문제는 독일부충협정 44조 6항에 규정되어 있는바
동규정에 의하면 독일법정 혹은 독립중재재판소에서
해결하게 되어 있으며 독일법정에서 분쟁해결을 할때
에는 독일연방이 파견국을 대신하여 재판에 임하게
되어 있다.

3. 에치오피아 (1953)
(1) 공무집행중에 일어난 모든 정부재산에 대한 손해
　는 상호 포기한다 (도로 유지비 제외)

0226

(2) 미국정부는 미국대외소청법에서 인정하는 미국
군대구성원이 행한 손해에 대하여 미국법에 따라
공정하고 합리적인 배상을 한다.

4. 리비아 (1954)

(1) 미국정부는 리비아 정부재산에 가한 손해에 대하여
공정하고 합리적인 배상을 한다.

(2) 미국정부는 본협정에 의거 리비아국에 주둔하는
군대구성원과 본협정의 문영과 관련하여 리비아국
에 있는 미국인 고용원 및 기타 고용원이 리비아
국민에게 가한 손해에 대하여 공정하고 합리적인
배상을 한다.

(3) 이러한 모든 청구는 미국법에 의거 처리한다.

(4) 미국군대구성원이 관련하게 되는 기타 모든 민사
사건에 대하여는 리비아법정이 재만관할건을 갖는다.

5. 비율빈 (1947)

(1) 우호관계를 유지 및 증진하기 위하여 미국은 군대
구성원, 군속 및 고용원이 가한 비율빈인에 대한
인명 및 사유재산에 대한 손해에 대하여 공정하고
합리적인 배상을 한다.

(2) 이러한 청구는 사고가 발생한 후로부터 1년이내에
제출하여야 한다.

6. West Indies (1961)

(1) 미국정부는 미국법에 의거 미국군대구성원의 공무
~~죽은 가정 항위~~로 일어나는 민사청구를 공정하고
합리적으로 해결, 보상금을 지불한다.

(2) 청구는 손해발생후 2년이내에 제출하여야 한다.

(3) 청구권자가 만족하지 않는한 청구권자의 현지법에
규정된 구제방법의 사용을 금지하지 않는다.

(4) 본조항이 만족스럽게 운영되지 못할 경우에는
West Indies 정부의 요청에 의거 "나토"
협정 8조 5항과 유사한 민사청구권 조항을 채택
한다.

0227

CLAIMS ARTICLE

1. 제 1 차 비공식 회의에서 미측이 제안한 합의의사록 1.

 (1) The costs under paragraph 5 to be borne by the United States shall not exceed 75% of the amounts mutually agreed upon by claims authorities of both governments as being properly payable under that paragraph.

2. 제 2 차 비공식 회의당시의 우리측 입장

 가. 거대한 액수가 관련된 사건 (예를 들면 2,3 만불 정도이상)에 대하여만 양국정부가 상호 합의토록 제의한다.

 나. 원칙적으로 분담율은 미·일협정선까지 양보할 용의가 있을수 있으나 우선 75퍼센트를 초과하지 않는다는 미국측안에 대한 명확한 해석을 요구한다. 75 퍼센트 선을 수락함은 언급하지는 않는다.

3. 제 2 차 비공식 회의시의 회답내용.

 가. 미측의 설명

 (1) 미측의 합의의사록 (1) , (2) 및 (3)은 한국측 안을 중심으로 토의한다는 전제하에 제안한 것이다.

 (2) 합의의사록 1은 case by case 로 문제를 해결하며 금액에 대하여 양국의 송무당국의 기관장간의 합의에 의하여 결정하여야 한다는 것이다. 75퍼센트를 초과하지 않는다는 말은 미국측의 부담액이 75퍼센트가 아니면 50퍼센트 가 됨을 의미한다.

 (3) 이는 미일 협정에 경우에서도 협정조문에는 명시되지 않았으나 Practice 에 의해 하나의 절차화 되었다. 최초 미일협정이 체결되었을 때에는 협정문에 의거 문제가 잘해결 되지 않아 결국 이러한 절차가 생기게 되었으며 지금은 원만히 해결되어 나가고 있다.

0228

그러나 최초 협정조문에 의거 해결코저 시도
하여 해결되지 못한 2,3건은 아직도 해결되지
않은체로 남아있는 실정이다.

나. 토의 요지

한국측 : 일정한 금액을 정하고 그한도 내에서는
　　　　양측의 합의없이 한국안에 의한 분담율
　　　　에 의거 해결토록 하고 그한도이상의 금액
　　　　에 대하여만 양국간의 합의로 결정토록
　　　　하는것이 어떻겠는가.

미국측 :(1)사건별 금액을 합의하여야 한다. 한도
　　　　액수를 정하고 한국측이 일방적으로 지불시
　　　　이에 대하여 미국측이 합의 못할경우가
　　　　있으면 곤란하다.
　　　　미국측은 금액에 대한 상호 합의문제를
　　　　제외하고는 한국안 5항 e (i) (ii)에 의한
　　　　그 해결 방법에는 동의한다.

　　　　(2)5항에 있어 가장 중요한 것은 1. Liability;
　　　　2. Amount 　　　　, 3. Distribution 문제
　　　　인바 이에 대한 결정은 일본에서도
　　　　관행(practice) 에 의해 양국정부
　　　　합의에 의거 결정하고 있다.
　　　　한국에는 이러한 practice 가 없는 나라
　　　　니까 미측이 제안한 합의의사록이 필요한
　　　　것이다.

　　　　(3)만약 한국측이 5 (e) (iii) Every half-year,
　　　　a statement of the sums paid by the Republic of
　　　　Korea in the course of the half-yearly period in
　　　　respect of every case regarding which the proposed
　　　　distribution on a percentage basis has been
　　　　accepted, shall be sent to the appropriate authorities

0229

of the United States, together with a request
for reimbursement. Such reimbursement shall be
made, in won, within the shortest possible time.

을 　Every half-year, a statement of the sums
paid by the Republic of Korea in the course of the
half-yearly period in respect of every case
regarding which the <u>liability of the U.S.,the
amount of payment and</u> the proposed distribution
on a percentage basis has been accepted, shall
be sent to the appropriate authorities of the United
States, together with a request for reimbursement.
Such reimbursement shall be made, in won, within
the shortest possible time. 　으로　수정한다면
미국측의　합의의사록　1을　철회하겠다.

한국측: 　고려한후　답변하겠다.

1. 제 1 차 비공식 회의에서 미측이 제출한 합의의사록 2.

(2) The provisions of paragraph 5 of this article will become
effective upon mutual agreement in the Joint Committee that
the claims service of the Government of the Republic of
Korea is prepared to undertake the procedures provided for
in that paragraph. Until such time the United States
agrees to pay just and reasonable compensation in settlement
of civil claims (other than contrastual claims) arising out
of acts or omissionsof members of the United States Forces
done in the performance of official duty or out of any
other act, omission or occurrence for which the United
States Forces are legally responsible. In making such
payments United States authorities would exercise the
broad authority provided under United States laws relating
to Foreign Claims and regulations issued thereunder. In
settling claims which are described as arising "... out of
any act, omission or occurrence for which the United States
Forces are legally responsible", United States authorities
will take into consideration local law and practice.

2. 제 2 차 비공식 회의를 위한 한국측의 입장.
조약발효후 일정한 기간 (예를 들면 6 개월 , 혹은 1 년 등)
을 정하고 그 기간이 경과하면 효력을 갖도록 한다 .

3. 제 2 차 비공식 회의내용 (요지)
한국측 : 미측안과 같이 막연하게 하는 것 보다는 조약
발효후 일정기간을 정하고 그 후부터는 이 규정을
적용토록 하는 것이 더 좋지않겠는가 .
미국측 : 미국측 합의의사록은 기간을 정하는 것보다
더욱 융통성이 있다 .
한국측 : 그러면 일정기간을 정한후 그 이내에 가능할시
에는 합동위원회에서 결정토록 하는 것이
좋지 않겠는가 .
미국측 : 고려해 보겠다 .

0231

1. 제1차 비공식 회의에서 미측이 재출한 합의의사록 3.

   (3) For the purposes of paragraph 5 of this Article, members

   of the Korean Augmentation to the United States Army (KATUSA)

   shall be considered as members of the United States armed

   forces, and members of the Korean Service Corps (KSC)

   shall be considered as employees of the armed forces of the
   Republic of Korea.

2. 제2차 비공식 회의를 위한 한국측의 입장.

   청구권 문제에 있어서는 KATUSA 나 KSC 가 모두

   미국측이 일종의 사용주에 해당되기 때문에 KSC 는

   미군당국의 피고용원으로 간주하여야 할것이다.

3. 제2차 비공식 회의내용 (요지)

   한국측 : KSC 는 미국측의 피고용잔로 간주하여야

   　　　　　하지 않겠는가.

   미국측 : 그사정을 이해하고 있다. 고려해 보겠다.

보통문서로 재분류 (1966. 12. 31.)

0232

SOFA NEGOTIATION

Agenda for the 76th Session

14:30 April 30, 1965

1. Continuation of Discussions on:

    a. Civil Claims Article

2. Other Business

3. Agenda and Date of the Next Meeting

4. Press Release

0233

PARAGRAPH 5

5.   (a) The military authorities of the United States
and the authorities of the Republic of Korea shall
assist each other in the arrest of members of the United
States armed forces, the civilian component, or their
dependents in the territory of the Republic of Korea and
in handing them over to the authority which is to have
custody in accordance with the following provisions.

(b) The authorities of the Republic of Korea shall
notify promptly the military authorities of the United
States of the arrest of any member of the United States
armed forces, or civilian component, or a dependent.
The military authorities of the United States shall
promptly notify the authorities of the Republic of Korea
of the arrest of a member of the United States armed
forces, the civilian component, or a dependent in any
case in which the Republic of Korea has the primary
right to exercise jurisdiction.

(c) The custody of an accused member of the United
States armed forces or civilian component, or of a dependent,
over whom the Republic of Korea is to exercise jurisdiction
shall, if he is in the hands of the military authorities
of the United States, remain with the military authorities

- 1 -

of the United States pending the conclusion of all
judicial proceedings and until custody is requested by
the authorities of the Republic of Korea. If he is in
the hands of the Republic of Korea, he shall, on _request_,
be handed over to the _military_ authorities of the United
States and remain in their custody pending completion
of all judicial proceedings and until custody is requested
by the authorities of the Republic of Korea. When an
accused has been in the custody of the military authorities of the United States, _the military authorities of_
the United States may transfer custody to the authorities
of the Republic of Korea at any time, and shall give
sympathetic consideration to any request for the transfer
of custody which may be made by the authorities of the
Republic of Korea in specific cases. The _military autho-_
rities of the United States _shall promptly_ make any such
accused available to the authorities of the Republic
of Korea upon their request for purposes of investigation
and trial, _and shall take all appropriate measures to_
that end and to prevent any prejudice to the course of
justice. They shall take full account of any special
request regarding custody made by the authorities of
the the Republic of Korea. The authorities of the
Republic of Korea shall give sympathetic consideration

- 2 -

0235

to a request from the military authorities of the United
States for assistance in maintaining custody of an accused
member of the United States armed forces, the civilian
component, or a dependent.

(d) In respect of offenses solely against the security
of the Republic of Korea provided in Paragraph 2(c),
an accused shall be in the custody of the authorities
of the Republic of Korea.

- 3 -

0236

Agreed Minute #1 Re Paragraph 3(a)(ii)

1. Where a member of the United States armed forces or civilian component is charged with an offense, a certificate issued by competent authorities of the United States armed forces stating that the alleged offense, if committed by him, arose out of an act or omission done in the performance of official duty shall be sufficient evidence of the fact for the purpose of determining primary jurisdiction.

In those exceptional cases where the chief prosecutor for the Republic of Korea considers that there is proof contrary to a certificate of official duty, it shall be made the subject of review through discussions between appropriate officials of the Government of the Republic of Korea and the diplomatic mission of the United States in the Republic of Korea.

Agreed Minute #2 Re Paragraph 3(a)(ii)

2. The term "official duty" as used in Article ___ and the Agreed Minute is not meant to include all acts by members of the Armed Forces and the civilian component during periods when they are on duty, but is meant to apply only to acts which are required to be done as

- 1 -

한·미국 간의 상호방위조약 제4조에 의한 시설과 구역 및 한국에서의 미국군대의 지위에 관한 협정(SOFA) 전59권. 1966.7.9 서울에서 서명 : 1967.2.9 발효(조약 232호) (V.29 실무교섭회의, 제73-76차, 1965.4월) 243

functions of those duties which the individuals are
performing. Thus, a substantial departure from the
acts a person is required to perform in a particular
duty usually will indicate an act outside of his "official
duty." (U.S. draft proposed at the 49th meeting)

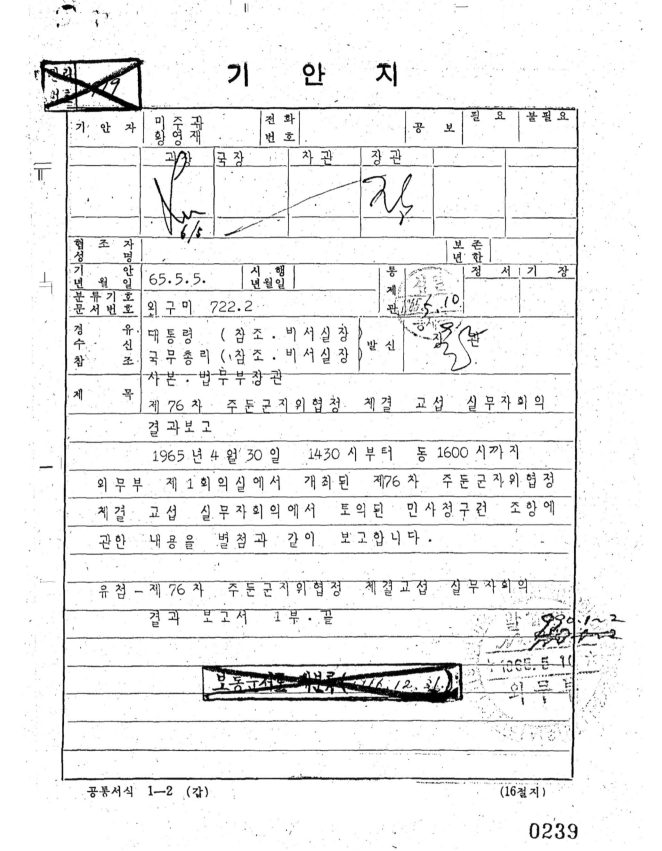

기 안 지

기 안 자	미주과 황영재	전 화 번 호			공 보	필 요	불 필 요

	과 장	국 장	차 관	장 관			

협 조 성 자 명					보 존 년 한		
기 안 년 월 일	65. 5. 5.	시 행 년월일		통 제 관		정 서	기 장
분 류 기 호 문 서 번 호	외구미 722.2						
경 수 유 신 조 참 조	대통령 (참조 · 비서실장 국무총리 (참조 · 비서실장		발신				
	사본 · 법무부장관						
제 목	제 76 차 주둔군지위협정 체결 교섭 실무자회의						

결과보고

1965 년 4 월 30 일 1430 시부터 동 1600 시까지

외무부 제 1 회의실에서 개최된 제76 차 주둔군지위협정

체결 교섭 실무자회의에서 토의된 민사청구권 조항에

관한 내용을 별첨과 같이 보고합니다.

유첨 - 제 76 차 주둔군지위협정 체결교섭 실무자회의

결과 보고서 1부 · 끝

공통서식 1—2 (갑)　　　　　　　　　　　　　　　(16절지)

기 안 지

기 안 자	미주과 황영재	전 화 번 호		공 보	필 요	불필요
	과장	국장	차관	장관		

협 조 자 성 명				보 존 년 한	
기 안 년 월 일	65.5.5.	시 행 년월일		통 제 관	정 서 기 장
분류기호 문서번호	외구미 722.2				
경 유 수 신	법무부장관			발 신	
참 조	참조 : 법무국장				장 관

제 목 제76차 주둔군지위협정 체결교섭 실무자회의

보고 사본 송부

　　　　1965년 4월 30일 당부에서 개최된 제76차 주둔

군지위협정 체결 교섭 실무자회의 보고서의 사본을

별첨과 같이 송부하오니 참고하시기 바랍니다.

　　유첨 ― 제76차 주둔군지위협정 체결 교섭 실무자회의

　　결과 보고서 사본 1부. 끝.

공통서식 1―2 (갑)

(16절지)

0240

제 76 차

한·미간 주둔군지위협정 체결 교섭 실무자회의
보고서

1. 일시   1965.4.30 . 1430 시부터 1800 시까지
2. 장소   외무부 제 1 회의실
3. 토의사항
가. 민사청구권 조항

1965 년 8 월 민사청구권 조항에 관한 토의가 시작된
이래 지금까지 미국측은 주한미군에 의한 손해로 발생
하는 모든 손해배상 청구는 현행 주한미군소청사무소에서
채택하고 있는 것과 동일한 절차, 즉 미국대외소청법에
규정된 절차에 따라 해결하여야 한다는 입장을 취하여
왔으나,

이번 회의에서 그들은 상기와 같은 입장을 포기
하고 한국측이 제안한 절차, 즉 공무집행중에 일어나는
손해에 대하여도 피해자에게 접수국의 민사재판권을 궁극
적으로는 존중하여 주는 "나토"및 미·일협정의 선례에
따른 손해배상청구에 대한 해결절차를 요지 아래와 같이
수정하도록 제안하였음:

(1) 2 (무)항, 공무집행중에 발생하는 양국정부가
소유하는 기타 재산에 (군대재산을 제외한) 대한 손해의
배상규정은 한국영토 밖에서 발생하는 손해에도 적용도록
하기 위하여 한국초안중에 포함되어 있는 "대한민국내에
위치한" 이라는 귀절을 삭제할것.

(2) 2 (f)항, 상기 기타 정부재산에 대한 손해에
있어, $1,400 이하의 손해는 상호 포기하며, 이와 대등한
한국화의 금액은 "외환통제에 관한 조항"에 규정된
환율에 따라 산출도록 할것. (한국초안은 $800 이하
혹은 W104,000 이하의 손해를 포기하며, 환율에 현격한
변동이 있을 때에는 양국정부가 동금액을 적절히 소절
하도록 되어 있음.)

0241

(3) 5 (e) (i)항, 공무집행중 제3자에 대하여
손해가 발생한 경우와 기타 정부재산에 손해가 발생한
경우로서 그손해에 대한책임이 미국측에만 있을때에 양국
정부가 분담하는 배상금의 분담율은 한국 25머선트 미국
75머선트로 할것. (한국초안은 이러한 경우의 분담율을
한국 15머선트 미국 85머선트로 되어 있음.)

(4) 5 (e) (iii)항, 한국정부가 지불한 배상금에 대한
미국정부의 만상책임은 그배상의 책임한계, 배상금 및
양국정부의 분담율에 대하여 미국정부가 인정한 청구사건에
한정한다. (한국초안은 미국정부가 양국정부의 분담율에
대하여 수락한 청구사건이면 이를 만상도록 되어 있음.)

(5) 5 (f)항, 공무집행중에 일어나는 사건에 대하여
한국에서 내려진 만결에 "한국국민인 혹은 한국에 통상
적으로 거주하는 고용원"도 미군군대구성원이나 고용원과
동등하게 복하지 않도록 할것. (한국초안에는 상기 만결에
복하게 되어 있음.)

(6) 6 (a)항, 한국초안의 "5 (f)항에 규정된 범위
를 제외하고는 미국은 그의 군대구성원과 고용원에 대한
한국민사재판으로 부터의 면제를 주장하지 못한다"를,
  (가) "공무집행중에 일어나는 사항에 대하여
      한국이 어떠한 만결을 내렸을 때에 그
      집행을 위한 절차와,"
  (나) "손해배상청구에 있어 완전히 만족하게
      배상금을 지불하였을때",
를 제외하고는 미국은 그의 군대구성원과 고용원에 대한
한국의 민사재판으로부터의 면제를 주장하지 못한다로
추정할것.

(7) 6 (b)항, 미군시설내에 한국의 법원에 의거
강제집행을 행하여야 할 사유동신이 있을때에 미국당국은
한국의 재판소의 요청이 있으면, "그재산을 차압하여

0243

미 둘 1123 (3)

0244

한국당국에 인도하여야 한다"를 "그재산이 한국당국에
인도되도록 그들의 권한내의 모든 원조를 제공한다."로
수정할것.

(8) 9 (d)항, "대한민국과 합중국의 당국은 본조의
규정에 의한 청구의 공평한 심리 및 처리를 위한 증거
를 수집하는데 협력하여야 한다"를 "대한민국과 합중국
의 당국은 본조의 규정에 의한 청구의 공명한 처리를
위한 증거를 수집하는데 협력하여야 한다"로 수정할것.

(9) 청구권 조항을 위하여 KATUSA는 미군의 구성원
으로 간주하며, KSC 는 한국군의 고용원으로 간주할것.

(10) 청구권 조항의 규정은 협정발효 이전에 발생한
여하한 청구에도 적용하지 않을것.

(11) 또한 미측은 한국측이 제안한 합의의사록을
삭제하고 오직 아래와 같은 내용의 합의의사록을 새로이
제안하였음.

  (가) 본조의 5,6,7및 8항의 규정은 서울특별시
    지역내에서 일어나는 사고에 대한 청구에
    관하여만 협정발효후 6개월부터 발효한다.

  (나) 본조의 5,6,7및 8항의 규정은 합동위원회
    의 결정에 따라 기타 지역에 점차적으로
    적용토록 한다.

  (다) 상기의 규정이 발효할때 까지는 미국정부가
    동규정에 해당되는 청구에 대한 해결을
    한다.

  이상 미국측 제안에 대하여 한국측은 신중히 검토
하여 차기회의시에 답변하겠다고 하였음.

4. 기타 참고사항
  차기회의일자 1965.5.7일 1500 시. 끝

0245

STATUS OF FORCES NEGOTIATIONS:

SUBJECTS:

PLACE:

PARTICIPANTS:

76th Meeting

Claims Article

Ministry of Foreign Affairs

April 30, 1965

Republic of Korea

CHANG Sang-mun
CHU Mun-ki
YI Nam-ki
Major YI Ke-hun, ROKA
~~KIxKx~~ KIM Ki-cho
HWANG Yong-chae
PAK Won-chol
YI Kun-pal (Interpreter)

United States

Philip C. Habib
Brig. General Carroll H. Dunn, USA
Colonel Allan G. Pixton, USA
Captain George Hagerman, USN
Colonel Kenneth C. Crawford, USA
Benjamin A. Fleck
Robert A. Kinney
Major Alton Harvey, USA
David Y.C. lee, (Interpreter)

Lt. Colonel C.M. Thompson, USA,
                    Observer

0247

1. Mr. Habib opened the meeting by stating that the U.S. negotiators had given careful consideration to the points raised by the Korean negotiators at previous sessions ~~regarding~~ regarding the Claims Article. The U.S. negotiators believed that the point had now been reached where a solution of the problem must be found. Not only should that solution be satisfactory to both sides, but it must provide [for] an equitable and timely settlement of all justified claims. In an effort to expedite agreement on this article, the U.S. negotiators were now prepared to accept the Korean draft, subject to some important modifications which would be explained.

2. In order to make the terminology of this article consistent with that of other articles of the Agreement, Mr. Habib continued, the U.S. negotiators wished to propose some minor changes in language. These would not affect the meaning of the article. They would apply throughout the article, wherever appropriate, as follows:

a. Change "armed services" to "armed forces" (Paragraphs 1, 4, 5(e)(ii));

b. Change "execution of its official duty" to "performance of his official duties" (Paragraph 1(a));

c. Change "in the execution of its official duty" to "for official purposes" (~~ ~~ Paragraph 1(b));

d. Change "counter-measures" to "counter-claims" (Paragraph 2(a)).

3. Mr. Habib noted that Paragraph 2(a) pertains to claims for damage to property owned by either government other than that to which Paragraph 1 applies. The U.S. negotiators proposed the deletion of the phrase "and located in the Republic of Korea". The forces of the United States and the Republic of Korea are jointly present in foreign countries and also on the high seas. Therefore, the U.S. negotiators believe that [it would be mutually advantageous to ~~xxxx~~ make] the terms of the paragraph ~~ ~~ applicable on a world-wide basis. ~~ ~~ With this modification, ~~the~~ Paragraph 2(a) of the Korean draft would be acceptable to the U.S. negotiators. 0248

4. Mr. Habib noted that ~~Paragraph~~ 4(f) ~~ ~~ would provide *for the waiver of* ~~ ~~ govern-

ment claims, other than those covered by the provisions of Paragraph 1, up to
$800.00 or Won 104,000. Through long experience, the U.S. authorities have found
this amount to be too small. Therefore, the U.S. negotiators proposed that this
paragraph be re-written as follows:

> "2(f). Each party waives its claim in any such case
> up to the amount of 1,400 United States dollars or its e-
> quivalent in Korean currency at the rate of exchange pro-
> vided for in the Agreed Minute to Article ____ at the time
> the claim is filed."

5. Mr. Habib noted that Paragraph 5(e)(i) of the Korean draft deals with
the proportionate cost in satisfying claims. The U.S. negotiators ppoposed that
the amounts be changed to provide for the standard distribution of 25% chargeable
to the host nation and 75% chargeable to the visiting nation.

6. Mr. Habib noted that Paragraph 5(e)(iii) provides for reimbursement of
the Republic of Korea for claims settled. The U.S. negotiators wished to change
the language of the Korean draft by inserting the words "liability, amount and"
before the words "proposed distribution" and by deleting the word "accepted" and
inserting in its place the words "approved by the United States". The subparagraph
would then read as follows:

> "5(e)(iii). Every half year, a statement of the sums paid by
> the Republic of Korea in the course of the half-yearly period in
> respect of every case regarding which the liability, amount, and
> proposed distribution on a percentage basis have been approved by
> the United States shall be sent to the appropriate authorities of
> the United States, together with a request for reimbursement. Such
> reimbursement shall be made in won within the shortest possible
> time."

7. Mr. Habib noted that the Korean draft of the Paragraph 5(e)(iii)
would require mutual agreement only on the distribution. At the 61st and 62nd negotiating sessions, the U.S. negotiators had pointed out that the actual practice under
the SOFA with Japan is to obtain mutual agreement as to liability, amount and proposed distribution. As the U.S. negotiators had explained at that time, no claims
has been paid in Japan unless approval of the U.S. authorities was obtained. This

0249

practice allows each side to determine liability and propriety of the award prior to settlement. Thereafter, mutual agreement is reached. The U.S. negotiators consider this a good system and one that fulfills the requirements of each country. It should be affirmatively stated in the text of the article. Therefore, the U.S. negotiators were proposing the modifications in the text of this subparagraph which they had just tabled.

8. With regard to Paragraph 5(f) of the Korean draft, Mr. Habib continued, the U.SS negotiators proposed the substitution of the word "including" for the word "excluding". This change is designed to accomplish two objectives. First, it would make the language of the subparagraph consistent with the rest of the article. Secondly, it would protect a Korean employee of the U.S. armed forces from becoming the subject of a civil action when he is already subject to claims pursuant to this paragraph. Therefore, the change proposed by the U.S. negotiators is designed to meet the requirements of consistency and fairness.

9. With regard to Paragraph 9(a) of the Korean draft, the U.S. negotiators believe that it would be preferable to (specifically) state the basis for an authorized claim of immunity from the civil jurisdiction of the courts of the Republic of Korea. The exceptions allowed in the modification proposed by the U.S. negotiators would permit a claim of immunity if the matter arose from the performance of official duty or if there has been full satisfaction of the claim in question. The U.S. negotiators believe this to be consistent with the intent of the Korean draft and urge, therefore, that the paragraph be modified as follows:

"9(a). The United States shall not claim immunity from the jurisdiction of the courts of the Republic of Korea for members or employees of the United States armed forces in respect of the civil jurisdiction of the courts of the Republic of Korea except in respect of proceedings for the enforcement of any judgment given against them in the Republic of Korea in a matter arising from the performance of their official duties or except after payment in full satisfaction of a claim."

0250

CONFIDENTIAL

10. Mr. Habib noted that Paragraph 9(b) of the Korean draft would require U.S. authorities to "possess and turn over" personal movable property subject to compulsory execution under Korean law and located within United States facilities and areas. The Korean negotiators were aware, Mr. Habib continued, that provisions of the United States Constitution and laws restrict the power of the military commanders over personal property. At the same time, the U.S. authorities wished to be of maximum assistance to the Korean authorities in this regard. Therefore, they proposed that Paragraph 6(b) of the U.S. draft, which covers the same subject matter, be substituted for Paragraph 9(b) of the Korean draft. The U.S. negotiators wished to assure the Korean negotiators that U.S. authorities would render all possible assistance to the Korean courts.

11. Mr. Habib then turned to Paragraph 9(c) of the Korean draft, dealing with U.S. and Korean cooperation in the procurement of evidence. The Korean draft implies that a hearing must be held in every case. The United States authorities have every intention of cooperating in procuring any necessary evidence but the U.S. negotiators doubted that the Korean negotiators were proposing that a hearing would be required in the disposition of every claim under this article. Therefore, the U.S. negotiators proposed that Paragraph 7 of the U.S. draft be substituted for Paragraph 9(c) of the Korean draft. This paragraph would provide for mutual cooperation in the procurement of evidence for fair disposition of a claim, regardless of whether a hearing, or some other procedure, is utilized. The U.S. negotiators believed that this would eliminate any possibility of misinterpretation while still meeting the requirements of the Korean negotiators. 0251

12. Mr. Habib said the U.S. negotiators wished to propose that Paragraph 10 of the U.S. draft be incorporated into the Korean draft as a new Paragraph 12. This paragraph would make clear the status of KATUSA and KSC personnel for claims purposes. This subject had been discussed at length; the U.S. negotiators

stop.

wished to point out that it provides for nothing more than a continuation of the present practices and policies. These individuals do generate claims. It is essential and only common sense to clarify in this article their status with respect to these claims.

13. Mr. Habib pointed out that the Korean draft contains no provision establishing liability for prior claims. To ensure that all parties understand what claims fall within the scope of the agreement, this article should clearly spell out ~~the factual situation~~ the fact that it does not apply to claims which [arise] ~~arise~~ before the Agreement comes into force. Therefore, the U.S. negotiators wished to propose a new Paragraph 13, reading as follows:

"13. The provisions of this Article shall not apply to any claims which arose before the entry into force of this Agreement."

14. Mr. Habib said that he had now come to the most important question of when the [responsibility ~~authority~~ for] settlement of claims ~~will~~ would be transferred to the authorities of the Republic of Korea. The U.S. negotiators believe that the present claims system has been performing this task in an efficient and timely fashion, with equitable awards made for all justified claims. As the Korean negotiators know, the U.S. authorities are deeply concerned with their obligation to settle these claims equitably and speedily. The U.S. negotiators, in previous meetings, have questioned the capability of the recently established Korean Claims Service to assume this task without an extended period for expansion and training of new employees. At ~~these~~ previous meetings, the Korean negotiators had consistently maintained that the task could be efficiently accomplished "with some enlargement and improvement of the present Korean system". In response to the Korean position, ~~we are~~ [the U.S. Negotiators were] now prepared to ~~make~~ make a major concession by tabling a new Agreed Minute to replace those previously tabled by the Korean negotiators. This Agreed Minute would read as follows:

"Agreed Minute

A. Unless otherwise provided,

1. The provisions of paragraphs five, six, seven and eight of this article will become effective six months from the date of entry into force of this agreement as to claims arising from incidents in the Seoul Special City area.

2. The provisions of paragraphs five, six, seven and eight will be progressively extended to other areas of Korea as determined and defined by the Joint Committee.

B. Until such time as the provisions of paragraphs five, six, seven and eight become effective in any given area

1. The United States shall process and settled claims (other than contractual claims) arising out of the acts or omissions of members or employees of the United States armed forces done in the performance of official duty or out of any other act, omission or occurence for which the United States armed forces are legally responsible, which cause damage in the Republic of Korea to parties other than the two governments;

2. The United States shall entertain other non-contractual claims against members or employees of the armed forces and may offer an ex gratia payment in such cases and in such amount as is determined by the appropriate United States authorities; and

3. Each party shall have the right to determine whether a member or employee of its armed forces was engaged in the performance of official duties and whether property owned by it was being used by its armed forces for official purposes.

C. For the purposes of subparagraph 2(d), subparagraph 5 (e) shall be effective throughout Korea from the date of entry into force of this agreement.

0253

"Agreed Minute.

"
"

15. Mr. Habib stated that Paragraph A1 of the proposed Agreed Minute would provide for transfer of claims settlement within the Seoul Special City area to the Korean Claims Service six months after the effective date of the Agreement. Approximately, 20% to 25% of the claims currently processed by the U.S. Claims Service arise in the Seoul Special City area. ~~The extension after the effective dates~~ The extension of this responsibility to the Korean Claims Service in other areas would then depend upon the effectiveness of the Service in processing claims in the Seoul Special City Area. At previous sessions, the Korean negotiators had asserted that the Korean Claims Service would overcome the problems envisaged by the U.S. negotiators without difficulty. If this proved correct, the extension of ~~the provisions of the Agreement concerns~~ Korean Claims Service jurisdiction to other areas would take place at an early date. The U.S. negotiators wished to assure the Korean negotiators that the U.S. authorities would agree to transfer claims settlement authority as soon as the capability of the Korean Claims Service was demonstrated to the satisfaction of the Joint Committee.

16. Mr. Habib noted that Paragraph B of the Agreed Minute pertains to claims arising prior to the time the settlement authority is transferred to the Korean Claims Service in the particular area concerned. Paragraph C covers "other government claims", which will be settled in accordance with Paragraph 2 of the Article, which will come into effect immediately when the Agreement becomes effective. Since Paragraph 5(e), which pertains to the proportionate shares of the cost incurred in settling these claims, is essential to the operation of Paragraph 2(d),

0254

it must also come into force as soon as the Agreement becomes operative.

17. Mr. Habib said he wished to summarize the position of the U.S. negotiators with regard to this article. ~~Nevertheless~~ At this meeting, they had presented a comprehensive proposal designed to meet the major requirements of both sides and to expedite agreement on this article. ~~They~~ Their proposals would meet the desires expressed by the Korean negotiators to the maximum extent possible consistent with the obligations which the U.S. authorities and negotiators feel to the Korean people. The modifications proposed by the U.S. negotiators are essential. The U.S. negotiators hope that the Korean negotiators, ~~~ after careful study, will accept the compromise proposal made by the U.S. negotiators.

18. Mr. Chang replied that the Korean negotiators appreciated the comprehensive nature of the U.S. proposals. They would give them careful consideration and respond at a later meeting.

19. It was agreed to hold the next meeting on May 7, 1965.

한·미국 간의 상호방위조약 제4조에 의한 시설과 구역 및 한국에서의 미국군대의 지위에 관한 협정(SOFA)
전59권. 1966.7.9 서울에서 서명 : 1967.2.9 발효(조약 232호) (V.29 실무교섭회의, 제73-76차, 1965.4월) 261

JOINT SUMMARU RECORD OF THE 76TH SESSION

1. Time and Place: 2:30-4:00 P.M., April 30, 1965 at the
                    Foreign Ministry's Conference Room(No.1)

2. Attendance:

   ROK Side:

   Mr.   Chang, Sang Moon   Director
                                   European and American Affairs
                                   Bureau

   Mr.   Choo Moon Ki   Chief
                                   Legal Affairs Section
                                   Ministry of Justice

   Maj. Lee Kye Hoon   Military Affairs Section
                                   Ministry of National Defense

   Mr.   Kim, Kee Joe   3rd Secretary
                                   Ministry of Foreign Affairs

   Mr.   Lee, Keun Pal   3rd Secretary
         (Interpreter)   Ministry of Foreign Affairs

   Mr.   Hwang, Young Jae   3rd Secretary
                                   Ministry of Foreign Affairs

   Mr.   Park, Won Chul   3rd Secretary
                                   Ministry of Foreign Affairs

   U.S. Side:

   Mr.   Philip C. Habib   Counselor
                                   American Embassy

   Brig. Gen. Carroll H.Dunn   Deputy Chief of Staff
                                   8th U.S. Army

   Col. Allan G. Pixton   Deputy Chief of Staff
                                   8th U.S. Army

   Capt. George Hagerman   Assistant Chief of Staff
                                   USN/K

   Col. Kenneth C. Crawford   Staff Judge Advocate
                                   8th U.S. Army

   Mr.   Benjamin A. Fleck   First Secretary
                                   American Embassy

   Mr.   Robert A. Kinney   J-5
                                   8th U.S. Army

   Maj. Alton H. Harvey   Staff Judge Advocate's Office
                                   8th U.S. Army

   Mr.   David Y.C. Lee   Second Secretary
         (Interpreter)   American Embassy

   Mr.   Lt. Col. Charles M. Thompson
         (Observer)
                                   Claims Service
                                   8th U.S. Army

0256

<u>CLAIMS ARTICLE</u>

1. Mr. Habib opened the meeting by stating that the U.S. negotiators had given careful consideration to the points raised by the Korean negotiators at previous sessions regarding the Claims Article. The U.S. negotiators believed that the point had now been reached where a solution of the problem must be found. Not only should that solution be satisfactory to both sides, but it must provide for an equitable and timely settlement of all justified claims. In an effort to expedite agreement on this article, the U.S. negotiators were now prepared to accept the Korean draft, subject to some important modifications which would be explained.

2. In order to make the terminology of this article consistent with that of other articles of the Agreement, Mr. Habib continued, the U.S. negotiators wished to propose some minor changes in language, These would not affect the meaning of the article. They would apply throughout the article, wherever appropriate, as follows:

a. Change "armed services" to armed forces" (Paragraphs 1, 4, 5(e)(ii);

b. Change "execution of its official duty" to "performance of his official duties" (Paragraph 1(a);

c. Change "in the execution of its official duty" to "for official purposes" (Paragraph 1(b));

d. Change "counter-measures" to "counter-claims" (Paragraph 2(a)).

3. Mr. Habib noted that Paragraph 2(a) pertains to claims for damage to property owned by either government other than that to which Paragraph 1 applies. The U.S. negotiators proposed the deletion of the phrase "and located in the Republic of Korea", The forces of the United States and the Republic of Korea are jointly present

0257

in foreign countries and also on the high seas. Therefore, the U.S. negotiators believe that it would be mutually advantageous to make the terms of the paragraph applicable on a world-wide basis. With this modification, Paragraph 2(a) of the Korean draft would be acceptable to the U.S. negotiators.

4. Mr. Habib noted that Paragraph 2(f) would provide for the waiver of government claims, other than those covered by the provisions of Paragraph 1, up to $800.00 or Won 104,000. Through long experience, the U.S. authorities have found this amount to be too small. Therefore, the U.S. negotiators proposed that this paragraph be re-written as follows:

> "2(f). Each party waives its claim in any such case up to the amount of 1,400 United States dollars or its equivalent in Korean currency at the rate of exchange provided for in the Agreed Minute to Article ------ at the time the claim is filed."

5. Mr. Habib noted that Paragraph 5(e)(i) of the Korean draft deals with the proportionate cost in satisfying claims. The U.S. negotiators proposed that the amounts be changed to provide for the standard distribution of 25% chargeable to the host nation and 75% chargeable to the visiting nation.

6. Mr. Habib noted that Paragraph 5(e)(iii) provides for reimbursement of the Republic of Korea for claims settled. The U.S. negotiators wished to change the language of the Korean draft by inserting the words "liability, amount and " before the words "proposed distribution" and by deleting the word "accepted" and inserting in its place the words "approved by the United States." The subparagraph would then read as follows:

> "5(e)(iii). Every half year, a statement of the sums paid by the Republic of Korea in the course of the half-yearly period in respect of every case regarding which the liability, amount, and *proposed* distribution on a percentage basis have been approved by the United States shall be sent to the appropriate authorities of

the United States, together with a request for reimbursement. Such reimbursement shall be made in won within the shortest possible time."

7. Mr. Habib noted that the Korean draft of the Paragraph 5(e)(iii) would require mutual agreement only on the distribution. At the 61st and 62nd negotiating sessions, the U.S. negotiators had pointed out that the actual practice under the SOFA with Japan is to obtain mutual agreement as to liability, amount and proposed distribution. As the U.S. negotiators had explained at that time, no claims has been paid in Japan unless approval of the U.S. authorities was obtained. This practice allows each side to determine liability and propriety of the award prior to settlement. Thereafter, mutual agreement is reached. The U.S. negotiators consider this a good system and one that fulfills the requirements of each country. It should be affirmatively stated in the text of the article. Therefore, the U.S. negotiators were proposing the modifications in the text of this subparagraph which they had just tabledd

8. With regard to Paragraph 5(f) of the Korean draft, Mr. Habib continued, the U.S. negotiators proposed the substitution of the word "including" for the word "excluding". This change is designed to accomplish two objectives. First, it would make the language of the subparagraph consistent with the rest of the article. Secondly, it would protect a Korean employee of the U.S. armed forces from becoming the subject of a civil action when he is already subject to claims pursuant to this paragraph. Therefore, the change propsed by the U.S. negotiators is designed to meet the requirements of consistency and fairness.

9. With regard to Paragraph 9(a) of the Korean draft, the U.S. negotiators believe that it would be preferable to

0259

state specifically the basis for an authorized claim of immunity from the civil jurisdiction of the courts of the Republic of Korea. The exceptions allowed in the modification proposed by the U.S. negotiators would permit a claim of immunity if the matter arose from the performance of official duty or if there has been full satisfaction of the claim in question. The U.S. negotiators believe this to be consistent with the intent of the Korean draft and urge, therefore, that the paragraph be modified as follows:

"9(a). The United States shall not claim

immunity from the jurisdiction of the courts of the Republic of Korea for members or employees of the United States armed forces in respect of the civil jurisdiction of the courts of the Republic of Korea except in respect of proceedings for the enforcement of any judgment given against them in the Republic of Korea in a matter arising from the performance of their official duties or except after payment in full satisfaction of claim."

10. Mr. Habib noted that Paragraph 9(b) of the Korean draft would require U.S. authorities to "possess and turn over" personal movable property subject to compulsory execution under Korean law and located within United States facilities and areas. The Korean negotiators were aware, Mr. Habib continued, that provisions of the United States Constitution and laws restrict the power of the military commanders over personal property. At the same time, the U.S. authorities wished to be of maximum assistance to the Korean authorities in this regard. Therefore, they proposed that Paragraph 6(b) of the U.S. draft, which covers the same subject matter, be substituted for Paragraph 9(b) of the Korean draft. The U.S. negotiators wished to assure the Korean negotiators that U.S. authorities would render all possible assistance to the Korean courts.

11. Mr. Habib then turned to Paragraph 9(c) of the Korean draft, dealing with U.S. and Korean cooperation

0260

in the procurement of evidence. The Korean draft implies
that a hearing must be held in every case. The United States
authorities have every intention of cooperating in procuring
any necessary evidence but the U.S. negotiators doubted
that the Korean negotiators were proposing that a hearing
would be required in the disposition of every claim under
this article. Therefore, the U.S. negotiators proposed that
Paragraph 7 of the U.S. draft be substituted for Paragraph
9(c) of the Korean draft. This paragraph would provide for
mutual cooperation in the procurement of evidence for fair
disposition of a claim, regardless of whether a hearing, or
some other procedure, is utilized. The U.S. negotiators
believed that this would eliminate any possibility of
misinterpretation while still meeting the requirements of the
Korean negotiators.

12. Mr. Habib said the U.S. negotiators wished to
propose that Paragraph 10 of the U.S. draft be incorporated
into the Korean draft as a new Paragraph 12. This paragraph
would make clear the status of KATUSA and KSC personnel
for claims purposes. This subject had been discussed at
length; the U.S. negotiators wished to point out that it
provides for nothing more than a continuation of the
present practices and policies. These individuals do
generate claims. It is essential and only common sense to
clarify in this article their status with respect to these
claims.

13. Mr. Habib pointed out that the Korean draft
contains no provision establishing liability for prior
claims. To ensure that all parties understand what
claims fall within the scope of the agreement, this article
should clearly spell out the fact that it does not apply
to claims which arise before the Agreement comes into force.
Therefore, the U.S. negotiators wished to propose a new
Paragraph 13, reading as follows:

0261

"13. The provisions of this Article shall not apply to any claims which arose before the entry into force of this Agreement."

14. Mr. Habib said that he had now come to the most important question of when the responsibility for settlement of claims would be transferred to the authorities of the Republic of Korea. The U.S. negotiators believe that the present claims system has been performing this task in an efficient and timely fashion, with equitable awards made for all justified claims. As the Korean negotiators know, the U.S. authorities are deeply concerned with their obligation to settle these claims equitably and speedily. The U.S. negotiators, in previous meetings, have questioned the capability of the recently established Korean Claims Service to assume this task without an extended period for expansion and training of new employees. At previous meetings, the Korean negotiators had consistently maintained that the task could be efficiently accomplished "with some enlargement and improvement of the present Korean system". In response to the Korean position, the U.S. negotiators were now prepared to make a major concession by tabling a new Agreed Minute to replace those previously tabled by the Korean negotiators. This Agreed Minute would read as follows:

Agreed Minute

A. Unless otherwise provided,

1. The provisions of paragraphs five, six, seven and eight of this article will become effective six months from the date of entry into force of this agreement as to claims arising from incidents in the Seoul Special City area.

2. The provisions of paragraphs five, six, seven and eight will be progressively extended to other areas of Korea as determined and defined by the Joint Committee.

B. Until such time as the provisions of paragraphs five, six, seven and eight become effective in any given area

1. The United States shall process and settled claims (other than contractual claims) arising out of the acts or omissions of members or employees of the United States armed

0262

forces done in the performance of official duty or out of any other act, omission or occurence for which the United States armed forces are legally responsible, which cause damage in the Republic of Korea to parties other than the two governments;

2. The United States shall entertain other noncontractual claims against members or employees of the armed forces and may offer an ex gratia payment in such cases and in such amount as is determined by the appropriate United States authorities; and

3. Each party shall have the right to determine whether a member or employee of its armed forces was engaged in the performance of official duties and whether property owned by it was being used by its armed forces for official purposes.

C. For the purposes of subparagraph 2(d), subparagraph 5(e) shall be effective throughout Korea from the date of entry into force of this agreement.

15. Mr. Habib stated that Paragraph A1 of the proposed Agreed Minute would provide for transfer of claims settlement within the Seoul Special City area to the Korean Claims Service six months after the effective date of the Agreement. Approximately, 20% to 25% of the claims currently processed by the U.S. Claims Service arise in the Seoul Special City area.
The extension of this responsibility to the Korean Claims Service in other areas would then depend upon the effectiveness of the Service in processing claims in the Seoul Special City Area. At previous sessions, the Korean negotiators had asserted that the Korean Claims Service would overcome the problems envisaged by the U.S. negotiators without difficulty. If this proved correct, the extension of Korean Claims Service jurisdiction to other areas would take place at an early date. The U.S. negotiators wished to assure the Korean negotiators that the U.S. authorities would agree to transfer claims settlement authority as soon as the capability of the Korean Claims Service was demonstrated to the satisfaction of the Joint Committee.

16. Mr. Habib noted that Paragraph B of the Agreed Minute pertains to claims arising prior to the time

0263

the settlement authority is transferred to the Korean Claims Service in the particular area concerned. Paragraph C covers "other government claims", which will be settled in accordance with Paragraph 2 of the Article, which will come into effect immediately when the Agreement becomes effective. Since Paragraph 5(e), which pertains to the proportionate shares of the cost incurred in settling these claims, is essential to the operation of Paragraph 2(d), it must also come into force as soon as the Agreement becomes operative.

17. Mr. Habib said he wished to summarize the position of the U.S. negotiators with regard to this article. At this meeting, they had presented a comprehensive proposal designed to meet the major requirements of both sides and to expedite agreement on this article. Their proposals would meet the desires expressed by the Korean negotiators to the maximum extent possible consistent with the obligations which the U.S. authorities and negotiators feel to the Korean people. The modifications proposed by the U.S. negotiators are essential. The U.S. negotiators hope that the Korean negotiators, after careful study, will accept the compromise proposal made by the U.S. negotiators.

18. Mr. Chang replied that the Korean negotiators appreciated the comprehensive nature of the U.S. proposals. They would give them careful consideration and respond at a later meeting.

19. It was agreed to hold the next meeting on May 7, 1965.

0264

기록물종류	문서-일반공문서철	등록번호	928 9601	등록일자	2006-07-27
분류번호	741.12	국가코드	US	주제	
문서철명	한.미국 간의 상호방위조약 제4조에 의한 시설과 구역 및 한국에서의 미국군대의 지위에 관한 협정 (SOFA) 전59권. 1966.7.9 서울에서 서명 : 1967.2.9 발효 (조약 232호) *원본				
생산과	미주과/조약과	생산년도	1952 - 1967	보존기간	영구
담당과(그룹)	조약	조약		서가번호	--
참조분류					
권차명	V.30 실무교섭회의, 제77-80차, 1965.5월				

내용목차

1. 제77차 회의. 5.6 (p.2~71)
2. 제78차 회의. 5.7 (p.72~91)
3. 제79차 회의. 5.12 (p.92~132)
4. 제80차 회의. 5.28 (p.133~224)

* 일지 :

1953.8.7	이승만 대통령-Dulles 미국 국무장관 공동성명 - 상호방위조약 발효 후 군대지위협정 교섭 약속
1954.12.2	정부, 주한 UN군의 관세업무협정 체결 제의
1955.1월, 5월	미국, 제의 거절
1955.4.28	정부, 군대지위협정 제의 (한국측 초안 제시)
1957.9.10	Hurter 미국 국무차관 방한 시 각서 수교 (한국측 제의 수락 요구)
1957.11.13, 26	정부, 개별 협정의 단계적 체결 제의
1958.9.18	Dawling 주한미국대사, 형사재판관할권 협정 제외 조건으로 행정협정 체결 의사 전달
1960.3.10	정부, 토지, 시설협정의 우선적 체결 강력 요구
1961.4.10	장면 국무총리-McConaughy 주한미국대사 공동성명으로 교섭 개시 합의
1961.4.15, 4.25	제1, 2차 한.미국 교섭회의 (서울)
1962.3.12	정부, 교섭 재개 촉구 공한 송부
1962.5.14	Burger 주한미국대사, 최규하 장관 면담 시 형사재판관할권 문제 제기 않는 조건으로 교섭 재개 통고
1962.9.6	한.미국 간 공동성명 발표 (9월 중 교섭 재개 합의)
1962.9.20~ 1965.6.7	제1-81차 실무 교섭회의 (서울)
1966.7.8	제82차 실무 교섭회의 (서울)
1966.7.9	서명
1967.2.9	발효 (조약 232호)

마/이/크/로/필/름/사/항

촬영연도	*롤 번호	화일 번호	후레임 번호	보관함 번호
2006-11-23	I-06-0069	07	1-224	

0001

1. 제77차 회의, 5.6

0002

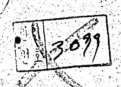

(1965. 5.3

韓·美間 駐屯軍地位協定締結交涉

I. 刑事裁判管轄權

韓國側案	美國側案
가. 第一次管轄權의 抛棄	① 韓國政府는 韓國當局에 賦與된 第一次管轄權을 美國을 爲하여 抛棄한다.
① 韓國當局은 美軍當局이 要請하면 韓國當局이 管轄權을 行使함이 特히 重要하다고 決定하는 境遇를 除外하고 第一次管轄權을 美軍當局에 抛棄한다.	② 韓國當局이 特定事件에 있어서 特殊한 事情을 理由로 韓國의 司法上의 重大한 利益이 韓國의 管轄權行使를 不可避하게 한다는 意見을 가질 境遇에는 美軍當局에 通告함으로서 權利抛棄를 撤回할수 있다.
② 韓國當局이 내리는決定에 關하여 異議가 提起된 境遇 美國外交使節에 韓國當局과 協議할수 있는 機會가 賦與된다.	가) 特定事件의 措置한後討와 그結果에 따를것을 條件으로 特히 다음과 같은事件에 있어서 韓國의 司法上의 重大한 利益이 韓國의管轄權行使를 不可避하게 할수 있는것으로 한다.
③ 諒解事項	(가). 韓國의 安全에 關한 犯罪
韓國의 管轄權을 行使함이 特히 重要하다고決定하는 事件의 範疇에 該當하는 犯罪는 다음과같은 犯罪을 包含한다.	2) 사람을 죽음에 이르게한 犯罪. 强姦罪. 强盜罪
가) 韓國의 安全에 關한犯罪	3) 上記各犯罪의 未遂또는 共犯
나) 사람을 죽음에 이르게한犯罪	③ 韓國當局이 特定事件에 對한 權利抛棄을 撤回하고 關係當局間의 諒解가 成立
다) 强姦罪	되지않을때에는 美國當局은 外交經路를
라) 强盜罪	

0003

韓 國 側 案	英 國 側 案
마) 韓美兩國中 어느管局이 特히 直要하다고 認定하는 犯罪 바) 上記 各犯罪의 未遂또는共犯	通하여 韓國政府에 異議를 提起할수 있다. 韓國政府는 韓國의 司法上의 利益과 英國의 利益을 充分히 考慮하 여 外交分野에 있어서의 그權限을 行使하여 意見差異를 解決하여야 한 다.
나. 公務執行中 犯罪 ① 美軍法務官이 發行한 證明書는 管 轄權決定을爲한 事實의充分한 證據가 된다. ② 韓國地方檢察廳 檢事長이 反證이 있다고 思料하는 例外的인境遇 韓美 關係官및 美國外交使節間에 再審되어 야 한다. ③ 諒解事項 가) 證明書는 修正되지 않는限 確 定的이다. 美軍當局은 韓國當局이 提示한異議에 對하여 正當한考慮를 하여야한다. ④ 公務의定義는 1956年度의 英極 東軍의 定義를 一部修正하여 合意議 事錄에 規定한다.	① 美軍의 權限있는 當局이 發行한 證 明書는 管轄權決定을爲한 事實의充分 한 證據가 된다. ② 韓國檢察總長이 反證이 있다고 思 料하는 例外的인境遇 韓國關係官및 英國外交使節間에 再審될수 있다. ③ 諒解事項 가) 證明書는 合意議事錄의 節次에 따라 修正되지 않는限 確定的이다 ④ 公務의 定義는 1956年度의 英極東軍의 定義대로 諒解事項으로 規定한다.

0004

韓 國 側 案	美 國 側 案
다. 被疑者의 裁判前身柄拘禁 ① 韓國當局이 拘禁할 正當한事由가있는限 모든司法節次가 끝나고 韓國當局이 要請할때까지 美國當局이 拘禁한다. ② 韓國의安全에關한 被疑者의 身柄은 韓國當局이 拘禁한다. ③ 韓國當局이 身柄의引渡을 要請하면 美國當局은 好意的考慮를 하여야한다	① 모든司法節次가 끝나고 韓國當局이 要請할때까지 美國當局이 拘禁한다. ② 韓國의安全에關한 被疑者의 身柄은 韓國當局이 拘禁하되 拘禁事情의 適否에關한 兩國間의 合意가 있어야 한다. ③ 同

II. 民事請求權

韓 國 側 案	美 國 側 案
1. 公務執行中 第3者에 對한 損害 韓國法에 依據 韓國當局이 解決하여 賠償金을 支拂하고 其後 兩國政府가 그支拂된金額을 分擔하며 美國當局에게 全的으로 損害의 責任이 있을때에는 韓國15% 美國85%의 比率로 分擔하되 個個의 請求事件에 關한 分擔案에 對하여 美國當局이 受諾한事件에 限하여 美國政府는 韓國政府에 辨償한다	韓國案과 同一한方法으로 解決하되 美國當局에게 全的으로 損害의責任이 있을때의 分擔率은 韓國25% 美國75%로하며 個個의 請求事件에 關한 分擔案 損害의責任限界및 賠償金額에 對하여 美國當局이 受諾한事件에 限하여 美國政府는 韓國政府에 辨償한다.

6-7

0005

한·미국 간의 상호방위조약 제4조에 의한 시설과 구역 및 한국에서의 미국군대의 지위에 관한 협정(SOFA)
전59권. 1966.7.9 서울에서 서명 : 1967.2.9 발효(조약 232호) (V.30 실무교섭회의, 제77-80차, 1965.5월) 275

韓 國 側 案	美 國 側 案
2. 請求權條項의 發効時期 第5項 公務執行中 第三者에對한 損害의 解決規定은 協定發効 6個月 後부터 發効한다.	第5項 公務執行中 第三者에 對한 損害 第6項 非公務乘의 損害 第7項 非 公務中의 車輛使用으로 發生하는損害및 第8項 公務執行與否에 關한 紛爭解決 規定은 서울特別市에서 일어나는 事件 에 限하여 協定發効6個月後부터 適用 하며 其他地域에 對하여는 合同委員會 의 決議에 따라 漸次的으로 適用도록 한다.
3. KSC의 行爲로 因한 損害 第5項 公務執行中 第三者에 對 한 損害의 解決을 爲하여 KSC 는 美軍의 雇傭員으로 看做한다.	本條의 規定을爲하여 KSC는 韓國軍 의 雇傭員으로 看做한다.

III 勞務調達

韓 國 側 案	美 國 側 案
합동위원회에서정하는 군요원계약서 1. 雇傭主는 美國軍(非歲出機關包含) KSC는 제51항 雇傭人은 美軍屬이 아닌 韓國國籍을 가진 民間人으로 한다.	1. 雇傭主는 美國軍(非歲出機關包含)및 軍招請契約書, 雇傭人은 美軍屬이 아닌 雇傭人(KSC 및 家事使用人은 除外) 但 準軍事的인

0006

韓 國 側 案	美 國 側 案
2. 勞動條件은 本條規定에 相反되지 않거나 別途合意(合同委에서 事前에) 되지않는限 韓國勞動法令을 遵守한다	2. 本條規定과 美軍의 軍事上 必要에 相反되지 않는限 韓國勞動法 慣習 傾例를 遵守한다. (必要時 可能한限 事前에 合同委에서 審議한다)
이상시 문조의 점용은 한국정부가 취하는 비상조치에 따르지 제한한컨다.	
3. 罷業權은 合同委에서 同行使를 禁止쫄한者를 除外한 雇傭人에게 賦與되어야 한다.	3. 罷業權은 韓國軍屬傭人과 同一한 法的規制를 받는다.
0동의 미비의 조정기간 ○ 참공기기시에 (紛爭解決期間中 特別委에)回附된 날 부터 起算하여 (冷却期間(勞動爭議 法14條依據)이) 經過하면 (罷業權을 行使할수있다.)	紛爭解決期間中에는 罷業을 包含한 一切의 正常業務防害行爲를 하지못한 다.
4. 美軍業務에 不可缺한 技術者에 對하여 事前에 要求하면 相互合意下에 戰時에 兵役義務를 延期한다.	4. 美軍業務에 不可缺한 技術者에 對하여 事前에 要求하면 戰時에 兵役 義務를 延期하여야 한다.

196◯.2◯ 에 예고문에 의거 일반문서로 재분류됨

0007

보통군사 재분류(1965.12.31.)

CONFIDENTIAL

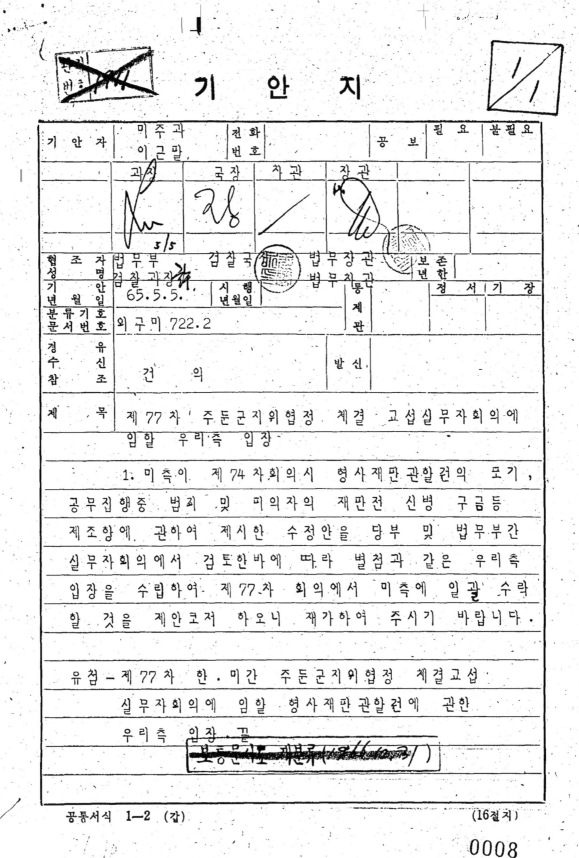

기 안 지

기안자	미주과 이근팔	전화 번호		공보	필요	불필요

	과장	국장	차관	장관

협조 자명	법무부 검찰과장	검찰국 	법무장관 법무차관		보존 년한	

기안 년월일	65.5.5.	시행 년월일		통 제 관	정서 기장	
분류기호 문서번호	외구미 722.2					
경유 수신 참조	건 의		발신			

제 목 : 제77차 주둔군지위협정 체결 교섭실무자회의에 임할 우리측 입장

　　1. 미측이 제74차회의시 형사재판관할건의 포기, 공무집행중 범죄 및 피의자의 재판전 신병 구금등 제조항에 관하여 제시한 수정안을 당부 및 법무부간 실무자회의에서 검토한바에 따라 별첨과 같은 우리측 입장을 수립하여 제77차 회의에서 미측에 일괄 수락 할 것을 제안코저 하오니 재가하여 주시기 바랍니다.

　　유첨 - 제77차 한·미간 주둔군지위협정 체결교섭 실무자회의에 임할 형사재판관할건에 관한 우리측 입장 끝

<del>보통문서로 재분류(1966.4.31)</del>

공통서식 1-2 (갑)　　　　　　　　　　　　　(16절지)

0008

제 77 차 주둔군지위협정 체결 고섭 실무자회의
에 임할 형사재판관할건에 관한 우리측 입장

1. 관할건의 포기

미측이 제 74 차 회의시 제시한 수정안을 원칙적으로
수락하되 다음과 같이 일부 수정 할것을 제안한다.

(1) 협정의 체제를 고려하여 미국이 요청하면 포기하는
것으로 하기 위하여 미측 합의의사록 제 1 항 서두에
"합중국이 요청하면" 이라는 어구를 삽입할 것을
제의한다.

(2) 한국측이 포기를 철회한후 만약에 미국측과 양해가
성립되지 아니하였을 때에는 한국정부가 외교분야에
있어서의 그의 건한을 행사하여 의견차이를 해결
하게 되어 있는바 한국당국이 포기를 철회하였을
때에 포기의 효과가 확정적인 것으로 하기 위하여
양국간의 의견차이와 해결에 관한 제 4 항 말미에
다음과 같은 구절을 추가 삽입할 것을 제안한다:
    "포기의 철회는 양국정부 간의 협의를
    통하여 철회를 위한 통고가 대한민국 정부에
    의하여 취소되지 않는한 확정적이며 또한
    최종적이다."

(3) 재판장소 및 대한민국대표의 참석에 관한 제 6 항의
규정은 한·미양측이 종전에 제시하였던 다음과
같은 안으로 대체할것을 제의한다:
    "대한민국이 관할건을 행사할 제 1 차적건리를
    포기하는 사건의 재판과 제 3 (a) (ii)항에
    규정된 범죄로서 대한민국 또는 대한민국
    국민에 대하여 범하여 진 범죄에 관련된
    사건의 재판은 별도의 약정이 상호 합의되지
    않는한 범죄가 행하여진 것으로 인정되는
    장소로부터 적당한 거리내에서 행하여 진다.
    대한민국의 대표는 그러한 재판에 참석할수있다."

0009

2. 공무집행중범죄

공무집행중 범죄에 관하여서는 양측 입장이 대동소이
한바,

(1) 공무집행증명서의 발행권자에 관하여 미측 주장
대로 "미국군대의 권한있는 당국"으로 하되
다음과 같은 양해사항을 제안한다:
"증명서는 반듯이 미군법무관의 의견을 들은
후에 발행되어야 하며 미측의 증명서 발행
기관은 장성급으로 한다."

(2) 반증이 있다고 사료하는 때에 이의를 제기할수
있는 한국기관은 미측 주장대로 "대한민국검찰총장"
으로 한다.

(3) 공무집행중 범죄의 정의는 미측 입장을 참작하여
1956년도의 미극동군의 정의를 문자그대로 수락
하되 합의의사록에 규정할것을 계속 주장한다:
"공무라 함은 미군대 구성원 및 군속이 공무
중 행한 모든 행위를 포함하는 것을 의미하는
것이 아니며 개인이 집행하는 공무의 기능
으로서 행하여 질것이 요구되는 행위에만
적용되는 것을 의미한다. 그러므로 어떤
자가 특정공무에 있어서 행할것이 요구되는
행위로부터 실질적으로 이탈된 행위는 통상
그의 공무밖의 행위이다."

(4) 공무집행증명서에 대한 반증이 있다고 사료하는
예외적인 경우에는 공무집행증명서는 대한민국
당국과 주한미국외교사절간의 협의를 통한 재심의
대상이 "되어야 한다"라는 우리측 입장을 계속
주장한다.

(5) 미측이 제시한 양해사항에 관하여서는 우리측 입장
을 계속 주장한다:

0010

"미군당국이 발행한 공무집행증명서는 미측이
수정하지 않는한 확정적이다. 그러나 미국당국은
대한민국이 제시한 이의에 대하여 정당한 고려
를 하여야 한다."

3. 피의자의 재판전 신병구금

　미측이 74차 회의에서 제안한 피의자의 신병구금에
관한 수정안은 다음과 같이 일부 수정할 것을 조건
으로 수락한다.

　(1) 피의자의 신병이 한국당국의 수중에 있을 때에
　　　"요청하면" 미군당국에 인도한다.

✓(2) 피의자의 신병이 미군당국의 수중에 있을 때에는
　　　"미군당국은 언제던지 신병을 대한민국당국에 인도할수"
　　　있는 것으로 한다.

✓(3) 미군당국은 대한민국당국이 요청하면 "즉시" 대한
　　　민국당국이 피의자에 대한 수사 또는 재판을 할수있게
　　　하여야 하며 "이러한 목적과 그리고 증거인멸의
　　　위험을 방지하기 위하여 제반 적절한 조치를 취
　　　하여야 한다."

　(4) 미측이 제시한 다음과 같은 2개의 양해사항을
　　　수락한다.

　　(가) 대한민국의 안전에 관한 피의자의 구금에
　　　　　관하여, 한국당국의 신병구금사정의 적당여부에
　　　　　관하여 한·미양국간의 상호합의가 있어야
　　　　　한다.

　　(나) 한국의 구금시설은 미국수준으로 보아 적당
　　　　　하여야 한다.

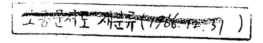

0011

<u>Agreed Minute Re Paragraph 3(b)</u>

<u>Revised Paragraph 1</u>

    1. <u>At the request of the United States</u>, the Government
of the Republic of Korea waives in favor of the United States
the primary right granted to the Korean authorities under
sub-paragraph (b) of Paragraph 3 of this Article in cases of
concurrent jurisdiction, in accordance with Paragraphs 2, 3, 4,
5, 6, and 7 of this Minute.

<u>Revised Paragraph 4</u>

    4. If, pursuant to Paragraph 3 of this Minute, the competent
Korean authorities have recalled the waiver in a specific case
and in such case an understanding cannot be reached in discussions
between the authorities concerned, the Government of the United
States may make representations to the Government of the Republic
of Korea through diplomatic channels. The Government of the
Republic of Korea, giving due consideration to the interests of
Korean administration of justice and to the interests of the
Government of the United States, shall resolve the disagreement
in the exercise of its authority in the field of foreign affairs.
<u>The recall of waiver shall be final and conclusive unless the</u>
<u>statement for recall referred to in Paragraph 3</u> ~of this Minute~ <u>is withdrawn</u>
<u>by the Government of the Republic of Korea through consultation</u>
<u>between both Governments</u>.

<u>Paragraph 6</u>

    6. Trials of cases in which the authorities of the Republic
of Korea waive the primary right to exercise jurisdiction,
and trials of cases involving offenses described in paragraph
3(a)(ii)committed against the State or nationals of the Republic
of Korea <u>shall</u> be held <u>promptly in the Republic of Korea</u> within
a reasonable distance from the place where the offenses are alleged
to have taken place unless other arrangements are mutually agreed
upon. Representatives of the Republic of Korea may be present
at such trials. (U.S. draft proposed at the 67th meeting) 0012

Agreed Minute #1 Re Paragraph 3(a)(ii)

1. Where a member of the United States armed forces or civilian component is charged with an offense, a certificate issued by competent authorities of the United States armed forces stating that the alleged offense, if committed by him, arose out of an act or omission done in the performance of official duty shall be sufficient evidence of the fact for the purpose of determining primary jurisdiction.

In those exceptional cases where the chief prosecutor for the Republic of Korea considers that there is proof contrary to a certificate of official duty, it <u>shall</u> be made the subject of review through discussions between appropriate officials of the Government of the Republic of Korea and the diplomatic mission of the United States in the Republic of Korea.

Agreed Minute # 2 Re Paragraph 3(a)(ii)

2. The term "official duty" as used in Article ___ and the Agreed Minute is not meant to include all acts by members of the Armed Forces and the civilian component during periods when they are on duty, but is meant to apply only to acts which are required to be done as functions of those duties which the individuals are performing. Thus, a substantial departure from the acts a person is required to perform in a particular duty usually will indicate an act outside of his "official duty". (U.S. draft proposed at the 49th meeting)

0013

한·미국 간의 상호방위조약 제4조에 의한 시설과 구역 및 한국에서의 미국군대의 지위에 관한 협정(SOFA)
전59권. 1966.7.9 서울에서 서명 : 1967.2.9 발효(조약 232호) (V.30 실무교섭회의, 제77-80차, 1965.5월) 283

5. (a) The <u>military</u> authorities of the United States and the
authorities of the Republic of Korea shall assist each other in
the arrest of members of the United States armed forces, the
civilian component, or their dependents in the territory of the
Republic of Korea and in handing them over to the authority which
is to have custody in accordance with the following provisions.

(b) The authorities of the Republic of Korea shall notify
promptly the <u>military</u> authorities of the United States of the
arrest of any member of the United States armed forces, or
civilian component, or a dependent. The military authorities of
the United States shall promptly notify the authorities of the
Republic of Korea of the arrest of a member of the United States
armed forces, the civilian component, or a dependent in any
case in which the Republic of Korea has the primary right to
exercise jurisdiction.

(c) The custody of an accused member of the United States
armed forces or civilian component, or of a dependent, over whom
the Republic of Korea is to exercise jurisdiction shall, if he is
in the hands of <u>the military authorities of</u> the United States,
remain with <u>the military authorities of</u> the United States pending
the conclusion of all judicial proceedings and until custody is
requested by the authorities of the Republic of Korea. If he is
in the hands of the Republic of Korea, he shall, <u>on request</u>, be
handed over to the <u>military</u> authorities of the United States and
remain in their custody pending completion of all judicial
proceedings and until custody is requested by the authorities of
the Republic of Korea. When an accused has been in the custody
of the military authorities of the United States, <u>the military</u>
<u>authorities of the United States may transfer custody to the</u>
<u>authorities of the Republic of Korea at any time, and</u> shall give
sympathetic consideration to any request for the transfer of
custody which may be made by the authorities of the Republic of
Korea in specific cases. The <u>military authorities of the United</u>

0014

States shall promptly make any such accused available to the authorities of the Republic of Korea upon their request for purposes of investigation and trial, and shall take all appropriate measures to that end and to prevent any prejudice to the course of justice. They shall take full account of any special request regarding custody made by the authorities of the Republic of Korea. The authorities of the Republic of Korea shall give sympathetic consideration to a request from the military authorities of the United States for assistance in maintaining custody of an accused member of the United States armed forces, the civilian component, or a dependent.

(d) In respect of offenses solely against the security of the Republic of Korea provided in Paragraph 2(c), an accused shall be in the custody of the authorities of the Republic of Korea.

한·미국 간의 상호방위조약 제4조에 의한 시설과 구역 및 한국에서의 미국군대의 지위에 관한 협정(SOFA) 전59권. 1966.7.9 서울에서 서명 : 1967.2.9 발효(조약 232호) (V.30 실무교섭회의, 제77-80차, 1965.5월) 285

SOFA NEGOTIATION

Agenda for the 77th Session

15:00 May 6, 1965

1. Continuation of Discussions on:
   a. Criminal Jurisdiction Article
2. Other Business
3. Agenda and Date of the Next Meeting
4. Press Release

0016

Agreed Minute Re Paragraph 3(b)

Revised Paragraph 1

1. (At the request of the United States,) the Government of the Republic of Korea waives in favor of the
United States the primary right granted to the Korean
authorities under sub-paragraph (b) of Paragraph 3 of
this Article in cases of concurrent jurisdiction, in
accordance with Paragraphs 2,3,4,5,6 and 7 of this Minute.

Revised Paragraph 4

4. If, pursuant to Paragraph 3 of this Minute, the
competent Korean authorities have recalled the waiver
in a specific case and in such case an understanding
cannot be reached in discussions between the authorities
concerned, the Government of the United States may make
representations to the Government of the Republic of
Korea through diplomatic channels. The Government of
the Republic of Korea, giving due consideration to the
interests of Korean administration of justice and to
the interests of the Government of the United States,
shall resolve the disagreement in the exercise of its
authority in the field of foreign affairs. The recall
of waiver shall be final and conclusive unless the
statement for recall referred to in Paragraph 3 of this

- 1 -

0017

Minute is withdrawn by the Government of the Republic
of Korea through consultation between both Governments.

Paragraph 6

6. Trials of cases in which the authorities of
the Republic of Korea waive the primary right to
exercise jurisdiction, and trials of cases involving
offenses described in paragraph 3(a) (ii) committed
against the State or nationals of the Republic of Korea
shall be held promptly in the Republic of Korea within
a reasonable distance from the place where the offenses
are alleged to have taken place unless other arrangements are mutually agreed upon. Representatives of the
Republic of Korea may be present at such trials.
(U.S. draft proposed at the 67th meeting)

- 2 -

0018

<u>Agreed Minute Re Paragraph 3(b)</u>

<u>Revised Paragraph 1</u>

1. <u>At the request of the United States</u>, the Government of the Republic of Korea waives in favor of the United States the primary right granted to the Korean authorities under sub-paragraph (b) of Paragraph 3 of this Article in cases of concurrent jurisdiction, in accordance with Paragraphs 2,3,4,5,6 and 7 of this Minute.

<u>Revised Paragraph 4</u>

4. If, pursuant to Paragraph 3 of this Minute, the competent Korean authorities have recalled the waiver in a specific case and in such case an understanding cannot be reached in discussions between the authorities concerned, the Government of the United States may make representations to the Government of the Republic of Korea through diplomatic channels. The Government of the Republic of Korea, giving due consideration to the interests of Korean administration of justice, and to the interests of the Government of the United States, shall resolve the disagreement in the exercise of its authority in the field of foreign affairs. <u>The recall of waiver shall be final and conclusive unless the statement for recall referred to in Paragraph 3 of this</u>

- 1 -

0019

Minute is withdrawn by the Government of the Republic of Korea through consultation between both Governments.

Paragraph 6

6. Trials of cases in which the authorities of the Republic of Korea waive the primary right to exercise jurisdiction, and trials of cases involving offenses described in paragraph 3(a) (ii) committed against the State or nationals of the Republic of Korea shall be held promptly in the Republic of Korea within a reasonable distance from the place where the offenses are alleged to have taken place unless other arrangements are mutually agreed upon. Representatives of the Republic of Korea may be present at such trials.
(U.S. draft proposed at the 67th meeting)

- 2 -

0020

Agenda for the 79th Session

16:00 May 12, 1965

1. Continuation of Discussions on:
   o a. Labor Article
   o b. Claims Article
2. Other Business
3. Agenda and Date of the Next Meeting
4. Press Release

In case where Korean Government, in resolving disagreement in accordance with the fore-going provisions, determines to exercise its jurisdiction, such determination shall final and conclusive.

大韓民国 政府와 上記 規定에 따라 意見差異를 解決함에 있어서 同 政府가 裁判管轄権을 行使하기로 決定하는 경우에는, 이러한 決定은 最終的이며 또한 確定的이어야 한다.

0022

Agreed Minute Re Paragraph 3(b)

Revised Paragraph 1

    1. At the request of the United States, the Government of the Republic of Korea waives in favor of the United States the primary right granted to the Korean authorities under sub-paragraph (b) of Paragraph 3 of this Article in cases of concurrent jurisdiction, in accordance with Paragraphs 2,3,4,5,6 and 7 of this Minute.

Revised Paragraph 4

    4. If, pursuant to Paragraph 3 of this Minute, the competent Korean authorities have recalled the waiver in a specific case and in such case an understanding cannot be reached in discussions between the authorities concerned, the Government of the United States may make representations to the Government of the Republic of Korea through diplomatic channels. The Government of the Republic of Korea, giving due consideration to the interests of Korean administration of justice and to the interests of the Government of the United States, shall resolve the disagreement in the exercise of its authority in the field of foreign affairs. The recall of waiver shall be final and conclusive unless the statement for recall referred to in Paragraph 3 of this

- 1 -

0023

Minute is withdrawn by the Government of the Republic of Korea through consultation between both Governments.

<u>Paragraph 6</u>

6. Trials of cases in which the authorities of the Republic of Korea waive the primary right to exercise jurisdiction, and trials of cases involving offenses described in paragraph 3(a) (ii) committed against the State or nationals of the Republic of Korea <u>shall</u> be held <u>promptly in the Republic of Korea</u> within a reasonable distance from the place where the offenses are alleged to have taken place unless other arrangements are mutually agreed upon. Representatives of the Republic of Korea may be present at such trials. (U.S. draft proposed at the 67th meeting)

- 2 -

<u>Criminal Jurisdiction Article</u>

<u>ROK Positions for the 77th Session of the Status</u>
<u>of Forces Negotiations</u>

The Korean negotiators together with competent
authorities of the Korean Government have given very
careful consideration to the U.S. proposals regarding
waiver formula, official duty certificates, and pre-trial
custody. As the results of such deliberation, the Korean
negotiators with a view to reach an early agreement on
the most important article of SOFA, are about to make
the most significant concessions by meeting requirement
of U.S. side and accepting in principle but with minor
modifications those drafts tabled by the U.S. side at
the 74th session.

However, before going into any detailed presentation,
the Korean negotiators wish to seek clarification from
the United States side regarding the provisions of
Paragraph 4 of the proposed waiver formula:

"In case where the Korean Government, in resolving
disagreement in accordance with the provisions of
Paragraph 4 of the U.S. draft, determines to exercise
its jurisdiction, can the determination be final and
conclusive?"

. . . .

The Korean negotiators appreciate very much for the
explanation to the question. In the past negotiations,
the Korean negotiators have repeatedly stressed their
intention that with the waiver discretion provided for
in the original draft of the Korean side the Korean
authorities would <u>exercise at most restraint in</u> implementing
the waiver provision. In other words, the Korean negotiators have given to the U.S. negotiators the assurances
that the Korean authorities would waive in as many cases

0025

as other countries do under their very simple SOFA. However,
they have firmly held their position that they would waive
except where they determine that it is of particular
importance that the jurisdiction be exercised by the
authorities of the Republic of Korea, whereas the U.S.
side held their position that the primary right to exercise
jurisdiction should be waived to the U.S. authorities with
the right of recall of waiver on Korean side.

With the/answer from/U.S. side to our question, just
raised, the Korean negotiators are now prepared to accept
the waiver formula, proposed by the U.S. side at the 74th
session. However, this concession by the Korean side is
made on condition that the U.S. negotiators would accept
the following modifications which the Korean negotiators
felt most essential:

(1) The Korean negotiators, noting again the affirmative
answer to the question with regard to the provisions of
Paragraph 4 of the Agreed Minute, and believing that the
U.S. negotiators would accept our minor condition, wish
to propose the following additional sentence to be
incorporated into the provisions of the Paragraph 4 as
the last sentence:

"The recall of waiver shall be final and conclusive
unless the statement for recall referred to in
Paragraph 3 of this Minute is withdrawn by the
Government of the Republic of Korea through consultation between both Governments."

The Korean negotiators firmly believe the above
assurances are absolutely necessary not only for the
Government to obtain understanding of the National
Assembly as well as of the people of the

0026

Republic of Korea but also for mutually satisfactory
implementation of the Waiver formula.

(2) With regard to the provisions of paragraph 1
of Agreed Minute Re Paragraph 3 (b), believing that the
waiver of primary right should be made following the
request of the United States, the Korean negotiators
propose the following phrase "At the request of the
United States" be placed at the start of the provisions
of Paragraph 1 of the Agreed Minute.

⟹(3) With regard to the provisions of Paragraph 6,
it is recalled that the U.S. negotiators had stated
at the 67th session that the second paragraph of the tabled
U.S. Agreed Minute was a new addition to the U.S. draft
and the provision was added in order to incorporate the
position set forth in the third paragraph of the Agreed
Minute Re Paragraph 3(c) of the Korean draft. They
had further stated that they viewed these provisions as
desirable and are pleased to be able to accede to the
wishes of the Government of the Republic of Korea by
incorporating them in the U.S. draft, naturally, the
Korean negotiators are completely at a loss to understand
the reasons why the U.S. negotiators, after reaching
agreement verbatim, substituted the of Paragraph 6 for
the provisions proposed by the U.S. side at the 67th
session and reaffirmed by the Korean negotiators at the
70th session. Accordingly, the Korean negotiators, in
the light of the trends of the past negotiations, maintain
that the following portion of the previous draft be
incorporated into the U.S. draft as the provisions of
Paragraph 6 in place of the present provisions of Paragraph 6:

0027

"Trials of cases in which the authorities of the Republic of Korea waive the primary right to exercise jurisdiction, and trials of cases involving offenses described in Paragraph 3(a)(ii) committed against the state or nationals of the Republic of Korea shall be held promptly in the Republic of Korea within a reasonable distance from the place where the offenses are alleged to have taken place unless other arrangements are mutually agreed upon. Representatives of the Republic of Korea may be present at such trials."

Any other detailed arrangements in addition to the above provisions should be left to the deliberation by the Joint Committee.

0028

2. Official Duty Certificate

Regarding official duty certificate, the Korean negotiators are now prepared to accept the U.S. proposals with the following minor conditions:

(1) With regard to the issuing authorities of the certificate, the Korean negotiators accept the phrase of the U.S. draft "competent authorities of the United States armed forces," provided that the U.S. side aceept the incorporation of additional sentences into the U.S. understanding the following understandings for the Joint Summary Record.

"A duty certificate shall be issued only upon the advice of a Staff Judge Advocate, and the competent authority issuing a duty certificate shall be a General grade officer."

(2) The Korean negotiators also accept the wording "the Chief Prosecutor for the Republic of Korea" as the Korean authority raising any objection if he considers that there is proof contrary to a certificate of official duty.

(3) With regard to the definition of official du ty, the Korean negotiators are ready to accept the definition of official duty proposed by the U.S. side at the 49th meeting verbatim. However, they still believe the definition should be placed as Agreed Minute so that the agreed and authentic definition be fully understood by all concerned, and serve as a guide line for those authorities concerned in determing whether or not an offense was committed in the performance of official duty.

(4) The Korean negotiators believe that if the Chief Prosecutor of the Republic of Korea raises any objection, it should be made obligatory for the authorities of both countries to review the matter.

0029

Accordingly, the Korean negotiators propose the substitution of the word "shall" for the word "may" in the last sentence of Agreed Minute Re Paragraph 3(a)(ii) of the U.S. draft.

(5) As regards the proposed U.S. understanding regarding validity of a duty certificate, the intention of the negotiators of both sides is in essential agreement, thus hinging on how to incorporate the Korean requirements into the U.S. understanding. On this regards, the Korean negotiators still believe that the Korean proposal is preferable to that of the U.S. side, since the Korean language is distinct and self-explanatory:

"The certificate will be conclusive unless modification is agreed upon. The United States authorities shall give due consideration to any objection which may be raised by the Chief Prosecutor for the Republic of Korea."

0030

3. Pre-trial Custody

With respect to the provisions of pre-trial custody, although there still exist substantial differences between the two drafts, the Korean negotiators, with a view to expediting the negotiations and to be responsive to the U.S. requirements, are now prepared to accept the U.S. draft. However, in order to be consistent with basic needs of the Korean negotiators, we propose that the following minor modifications be incorporated into the proposed U.S. draft:

(1) The words "the authorities of the United States" should read "the military authorities of the United States" pending final agreement on the problems of the authorities of both sides referred to in the provisions of Paragraph 1 of the text.

(2) It has been the firm position of the Korean negotiators that an accused, if he is in the hands of the authorities of the Republic of Korea, will be handed over to the military authorities, if the military authorities of the United States request, and unless there are adequate cause and necessity to retain him. Nevertheless, to expedite the negotiations, the Korean negotiators are prepared to make one of the major concessions, and accept the U.S. draft provided that the U.S. authorities take full account of any special request for transfer of custody which may be made by the Korean authorities. It is requested that the words "on request" the included between the words "shall" and "be", and the wording "They shall take full account of any special request regarding custody made by the authorities of the Republic of Korea" is incorporated into the proposed U.S. draft, and that the U.S. military authorities exert their best efforts to maintain custody and to prevent any prejudice against

0031

the course of criminal proceedings, such as destroying valuable evidences, or escape from confinement. It is also self-explanatory that the U.S. negotiators may, if and whenever they so desire, transfer the custody of an accused to the Korean authorities.

(3) As regards the custody of an accused in the hands of Korean authorities relating to security offenses, the Korean negotiators, ~~in view of our brotherly relations existing between the two countries and of common efforts~~ for mutual defense, accept the two proposed U.S. understandings for the Joint Summary Record:

(a) There must be mutual ROK-U.S. agreement as to the circumstances in which such custody is appropriate;

(b) Korean confinement facilities must be adequate by U.S. standards.

As stated at the outset, to meet the requirements of the U.S. side and at the same time to be consistent with the minimum needs of the Korean Government, the Korean negotiators are accepting the U.S. proposals with minor modifications which we hope U.S. negotiation will accept. Moreover, the Korean negotiators, believing that any further delay of conclusion of the negotiations would be neither for the interests of the Korean side nor for those of the U.S. side as well, request the U.S. negotiators to take into full account the positions outlined by the Korean negotiators and accept them, thus paving the way for an early conclusion of the negotiations.

0032

<u>Criminal Jurisdiction Article</u>

<u>ROK Positions for the 77th Session of the Status
of Forces Negotiations</u>

The Korean negotiators together with competent
authorities of the Korean Government have given very
careful consideration to the U.S. proposals regarding
waiver formula, official duty certificates, and pre-trial
custody. As the results of such deliberation, the Korean
negotiators with a view to reach an early agreement on
the most important article of SOFA, are about to make
the most significant concessions by meeting requirement
of U.S. side and accepting in principle but with minor
modifications those drafts tabled by the U.S. side at
the 74th session.

However, before going into any detailed presentation,
the Korean negotiators wish to seek clarification from
the United States side regarding the provisions of
Paragraph 4 of the proposed waiver formula:

"In case where the Korean Government, in resolving
disagreement in accordance with the provisions of
Paragraph 4 of the U.S. draft, determines to exercise
its jurisdiction, can the determination be final and
conclusive?"

. . . .

The Korean negotiators appreciate very much for the
explanation to the question. In the past negotiations,
the Korean negotiators have repeatedly stressed their
intention that with the waiver discretion provided for
in the original draft of the Korean side the Korean
authorities would exercise at most restraint in implementing
the waiver provision. In other words, the Korean negotiators have given to the U.S. negotiators the assurances
that the Korean authorities would waive in as many cases

0033

as other countries do under their very simple SOFA. However, they have firmly held their position that they would waive except where they determine that it is of particular importance that the jurisdiction be exercised by the authorities of the Republic of Korea, whereas the U.S. side held their position that the primary right to exercise jurisdiction should be waived to the U.S. authorities with the right of recall of waiver on Korean side.

With the/answer from/U.S. side to our question, just raised, the Korean negotiators are now prepared to accept the waiver formula, proposed by the U.S. side at the 74th session. However, this concession by the Korean side is made on condition that the U.S. negotiators would accept the following modifications which the Korean negotiators felt most essential:

(1) The Korean negotiators, noting again the affirmative answer to the question with regard to the provisions of Paragraph 4 of the Agreed Minute, and believing that the U.S. negotiators would accept our minor condition, wish to propose the following additional sentence to be incorporated into the provisions of the Paragraph 4 as the last sentence:

"The recall of waiver shall be final and conclusive unless the statement for recall referred to in Paragraph 3 of this Minute is withdrawn by the Government of the Republic of Korea through consultation between both Governments."

The Korean negotiators firmly believe the above assurances are absolutely necessary not only for the Government to obtain understanding of the National Assembly as well as of the people of the

0034

Republic of Korea but also for mutually satisfactory
implementation of the Waiver formula.

(2) With regard to the provisions of paragraph 1
of Agreed Minute Re Paragraph 3 (b), believing that the
waiver of primary right should be made following the
request of the United States, the Korean negotiators
propose the following phrase "At the request of the
United States" be placed at the start of the provisions
of Paragraph 1 of the Agreed Minute.

(3) With regard to the provisions of Paragraph 6,
it is recalled that the U.S. negotiators had stated
at the 67th session that the second paragraph of the tabled
U.S. Agreed Minute was a new addition to the U.S. draft
and the provision was added in order to incorporate the
position set forth in the third paragraph of the Agreed
Minute Re Paragraph 3(c) of the Korean draft. They
had further stated that they viewed these provisions as
desirable and are pleased to be able to accede to the
wishes of the Government of the Republic of Korea by
incorporating them in the U.S. draft, naturally, the
Korean negotiators are completely at a loss to understand
the reasons why the U.S. negotiators, after reaching
agreement verbatim, substituted the Paragraph 6 for
the provisions proposed by the U.S. side at the 67th
session and reaffirmed by the Korean negotiators at the
70th session. Accordingly, the Korean negotiators, in
the light of the trends of the negotiations, maintain
that the following portion of the previous draft be
incorporated into the U.S. draft as the provisions of
Paragraph 6 in place of the present provisions of Paragraph 6:

0035

2. **Official Duty Certificate**

Regarding official duty certificate, the Korean negotiators are now prepared to accept the U.S. proposals with the following minor conditions:

(1) With regard to the issuing authorities of the certificate, the Korean negotiators accept the phrase of the U.S. draft "competent authorities of the United States armed forces," provided that the U.S. side accept the incorporation of additional sentences into the U.S. understanding the following understandings for the Joint Summary Record.

"A duty certificate shall be issued only upon the advice of a Staff Judge Advocate, <u>and the competent authority issuing a duty certificate shall be a General grade officer.</u>"

(2) The Korean negotiators also accept the wording "the Chief Prosecutor for the Republic of Korea" as the Korean authority raising any objection if he considers that there is proof contrary to a certificate of official duty.

(3) With regard to the definition of official duty, the Korean negotiators are ready to accept the definition of official duty proposed by the U.S. side at the 49th meeting verbatim. However, they still believe the definition should be placed as Agreed Minute so that the agreed and authentic definition be fully understood by all concerned, and serve as a guide line for those authorities concerned in determing whether or not an offense was committed in the performance of official duty.

(4) The Korean negotiators believe that if the Chief Prosecutor of the Republic of Korea raises any objection, it should be made obligatory for the authorities of both countries to review the matter.

0037

Accordingly, the Korean negotiators propose the substitution of the word "shall" for the word "may" in the last sentence of Agreed Minute Re Paragraph 3(a)(ii) of the U.S. draft.

(5) As regards the proposed U.S. understanding regarding validity of a duty certificate, the intention of the negotiators of both sides is in essential agreement, thus hinging on how to incorporate the Korean requirements into the U.S. understanding. On this regards, the Korean negotiators still believe that the Korean proposal is preferable to that of the U.S. side, since the Korean language is distinct and self-explanatory:

> "The certificate will be conclusive unless modification is agreed upon. The United States authorities shall give due consideration to any objection which may be raised by the Chief Prosecutor for the Republic of Korea."

한·미국 간의 상호방위조약 제4조에 의한 시설과 구역 및 한국에서의 미국군대의 지위에 관한 협정(SOFA)
전59권. 1966.7.9 서울에서 서명 : 1967.2.9 발효(조약 232호) (V.30 실무교섭회의, 제77-80차, 1965.5월) 307

"Trials of cases in which the authorities of the Republic of Korea waive the primary right to exercise jurisdiction, and trials of cases involving offenses described in Paragraph 3(a)(ii) committed against the state or nationals of the Republic of Korea shall be held promptly in the Republic of Korea within a reasonable distance from the place where the offenses are alleged to have taken place unless other arrangements are mutually agreed upon. Representatives of the Republic of Korea may be present at such trials."

Any other detailed arrangements in addition to the above provisions should be left to the deliberation by the Joint Committee.

0036

3. Pre-trial Custody

With respect to the provisions of pre-trial custody, although there still exist substantial differences between the two drafts, the Korean negotiators with a view to expediting the negotiations and to be responsive to the U.S. requirements, are now prepared to accept the U.S. draft. However, in order to be consistent with basic needs of the Korean negotiators, we propose that the following minor modifications be incorporated into the proposed U.S. draft:

(1) The words "the authorities of the United States" should read "the military authorities of the United States" pending final agreement on the problems of the authorities of both sides referred to in the provisions of Paragraph 1 of the text.

(2) It has been the firm position of the Korean negotiators that an accused, if he is in the hands of the authorities of the Republic of Korea, will be handed over to the military authorities, if the military authorities of the United States request, and unless there are adequate cause and necessity to retain him. Nevertheless, in order to reach prompt and final agreement, the Korean negotiators are prepared to make one of the major concessions, and accept the U.S. draft provided that the U.S. authorities take full account of any special request for transfer of custody which may be made by the Korean authorities. It is requested that the words "on request" the included between the words "shall" and "be", and the wording "They shall take full account of any special request regarding custody made by the authorities of the Republic of Korea" is incorporated into the proposed U.S. draft, and that the U.S. military authorities exert their best efforts to maintain custody and to prevent any prejudice against

0039

the course of criminal proceedings, such as destroying valuable evidences, or escape from confinement. It is also self-explanatory that the U.S. negotiators may, if and whenever they so desire, transfer the custody of an accused to the Korean authorities.

(3) As regards the custody of an accused in the hands of Korean authorities relating to security offenses, the Korean negotiators, ~~in view of our brotherly relations existing between the two countries and of common efforts for mutual defense~~, accept the two proposed U.S. understandings for the Joint Summary Record:

    (a) There must be mutual ROK-U.S. agreement as to the circumstances in which such custody is appropriate;

    (b) Korean confinement facilities must be adequate by U.S. standards.

As stated at the outset, to meet the requirements of the U.S. side and at the same time to be consistent with the minimum needs of the Korean Government, the Korean negotiators are accepting the U.S. proposals with minor modifications which we hope U.S. negotiation will accept. Moreover, the Korean negotiators, believing that any further delay of conclusion of the negotiations would be neither for the interests of the Korean side nor for those of the U.S. side as well, request the U.S. negotiators to take into full account the positions outlined by the Korean negotiators and accept them, thus paving the way for an early conclusion of the negotiations.

1.　　Regarding Paragraph 1 of the U.S. draft, the Korean negotiators had proposed at the 77th session the inclusion of the phrase "at the request of the United States" as one of our condition for acceptance of waiver formula which the U.S. side tabled at the 74th session, because they believe that request for waiver should be made in each cases but not at the time of entry into force for waiver en masse. This modification was made to meet the requirements of the United States side, and at the same time to be consistent with out basic requirements. The Korean negotiators believe this modification is absolutely necessary as a sovereign state hosting U.S. armed forces, and, as the Korean negotiators had already reiterated at the previous session, to obtain understanding of the National Assembly as well as the Korean people.

　　We request the U.S. negotiators to take into full consideration the basic requirements of the Korean Government.

2.　　As regards the additional sentence to the provisions of Paragraph 4, the Korean negotiators, believing that final settlement of disagreement between the two sides should not be delayed indefinitely, propose the following amendment to the Korean proposal so that the proposal should read:

　　"The recall of waiver shall be final and conclusive unless the statement for recall referred to in Paragraph 3 of this Minute is withdrawn by the Government of Republic of Korea <u>within a period of Twenty-one days after such statement for recall is made.</u>"

in place of the phrase "through consultation between both Governments."

recall "within a period of Twenty-one days after such statement for

This is proposed with the view to wipe off any ambiguity which may arise between the two sides.

한·미국 간의 상호방위조약 제4조에 의한 시설과 구역 및 한국에서의 미국군대의 지위에 관한 협정(SOFA)
전59권. 1966.7.9 서울에서 서명 : 1967.2.9 발효(조약 232호) (V.30 실무교섭회의, 제77-80차, 1965.5월)　311

1. Regarding Paragraph 1 of the U.S. draft, the Korean negotiators had proposed at the 77th session the inclusion of the phrase "at the request of the United States" as one of our condition for acceptance of waiver formula which the U.S. side tabled at the 74th session, because they believe that request for waiver should be made in each cases but not at the time of entry into force for waiver en masse. This modification was made to meet the requirements of the United States side, and at the same time to be consistent with out basic requirements. The Korean negotiators believe this modification is absolutely necessary as a sovereign state hosting U.S. armed forces, and, as the Korean negotiators had already reiterated at the previous session, to obtain understanding of the National Assembly as well as the Korean people.

We request the U.S. negotiators to take into full consideration the basic requirements of the Korean Government.

2. As regards the additional sentence to the provisions of Paragraph 4, the Korean negotiators, believing that final settlement of disagreement between the two sides should not be delayed indefinitely, propose the following amendment to the Korean proposal so that the proposal should read:

"The recall of waiver shall be final and conclusive unless the statement for recall referred to in Paragraph 3 of this Minute is withdrawn by the Government of Republic of Korea within a period of Twenty-one days after such statement for recall is made."

0042

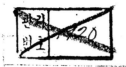

기 안 지

기 안 자	미주과 이근팔	전 화 번 호		공 보	필 요	불필요
	과장	국장	차관	장관		
협 조 자 서 명					보 존 년 한	
기 안 년 월 일	1965. 5. 10	시 행 년월일		통제관	정 서	기 장
분 류 기 호 문 서 번 호	외구미 722.2 —			5.10		
경 유 수 신 참 조	대통령 참조: 비서실장 국무총리 참조: 비서실장 사본: 법무부장관 참조:검찰국장		발신		장	관
제 목	제 77 차 주둔군지위협정 체결 교섭실무자회의 결과 보고					

1965년 5월 6일 하오 3시부터 동 4시 30분까지

외무부 제 1 회의실에서 개최된 제 77 차 주둔군지위협정 체결

교섭실무자회의 에서 토의된 형사재판관할권에 관한 내용을

별첨과 같이 보고합니다.

유 첨: 제 77 차 주둔군지위협정 체결 교섭실무자회의 결과

보고서 1부. 끝.

1965. 5. 10

한·미국 간의 상호방위조약 제4조에 의한 시설과 구역 및 한국에서의 미국군대의 지위에 관한 협정(SOFA)　313
전59권. 1966.7.9 서울에서 서명 : 1967.2.9 발효(조약 232호) (V.30 실무교섭회의, 제77-80차, 1965.5월)

기 안 지

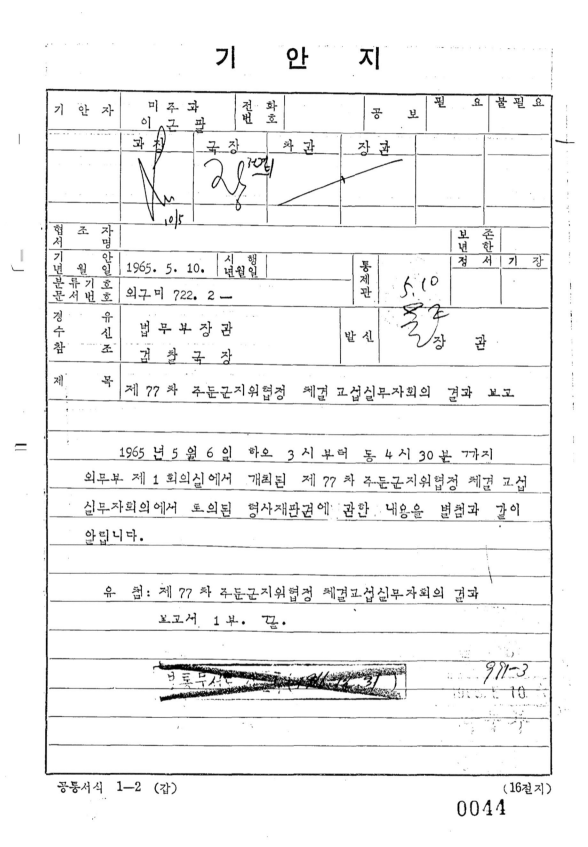

기 안 자	미주과 이 근 팔	전 화 번 호		공 보	필 요	불필요
	과 장	국 장	차 관	장 관		

협 조 자 서 명			보 존 년 한	
기 안 년 월 일	1965. 5. 10.	시 행 년월일	통 제 관	정 서 기 장
분 류 기 호 문 서 번 호	의구미 722. 2 —			
경 유 수 신 참 조	법무부장관 검찰국장		발신	장 관

제 목 | 제 77 차 주둔군지위협정 체결 교섭실무자회의 결과 보고

1965 년 5 월 6 일 하오 3 시부터 동 4 시 30 분 까지

외무부 제 1 회의실에서 개최된 제 77 차 주둔군지위협정 체결 교섭

실무자회의에서 토의된 형사재판권에 관한 내용을 별첨과 같이

알립니다.

유 첩: 제 77 차 주둔군지위협정 체결교섭실무자회의 결과

보고서 1부. 끝.

제 77 차
한·미간 주둔군지위협정 체결 교섭실무자회의
보 고 서

1. 일 시: 1965 년 5 월 6 일 하오 3 시 부터 동 4 시 30 분 까지.

2. 장 소: 외무부 제 1 회의실

3. 토의사항:

헝사재판관할권

I. 우리측은 미측이 제 74 차 교섭실무자회의 시 제 1 차관할권의 포기,
공무집행중 범죄, 및 피의자의 재판전 신병구금등 문제에 관하여 제안한
수정안에 대하여 관게부처와 더불어 검토한바에 따라 우리측 입장을
다음과 같이 제시하였다:

가. 제 1 차 관할권의 포기

미측이 독·일보충협정의 포기조항의 내용에 따라 제안한 수정안에
관하여 우리측은 미측 제안이 우리측 입장과는 상당한 거리가
있지만 미측 입장을 참작함과 아울러 현안인 협정을 조속한 시일내에
체결하기 위하여 다음과 같은 몇 가지 수정안을 미측이 수락하는 것을
조건으로 미측 제안을 원칙적으로 수락한다는 우리측 입장을 밝혔다:

(1) 우리측은 "대한민국정부가 포기를 철회하였을 때 미국당국과
의견차이를 해결함에 있어서 대한민국이 관할권을 행사하기로
결정하는 경우 그 결정은 최종적이며 또한 확정적일수 있는가"
라고 질문하여 이에 대한 미측의 긍정적인 답변을 받은 다음
국회와 국민의 이해를 획득하기 위하여서 뿐 만 아니라 관할권의
포기조항의 상호 만족할 만한 운영을 위하여서도 한국정부가
내리는 결정이 최종적이며 확정적이어야함을 강조하고 다음과
같은 규정을 미측 제안 제 4 항 말미에 삽입할 것을 제안하였다:
        "포기의 철회는 양국정부간의 협의를 통하여 철회를 위한
통고가 대한민국정부에 의하여 취소되지 않는 한 확정적이며
최종적이어야 한다"

(2) 한국당국에 부여된 제 1 차관할권의 포기를 규정한 미측 제안
제 1항은 원칙적으로 수락하되 관할권의 포기는 미측주장대로
자동적이며 전면적으로 일시에 할 것이 아니라 개개특정사건 마다

5월 1   0045

65-5-11 (4)   미국·문 112-2 (나)

0046

미측이 요청하면 포기하는 것으로 하기 위하여 "미국이 요청하면" 이라는 문구를 동규정 서두에 삽입할 것을 제안하였다.

(3) 또한 재판의 장소와 한국대표의 참석에 관한 미측제안 제6항은 미측의 재량권의 여지가 광범위하기 때문에 이를 제한하기 위하여 미측이 제 67 차회의 때에 우리측 포기조항 중 재판의 장소와 한국대표의 참석에 관한 초안부분을 "타당한 것으로 인정하고" 수락한바 있음을 지적하고 이미 측조적으로 합의되었던 다음과 같은 규정을 미측 수정안 제 6 항의 규정에 대체할 것을 주장하고 기타 상세한 것은 합동위원회에서 상호 합의하여 처리할 수 있음을 강조하였다.

"대한민국이 관할권을 행사할 제 1 차적권리를 포기하는 사건의 재판과 제 3 (a)(ii)항에 규정된 범죄(공무집행중 범죄)로서 대한민국 또는 대한민국국민에 대하여 범하여진 범죄에 관련된 사건에 대한 재판은 별도의 약정이 상호 합의되지 않는 한 범죄가 행하여진 것으로 인정되는 장소로 부터 적당한 거리 내에서 즉시 행하여져야 한다. 대한민국의 대표는 그러한 재판에 참석할 수 있다."

나. 공무집행중 범죄

공무집행중 범죄에 관하여서는 한.미간 입장이 거의 합의에 도달한 바 우리측은 미측 제안을 수락하는 대신 다음과 같은 조건을 미측이 수락할 것을 촉구하였다.

(1) 공무집행중명서의 발행권자에 관하여 미측 주장대로 "미국군대의 권한있는 당국"으로 하되 다음과 같은 양해사항을 제안하였다:

"공무집행중명서는 반듯이 미군법무관의 의견을 들은 후에 발행되어야 하며 미군당국의 증명서 발행기관은 장성급으로 하여야 한다."

(2) 반증이 있다고 사려하는 예외적인 경우에 이의를 제기할 수 있는 한국기관은 미측주장 대로 "대한민국검찰총장"으로 하되 그러한 때에 공무집행중명서는 "반듯이" 대한민국당국과 주한미국외교사절간의 협의를 통한 재심의 대상이 "되어야"한다는 우리 입장을 계속 주장하였다.

4 의 2

0047

65 - 5 - 11   어문 112-2

0048

(3) 공무의 정의는 미측 주장을 참작하여 다음과 같은 1956 년도의 미국동군의 정의를 수락하되 실지 운영상의 지침이 되기 위하여 합의의사록에 규정함이 타당함을 주장하였다.

"공무타함은 미군대구성원 및 군속이 공무중 행한 모든 행위를 포함하는 것을 의미하는 것이 아니며 개인이 집행하는 공무의 기능으로서 행하여 질 것이 요구되는 행위에 만 적용되는 것을 의미한다. 그러므로 어떤 자가 특정공무에 있어서 행할 것이 요구되는 행위로 부터 실질적으로 이탈한 행위는 통상 공무 밖 의 행위이다."

(4) 우리는 공무집행증명서의 효력에 관한 미측 양해사항을 수락하는 대신 우리측 양해사항을 미측제안에 추가 삽입하여 다음과 같이 규정할 것을 주장하였다.

"미군당국이 발행한 공무집행증명서는 수정에 합의되지 않는 한 확정적이다. 그러나 미국당국은 대한민국이 제기하는 이의에 대하여 정당한 고력를 하여야 한다."

다. 피의자의 재판전 신병 구급

미측이 제 74 차 회의에서 제안한 피의자의 재판전 신병구급에 관한 수정안은 다음과 같이 입부 수정할 것을 조건으로 수락하였다.

(1) 피의자의 신병이 한국당국 수중에 있을 때에는 미군당국이 "요청하면" 미군당국에 인도한다.

(2) 피의자의 신병이 미군당국의 수중에 있을 때에는 "미군당국은 언제먼지 신병을 대한민국당국에 인도 할 수 있는 것"으로 한다.

(3) 미군당국은 대한민국이 요청하면 "즉시" 대한민국당국이 피의자에 대한 수사 또는 재판을 할 수 있게 하여야 하며 "이러한 목적과 사법절차진행에 대한 장해를 제거하기 위하여 제반 적절한 조치를 취하여야 한다."

(4) 미측이 주장하는 다음과 같은 두개의 양해사항은 이를 수락하였다.

(가) 대한민국의 안전에 관한 피의자의 신병구급에 관하여 한국당국의 구급사정의 적당여부에 관하여 한.미양국간의 상호 합의가 있어야 한다.

0049

4 의 3

0050

(나) "한국의 구급시설은 미국수준으로 보아 적당하여야 한다."

II. 미측은 우리측 제안설명에 대하여 공무집행중 범죄 및 피의자의 신병 구금문제에 관한 양측 입장이 합의에 가까와졌음을 시인하고나서 관할권의 포기에 관한 우리측 수정안에 대하여 다음과 같이 미측 입장을 밝혔다.

    (1) 독일보충협정중 포기조항의 형태와 같은 미측 초안은 한국당국이
        그에게 부여된 제1차 관할권을 협정 발효와 동시에 포괄적으로
        미국당국에 포기할 것을 요구하는 것이며 따라서 개개 사건이
        발생할 때 마다 미국이 포기를 요청할 것을 요구하고 이에 따라
        관할권을 포기할 것이라는 한국측 입장은 미측 제안 취지와 상반
        되는 것으로 도저히 수락할 수 없다.

    (2) "포기의 철회는 양국정부간의 협의를 통하여 철회를 위한 통고가
        대한민국정부에 의하여 취소되지 않는 한 확정적이며 최종적이어야
        한다"는 한국측 제안에 대하여서는 본국정부의 훈령을 기다려
        답변할 것이라고 말하였다.

    (3) 또한 미측은 재판의 장소와 대한민국정부대표의 참석에 관한
        한국측 제안에 대하여 미국은 그러한 재판은 원칙적으로 한국내
        에서 행할 것이지만 미국의 안전에 관한 피의자에 대한 재판으로서
        미국법률이 그와 달리 요구할 때, 또는 군사상의 필요성 기타
        관계 증인이 전부 귀국하여 사실상 재판이 불가능할 때와 같은
        사법상의 이유가 있을 때에는 피의자를 미본국으로 이송하여
        재판할 수 있는 길이 마련되어야 한다고 미측입장을 말하였다.

4. 기타 사항:

가. 차기 회의 일자: 1965 년 5 월 7 일 하오 4시 부터.   끝

4 의 4

0051

65-5-25

45-5-11(4)

대중은 112-2(4)

0052

STATUS OF FORCES NEGOTIATIONS: 77th Meeting

SUBJECT: Criminal Jurisdiction Article

PLACE: Ministry of Foreign Affairs

DATE: May 6, 1965

PARTICIPANTS:

Republic of Korea	United States
CHANG Sang-mun	Philip C. Habib
YUN Wun-yong	Brig. General Carroll H. Dunn, USA
YI Nam-ki	Colonel Allan G. Pixton, USA
Major YI Ke-hun, ROKA	Captain George Hagerman, USN
KIM Ki-cho	Colonel Kenneth C. Crawford, USA
HWANG Yong-chae	Benjamin A. Fleck
PAK Won-chol	Robert A. Kinney
YI Kun-pal (Interpreter)	Frank R. LaMacchia
	Goodwin Shapiro
KIM Tong-hui	Major Alton Harvey, USA
HO Sung-chun	David Y.C. Lee (Interpeeter)

0053

1. Mr. Chang opened the meeting by stating that the Korean negotiators, together with competent authorities of the Korean Government, had given very careful consideration to the U.S. proposals regarding the waiver formula, duty certificates, and pre-trial custody. As the result of ~~this~~ this deliberation, the Korean negotiators, with a view to reaching early agreement on this, the most important article in the SOFA, were about to make most significant concessions by meeting the requirement of the U.S. and accepting in principle, with minor modifications, the drafts tabled by the U.S. negotiators at the 74th negotiating session.

2. However, Mr. Chang continued, before giving a detailed presentation of /their\ ~~the~~ views, ~~of~~ the Korean negotiators wished to seek clarification by the U.S. negotiators regarding the provisions of Paragraph 4 of the Agreed Minute Re Paragraph 3(b) tabled by the U.S. negotiators. In case the Korean Government, in resolving disagreement in accordance with the provisions of Paragraph 4, determines to exercise its jurisdiction, can the determination be final and conclusive?

3. Mr. Habib replied that the answer to Mr. Chang's question was yes. However, in presenting this draft, the U.S. negotiators had taken into account repeated statements by the Korean negotiators that due restraint would be observed by the Korean authorities in (exercising their jurisdiction under their waiver clause when they considered ~~recalling the waiver when the interests of Korean justice made imperative~~ that it was of particular importance that jurisdiction be exercised by the Korean ~~the exercise of Korean jurisdiction.~~ authorities.

4. Mr. Chang expressed appreciation for Mr. Habib's reply. During the course of the negotiations, he said, the Korean negotiators had repeatedly stressed that under the terms of waiver discretion provided for in the original draft tabled by them, the Korean authorities would exercise utmost restraint in implementing the waiver provision. In other words, the Korean negotiators had given assurances that the Korean authorities would waive in as many cases as other countries do under their very simple status of forces agreements. However, the Korean negotiators had firmly held their position that the Korean authorities would waive ~~except~~ when ~~they~~ determined that it is of particular

0054

importance that jurisdiction be exercised by the authorities of the Republic of Korea, whereas the U.S. negotiators had held the position that the primary right to exercise jurisdiction should be waived to the U.S. authorities, with the right of recall retained by the Korean authorities.

5. Having received the affirmative answer which the U.S. negotiators had just given to the Korean negotiators' question, Mr. Chang said, the Korean negotiators were now prepared to accept the waiver formula proposed by the U.S. side at the 74th meeting. However, this concession by the Korean negotiators was made on condition that the U.S. negotiators accept the following modifications which were felt to be most essential by the Korean negotiators.

6. Noting again the affimative answer of the U.S. negotiators with regard to the provisions of Paragraph 4 of the Agreed Minute Re Paragraph 3(b), and believing that the following minor modification would be acceptable to the U.S. negotiators, the Korean negotiators proposed the addition of the following sentence to Paragraph 4:

> "The recall of waiver shall be final and conclusive unless the statement for recall referred to in Paragraph 3 of this Minute is withdrawn by the Government of the Republic of Korea through consultation between both Governments."

Mr. Chang said the Korean negotiators firmly believe the above sentence to be absolutely necessary not only to enable the ROK Government to obtain the understanding of the National Assembly and the Korean people but also for mutually satisfactory implementation of the waiver formula.

7. Mr. Chang referred to Paragraph 1 of the Agreed Minute Re Paragraph 3(b) and said that the Korean negotiators believe that the waiver of the primary right of jurisdiction should be made following a request by the United States. Therefore, the Korean negotiators proposed the insertion at the beginning of the paragraph of the phrase "At the request of the United States,".

8. Mr. Habib asked for clarification of this proposal. Did the phrase

0055

refer to a one-time request for a blanket waiver or were the Korean negotiators proposing that the United States authorities request waiver in each individual
case? Mr. Chang replied that the Korean proposal was that the United States authorities make a separate request for waiver in each case.

   9. Resuming his discussion of the drafts tabled by the U.S. negotiators
at the 74th meeting, Mr. Chang turned to Paragraph 6 of the Agreed Minute Re Paragraph
3(b). He recalled that at the 67th meeting the U.S. negotiators had tabled a revision
of what was then their Agreed Minute Re Paragraph 3. They had stated that the second
paragraph of that revision was a new paragraph incorporated into the U.S. draft
in order to include the position set forth in the third paragraph of the Agreed Minute
Re Paragraph 3 of the Korean draft. They had further stated that they viewed these
provisions as desirable and were pleased to be able to accede to the wishes of the
KOK Government by incorporating them into the U.S. draft. Mr. Chang said that the
Korean negotiators were completely at a loss to understand the reasons why the
U.S. negotiators, after agreeing to the Korean language at the 67th meeting, had
now substituted a new Paragraph 6 in place of that language. Accordingly, the Korean
negotiators, in the light of the trend of the past negotiations, proposed that in
place of the Paragraph 6 contained in the U.S. draft, the following portion of the
previous draft be adopted as Paragraph 6:

> "Trials of cases in which the authorities of the
> Republic of Korea waive the primary right to exercise juris-
> diction, and trials of cases involving offenses described in
> Paragraph 3(a)(ii) committed against the state or nationals
> of the Republic of Korea shall be held promptly in the Repub-
> lic of Korea within a reasonable distance from the place
> where the offenses are alleged to have taken place unless
> other arrangements are mutually agreed upon. Representatives
> of the Republic of Korea may be present at such trials.

Mr. Chang said that any detailed arrangements in addition to the above provisions should be left to deliberation by the Joint Committee.

0056

10. Mr. Habib replied that the new Paragraph 6, which was based on Article 26 of the German Supplementary Agreement, was necessary because with the tabling by the U.S. negotiators of the German waiver formula there now existed an entirely different basis for the exercise of waiver.

11. Mr. Habib explained that subparagraph (a)(i) of Paragraph 6 related to trials of transitory offenses - offenses triable in the United States Federal Courts regardless of where committed. Under the existing U.S. laws, this provisions would be operative only upon civilians, since any offense by personnel of the armed forces may be tried by court-martial in the Republic of Korea. The number of different offenses classified as transitory is very limited. Therefore, it is anticipated that there would be only rare instances when this provision would be applicable. Transitory offenses, Mr. Habib continued, would include treason and conspiracy against the United States. They would only involve Korean interests in a very exceptional case. An example would be a case in which a member of the civilian component committed an act of treason against the United States and in the process injured a Korean national. Jurisdiction to try this case would rest only with a United States Federal Court located in the United States. Such a case would be rare and this provision, therefore, would rarely be utilized.

12. Explaining the terms of subparagraph (a)(ii) of Paragraph 6, Mr. Habib stated that this provision meant that in a few cases, military requirements or the necessity of assuring a fair trial might require the trial to be held elsewhere than in Korea. For example, if all the witnesses in a given case had returned to the United States, it might be necessary to try the case in the United States in order to secure testimony, for if the witnesses were civilians, the U.S. armed forces could not compel them to return to Korea to testify. Also, if a division were rotated to the United States, it might be more suitable or feasible to try the case of a member of the division in the United States. This provision, Mr. Habib explained, would cover unforeseen situations which would make the trial of a case in the Republic of Korea

impractical.

13. With regard to subparagraph (b) of Paragraph 6, Mr. Habib said that the presence of a representative of the Republic of Korea would be incompatible with the rules of the court in only very rare cases. If, by chance, the representative were to be called as a witness, he might be excluded from the trial. The U.S. negotiators seriously doubted whether such a very exceptional circumstance, precluding the attendance of the ROK Government representative ~~at~~ [from] the trial, would ever arise, [except in cases involving security.] However, it might arise; thus it must be provided for in the Agreement.

14. Mr. Habib said that to the knowledge of the U.S. negotiators, no problem had been encountered in connection with the similar provisions in the German Agreement.

15. Mr. Chang thanked Mr. Habib for his thorough explanation of these provisions. He said the Korean negotiators were concerned only with crimes against Korean nationals or interests. The ~~Xxxxxx~~ alternative language proposed by the Korean negotiators provided for "other arrangements". [Disposition of] ~~T~~The rare types of cases mentioned by Mr. Habib could be settled by the Joint Committee.

16. Mr. Habib replied that the U.S. draft provided for the same result, but in more exact legal terminology. The U.S. negotiators were trying to provide for every conceivable circumstance.

17. Mr. Chang said the Korean negotiators were now prepared to accept the U.S. proposals regarding official duty certificates, with the following minor conditions:

a. With regard to the question of who should be designated as issuing authorities, the Korean negotiators would accept the phrase "competent authorities of the United States armed forces", provided the U.S. negotiators would accept the following of the understanding to be included in the Agreed Joint Summary:

"A duty certificate shall be issued only upon the advice of a Staff Judge Advocate, and the competent authority issuing a duty certificate shall be a General grade officer."

b. The Korean negotiators accept the wording "the Chief Prosecutor for the Republic of Korea" as the definition of the Korean authority who will raise objection if he considers that there is proof contrary to a certificate of official duty.

c. The Korean negotiators are ready to accept the definition of official duty proposed by the U.S. negotiators at the 49th meeting. However, they still believe the definition should be ~~placed~~ included in ~~the agreement~~ an Agreed Minute so that it would serve as a guide line for those authorities concerned in determining whether or not an offense was committed in the performance of official duty.

0059

d. The Korean negotiators believe that if the Chief Prosecutor of the Republic of Korea raises any objection, it should be made obligatory for the authorities of both countries to review the case. Accordingly, they propose the substitution of the word "shall" for the word "may" in the last sentence of Agreed Minute #2 Re Paragraph 3(a) of the U.S. draft.

e. With regard to the understanding proposed by the U.S. negotiators regarding the validity of the duty certificate, both sides are in essential agreement as to intention. Thus the question is how to incorporate the Korean requirements into the understanding. The Korean negotiators still believe that the Korean proposal is preferable to that of the U.S. negotiators. They ~~xxxxxx~~ continue to support the following version of the understanding, the language of which is distinct and self-explanatory:

> "The certificate will be conclusive unless modification is agreed upon. The United States authorities shall give due consideration to any objection which may be raised by the Chief Prosecutor for the Republic of Korea."

18. Mr. Habib said that he wished to revert for a moment to the Korean proposal regarding the ~~xxxx~~ Paragraph 1 of the Agreed Minute Re Paragraph 3(b). Did the Korean negotiators really intend that the provision should require a U.S. request for waiver in ~~xxx~~ every individual case? Mr. Chang replied that this was a correct interpretation the Korean proposal. Mr. Habib stated that such a proposal was unacceptable to the U.S. Government.

19. Mr. Chang then referred to the reference to ~~xxxx~~ the notification of individual cases by the U.S. military authorities in Paragraph 2 of the Agreed Minute. If the U.S. authorities were obliged to notify the Korean authorities of the occurrence of each offense, why could they not at the same time request a waiver of the exercise of ~~xxxxx~~ jurisdiction by the Korean authorities?

20. Mr. Habib replied that the provisions of Paragraph 2 would impose on the U.S. authorities the obligation not to conceal offenses from the Korean authorities.

0060

To require the U.S. authorities to request a waiver in each case would completely alter the nature of the waiver formula, was in no way similar to the G_{e}rman waiver formula which the U.S. negotiators had proposed, and was unacceptable to the U.S. negotiators.

21. Turning to the provisions regarding pre-trial custody, Mr. Chang said that although there still existed substantial differences between the two drafts, the Korean negotiators, with a view to expediting the negotiations and in order to be responsive to the U.S. requirements, were now prepared to accept the U.S. draft. However, in order to be consistent with the basic needs of the Korean negotiators, they proposed that the following minor modifications be incorporated into the ~~xxxx~~ ~~xxxx~~ U.S. draft:

a. The words ~~xxxx~~ "the authorities of the United States" should read "the military authorities of the United States", pending final agreement on the ~~xxxx~~ definition of authorities of both sides exercising jurisdiction in the provisions of Paragraph 1 of the Article.

b. It has been the firm position of the Korean negotiators that an accused, if he is in the hands of the authorities of the Republic of Korea, will be handed over to the military authorities of the United States, if the latter so request and unless there is adequate cause or necessity to retain him. Nevertheless, in order to reach prompt and final agreement, the Korean negotiators are prepared to make one of their major concessions by accepting the U.S. draft, provided that the U.S. authorities take full account of any special request for transfer of custody which may be made by the Korean authorities. The Korean negotiators propose that the words "on request" be ~~xxxx~~ (inserted) between the words "shall" and "be" in the second sentence of subparagraph (c). They also propose the insertion in the third sentence

0061

of the wording "They shall take full account of any special request regarding custody made by the authorities of the Republic of Korea". The Korean negotiators also propose that the U.S. military authorities exert their best efforts to maintain custody and to prevent any prejudice against the course of criminal proceedings, such as the destruction of valuable evidence or the escape of an accused from confinement. Of course, the U.S. negotiators may, if and whenever they so desire, transfer the custody of an accused to the Korean authorities .

c. With regard to the custody of an accused in the hands of the Korean authorities in connection with security offenses, the Korean negotiators accept the following two understandings proposed by the U.S. negotiators for inclusion in the Agreed Joint Summary:

> (1) There must be mutual ROK-US agreement as to the circumstances in which such custody is appropriate;

> (2) Korean confinement facilities must be adequate by U. S. standards.

22. Mr. Chang summarized his presentation by stating that, as he had said in the beginning, the Korean negotiators, in order to meet the requirements of the U.S. negotiators and at the same time to be consistent with the minimum needs of the Korean Government, were accepting the U.S. proposals with minor modifications which they hoped the U.S. negotiators would accept. Moreover, the Korean negotiators, believing that any further delay in the conclusion of the negotiations would be in the interest of neither the Korean side or the U.S. side, requested the U.S. negotiators to take into full account the positions outlined by the Korean negotiators and to accept them, thus paving the way for an early conclusion of the negotiations.

23. Mr. Habib replied that the U.S. negotiators would consider the Korean

proposals very carefully. He believed that the negotiators were very close to agreement on these provisions of the Criminal Jurisdiction Article.

24. The next meeting was scheduled for May 7 at 3:00 p.m.

0063

JOINT SUMMARY RECORD OF THE 77TH SESSION

1. Time and Place: 3:00-4:30 P.M., May 6, 1965 at the
    Foreign Ministry's Conference Room.
    (No.1)

2. Attendance:

    ROK Side:

    Mr. Chang, Sang Moon   Director
                                European and American Affairs
                                Bureau

    Mr. Lee, Nam Ki   Chief
                                America Section
                                Ministry of Foreign Affairs

    Mr. Hur, Hyong Koo   Chief
                                Prosecutors Section
                                Ministry of Justice

    Mr. Kim, Dong Hwi   Chief
                                Treaty Section
                                Ministry of Foreign Affairs

    Maj. Lee, Key Hoon   Military Affairs Section
                                Ministry of National Defense

    Mr. Kim, Kee Joe   3rd Secretary
                                Ministry of Foreign Affairs

    Mr. Lee, Keun Pal   3rd Secretary
    (Interpreter)   Ministry of Foreign Affairs

    Mr. Hwang, Young Jae   3rd Secretary
                                Ministry of Foreign Affairs

    Mr. Park, Won Chul   3rd Secretary
                                Ministry of Foreign Affairs

    U.S. Side:

    Mr. Philip C. Habib   Counselor
                                American Embassy

    Brig. Gen. Carroll H. Dunn Deputy Chief of Staff
                                8th U.S. Army

    Col. Allan G. Pixton   Deputy Chief of Staff
                                8th U.S. Army

    Capt. George Hagerman   Assistant Chief of Staff
                                USN/K

    Col. Kenneth C. Crawford   Staff Judge Advocate
                                8th U.S. Army

0064

Mr. Frank R. LaMacchia	First Secretary American Embassy
Mr. Benjamin A. Fleck	First Secretary American Embassy
Mr. Robert A. Kinney	J-5 8th U.S. Army
Mr. Goodwin Shapiro	Second Secretary American Embassy
Maj. Alton H. Harvey	Staff Judge Advocate's Office 8th U.S. Army
Mr. David Y.C. Lee (Interpreter)	Second Secretary American Embassy

1. Mr. Chang opened the meeting by stating that
the Korean negotiators, together with competent authorities
of the Korean Government, had given very careful consideration to the U.S. proposals regarding the waiver formula,
duty certificates, and pre-trial custody. As the result
of this deliberation, the Korean negotiators, with a
view to reaching early agreement on this, the most
important article in the SOFA, were about to make most
significant concessions by meeting the requirement of
the U.S. and accepting in principle, with minor modifications, the drafts tabled by the U.S. negotiators at the
74th negotiating session.

2. However, Mr. Chang continued, before giving a
detailed presentation of their views, the Korean negotiators
wished to seek clarification by the U.S. negotiators
regarding the provisions of Paragraph 4 of the Agreed
Minute Re Paragraph 3(b) tabled by the U.S. negotiators.
In case the Korean Government, in resolving disagreement
in accordance with the provisions of Paragraph 4, determines
to exercise its jurisdiction, can the determination be
final and conclusive?

0065

3. Mr. Habib replied that the answer to Mr. Chang's question was yes. However, in presenting this draft, the U.S. negotiators had taken into account repeated statements by the Korean negotiators that due restraint would be observed by the Korean authorities in exercising their jurisdiction under their waiver clause when they considered that it was of particular importance that jurisdiction be exercised by the Korean authorities.

4. Mr. Chang expressed appreciation for Mr. Habib's reply. During the course of the negotiations, he said, the Korean negotiators had repeatedly stressed that under the terms of waiver discretion provided for in the original draft tabled by them, the Korean authorities would exercise utmost restraint in implementing the waiver provision. In other words, the Korean negotiators had given assurances that the Korean authorities would waive in as many cases as other countries do under their very simple status of forces agreements. However, the Korean negotiators had firmly held their position that the Korean authorities would waive except when they determined that it is of particular importance that jurisdiction be exercised by the authorities of the Republic of Korea, whereas the U.S. negotiators had held the position that the primary right to exercise jurisdiction should be waived to the U.S. authorities, with the right of recall retained by the Korean authorities.

5. Having received the affirmative answer which the U.S. negotiators had just given to the Korean negotiators' question, Mr. Chang said, the Korean negotiators were now prepared to accept the waiver formula

0066

proposed by the U.S. side at the 74th meeting. However, this concession by the Korean negotiators was made on condition that the U.S. negotiators accept the following modifications which were felt to be most essential by the Korean negotiators.

6. Noting again the affirmative answer of the U.S. negotiators with regard to the provisions of Paragraph 4 of the Agreed Minute Re Paragraph 3(b), and believing that the following minor modification would be acceptable to the U.S. negotiators, the Korean negotiators proposed the addition of the following sentence to Paragraph 4:

> "The recall of waiver shall be final and conclusive unless the statement for recall referred to in Paragraph 3 of this Minute is withdrawn by the Government of the Republic of Korea through consultation between both Governments."

Mr. Chang said the Korean negotiators firmly believe the above sentence to be absolutely necessary not only to enable the ROK Government to obtain the understanding of the National Assembly and the Korean people but also for mutually satisfactory implementation of the waiver formula.

7. Mr. Chang referred to Paragraph 1 of the Agreed Minute Re Paragraph 3 (b) and said that the Korean negotiators believe that the waiver of the primary right of jurisdiction should be made following a request by the United States. Therefore, the Korean negotiators proposed the insertion at the beginning of the paragraph of the phrase "At the request of the United States."

8. Mr. Habib asked for clarification of this proposal. Did the phrase refer to a one-time request for a blanket waiver or were the Korean negotiators proposing that the United States authorities request waiver in each individual

0067

case? Mr. Chang replied that the Korean proposal was
that the United States authorities make a separate
request for waiver in each case.

   9. Resuming his discussion of the drafts tabled
by the U.S. negotiators at the 74th meeting, Mr. Chang
turned to Paragraph 6 of the Agreed Minute Re Paragraph
3(b). He recalled that at the 67th meeting the U.S.
negotiators had tabled a revision of what was then their
Agreed Minute Re Paragraph 3. They had stated that the
second paragraph of that revision was a new paragraph
incorporated into the U.S. draft in order to include the
position set forth in the third paragraph of the Agreed
Minute Re Paragraph 3 of the Korean draft. They had
further stated that they viewed these provisions as
desirable and were pleased to be able to accede to the
wishes of the ROK Government by incorporating them into
the U.S. draft. Mr. Chang said that the Korean negotiators
were completely at a loss to understand the reasons why
the U.S. negotiators, after agreeing to the Korean
language at the 67th meeting, had now substituted a new
Paragraph 6 in place of that language. Accordingly, the
Korean negotiators, in the light of the trend of the
past negotiations, proposed that in place of the Paragraph
6 contained in the U.S. draft, the following portion of
the previous draft be adopted as Paragraph 6:

> "Trials of cases in which the authorities of
> the Republic of Korea waive the primary right
> to exercise jurisdiction, and trials of cases involving
> offenses described in Paragraph 3(a)(ii) committed
> against the state or nationals of the Republic
> of Korea shall be held promptly in the Republic
> of Korea within a reasonable distance from the place
> where the offenses are alleged to have taken place
> unless other arrangements are mutually agreed upon.
> Representatives of the Republic of Korea may be
> present at such trials.

0068

Mr. Chang said that any detailed arrangements in addition
to the above provisions should be left to deliberation
by the Joint Committee.

10. Mr. Habib replied that the new Paragraph 6,
which was based on Article 26 of the German Supplementary
Agreement, was necessary because with the tabling by
the U.S. negotiators of the German waiver formula there
now existed an entirely different basis for the exercise
of waiver.

11. Mr. Habib explained that subparagraph (a)(i)
of Paragraph 6 related to trials of transitory offenses -
offenses triable in the United States Federal Courts
regardless of where committed. Under the existing U.S.
laws, this provisions would be operative only upon
civilians, since any offense by personnel of the armed
forces may be tried by court-martial in the Republic
of Korea. The number of offenses classified as transitory
is very limited. Therefore, it is anticipated that
there would be only rare instances when this provision
would be applicable. Transitory offenses, Mr. Habib
continued, would include treason and conspiracy against
the United States. They would only involve Korean
interests in a very exceptional case. An example would
be a case in which a member of the civilian component
committed an act of treason against the United States
and in the process injured a Korean national. Jurisdiction
to try this case would rest only with a United States
Federal Court located in the United States. Such a case
would be rare and this provision, therefore, would rarely
be utilized.

12. Explaining the terms of subparagraph (a)(ii) of Paragraph 6, Mr. Habib stated that this provision meant that in a few cases, military requirements or the necessity of assuring a fair trial might require the trial to be held elsewhere than in Korea. For example, if all the witnesses in a given case had returned to the United States, it might be necessary to try the case in the United States in order to secure testimony, for if the witnesses were civilians, the U.S. armed forces could not compel them to return to Korea to testify. Also, if a division were rotated to the United States, it might be more suitable or feasible to try the case of a member of the division in the United States. This provision, Mr. Habib explained, would cover unforeseen situations which would make the trial of a case in the Republic of Korea impractical.

13. With regard to subparagraph (b) of Paragraph 6, Mr. Habib said that the presence of a representative of the Republic of Korea would be incompatible with the rules of the court in only very rare cases. If, by chance, the representative were to be called as a witness, he might be excluded from the trial. The U.S. negotiators seriously doubted whether such a very exceptional circumstance, precluding the attendance of the ROK Government representative from the trial, would ever arise, except in cases involving security. However, it might arise; thus it must be provided for in the Agreement.

14. Mr. Habib said that to the knowledge of the U.S. negotiators, no problem had been encountered in connection with the similar provisions in the German Agreement.

0070

15. Mr. Chang thanked Mr. Habib for his thorough explanation of these provisions. He said the Korean negotiators were concerned only with crimes against Korean nationals or interests. The alternative language proposed by the Korean negotiators provided for "other arrangements". Disposition of the rare types of cases mentioned by Mr. Habib could be settled by the Joint Committee.

16. Mr. Habib replied that the U.S. draft provided for the same result, but in more exact legal terminology. The U.S. negotiators were trying to provide for every conceivable circumstance.

17. Mr. Chang said the Korean negotiators were now prepared to accept the U.S. proposals regarding official duty certificates, with the following minor conditions:

a. With regard to the question of who should be designated as issuing authorities, the Korean negotiators would accept the phrase "competent authorities of the United States armed forces", provided the U.S. negotiators would accept the following of the understanding to be included in the Agreed Joint Summary:

"A duty certificate shall be issued only upon the advice of a Staff Judge Advocate, and the competent authority issuing a duty certificate shall be a General grade officer."

b. The Korean negotiators accept the wording "the Chief Prosecutor for the Republic of Korea" as the definition of the Korean authority who will raise objection if he considers that there is proof contrary to a certificate of official duty.

0071

c. The Korean negotiators are ready to accept the definition of official duty proposed by the U.S. negotiators at the 49th meeting. However, they still believe the definition should be included in an Agreed Minute so that it would serve as a guide line for those authorities concerned in determining whether or not an offense was committed in the performance of official duty.

d. The Korean negotiators believe that if the Chief Prosecutor of the Republic of Korea raises any objection, it should be made obligatory for the authorities of both countries to review the case. Accordingly, they propose the substitution of the word "shall" for the word "may" in the last sentence of Agreed Minute #2 Re Paragraph 3(a) of the U.S. draft.

e. With regard to the understanding proposed by the U.S. negotiators regarding the validity of the duty certificate, both sides are in essential agreement as to intention. Thus the question is how to incorporate the Korean requirements into the understanding. The Korean negotiators still believe that the Korean proposal is preferable to that of the U.S. negotiators. They continue to support the following version of the understanding, the language of which is distinct and self-explanatory:

> "The certificate will be conclusive unless modification is agreed upon. The United States authorities shall give due consideration to any objection which may be raised by the Chief Prosecutor for the Republic of Korea."

0072

18. Mr. Habib said that he wished to revert for a moment to the Korean proposal regarding the Paragraph 1 of the Agreed Minute Re Paragraph 3(b). Did the Korean negotiators really intend that the provision should require a U.S. request for waiver in every individual case? Mr. Chang replied that this was a correct interpretation of the Korean proposal. Mr. Habib stated that such a proposal was unacceptable to the U.S. Government.

19. Mr. Chang then referred to the reference to the notification of individual cases by the U.S. military authorities in Paragraph 2 of the Agreed Minute. If the U.S. authorities were obliged to notify the Korean authorities of the occurrence of each offense, why could they not at the same time request a waiver of the exercise of jurisdiction by the Korean authorities.?

20. Mr. Habib replied that the provisions of Paragraph 2 would impose on the U.S. authorities the obligation not to conceal offenses from the Korean authorities. To require the U.S. authorities to request a waiver in each case would completely alter the nature of the waiver formula, was in no way similar to the German waiver formula which the U.S. negotiators had proposed, and was unacceptable to the U.S. negotiators.

21. Turning to the provisions regarding pre-trial custody, Mr. Chang said that although there still existed substantial differences between the two drafts, the Korean negotiators, with a view to expediting the negotiations and in order to be responsive to the U.S. requirements, were now prepared to accept the U.S. draft. However, in order to be consistent with the basic needs of the Korean negotiators, they proposed that the following minor modifications be incorporated into the U.S. draft:

0073

a. The words "the authorities of the United
States" should read "the military authorities of
the United States", pending final agreement on the
definition of authorities of both sides exercising
jurisdiction in the provisions of Paragraph 1 of
the Article.

b. It has been the firm position of the Korean
negotiators that an accused, if he is in the hands
of the authorities of the Republic of Korea, will be
handed over to the military authorities of the United
States, if the latter so request and unless there
is adequate cause or necessity to retain him.
Nevertheless, in order to reach prompt and final
agreement, the Korean negotiators are prepared
to make one of their major concessions by accepting
the U.S. draft, provided that the U.S. authorities
take full account of any special request for transfer
of custody which may be made by the Korean authorities.
The Korean negotiators propose that the words "on
request" be inserted between the words "shall" and
"be" in the second sentence of subparagraph (c).
They also propose the insertion in the third sentence
of the wording "They shall take full account of any
special request regarding custody made by the
authorities of the Republic of Korea." The Korean
negotiators also propose that the U.S. military
authorities exert their best efforts to maintain
custody and to prevent any prejudice against the
course of criminal proceedings, such as the destruction of valuable evidence or the escape of an accused
from confinement. Of course, the U.S. negotiators

0074

may, if and whenever they so desire, transfer the custody of an accused to the Korean authorities.

c. With regard to the custody of an accused in the hands of the Korean authorities in connection with security offenses, the Korean negotiators accept the following two understandings proposed by the U.S. negotiators for inclusion in the Agreed Joint Summary:

(1) There must be mutual ROK-US agreement as to the circumstances in which such custody is appropriate;

(2) Korean confinement facilities must be adequate by U.S. standards.

22. Mr. Chang summarized his presentation by stating that, as he had said in the beginning, the Korean negotiators, in order to meet the requirements of the U.S. negotiators and at the same time to be consistent with the minimum needs of the Korean Government, were accepting the U.S. proposals with minor modifications which they hoped the U.S. negotiators would accept. Moreover, the Korean negotiators, believing that any further delay in the conclusion of the negotiations would be in the interest of neither the Korean side or the U.S. side, requested the U.S. negotiators to take into full account the positions outlined by the Korean negotiators and to accept them, thus paving the way for an early conclusion of the negotiations.

23. Mr. Habib replied that the U.S. negotiators would consider the Korean proposals very carefully. He believed that the negotiators were very close to agreement on these provisions of the Criminal Jurisdiction Article.

24. The next meeting was scheduled for May 7 at 3:00 p.m.

0075

2. 제78차 회의, 5.7

0076

기 안 지

기 안 자	미주과 이근팔	전 화 번 호		공 보	필 요	불필요
	과 장	국 장	차 관	장 관		
			후열			

협 조 자 서 명					보 존 년 한	
기 안 년 월 일	1965. 5. 11.	시 행 년월일		통제관	정 서	기 장
분류기호 문서번호	외구미 722.2 —					
경 유 수 신 참 조	대통령 참조: 비서실장 국무총리 참조: 비서실장 발신 사본: 법무부장관 참조: 검찰국장 사본: 보건사회부장관 참조: 노동청장				장 관	
제 목	제 78 차 주둔군지위협정 체결 교섭실무자회의 결과 보고					

1965 년 5 월 7 일 하오 4 시 부터 동 5 시 30 분 까지

외무부 제 1 회의실에서 개최된 제 78 차 한·미간 주둔군지위협정

체결 교섭실무자회의에서 토의된 형사재판관할권 및 노무 조항에

관한 내용을 별첨과 같이 보고합니다.

유 첨: 제 78 차 한·미간 주둔군지위협정 체결 교섭실무자회의

결과 보고서. 1 부. 끝.

공통서식 1—2 (갑)   (16절지)

0077

한·미국 간의 상호방위조약 제4조에 의한 시설과 구역 및 한국에서의 미국군대의 지위에 관한 협정(SOFA)
전59권. 1966.7.9 서울에서 서명 : 1967.2.9 발효(조약 232호) (V.30 실무교섭회의, 제77-80차, 1965.5월)   347

기 안 지

기 안 자	미주과 이 구 팔	전 화 번 호		공 보	필 요	불필요
	과 장	국 장	차 관	장 관		
			휴식			

협 조 자 서 명				보 존 년 한	
기 안 년 월 일	1965. 5. 11.	시 행 년월일	통제 제관	5 13	정 서	기 장
분류기호 문서번호	외구미 722.2 —					
경 수 참 조	유신조	법무부장관 참조: 검찰국장	발신	장 관	
		보건사회부장관 참조: 노동청장			
제 목		제 78 차 주둔군지위협정 체결 교섭실무자회의 결과 보고			

　　1965 년 5월 7일 하오 4시 부터 동 5 시 30 분 까지

외무부 제 1 회의실에서 개최된 제 78 차 주둔군지위협정 체결

교섭실무자회의에서 토의된 형사재판관할권 및 노무 조항에

관한 내용을 별첨과 같이 알립니다.

　　유 첨: 제 78 차 주둔군지위협정 체결 교섭실무자회의 결과

　　　　　　보고서 1 부. 끝.

제 78 차
한.미간 주둔군지위협정 체결 교섭실무자회의
보 고 서

1. 일 시: 1965 년 5 월 7 일 하오 4 시 부터 동 5 시 30 분 가지.

2. 장 소: 외무부 제 1 회의실.

3. 토의사항:

가. 형사재판관할권

우리측이 제 77 차 회의 때대 미측에 제시한 제 1 차 관할권의
포기조항에 관한 제안에 의하여 우리측 입장을 재차 강조하는 한편
일부 수정할 것을 다음과 같이 제안하였다.

(1) 우리측이 제 77 차 회의 때대 "포기의 철회는 양국정부간의
협의를 통하여 철회를 위한 통고가 대한민국정부에 의하여
취소되지 않는 한 최종적이며 확정적이어야 한다"고 제안한바
있는데 한국정부가 포기를 철회한 경우 한.미간의 의견차이로
말미아마 포기의 철회에 관한 한국정부의 최종적 결정이
부당히 지연되는 것을 방지하기 위하여 다음과 같이 일부
수정할 것을 제안하였다.

"포기의 철회는 본합의의사록 제 3 항에 규정된 포기의
철회를 위한 통고가(그러한 통고 발행후 21 일 이내에)
대한민국정부에 의하여 취소되지 않는 한 최종적이며 확정적
이어야 한다."

(영 문)

"The recall of waiver shall be final and conclusive
unless the statement for recall referred to in Paragraph
3 of this Minute is withdrawn by the Government of
the Republic of Korea within a period of Twenty-one
days after such statement for recall is made."

(2) 우리 나락에 부여된 제 1 차 관할권의 일괄적 포기를 규정한
미측 제안에 대하여 우리측은 제 77 차 회의 시 개개특정
사건이 발생할 때 마다 미국당국이 요청하면 포기하는 것으로

0079

65-5-30

65-5-12 (3)

미줄도1121(3)

0080

하게 위하여 "미국이 요청하면"(At the request of the United States)이란 문구를 동 규정 서두에 삽입할 것을 제안 하였는바 미측이 즉석에서 이를 수락할 수 없다는 태도를 표명 한데 감하여 우리측은 협정의 조속한 체결을 위하여 미측의 포기조항을 원칙적으로 수락하지만 제 1 차관할권을 협정 발효와 동시에 포괄적으로 포기할 것을 요구하는 미측 제안은 주권국가 로서 수락할 수 없을 뿐만 아니라 국회나 국민이 이해할 수 없을 것임을 재강조하고 우리측 입장을 수락할 것을 촉구 하였다.

미측은 이에 대하여 미측의 금번 제안이 결코 한국의 주권을 침해하려는 것은 아니며 독일국도 동일한 포기조항을 수락 운영하고 있지만 주권침해문제는 야기되지 않았으며 한국이 미측 제안을 수락할 수 없다는 것은 이해하기 곤란하다. 미군이 지금 까지 배타적으로 행사하여 온 재판권을 한국이 포기하는 경우에도 철회할 수 있게 한 것은 미측으로서는 큰 양보이다. 더욱이 한국측이 국회와 국민이 이해할 수 없을 것이라고 하지만 미측도 미국회와 국민에 대하여 동일한 입장에 있으며 따라서 미측은 한국측 제안을 수락할 수 없다고 답변하였다.

나. <u>노무조항</u>

제 75 차 회의 시 우리측이 제시한 미군노무자의 파업권에 관한 대안에 대하여 미측은 노무조항 전반의 해결여부가 노무자의 파업권 한정 여부에 달려 있다고 지적하고 미측 입장을 다음과 같이 강조하였다.

(1) 한국측이 "파업에 관한 권리는 권리행사가 합동위원회에서 금지된 자를 제외한 노무자에게 부여되어야 한다"고 제안한데 관하여 주한미군은 영리를 목적으로 하는 일반 기업체는 아니며,

(2) 한국을 공산침략으로부터 방위하는 미군의 사명은 한국군의 사명과 동일할 뿐만 아니라 한.미양국군대가 동일한 지휘권에 복하고 있는 이상 한국군에 근무하는 고용인이 파업을 할 수 없다면 미군의 고용인도 파업권을 행사할 수 없어야 하며

(3) 더욱이 양측의 분쟁해결절차의 결정이 최종적인 구속력이 있음을

0081

0082

인정하는 취지와 모순되는 것이며 따라서 미군노무자에게 파업권을
인정하려는 한국측 주장은 수락할 수 없다고 말하였다.

4. 기타 사항:

　가. 차기 회의 일자: 1965 년 5 월 12 일 하오 4 시 부터. 끝.

0083

STATUS OF FORCES NEGOTIATIONS: 78th Meeting

SUBJECTS: 1. Labor Article
                                        2. Criminal Jurisdiction Article

PLACE: Ministry of Foreign Affairs

DATE: May 7, 1965

PARTICIPANTS:

Republic of Korea   United States

CHANG Sang-mun   Philip C. Habib
X HO Sung-chung   Brig. General Carroll H. Dunn, USA
YI Nam-ki   Colonel Allan G. Pixton, USA
Major YI Ke-hun, ROKA   Captain George Hagerman, USN
KIM Ki-cho   Colonel Kenneth C. Crawford, USA
HWANG Yong-chae   Benjamin A. Fleck
X KIM Tong-hui   Robert A. Kinney
PAK Won-chol   Major Alton Harvey, USA
YI Kun-pal   (Interpreter)   David Y.C. Lee (Interpreter)

                                        Ogden C. Reed, Observer
                                        G.W. Flowers, Observer

0085

CONFIDENTIAL

Labor Article

1. Mr. Habib opened the meeting by stating that at this session the U.S. negotiators wished to concentrate on the principal remaining point at issue in the Labor Article. There were a number of differences still unresolved but at this meeting the U.S. negotiators wished to present their views on the question of the status of the Korean employees of the U.S. armed forces. The U.S. *negotiators* have been seeking to establish a relationship *in this Article between the U.S. armed forces and* their employees which would support the mission of the armed forces and at the same time safeguard the rights and privileges of their employees. The U.S. draft of the Labor Article would protect and preserve all of the basic rights currently enjoyed by those employees. The principal difference between the two drafts centers on the question of the right to strike.

2. This question, Mr. Habib continued, should be viewed in connection with the disputes settlement procedures established in the U.S. draft. Through these procedures, the U.S. negotiators have sought to provide for the amicable settlement of any disputes which may arise. They would establish a consultative and conciliation process which would operate at the governmental and Joint Committee level. Provision would be made for representation of the employees through recognition of the right to organize.

3. The Korean negotiators recognize the necessity for procedures for the settlement of disputes but the Korean draft goes beyond this, Mr. Habib continued. The Korean draft contradicts the settlement procedures provided for by quoting the Korean Labor Dispute Adjustment Law, which, in effect, says that a decision of the Joint Committee would not be binding. The Korean draft also provides that employees of the U.S. armed forces shall have the right to strike. Nowhere in their draft have the Korean negotiators recognized what the U.S. negotiators have been trying to stress - that Korean employees of the U.S. armed forces are not comparable to ordinary employees of commercial enterprises.

0086

CONFIDENTIAL

4. Mr. Habib reiterated the position of the U.S. negotiators that the Korean employees of the U.S. armed forces have a status and importance comparable to that of employees of the Korean armed forces. The U.S. armed forces [in Korea have] ~~perform~~ exactly the same mission as the ROK armed forces - the defense of the Republic of Korea.

5. Mr. Habib pointed out that the paragraph in the U.S. draft dealing with strikes (Paragraph 4(e)) simply states that "an employee shall be subject to the same legal provisions concerning strikes and other work stoppages as an employee in a comparable ~~position~~ position in the employment of the armed forces of the Republic of Korea". This provision is not only sound with respect to the mission of the U.S. armed forces. It is also justifiable, not only in terms of military requirements but also in comparability with Korean procedures. Korean recognition that certain operations require special provisions extends beyond the armed forces, for employees of certain utilities in the Republic of Korea do not have the right to strike. The U.S. negotiators would also like to point out that staff functions of certain of the Korean employees of the U.S. armed forces ~~also~~ serve the Korean armed forces as well as the U.S. armed forces, particularly in the fields of supply and transport. The U.S. negotiators ~~also~~ do not understand why the Korean negotiators attempt to apply different sets of rules to employees of the U.S. armed forces and employees of the Korean armed forces when the mission, functions, and command of the two armed forces are identical.

6. Mr. Habib stated that the U.S. negotiators agree with the reasoning that leads the Korean negotiators to the conclusion that a requirement exists to restrict the rights of Korean employees of the ROK armed forces. The U.S. armed forces desire the same treatment, not discriminatory treatment, so that the achievement of the mission of the U.S. armed forces is not interfered with. The position of the U.S. negotiators is consistent with the past and present practice and rules of both the U.S. and ROK governments.

7. Mr. Habib pointed out that the U.S. negotiators were not attempting to

0087

deny the rights of labor to organize and to be dealt with through established procedures. They were trying to preserve rights equivalent to those held by employees of the Korean armed forces in order to permit the U.S. armed forces to fulfill their mission without unnecessary interference. The mission of the U.S. armed forces is all-important.

8. The U.S. negotiators believe that disputes should be conciliated, Mr. Habib continued. The formula contained in the U!S. draft permits the U.S· armed forces to meet their requirements and enables the Korean negotiators to justify these provisions to the Korean authorities and people. That justification is found in the phraseology which ~~provides for resolution of~~ the issue in the same fashion in both armed forces.

9. Mr. Habib remarked that the principal argument of the Korean negotiators has been that the right to strike exists elsewhere. This argument is not persuasive for a number of reasons. The primary mission of the U.S. armed forces in Korea is considerably different than that of such forces elsewhere. The U.S. negotiators believe that the procedures set forth in the U.S. draft will fully meet the requirements of both sides for amicable relations. For all of the reasons which he had just cited, Mr. Habib concluded, the U.S. negotiators are unable to agree to the Korean proposal to delete Paragraph 4(e) from the U.S. draft.

10. Mr. Chang replied that the Korean negotiators would consider the position stated by the U.S. negotiators and would respond at a later meeting.

Criminal Jurisdiction Article

11. Turning to the Criminal Jurisdiction Article, Mr. Chang said the Korean negotiators were waiting to hear the views of the U.S negotiators regarding the latest proposals made by the Korean negotiators. In the meantime, the Korean negotiators wished to clarify their position and propose a minor modification of their latest proposal. In order to eliminate possible ambiguity, they wished to

alter the ~~additional~~ sentence which they had proposed for addition to Paragraph 4 of the Agreed Minute Re Paragraph 3(b). The phrase "through consultation between both governments" should be deleted and in its place should be added the phrase "within a period of 21 days after such statement for recall is made".

12. With regard to the phrase "At the request of the United States" which they had proposed for insertion in Paragraph 1 of the Agreed Minute Re Paragraph 3(b), Mr. Chang said that this proposal had been made in order to meet the basic requirements of the Korean negotiators as well as the requirements of the U.S. negotiators. The additional phrase was absolutely necessary to ~~enable~~ permit the ROK Government to maintain its dignity as a sovereign government and to enable the Korean negotiators to explain the provisions of this Agreed Minute to the National Assembly.

13. Mr. Habib replied that the U.S. negotiators had presented a formula which provided for the waiver of jurisdiction and the right of recall of that waiver in extremely important cases. They were not prepared to accept any requirement that the U.S. authorities should request waiver in every case. The question of waiver had nothing to do with sovereignty. The German waiver formula in operation has not detracted from German sovereignty. It will not detract from the sovereignty of the Republic of Korea. The formula proposed by the U.S. negotiators had been designed to meet the oft-repeated indication by the Korean negotiators of the Korean requirement to exercise jurisdiction when it was imperative to do so in the interests of Korean justice. The ~~phrase~~ additional phrase proposed by the Korean negotiators ~~~~ would completely reverse the formula proposed by the U.S. negotiators. Paragraph 4 of the proposed Agreed Minute Re Paragraph 3(b) would give the ROK Government the final determination of the exercise of jurisdiction This is what the Korean negotiators had repeatedly said ~~~~ at past meetings they needed. The waiver formula was a fundamental issue. The U.S. negotiators hoped, therefore, that the Korean negotiators would reconsider their position with regard to their proposed additional phrase in Paragraph 1 of the Agreed Minute.

14. Mr. Chang again ~~referred to the necessity~~ of being able to explain the

waiver provision to the National Assembly and reiterated the Korean position that the Korean authorities would be prepared to waive when requested to do so by the U.S. authorities. Mr. Habib reminded the Korean negotiators that not only the National Assembly but also the U.S. Congress was interested in this agreement and would examine its provisions carefully. He ~~reminded~~ [pointed out to] the Korean negotiators that the present U.S. draft was actually a compromise between the earlier Korean position and the earlier U.S. position. The U.S. negotiators believed it to be a workable compromise which could be satisfactorily explained to the legislatures of both countries.

15. Mr. Chang then referred to Article 19 of the German ~~Supplementary~~ Supplementary Agreement, which begins "At the request of the sending state,...". Mr. Habib, in reply, explained the significance of this language in connection with the related Agreed Minute. He explained that, in reality, this was a provision for a blanket waiver which was made (by the German Government) insofar as the U.S. armed forces were concerned, at the time when the German Supplementary Agreement became operative. He assured the Korean negotiators that the formula which the U.S. negotiators had presented was the German waiver formula.

0090

JOINT SUMMARY RECORD OF THE 78TH SESSION

1. Time and Place: 4:30-5:30 P.M., May 7, 1965 at the
                     Foreign Ministry's Conference Room
                     (No.1)

2. Attendance:

    ROK Side:

    Mr. Chang, Sang Moon   Director
                                European and American Affairs
                                Bureau
                                Ministry of Foreign Affairs

    Mr. Yoon, Woon Young   Director
                                Prosecutors Bureau
                                Ministry of Justice

    Mr. Hur Hyong Koo   Chief
                                Prosecutors Section
                                Ministry of Justice

    Mr. Lee, Nam Ki   Chief
                                America Section
                                Ministry of Foreign Affairs

    Maj. Lee, Kye Hoon   Military Affairs Section
                                Ministry of National Defense

    Mr. Kim, Kee Joe   3rd Secretary
                                Ministry of Foreign Affairs

    Mr. Lee, Keun Pal   3rd Secretary
    (Interpreter)   Ministry of Foreign Affairs

    Mr. Lee, Chung Bin   3rd Secretary
                                Ministry of Foreign Affairs

    Mr. Hwang, Young Jae   3rd Secretary
                                Ministry of Foreign Affairs

    Mr. Cho, Yong Si   Office of Labor Affairs
    (Observer)

    U.S. Side:

    Mr. Philip C. Habib   Counselor
                                American Embassy

    Brig. Gen. Carroll H. Dunn Deputy Chief of Staff
                                8th U.S. Army

    Col. Allan G. Pixton   Deputy Chief of Staff
                                8th U.S. Army

    Capt. George Hagerman   Assistant Chief of Staff
                                USN/K

                                                    0091

Col. Kenneth C. Crawford	Staff Judge Advocate 8th U.S. Army
Mr. Benjamin A. Fleck	First Secretary American Embassy
Mr. Robert A. Kinney	J-5 8th U.S. Army
Mr. Goodwin Shapiro	Second Secretary American Embassy
Maj. Alton H. Harvey	Staff Judge Advocate's Office 8th U.S. Army
Mr. David Y.C. Lee (Interpreter)	Second Secretary American Embassy
Mr. Ogden C. Reed (Observer)	Civilian Personnel Director 8th U.S. Army
Mr. G.W. Flower (Observer)	8th U.S. Army

Labor Article

1. Mr. Habib opened the meeting by stating that at
this session the U.S. negotiators wished to concentrate on
the principal remaining point at issue in the Labor Article.
There were a number of differences still unresolved but at
this meeting the U.S. negotiators wished to present their
views on the question of the status of the Korean employees
of the U.S. armed forces. The U.S. negotiators have been
seeking to establish in this Article a relationship between
the U.S. armed forces and their employees which would
support the mission of the armed forces and at the same time
safeguard the rights and privileges of their employees.
The U.S. draft of the Labor Article would protect and preserve
all of the basic rights currently enjoyed by those employees.
The principal difference between the two drafts centers
on the question of the right to strike.

0092

2. This question, Mr. Habib continued, should be
viewed in connection with the disputes settlement procedures
established in the U.S. draft. Through these procedures,
the U.S. negotiators have sought to provide for the amicable
settlement of any disputes which may arise. They would
establish a consultative and conciliation process which
would operate at the governmental and Joint Committee
level. Provision would be made for representation of the
employees through recognition of the right to organize.

3. The Korean negotiators recognize the necessity
for procedures for the settlement of disputes but the
Korean draft goes beyond this, Mr. Habib continued. The
Korean draft contradicts the settlement procedures provided
for by quoting the Korean Labor Dispute Adjustment Law,
which, in effect, says that a decision of the Joint Committee
would not be binding. The Korean draft also provides that
employees of the U.S. armed forces shall have the right to
strike. Nowhere in their draft have the Korean negotiators
recognized what the U.S. negotiators have been trying to
stress - that Korean employees of the U.S. armed forces
are not comparable to ordinary employees of commercial
enterprises.

4. Mr. Habib reiterated the position of the U.S.
negotiators that the Korean employees of the U.S. armed forces
have a status and importance comparable to that of
employees of the Korean armed forces. The U.S. armed forces
in Korea have exactly the same mission as the ROK armed
forces - the defense of the Republic of Korea.

5. Mr. Habib pointed out that the paragraph in the
U.S. draft dealing with strikes (Paragraph 4(e)) simply

0093

states that "an employee shall be subject to the same
legal provisionsíconcerning strikes and other work stoppages
as an employee in a comparable position in the employment
of the armed forces óf the Republic of Korea". This
provision is not only sound with respect to the mission of
the U.S. armed forces. It is also justifiable, not only
in terms of military requirements but also in comparability
with Korean procedures. Korean recognition that certain
operations require special provisions extends beyond the
armed forces, for employees of certain utilities in the
Republic of Korea do not have the right to strike. The
U.S. negotiators would also like to point out that staff
functions of certain of the Korean employees of the
U.S. armed forces serve the Korean armed forces as well as
the U.S. armed forces, particularly in the fields of supply
and transport. The U.S. negotiators do not understand why
the Korean negotiators attempt to apply different sets of
rules to employees of the U.S. armed forces and employees
of the Korean armed forces when the mission, functions,
and command of the two armed forces are identical.

6. Mr. Habib stated that the U.S. negotiators agree
with the reasoning that leads the Korean negotiators to the
conclusion that a requirement exists to restrict the rights
of Korean employees of the ROK armed forces. The U.S.
armed forces desire the same treatment, not discriminatory
treatment, so that the achievement of the mission of the
U.S. armed forces is not interfered with. The position of
the U.S. negotiators is consistent with the past and
present practice and rules of both the U.S. and ROK
governments.

0094

7. Mr. Habib pointed out that the U.S. negotiators were not attempting to deny the rights of labor to organize and to be dealt with through established procedures. They were trying to preserve rights equivalent to those held by employees of the Korean armed forces in order to permit the U.S. armed forces to fulfill their mission without unnecessary interference. The mission of the U.S. armed forces is all-important.

8. The U.S. negotiators believe that disputes should be conciliated, Mr. Habib continued. The formula contained in the U.S. draft permits the U.S. armed forces to meet their requirements and enables the Korean negotiators to justify these provisions to the Korean authorities and people. That justification is found in the phraseology which provides for resolution of the issue in the same fashion in both armed forces.

9. Mr. Habib remarked that the principal argument of the Korean negotiators has been that the right to strike exists elsewhere. This argument is not persuasive for a number of reasons. The primary mission of the U.S. armed forces in Korea is considerably different than that of such forces elsewhere. The U.S. negotiators believe that the procedures set forth in the U.S. draft will fully meet the requirements of both sides for amicable relations. For all of the reasons which he had just cited, Mr. Habib concluded, the U.S. negotiators are unable to agree to the Korean proposal to delete Paragraph 4(e) from the U.S. draft.

10. Mr. Chang replied that the Korean negotiators would consider the position stated by the U.S. negotiators and would respond at a later meeting.

<u>Criminal Jurisdiction Article</u>

11. Turning to the Criminal Jurisdiction Article, Mr. Chang said the Korean negotiators were waiting to hear the views of the U.S. negotiators regarding the latest proposals made by the Korean negotiators. In the meantime, the Korean negotiators wished to clarify their position and propose a minor modification of their latest proposal. In order to eliminate possible ambiguity, they wished to alter the sentence which they had proposed for addition to Paragraph 4 of the Agreed Minute Re Paragraph 3(b). The phrase "through consultation between both governments" should be deleted and in its place should be added the phrase "within a period of 21 days after such statement for recall is made."

12. With regard to the phrase "At the request of the United States" which they had proposed for insertion in Paragraph 1 of the Agreed Minute Re Paragraph 3(b), Mr. Chang said that this proposal had been made in order to meet the basic requirements of the Korean negotiators as well as the requirements of the U.S. negotiators. The additional phrase was absolutely necessary to permit the ROK Government to maintain its dignity as a sovereign government and to enable the Korean negotiators to explain the provisions of this Agreed Minute to the National Assembly.

13. Mr. Habib replied that the U.S. negotiators had presented a formula which provided for the waiver of jurisdiction and the right of recall of that waiver in extremely important cases. They were not prepared to accept any requirement that the U.S. authorities should request waiver in every case. The question of waiver had nothing to do with sovereignty. The German waiver formula in operation has not detracted from German sovereignty. It will not detract

0096

from the sovereignty of the Republic of Korea. The formula proposed by the U.S. negotiators had been designed to meet the often-repeated indication by the Korean negotiators of the Korean requirement to exercise jurisdiction when it was imperative to do so in the interests of Korean justice. The additional phrase proposed by the Korean negotiators would completely reverse the formula proposed by the U.S. negotiators. Paragraph 4 of the proposed Agreed Minute Re Paragraph 3(b) would give the ROK Government the final determination of the exercise of jurisdiction. This is what the Korean negotiators had repeatedly said at past meetings they needed. The waiver formula was a fundamental issue. The U.S. negotiators hoped, therefore, that the Korean negotiators would reconsider their position with regard to their proposed additional phrase in Paragraph 1 of the Agreed Minute.

14. Mr. Chang again referred to the necessity of being able to explain the waiver provision to the National Assembly and reiterated the Korean position that the Korean authorities would be prepared to waive when requested to do so by the U.S. authorities. Mr. Habib reminded the Korean negotiators that not only the National Assembly but also the U.S. Congress was interested in this Agreement and would examine its provisions carefully. He pointed out to the Korean negotiators that the present U.S. draft was actually a compromise between the earlier Korean position and the earlier U.S. position. The U.S. negotiators believed it to be a workable compromise which could be satisfactorily explained to the legislatures of both countries.

0097

15. Mr. Chang then referred to Article 19 of the German Supplementary Agreement, which begins "At the request of the sending state,...". Mr. Habib, in reply, explained the significance of this language in connection with the related Agreed Minute. He explained that, in reality, this was a provision for a blanket waiver which was made by the German Government, insofar as the U.S. armed forces were concerned, at the time when the German Supplementary Agreement became operative. He assured the Korean negotiators that the formula which the U.S. negotiators had presented was the German waiver formula.

0098

3. 제79차 회의, 5.12

0099

기 안 용 지

관리번호 /924

자체통제		기안처	미주과 김기조	전화번호	근거서류접수일자

	과장	국장	차관	장관		

관계관 서명	노정과장	노정국장	노동청차장	노동청장	보사부차관	보사부장관

기안년월일	65. 5. 11.	시행년월일		보존년한		접서기장
분류기호	외구미 722.2	전체통제		종결		
경유수신참조	건의			발신		

제목 제 79차 미주둔군지위협정 체결교섭 실무자회의에

제안할 우리측 노무조항 개정안

우리측이 제 78차회의에서 제안한 노무조항중

고용인의 분쟁해결절차와 파업건에 대하여 미국측은

제 78차 회의에서 이의를 제기함에 당부와 보건사회부

실무자간에 검토한바에 따라 별첨과 같은 우리입장을

수립하여 제 79차회의에서 미측에 수락할것을 제안코저

하오니 재가하여 주시기 바랍니다.

유첨 - 제 79차 회의에 제안할 우리측 노무조항 개정안. 끝

~~~~~~~~~~~~ (66. 12. 31.)

1966. 12. 3에 예고문에
의거 일반문서로 재분류됨

승인서식 1-1-3   (11-00900-03) 3-1   (195mm×265mm16절지)

0100

제 79 차 미주둔군지위협정 체결 교섭 실무자
회의에 제안할 우리측 노무조항 개정안

1. 노동조건의 적용범위

   별도 합의되지 않는한 한국노동법령을 준수하되 준수
   하지 못할 경우에는 가능한한 사건에 합의하도록
   함으로서 전시 혹은 그에 준하는 사태하에서 긴급
   조치를 취할수 있는 여지를 미군에게 부여한다.
   따라서 한국원안 제5항 비상조치항은 삭제한다.

2. 분쟁해결절차

   분쟁해결 절차중 미측은 무기한 고용인의 정상업무
   방해 행위를 금지하자는 안에 대하여 동기간을 70일
   로 한정하기로 하고 다음과 같이 제안한다.

   (1) "분쟁은 대한민국 노동청에 조정을 위하여 회부
       되어야 한다."

       "The dispute shall be referred to the Office of
       Labor Affairs of the Republic of Korea for conciliation."

   (2) "상기 (1)의 절차에 의하여 분쟁이 20일이내에
       해결되지 않을 경우에는 그분쟁은 합동위원회에
       조정을 위하여 회부되어야 하며 합동위원회는
       동건을 노동분과위원회 혹은 특정위원회에 회부
       할수 있다."

       "In the event that the dispute is not settled by the
       procedures described in (1) above within twenty (20)
       days, the dispute shall be referred to the Joint
       Committee, which may refer the matter to the Labor
       Sub-Committee or to a specially-designated Committee
       for further conciliation efforts."

   (3) "상기 절차에 의하여 분쟁이 해결되지 않을 경우
       합동위원회는 동분쟁을 해결한다. 합동위원회의
       결정은 구속력을 갖는다."

3-2   0101

"In the event that the dispute is not settled by
the procedures outlined above, the Joint Committee
will resolve the dispute. The decisions of the
Joint Committee shall be binding."

(4) " 고용인과 고용인 단체는 분쟁이 상기 (1) 의
    노동청에 회부된후 해결없이 70 일의 기간이
    경과하지않는한 정상업무를 방해하는 행위를 하여
    서는 아니된다. "

"Neither employees or employee organizations shall
engage in any practice disruptive of normal work
requirements requirements unless a period of
seventy (70) days has elapsed without settlement after
the dispute is referred to the Office of Labor Affairs
mentioned in (1) above."

(5) 고용인 혹은 고용인 단체가 합동위원회 결정에
    복하지 않거나 전기 (4) 의 규정에 위반하여 정상
    업무를 방해하는 행위를 행하는 것은 대한민국
    노동법령에 의하여 부여된 권리와 보호를 박탈
    하는 원인으로 간주한다.

"Failure of any employee or employee organization
to abide by the decision of the Joint Committee on
any dispute, or engaging in practices disruptive of
normal work requirements in violation of the provisions
laid down in (4) above, shall be considered cause
for depriviation of the rights and protection accorded
by the relevant labor legislation of the Republic of
Korea."

3. 파업권의 행사

제 1 안

미측에서는 파업권을 가능한 최대한도로 제한하려는
것이 기본입장임에 우리측은 원칙적으로 파업권은
인정하되 동행사는 합동위원회의 결정에 따라
          미군의 군사임무수행에 불가결 한자에 대하여는
파업권 행사를 사전에 금하는데 합의할수 있도록 한다.

3-3

0102

LABOR ARTICLE

(Underlining indicates modifications from Korean
draft of the Article tabled at 75th session)

4.   (a) With regard to any dispute between employers and
employees or labor unions which cannot be settled through
the use of existing procedures of the United States Armed
Forces, settlement shall be accomplished in the following
manner:

(1) The dispute shall be referred to the Office of
Labor Affairs of the Republic of Korea for conciliation.

(2) In the event that the dispute is not settled by
the procedures described in (1) above within twenty (20)
days, the dispute shall be referred to the Joint Committee,
which may refer the matter to the Labor sub-Committee or
to a specially-designated Committee, for further conciliation efforts.

(3) In the event that the dispute is not settled by
the procedures outlined above, the Joint Committee will
resolve the dispute. The decisions of the Joint Committee
shall be binding.

(4) Neither employee organizations nor employees
shall engage in any practice disruptive of normal work
requirements unless a period of seventy (70) days has
elapsed without settlement after the dispute is referred
to the Office of Labor Affairs mentioned in (1) above.

(5) Failure of any employee organization or employee
to abide by the decision of the Joint Committee on any
dispute, or engaging in practices disruptive of normal
work requirements in violation of the provisions laid down
in (4) above, shall be considered cause for deprivation
of the rights and protection accorded by the relevant labor
legislation of the Republic of Korea.

0103

6-9

<u>LABOR ARTICLE</u>

(Presentation at the 79th session) *1965. 5. 12.*

1.   The Korean negotiators have carefully reconsidered the
position of U.S. negotiators taken at the 78th session in
order to paye a way to solving the stalemate with a view
to concluding the SOFA negotiations as early as possible.
To this end, intensive consultation has taken place among
the responsible authorities of the Korean Government with
respect to the labor problem. As a result of this consultation, our new proposal is before you, which is the honest
evidence of Korean side to make significant concession with
regard to the Labor Article.

2.   Prior to making explanation on the new proposal, the
Korean negotiators would like to make two principles clear
to the U.S. negotiators. First, we are now negotiating to
frame the status of Korean laborers working for the United
States Armed Forces, ~~whom no one shall consider in any way~~
~~for the purpose of this Article~~ as ~~neither~~ Korean Government employees nor (simple) military personnel of ~~two states~~.
Secondly, since they are laborers working for emoluments,
their rights concerning labor relations ~~shall~~ be protected
along the lines of ~~world-widely recognised~~ standards.
~~We assert once again that these basic principles should be~~
~~fully taken into consideration in our SOFA negotiations.~~
As have been shown, the Korean negotiators, ~~however,~~
are prepared to cooperate with the U.S. Armed Forces
to enable them to carry out common defense mission to the
maximum extent ~~without greatly harming the above-cited~~ two
basic principles. Therefore, we have already agreed to
~~certain~~ deviation of the U.S. Armed Forces from our labor
legislation on account of the military requirements ~~at the~~
~~time~~ of normal situation ~~and~~ emergency.

0104

3.   In this spirit and with the principles in mind,
the Korean side ~~has~~ now ~~made~~ further significant concession
in relation to ~~deviation from our labor legislation~~ labor
dispute settlement procedures, and the exercise of the
right concerning strike. ~~As first instance,~~ we now modify
the Agreed Minute #4 by inserting a phrase "whenever possible"
to meet the U.S. requirements. With this amendment, there
leaves no worry on the part of U.S. side regarding deviation
from our law at the times of unforeseeable circumstances
such as those of emergency situations. Together with this
modification, we delete the first sentence of Paragraph 5
which is no more ~~un~~necessary in light of the former inclusion
of the phrase "whenever possible" in the Agreed Minute #5.

4.   With regard to the settlement procedure of any
labor disputes, we ~~have again made significant~~ modification,
as is shown in the Paragraph 4(a). Our new proposal is
simple and self-explanatory. It provides a ~~complete~~ prohibition of disruptive practice for a maximum period of
70 days while any dispute is referred for settlement to
the ROK Labor Office and the Joint Committee. ~~Under our
new formula, the Labor Office is accorded 20 days limit
for conciliation.~~ This new proposal is based on ~~the fact~~
that there would be no dispute which could not be settled
during 70 days. ~~It implies that there would be a very few~~
~~strikes in the future. This is also the evidence that the~~
~~Korean Government can~~ ~~in cooperation with the U.S.~~
~~side to the fullest extent possible.~~

5.   As for the right concerning strike, the Korean side
hold the view that there would be no need to set forth
special provisions on the right, because the exercise of
the right is heretofore prohibited for 70 days under the

한·미국 간의 상호방위조약 제4조에 의한 시설과 구역 및 한국에서의 미국군대의 지위에 관한 협정(SOFA)
전59권. 1966.7.9 서울에서 서명 : 1967.2.9 발효(조약 232호) (V.30 실무교섭회의, 제77-80차, 1965.5월) 375

provisions of Paragraph 4(a). ~~But, taking into account of the U.S. position held at the previous session~~, the Korean side again modifies the Paragraph 4(b) to the effect that the right to strike shall not be ~~exercised~~ when the Joint Committee so (directs) to certain numbers of employees on account of the U.S. military requirements. As we have already committed at the 75th session, we are prepared to agree with the U.S. side to prohibit the exercise of the right to strike by certain members of the Korean employees working for the U.S. Armed Forces, whose disruptive practice would be greatly detrimental to the military mission of the U.S. Armed Forces.

In concluding, the Korean negotiators believe that the above proposal will meet the satisfaction of the U.S. side and hope that the U.S. side will accept our new proposal as a whole.

~~But, the Korean~~ side ~~negotiators again modify the Para. 4(b) which adds as follows:~~

6-6

0106

기 안 지

기 안 자	미 주 과 이 군 판	전 화 번 호		공 보	필 요	불필요
	과	국 장	차 관	장 관		

협 조 자 서 명					보 존 년 한	
기 안 년 월 일	1965. 5. 18.	시 행 년월일		통 제 관	정 서	기 장
분류기호 문서번호	외구미 722. 2 ―					
경 유 수 신 참 조	대 통 령 참조: 비서실장 국 무 총 리 참조: 비서실장 발 신 사본: 법무부장관 및 보건사회부장관					
제 목	제 79 차 주둔군지위협정 체결 교섭실무자회의 결과 보고					

1965 년 5 월 12 일 하오 4 시 부터 동 5 시 30 분 까지

외무부 제 1 회의실에서 개최된 제 79 차 주둔군지위협정 체결 교섭

실무자회의에서 토의된 노무조항 및 민사청구권조항에 관한

내용을 별첨과 같이 보고합니다.

유 첩: 제 79 차 주둔군지위협정 체결 교섭실무자회의 결과

보고서 1부. 끝.

보통문서로 재분류(1966.12. 31.)

기 안 지

기 안 자	미주과 이 근 팔	전 화 번 호		공 보	필 요	불필요
	과 정	국 장	차 관	장 관		

협조 서명 자명				보 존 년 한	
기안 년월일	1965. 5. 18.	시 행 년월일	~	통제 판	정 서 기 장
분류기호 문서번호	외구미 722.2 —				
경수 참 조	법 무 부 장 관, 참조: 법무국장 보건사회부장관 참조 : 노동청장		발신		장 관
제 목	제 79 차 주둔군지위협정 체결 교섭실무자회의 개최				

　　　　1965 년 5 월 18일 하오 4 시 부터 동 5 시 30 분 까지 의무부

제 1 회의실에서 개최된 제 79 차 주둔군지위협정 체결 교섭실무자회의

에서 토의된 노무조항 및 민사청구권조항에 관한 내용을 별첨과 같이

알리오니 참고하시기 바랍니다.

　　유 첨: 제 79 차 주둔군지위협정 체결 교섭실무자회의 결과보고서

　　　　사본. 1 부. 끝.

보통문서로 재분류(1966 12 31)

공통서식 1—2 (갑)　　　　　　　　　　　　　　　　　　　(16절지)

제 79 차
한·미 주둔군지위협정 체결교섭 실무자회의
보고서

1. 일시   1965년 5월 12일   하오 4시부터 동 5시 30분까지
2. 장소   외무부 제 1 회의실
3. 토의사항

    가. 노무조항 :

        (1) 우리측은 미국측이 제 78 차 회의에서 미군고용인의
파업권 행사에 대하여 주한미군은 한국군과 동일한
임무를 수행함으로 그 고용인의 파업권도 한국군 고용인과
동일하게 규제되어야 한다고 주장한데 대하여 새로운
개정안을 제안하였음. 새로운 제안에 앞서 우리측은
다음과 같은 원칙하에 고용인의 지위와 권리가 규정되어야
한다고 주장함.

            (가) 한국인 노무자는 대한민국 정부고용인도
아니며 어느국가의 군인도 아니다.

            (나) 따라서 그들은 급료를 목적으로 하는 단순한
노무자임으로 노자관계에 있어서의 그들의 권리는 국제적
으로 확립된 기준에 따라 보호되어야 한다.

        (2) 이상 2개원칙을 전제로 하여 다음과 같은
개정안을 제안함.

            (가) 제 4 항 (a) (2) "분쟁이 전기 (1) 절차에 의하여
20일동안에 해결되지 않을 경우, 그본쟁은 합동위원회의
새로운 조정노력을 위하여 합동위원회에 회부되어야 하며
합동위원회는 그사건을 노동분과위원회 혹은 특정위원회에
회부할수 있다.

        (2) In the event that the dispute is not settled
by the procedures described in (1) above within twenty (20)
days, the dispute shall be referred to the Joint Committee,
which may refer the matter to the Labor sub-Committee or
to a specially-designated Committee, for further conciliation
efforts.

0109

65-(→3/3)

앙홍113-7 (5)

0110

(나) 제 4 항 (a) (4) : " 고용인단체 혹은 고용인은 분쟁이 전기 (1)항의 노동청에 회부된 날로부터 해결없이 70일의 기간이 경과하지 않는한 정상업무를 방해하는 행위에 종사하지 못한다. "

(4) Neither employee organizations nor employees shall engage in any practice disruptive of normal work requirements <u>unless a period of seventy (70) days has elapsed without settlement after the dispute is referred to the Office of Labor Affairs mentioned in (1) above.</u>

(3) 이상의 제안으로 어느분쟁이든 조정을 위하여 노동청에 회부되면 그후 70일간은 무조건 고용인은 파업을 포함한 정상업무방해행위를 자행하지 못하게 됨으로서 미군측의 요망을 어느정도 성취시키도록 하였음.
한편 파업권행사에 대하여는 종전안 즉 " 합동위원회가 별도 파업권 행사를 금지한자를 제외하고는 파업권은 고용인에게 부여되어야 한다 " 라는 입장 (75차회의에서 제안) 을 계속 주장함으로서 기본권의 확보를 고수하였음.

나. 민사청구권 조항 :

우리측은, 제 76차회의 때에 미국측이 제안한 민사 청구권조항에 대한 미국측 수정안 중에서 아래와 같은 사항에 관한 한국측 입장에 미국이 합의할 경우, 한국측은 미국측 제안에 동의할 용의가 있음을 밝혔음.

(1) 손해에 대한 책임이 미국에만 있을때의 양국정부 의 분담율은 한국안과 같이 한국 15 퍼센트 미국 85 퍼센트 로 할것.

(2) 한국정부가 지불한 배상금에 대하여는 미국측은 손해배상 책임한계, 배상금액 및 양국정부의 분담안에 대하여 미국이 인정하는 사건에 한하여 한국정부에 청산 하여 주겠다는 입장은, 한국의 민사재판의 판결에 의하여 한국정부가 지불한 배상금도 미국의 인정을 받아야 하는

0111

65-5-13

미문113-7

0112

결과를 초래하므로 한국측으로서는 수락할수 없음.

따라서 그댓신 재판을 제외한 한국정부당국에서 해결하는 경우에 한하여 사전에 손해배상 책임한계와 배상금액에 대하여 합의한다는 아래와 같은 합의의사록을 채택할것.

합의의사록 :

"본조 제5항에 해당되는 청구에 관하여는 대한민국당국이 해결하기 전에 손해배상의 책임과 그손해에 사정할 배상금에 관하여 대한민국과 합중국의 당국이 상호 합의하여야 한다. 그러나, 청구자가 제기할수 있는 고소의 결과로 대한민국의 권위있는 재판소에 의한 그사건에 대한 어떠한 판결도 본협정의 당사국에 대하여 구속력을 가지며 또한 최종적인 것이다. "

Agreed Minute:

"Regarding the claims falling under the provisions of paragraph five of this Article, the authorities of the Republic of Korea and the United States shall seek mutual agreement as to the liability for damages and compensation to be awarded prior to the settlement by the authorities of the Republic of Korea. However, any adjudication of the case by a competent court of the Republic of Korea as a result of a suit which may be instituted by the claimant shall be binding and conclusive upon the Parties of this Agreement."

(3) 민사청구권 조항의 목적을 위하여 KSC 는 한국측 합의의사록 3항과 같이 미군의 고용원으로 간주 할것.

(4) 협정발효전의 청구권에 대한 해결책임은 미국 당국에 있다는 내용을 명시하기 위하여 미측이 제안한 13항을 아래와 같이 수정할것.

Paragraph 13

"The provisions of this Article shall not apply to any claims which arose before the entry into force of this Agreement. Such claims shall be processed and settled by the authorities of the United States."

0113

65-5-13

계속 113-7

0114

(5) 기타 지역에 대한 발효시기는 협정발효 1년후로 할것이며, 그때까지 한국당국에서 청구건 해결 업무를 담당할 준비를 갖추지 못할 경우에는 한국당국은 연기요청을 할수있다는 요지로 미국측이 제안한 합의의사록 "A 2"를 아래와 같이 수정할것:

합의의사록 2항:

"대한민국의 기타지역 내에서의 사고로 부터 발생하는 청구건에 관하여 본조제 5,6,7 및 8항의 규정은 이협정이 효력을 발생하는 날자로부터 12개월후에 효력을 갖는다. 그렇지만, 대한민국당국이 상기 12개월 기간내에 전기각항에 규정된 책임을 담당할 준비가 되지 않았을 경우에는, 대한민국 당국은 합중국의 책임을 연장하기 위하여 대한민국 당국이 준비를 위하여 추가적으로 필요한 기간을 합동위원회에 통보할수 있다."

Agreed Minute A2:

"As to claims arising from incidents in the other areas of the Republic of Korea, the provisions of paragraphs five, six, seven and eight of this Article will become effective twelve months from the date of entry into force of this Agreement. However, in case the authorities of the Republic of Korea are not prepared to assume the responsibility provided for in the preceding paragraphs within the twelve month period, the authorities of the Republic of Korea may notify additional period required for the preparation to the Joint Committee for extention of the responsibility of the United States."

이상과 같은 우리측 주장에 관하여 미국측은 다음과 같은 질의를 함:

(1) 한국측은 양국정부의 손해배상 분담율을 한국 15퍼센트 미국 85퍼센트로 주장하고 있으나 다른 나라에서

0115

65-5-13   메모 113-7

0116

적용하고 있는 표준비율은 접수국이 25퍼센트를 부담하는데 한국은 무슨 이유로 이러한 표준비율에서 이탈하려는가.

　　한국측 답변요지:

　　한국이 15퍼센트만을 부담하려는 것은 한국이 다른나라에 비하여 아직 경제적으로 부유하지 못하며, 현재 외국으로 부터 많은 원조를 받고 있는 입장이기 때문이다.

　　(2) 재판에 의하여 결정된 배상금액이 미국정부가 인정하는 배상금액보다 많을시에 한국정부는 그 차액을 부담하려는 것인가.

　　한국측 답변요지:

　　그렇지 않다. 본조 5(c)항에 의하여 재판에 의한 결정은 당연히 양국정부에 대하여 구속력을 가지게 되어있어, 양국정부는 규정된 비율에 따라 모두 배상금을 부담하여야 한다.

미국측은 한국측이 제안한 수정안에 대하여 다음회의에서 답변하기로 하였음.

　　다. 기타사항

　　차기회의는 양측 실무자대표간에 결정키로 하고 폐회하였음.

0117

43 - 5 - 13 (5)　　　　　　　　　　맥조 13-1 (5)

0118

LABOR ARTICLE

1. Mr. Chang opened the 79th meeting by indicating that the Korean negotiators have carefully reviewed the position taken by the U.S. negotiators at the 78th session in order to pave a way for resolving the stalemate, with a view to concluding the SOFA negotiations as early as possible. To this end, intensive consultation has taken place among the responsible authorities of the Korean Government with respect to the labor problem. As a result of this consultation, the new ROK proposal is ready to present. This proposal is an honest evidence of Korean side's desire to make a significant concession with regard to the Labor Article.

2. Prior to explaining the new proposal, Mr. Chang stated that the Korean negotiators would like to make two principles clear to the U.S. negotiators. First, the two sides are now negotiating to decide the status of Korean laborers working for the United States Armed Forces. Such laborers should not be considered either as Korean Government employees or military personnel of any state. Secondly, since they are simple laborers working for emoluments, their rights concerning labor relations should be protected along the lines of established and world-wide standards. The Korean negotiators, however, are prepared to cooperate with the U.S. Armed Forces to enable them to carry out our common defense mission to the maximum extent possible on the basis of the foregoing two basic principles. Therefore, the ROK negotiators have already agreed to possible deviation of the U. S. Armed Forces from ROK labor legislation on account of the military requirements under normal situation as well as in time of emergency.

3. Mr. Chang stated, that, in this spirit of cooperation and with the foregoing two principles in mind, the Korean side now wishes to make further

0113

significant concessions relating to procedures to settle labor disputes and concerning the exercise of the right to strike.

4. With regard to procedures to settle any labor dispute, the ROK side propose/amendments to paragraph 4 (a), as follows:

Paragraph 4. (a)

"(2) In the event that the dispute is not settled by the procedures described in (1) above within twenty (20) days, the dispute shall be referred to the Joint Committee, which may refer the matter to the Labor Sub-Committee or to a specially-designated committee, for further conciliation efforts."

"(4) Neither employee organizations nor employees shall engage in any practice disruptive of normal work requirements unless a period of seventy (70) days has elapsed without settlement after the dispute is referred to the Office of Labor Affairs mentioned in (1) above."

Mr. Chang explained that
5. /this new language provides for a complete prohibition of disruptive practices for a maximum period of 70 days while any dispute is referred for settlement to the ROK Labor Office and to the Joint Committee. This new proposal is based on the ROK belief that there would be no dispute which could not be settled during 70 days. Under this formula, the ROK negotiators envisage no dispute would lead to a strike in a practical sense, although employees would retain the ultimate, but almost non-practical, right to strike.

2

0120

5. Concerning the right to strike, Mr. Chang said that the Korean side holds the view that there would be no need to set forth special provisions on this right, because the exercise of this right had heretofore been prohibited for 70 days under the provisions of Paragraph 4(a). As the ROK negotiators have already committed themselves at the 75th session, they are prepared to agree with the US side to prohibit the exercise of the right to strike by certain categories of Korean employees working for the US Armed Forces, when such disruptive practices would be greatly detrimental to the military mission of the US Armed Forces.

6. In conclusion, Mr. Chang emphasized that the Korean negotiators believe that the foregoing proposal will meet the requirements of the US Armed Forces, and they hope that the US side will accept these new proposals as a whole.

7. Mr. Habib asked to have the two principles enunciated in paragraph 2 above repeated and then he asked, if these principles were consistent with paragraph 4 (b) of the ROK draft? Mr. Chang stated that these principles are subject to (modification) and in paragraph 4 (b) the ROK Government agrees that the right to strike shall be accorded to employees, except those whose exercise of this right is prohibited by the Joint Committee.

8. Mr. Habib asked if these two principles are consistent with US-ROK military requirements for the defense of the Republic of Korea? The US has consistently maintained the position that the US military are in Korea solely to assist in the defense of the Republic of Korea, and that the USFK Korean employees are a vital part of this defense. The Korean negotiators refer

3

한·미국 간의 상호방위조약 제4조에 의한 시설과 구역 및 한국에서의 미국군대의 지위에 관한 협정(SOFA) 전59권. 1966.7.9 서울에서 서명 : 1967.2.9 발효(조약 232호) (V.30 실무교섭회의, 제77-80차, 1965.5월) 391

to these USFK employees as laborers, but as explained at the 72nd negotiating session, less than 5 percent of the present USFK employees are in the unskilled labor-pool category, while most are skilled workers performing functions important to the joint defense position of the US and ROK armed forces.

9. Mr. Habib emphasized that it was in the mutual interest of our two governments to establish procedures for settling labor disputes amicably and without adversely affecting the defense of the Republic of Korea. That is what the US draft is designed to accomplish. We seek non-discrimination against USFK employees. We compare the USFK employees with ROK armed forces employees because they are similar employees performing similar functions for similar objectives. The US has agreed to conform to ROK labor legislation, taking into consideration special military requirements. We recognize the right of USFK employees to have a union and the USFK deals with it on matters of mutual concern. We have proposed comprehensive procedures for the amicable settlement of disputes. All the US is asking is that the ROK Government apply the same legal provisions in the one area of strikes and work stoppages to USFK employees working in the defense of their country as the ROK applies to Korean Government armed forces employees. We do not think this position is unreasonable. What's wrong with this US position?

10. Mr. Chang replied that the ROK negotiators had agreed that special conditions and procedures would be applicable to USFK employees in the Labor Article because of the role of such employees in the defense of the Republic. understand ~~The Korean negotiators recognize the strength and logic of the US position that US and ROK armed forces workers are in a comparable position.~~ But the ROK Government cannot agree that such USFK employees are comparable to ROK

army employees including the civilian components (Mun-Kwan)

4

(and its employees)

Government officials and it cannot agree that such employees will be denied their constitutional rights. Mr. Chang emphasized that, in providing for 70 days for the arbitration procedures to operate, the Korean negotiators firmly believe that chances of strikes would be wiped out. *almost non-existent in practical sense.* In the past the ROK Office of Labor Affairs has cooperated with USFK authorities to prevent strikes and they will continue to do so. *this Office* *Furthermore,* The ROK Government has provided that the Joint Committee can establish categories of essential employees, who because of their important defense work will be prohibited from exercising the right to strike. Thus, although the ROK draft avoid any *particular* provision which specifically denies all USFK workers the right to strike, the ROK proposal in effect almost *limits* eliminates the possibility of strikes. *(to the extent reasonable)* Mr. Chang urged that the US side give careful consideration to these Korean views.

(proposal and)

11. Mr. Habib answered that the Korean views would be carefully considered. He asked *in turn,* for the ROK Government's understanding of the role of USFK's Korean employees. The US side firmly believes that the long term interests of both the US and ROK Governments, as well as the welfare of USFK employees, requires that both sides accept the realities of their important role in the defense of the Republic of Korea.

5

0123

한·미국 간의 상호방위조약 제4조에 의한 시설과 구역 및 한국에서의 미국군대의 지위에 관한 협정(SOFA) 전59권. 1966.7.9 서울에서 서명 : 1967.2.9 발효(조약 232호) (V.30 실무교섭회의, 제77-80차, 1965.5월) 393

Claims Article

12. Mr. Chang ~~opened the meeting by stating~~ stated that the Korean negotiators
have given the most careful consideration to the proposal of the United
States negotiators regarding the Claims Article made at the 76th session.

14 ~~13.~~ Mr. Chang indicated that the Korean negotiators agree with the
views of the United States negotiators, expressed at the previous session,
that the point has now been reached where a solution of the problem with
respect to this Article must be found. Accordingly, the Korean negotiators
are prepared to accept the proposed changes in Korean draft as proposed by
the United States side as well as the new paragraphs and Agreed Minute
tabled by the United States side, subject to the following conditions and
modifications as set forth below.

5 ~~14.~~ Regarding paragraph 5(e) (i), the Korean negotiators still stand on
their original position that the Korean Government should share 15% of the
cost of satisfying the claims for which the United States alone is responsible.

6 ~~15.~~ Regarding paragraph 5(e) (iii), Mr. Chang stated that the changes
proposed by the United States negotiators are unacceptable. The proposed
changes in this subparagraph directly contradict the basic principles of
the claims settlement procedures laid down by the subparagraphs (a), (b) and
(c) of paragraph 5, which the United States negotiators have already accepted
at an earlier session. However, to accommodate the concern of the United
States side to the maximum extent practicable, the Korean negotiators are
prepared to propose the following sentences as an Agreed Minute for
paragraph 5 of this Article:

6

0124

"Regarding the claims falling under the
provisions of paragraph five of this Article,
the authorities of the Republic of Korea and
the United States shall seek mutual agreement
as to the liability for damages and compensation
to be awarded prior to the settlement by the
authorities of the Republic of Korea. However,
any adjudication of the case by a competent
court of the Republic of Korea as a result of
a suit which may be instituted by the claimant
shall be binding and conclusive upon the Parties
of this Agreement."

16. This new Agreed Minute, the Korean negotiators believe, would fully

meet the requirements of both sides. This system would allow each side to

review the liability and propriety of the award, and guarantee mutual agree-

ment between the two parties prior to the settlement by the authorities of

the Republic of Korea.

17. Regarding any case which would be decided by a competent court,

Mr. Chang emphasized that it is logical that the judgement of such a court and

payment of an award in accordance with the judgement should be binding upon

both parties in the light of the principle agreed upon by the provisions set

forth in subparagraph 5(c).

18. Regarding paragraph 12 of the United States draft, Mr. Chang stated

that the Korean negotiators still believe that the Korean Service Corps (KSC)

employees should be considered to be employees of the United States armed

forces for the purposes of this Article, as proposed in Agreed Minute 3 of

the Korean draft. The Korean negotiators would like to point out that it is

delete not the present practice or policy of the Korean Government, as the United

States side mentioned at the previous session, to assume responsibility for

any claims which arise out of the acts or omissions of the KSC in the course

of their performance of the duties which are directed by the United States

7

한·미국 간의 상호방위조약 제4조에 의한 시설과 구역 및 한국에서의 미국군대의 지위에 관한 협정(SOFA)
전59권. 1966.7.9 서울에서 서명 : 1967.2.9 발효(조약 232호) (V.30 실무교섭회의, 제77-80차, 1965.5월)   395

armed forces.

19. Regarding paragraph 13, the Korean negotiators accept the United States proposal with the addition of a few more words which will more clearly spell out the liability for claims which arose before the Agreement comes into force. Therefore, the Korean negotiators wish to propose an additional sentence so that the revised paragraph 13 should read as follows:

> "The provisions of this Article shall not apply to any claims which arose before the entry into force of this Agreement. Such claims shall be processed and settled by the authorities of the United States."

20. Regarding the Agreed Minute A2, Mr. Chang indicated that the Korean negotiators wished to clearly set forth a definite effective date of the provisions of the paragraphs covered in the Agreed Minute. Therefore, the Korean negotiators propose x to modify the paragraph A2 of the proposed Agreed Minute of the United States negotiators as follows:

> "As to claims arising from incidents in the
>
> other areas of the Republic of Korea, the provisions of paragraphs five, six, seven and eight of this Article will become effective twelve months from the date of entry into force of this Agreement. However, in case the authorities of the Republic of Korea are not prepared to assume the responsibility provided for in the preceding paragraphs within the twelve-month period, the authorities of the Republic of Korea may notify additional period required for the preparation to the Joint Committee for extention of the responsibility of the United States."

21. Mr. Chang stated that the Korean negotiators believe that the twelve-month period provided for in the Korean proposal is long enough to adopt the system in the other areas of the Republic of Korea. Nevertheless, the Korean negotiators would be willing to postpone the effective date of those

0126

provisions until such time as the Korean authorities are prepared to take
over the claims responsibilities. This, the Korean negotiators believe,
would suffice to meet the expressed concern of the United States negotiators.

28 11. Mr. Habib replied that the United States side would take these
proposals under consideration, but that he could say right now he was sure
some of the proposed ROK modifications of the Claims Article draft were not
acceptable. For example, the payment of claims on a 75% - 25% has become
standard for almost all such ~~agreements~~ and he could see no reason to make an
exception in Korea. Mr. Chang mentioned Korea was an aid receiving country,
receiving generous assistance from the US in many fields, and that therefore
the 85% - 15% formula proposed by the ROK authorities would be appropriate. Mr.
Habib replied that the US offered the ROK authorities a proposal that would
have required that the US Claims Service pay 100% of the claims against the
USFK, but the ROK negotiators rejected such a proposal. If you want to
play the game, you have to pay the cost, Mr. Habib remarked.

26 12. Mr. Habib inquired about the meaning of the new ROK proposed Agreed
Minute Re Para 5. Mr. Chang explained the new proposal was designed to insure
respond to the U.S. requirement to the maximum extent practicable by insuring
that while ROK and US authorities shall seek mutual agreement as to the
and propriety of the award prior to the settlement by claims authorities of the Government of RO
liability ~~(regarding claims)~~ any adjudication by a competent ROK court shall be
binding upon both parties to this agreement. Mr. Habib indicated that such
language was unnecessary, for this point was covered in paragraph 5.(c). The
new Agreed Minute creates a problem where none previously existed. However,
deletion of the US Paragraph 5(e) (iii), as proposed by the ROK, was
unacceptable, Mr. Habib emphasized. Mr. Chang replied that the Agreed Minute
was (needed to ratify an apparent contradiction in the US proposal.) Mr. Habib
proposed with a view to replacing the U.S proposal regarding para 5(c) (iii).

0127

reminded the ROK negotiators that the new ROK language did not provide for mutual agreement on the liability, amount, and proposed distribution as is the actual practice under the US—Japan SOFA. Mr. Habib indicated that the US side would make a formal response to the new ROK proposals regarding Claims Article at an early meeting, after studying them in detail.

10.

0128

<u>LABOR ARTICLE</u>   *Copy give to Fleek*

(Presented at the 79th session, May 12, 1965)

1. The Korean negotiators have carefully reconsidered the position of U.S. negotiators taken at the 78th session in order to pave a way to solving the stalemate with a view to concluding the SOFA negotiations as early as possible. To this end, intensive consultation has taken place among the responsible authorities of the Korean Government with respect to the labor problem. As a result of this consultation, our new proposal is ready to present to you, which is the honest evidence of Korean side to make significant concession with regard to the Labor Article.

2. Prior to making explanation on the new proposal, the Korean negotiators would like to make two principles clear to the U.S. negotiators. First, we are now negotiating to frame the status of Korean laborers working for the United States Armed Forces. They should not be considered as either Korean Government employees or military personnel of any state. Secondly, since they are simple laborers working for emoluments, their rights concerning labor relations should be protected along the lines of established and world-wide standards. The Korean negotiators, however, are prepared to cooperate with the U.S. Armed Forces to enable them to carry out common defense mission to the maximum extent on the basis of the two basic principles. Therefore, we have already agreed to possible deviation of the U.S. Armed Forces from our labor legislation on account of the military requirements under normal situation as well as in time of emergency.

3. In this spirit of cooperation and with the principles in mind, the Korean side now makes further significant concession in relation to labor dispute settlement procedures and the exercise of the right concerning strike.

4. With regard to the settlement procedure of any labor dispute, we make amendment, but last modifications which read as follows:

6-1

0129

Paragraph 4. (a)

"(2) In the event that the dispute is not settled by the procedures described in (1) above, within twenty (20) days, the dispute shall be referred to the Joint Committee, which may refer the matter to the Labor Sub-Committee or to a specially-designated committee, for further conciliation efforts."

"(4) Neither employee organizations nor employees shall engage in any practice disruptive of normal work requirements unless a period of seventy (70) days has elapsed without settlement after the dispute is referred to the Office of Labor Affairs mentioned in (1) above."

This provides a complete prohibition of disruptive practice for a maximum period of 70 days while any dispute is referred for settlement to the ROK Labor Office and the Joint Committee. This new proposal is based on our belief that there would be no dispute which could not be settled during 70 days. Under this formula, we envisage no dispute would lead to strike in practical sense, while retaining ultimate, but almost non-practical right to strike for the employees.

5. As for the right concerning strike, the Korean side holds the view that there would be no need to set forth special provisions on the right, because the exercise of the right is heretofore prohibited for 70 days under the provisions of Paragraph 4 (a). As we have already committed at the 75th session, we are prepared to agree with the U.S. side to prohibit the exercise of the right to strike by certain members of the Korean employees working for the U.S. Armed Forces, whose disruptive practice would be greatly detrimental to the military mission of the U.S. Armed Forces.

In concluding, the Korean negotiators believe that the above proposal will meet the satisfaction of the U.S. Armed Forces and hope that the U.S. side will accpet our new proposal as a whole.

- 2 -

0130

<u>Claims Article</u>

(79th Session)

The Korean negotiators have given most careful consideration to the proposal of the United States negotiators made at the 76th session regarding the Claims Article.

The Korean negotiators are of the same belief as the United States negotiators expressed at the previous session that the point has now been reached where a solution of the problem with respect to this Article must be found.

Accordingly, the Korean negotiators are prepared to accept the proposed changes in Korean draft as proposed by the United States side as well as the new paragraphs and Agreed Minute tabled by the United States side, subject to the following conditions and modifications.

1. Regarding paragraph 5(e)(i), the original position of the Korean negotiators that the Korean Government should share 15% of the cost satisfying the claims for which the United States alone is responsible still stand.

2. Regarding paragraph 5(e)(iii), the changes proposed by the United States negotiators is unacceptable. The proposed changes regarding this subparagraph contradicts directly with the basic principles of the claims settlement procedures laid down by the subparagraphs (a), (b) and (c) of paragraph 5, which the United States negotiators have already accepted at the previous session. However, to accomodate the concerns of the United States side to the maximum extent practicable, the Korean negotiators are prepared to propose the following sentences as an Agreed Minute for paragraph 5 of this Article.

0131

"Regarding the claims falling under the
provisions of paragraph five of this Article,
the authorities of the Republic of Korea and
the United States shall seek mutual agreement
as to the liability for damages and compensation
to be awarded prior to the settlement by the
authorities of the Republic of Korea. However,
any adjudication of the case by a competent
court of the Repbulic of Korea as a result of
a suit which may be instituted by the claimant
shall be binding and conclusive upon the Parties
of this Agreement."

This new Agreed Minute, the Korean negotiators believe,
would fully meet the requirements of both sides. This system
would allow each side to review liability and propriety of
the award, and guarantee mutual agreement between the two
parties prior to the settlement by the authorities of the
Republic of Korea.

As to any case which would be decided at the court, it
is logical that the judgement of any competent court and payment of award in accordance with the judgement should be binding upon the both parties in the light of principle agreed
upon by the provisions set forth in subparagraph 5(c).

3. Regarding paragraph 12 of the United States draft, the
Korean negotiators still believe that the Korean Service Corps
(KSC) should be considered as employee of the United States
armed forces for the purposes of this Article as proposed by
Agreed Minute 3 of the Korean draft. The Korean negotiators
would like to point out that it is not the present practices
or policies of the Korean Government, as the United States
side mentioned at the previous session, to assume responsibility for any claims which arose by the acts or omissions
of the KSC in the course of their performance of the duties
which are directed by the United States armed forces.

0132

4. Regarding paragraph 13, the Korean negotiators accept the
United States proposal with a few more words which will more
clearly spell out the liability for claims which arose before
the Agreement comes into force. Therefore, the Korean negotiators wish to propose an additional sentence so that the
provisions of paragraph 13 should read as following:

> "The provisions of this Article shall not
> apply to any claims which arose before the entry
> into force of this Agreement. Such claims shall be
> processed and settled by the authorities of the
> United States."

5. Regarding the Agreed Minute A2, the Korean negotiators
wish to clearly set forth a definite effective date of the
provisions of the paragraphs covered in the Agreed Minute.
Therefore, the Korean negotiators propose to modify the
paragraph A2 of the proposed Agreed Minute of the United
States negotiators as following:

> "As to claims arising from incidents in the
> other areas of the Republic of Korea, the provisions
> of paragraphs five, six, seven and eight of this
> Article will become effective twelve months from
> the date of entry into force of this Agreement.
> However, in case the authorities of the Republic of
> Korea are not prepared to assume the reponsibility
> provided for in the preceding paragraphs within
> the twelve month period, the authorities of the
> Republic of Korea may notify additional period
> required for the preparation to the Joint Committee
> for extention of the responsibility of the United
> States."

The Korean negotiators believe that the twelve month
period provided for in the Korean proposal is long enough
to adopt the system in the other areas of the Republic of
Korea. Nevertheless, the Korean negotiators would be willing to postpone the effective date of those provisions until
such time as the Korean authorities are prepared to take
over the claims responsibilities. This, the Korean negotiators
believe, would suffice the expressed concern of the United
States negotiators.

0133

<u>JOINT SUMMARY RECORD OF THE 79TH SESSION</u>

1. Time and Place: 4:00-5:30 P.M., May 12, 1965 at the
   Foreign Ministry's Conference Room
   (No.1)

2. Attendance:

ROK Side:

Mr. Chang, Sang Moon	Director European and American Affairs Bureau
Mr. Kim, Dong Hwi	Chief Treaty Section Ministry of Foreign Affairs
Mr. Choo, Moon Ki	Chief Legal Affairs Section Ministry of Justice
Mr. Kim, Tai Chung	Chief Labor Administration Section Office of Labor Affairs
Maj. Lee, Key Hoon	Military Affairs Section Ministry of National Defense
Mr. Kim, Kee Joe	3rd Secretary Ministry of Foreign Affairs
Mr. Lee, Keun Pal (Interpreter)	3rd Secretary Ministry of Foreign Affairs
Mr. Hwang, Young Jae	3rd Secretary Ministry of Foreign Affairs
Mr. Park, Won Chul	3rd Secretary Ministry of Foreign Affairs

U.S. Side:

Mr. Philip C. Habib	Counselor American Embassy
Brig. Gen. Carroll H. Dunn	Deputy Chief of Staff 8th U.S. Army
Col. Allan G. Pixton	Deputy Chief of Staff 8th U.S. Army
Capt. George Hagerman	Assistant Chief of Staff USN/K
Col. Kenneth C. Crawford	Staff Judge Advocate 8th U.S. Army

0134

Mr. Frank R. LaMacchia	First Secretary American Embassy
Mr. Benjamin A. Fleck	First Secretary American Embassy
Mr. Robert A. Kinney	J-5 8th U.S. Army
Mr. Goodwin Shapiro	Second Secretary American Embassy
Maj. Alton H. Harvey	Staff Judge Advocate's Office 8th U.S. Army
Mr. David Y.C. Lee	Second Secretary American Embassy
Mr. Ogden C. Reed	Civilian Personnel Director 8th U.S. Army

Labor Article

1. Mr. Chang opened the 79th meeting by indicating
that the Korean negotiators have carefully reviewed the
position taken by the U.S. negotiators at the 78th session
in order to pave a way for resolving the stalemate, with
a view to concluding the SOFA negotiations as early as
possible. To this end, intensive consultation has taken
place among the responsible authorities of the Korean
Government with respect to the labor problem. As a result
of this consultation, the new ROK proposal is ready to
present. This proposal is honest evidence of Korean side's
desire to make a significant concession with regard to the
Labor Article.

2. Prior to explaining the new proposal, Mr. Chang
stated that the Korean negotiators would like to make two
principles clear to the U.S. negotiators. First, the two
sides are now negotiating to decide the status of Korean
laborers working for the United States armed forces.
Such laborers should not be considered either as Korean

0135

Government employees or military personnel of any state. Secondly, since they are simple laborers working for emoluments, their rights concerning labor relations should be protected along the lines of established and world-wide standards. The Korean negotiators, however, are prepared to cooperate with the U.S. Armed Forces to enable them to carry out our common defense mission to the maximum extent possible on the basis of the foregoing two basic principles. Therefore, the ROK negotiators have already agreed to possible deviation of the U.S. armed forces from ROK labor legislation on account of the military requirements under normal situation as well as in time of emergency.

3. Mr. Chang stated, that, in this spirit of cooperation and with the foregoing two principles in mind, the Korean side now wishes to make further significant concessions relating to procedures to settle labor disputes and concerning the exercise of the right to strike.

4. With regard to procedures to settle any labor dispute, the ROK side proposes amendments to paragraph 4(a), as follows:

Paragraph 4(a)

"(2) In the event that the dispute is not settled by the procedures described in (1) above within twenty (20) days, the dispute shall be referred to the Joint Committee, which may refer the matter to the Labor Sub-Committee or to a specially-designated committee, for further conciliation efforts."

"(4) Neither employee organizations nor employees shall engage in any practice disruptive of normal work requirements unless a period of seventy (70) days has elapsed without settlement after the

0136

dispute is referred to the Office of Labor
Affairs mentioned in (1) above."

5. Mr. Chang explained that this new language provides
for a complete prohibition of disruptive practices for
a maximum period of 70 days while any dispute is referred
for settlement to the ROK Labor Office and to the Joint
Committee. This new proposal is based on the ROK belief
that there would be no dispute which could not be settled
during 70 days. Under this formula, the ROK negotiators
envisage no dispute would lead to a strike in a practical
sense, although employees would retain the ultimate, but
almost non-practical, right to strike.

6. Concerning the right to strike, Mr. Chang said
that the Korean side holds the view that there would be no
need to set forth special provisions on this right, because
the exercise of this right had heretofore been prohibited
for 70 days under the provisions of Paragraph 4(a). As
the ROK negotiators have already committed themselves at
the 75th session, they are prepared to agree with the US
side to prohibit the exercise of the right to strike by
certain categories of Korean employees working for the
US Armed Forces, when such disruptive practices would be
greatly detrimental to the military mission of the US
Armed Forces.

7. In conclusion, Mr. Chang emphasized that the
Korean negotiators believe that the foregoing proposal will
meet the requirements of the US Armed Forces, and they
hope that the US side will accept these new proposals as
a whole.

8. Mr. Habib asked to have the two principles enunciated
in paragraph 2 above repeated and then he asked if these
principles were consistent with paragraph 4(b) of the ROK

0137

draft? Mr. Chang stated that these principles are subject
to modification, and in paragraph 4(b) the ROK Government
agrees that the right to strike shall be accorded to
employees, except those whose exercise of this right is
prohibited by the Joint Committee.

9. Mr. Habib asked if these two principles are
consistent with US-ROK military requirements for the defense
of the Republic of Korea? The US has consistently maintained
the position that the US military are in Korea solely to
assist in the defense of the Republic of Korea, and that the
USFK Korean employees are a vital part of this defense.
The Korean negotiators refer to these USFK employees
as laborers, but as explained at the 72nd negotiating
session, less than 5 percent of the present USFK employees
are in the unskilled labor-pool category, while most are
skilled workers performing functions important to the
joint defense position on the US and ROK armed forces.

10. Mr. Habib emphasized that it was in the mutual interest
of our two governments to establish procedures for settling
labor disputes amicably and without adversely affecting
the defense of the Republic of Korea. That is what the
US draft is designed to accomplish. We seek non-discrimination against USFK employees. We compare the USFK employees
with ROK armed forces employees because they are similar
employees performing similar functions for similar
objectives. The US has agreed to conform to ROK labor
legislation, taking into consideration special military
requirements. We recognize the right of USFK employees to
have a union and the USFK deals with it on matters of
mutual concern. We have proposed comprehensive procedures

0138

for the amicable settlement of disputes. All the US is
asking is that the ROK Government apply the same legal
provisions in the one area of strikes and work stoppages
to USFK employees working in the defense of their country
as the ROK applies to Korean Government armed forces employees.
We do not think this position is unreasonable.

11. Mr. Chang replied that the ROK negotiators had
agreed that special conditions and procedures would be
applicable to USFK employees in the Labor Article because
of the role of such employees in the defense of the
Republic. But the ROK Government cannot agree that such
USFK employees are comparable to ROK army employees including the
civilian components (Mun-Kwan) and Government officials
or employees and it cannot agree that such employees will
be denied their constitutional rights. Mr. Chang emphasized
that, in providing for 70 days for the arbitration procedures
to operate, the Korean negotiators firmly believe that chances
of strikes would be almost non-existent in practical sense.
In the past the ROK Office of Labor Affairs has cooperated
with USFK authorities to prevent strikes and this office
will continue to do so. Furthermore, the ROK Government
has provided that the Joint Committee can establish categories
of essential employees who will be prohibited from exercising
the right to strike. Thus, although the ROK draft avoids
any particular provision which specifically denies all
USFK workers the right to strike, the ROK proposal in
effect limits the possibility of strikes to the extent
reasonable. Mr. Chang urged that the US side give careful
consideration to these Korean proposal and views.

0139

12. Mr. Habib answered that the Korean views would be carefully considered. He asked in turn, for the ROK Government's understanding of the role of USFK's Korean employees. The US side firmly believes that the long term interests of both the US and ROK Governments, as well as the welfare of USFK employees, requires that both sides accept the realities of their important role in the defense of the Republic of Korea.

Claims Article

13. Mr. Chang stated that the Korean negotiators have given the most careful consideration to the proposal of the United States negotiators regarding the Claims Article made at the 76th session.

14. Mr. Chang indicated that the Korean negotiators agree with the views of the United States negotiators, expressed at the previous session, that the point has now been reached where a solution of the problem with respect to this Article must be found. Accordingly, the Korean negotiators are prepared to accept the proposed changes in Korean draft as proposed by the United States side as well as the new paragraphs and Agreed Minute tabled by the United States side, subject to the following conditions and modifications as set forth below.

15. Regarding paragraph 5(e)(i), the Korean negotiators still stand on their original position that the Korean Government should share 15% of the cost of satisfying the claims for which the United States alone is responsible.

16. Regarding paragraph 5(e)(iii), Mr. Chang stated that the changes proposed by the United States negotiators are unacceptable. The proposed changes in this subparagraph

0140

directly contradict the basic principles of the claims
settlement procedures laid down by the subparagraphs (a),
(b) and (c) of paragraph 5, which the United States
negotiators have already accepted at an earlier session.
However, to accommodate the concern of the United States
side to the maximum extent practicable, the Korean
negotiators are prepared to propose the following sentences
as an Agreed Minute for paragraph 5 of this Article:

> "Regarding the claims falling under the
> provisions of paragraph five of this Article, the
> authorities of the Republic of Korea and the
> United States shall seek mutual agreement as to
> the liability for damages and compensation to be
> awarded prior to the settlement by the authorities
> of the Republic of Korea. However, any adjudication
> of the case by a competent court of the Republic of
> Korea as a result of a suit which may be instituted
> by the claimant shall be binding and conclusive upon
> the Parties of this Agreement."

17. This new Agreed Minute, the Korean negotiators
believe, would fully meet the requirements of both sides.
This system would allow each side to review the liability
and propriety of the award, and guarantee mutual agreement
between the two parties prior to the settlement by the
authorities of the Republic of Korea.

18. Regarding any case which would be decided by a
competent court, Mr. Chang emphasized that it is logical that
the judgement of such a court and payment of an award in
accordance with the judgement should be binding upon both
parties in the light of the principle agreed upon by the
provisions set forth in subparagraph 5(c).

19. Regarding paragraph 12 of the United States
draft, Mr. Chang stated that the Korean negotiators still
believe that the Korean Service Corps (KSC) employees
should be considered to be employees of the United States
armed forces for the purposes of this Article, as proposed

in Agreed Minute 3 of the Korean draft. The Korean
negotiators would like to point out that it is not
the present practice or policy of the Korean Government,
to assume responsibility for any claims which arise out
of the acts or omissions of the KSC in the course of their
performance of the duties which are directed by the United
States armed forces.

20. Regarding paragraph 13, the Korean negotiators
accept the United States proposal with the addition of
a few more words which will more clearly spell out the
liability for claims which arose before the Agreement
comes into force. Therefore, the Korean negotiators wish
to propose an additional sentence so that the revised
paragraph 13 should read as follows:

> "The provisions of this Article shall not
> apply to any claims which arose before the entry
> into force of this Agreement. Such claims shall be
> processed and settled by the authorities of the
> United States."

21. Regarding the Agreed Minute A2, Mr. Chang
indicated that the Korean negotiators wished to clearly
set forth a definite effective date of the provisions of
the paragraphs covered in the Agreed Minute. Therefore,
the Korean negotiators propose to modify the paragraph A2
of the proposed Agreed Minute of the United States negotiators
as follows:

> "As to claims arising from incidents in the
> other areas of the Republic of Korea, the provisions
> of paragraphs five, six, seven and eight of this Article
> will become effective twelve months from the date of
> entry into force of this Agreement. However, in case
> the authorities of the Republic of Korea are not
> prepared to assume the responsibility provided for
> in the preceding paragraphs within the twelve-month
> period, the authorities of the Republic of Korea may
> notify additional period required for the preparation
> to the Joint Committee for extention of the responsibi-
> lity of the United States."

0142

22. Mr. Chang stated that the Korean negotiators believe that the twelve-month period provided for in the Korean proposal is long enough to adopt the system in the other areas of the Republic of Korea. Nevertheless, the Korean negotiators would be willing to postpone the effective date of those provisions until such time as the Korean authorities are prepared to take over the claims responsibilities. This, the Korean negotiators believe, would suffice to meet the expressed concern of the United States negotiators.

23. Mr. Habib replied that the United States side would take these proposals under consideration, but that he could say right now he was sure some of the proposed ROK modifications of the Claims Article draft were not acceptable. For example, the payment of claims on a 75% - 25% has become standard for almost all such agreements and he could see no reason to make an exception in Korea.

24. Mr. Habib inquired about the meaning of the new ROK proposed Agreed Minute Re Para 5. Mr. Chang explained the new proposal was designed to respond to the U.S. requirement to the maximum extent practicable by insuring that while ROK and US authorities shall seek mutual agreement as to the liability and propriety of the award prior to the settlement by claims authorities of the Government of ROK, any adjudication by a competent ROK court shall be binding upon both parties to this agreement. Mr. Habib indicated that such language was unnecessary, for this point was covered in paragraph 5.(c). The new Agreed Minute creates a problem where none previously existed. However, deletion of the US Paragraph 5(e) (iii), as proposed by the ROK, was unacceptable, Mr. Habib emphasized. Mr. Chang replied that the Agreed Minute was

0143

proposed with a view to replacing the U.S. proposal regarding
Para 5(e)(iii). Mr. Habib reminded the ROK negotiators
that the new ROK language did not provide for mutual agreement on the liability, amount, and proposed distribution
as is the actual practice under the US-Japan SOFA. Mr.
Habib indicated that the US side would make a formal
response to the new ROK proposals regarding Claims Article
at an early meeting, after studying them in detail.

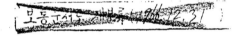

0144

4. 제80차 회의, 5.28

0145

기 안 지

폐안 65/5/11

기 안 자	미주과 황영재	전 화 번 호		공 보	필 요	불필요
		과 장	국 장	차 관	장 관	
협 조 자 서 명	법무부: 법무과장	법무국장	법무차관	법무장관	보 존 년 한	
기 안 년 월 일	65. 5. 11.	시 행 년월일		통제관	정 서	기 장
분류기호 문서번호	외구미 722.2					
경 수 참 조	유 신	건 의	발 신			
제 목	민사청구권 조항의 일괄 타결을 위한 우리측 입장					

주둔군지위협정 체결교섭에 있어 민사청구권조항에 관한

미해결 문제를 일괄 타결하기 위하여, 제 76 차 실무자 회의에서

미국측이 한국측 초안을 수락할 조건을 제시한 수정안에 대하여 별첨과

같이 우리측의 입장을 수립하여 차기 회의에서 미국측에 제안코저

하오니 재가 하여주시기 바랍니다.

유첨: 민사청구권조항에 대한 우리측 입장, 1부 끝

보통문서로 재분류(1966.12.31)

1.6

공통서식 1—2 (갑)   (16절지)

제76차 회의에서 미국측이 제안한 민사청구권 조항에 대한 수정안에 대하여 아래와 같이 우리측의 입장을 수립한다:

1. 용어의 수정

   가. 미국측 제안:

     조문해석상 의미의 차이는 없으나 다른 조항과 일치되는 용어를 사용하기 위하여 아래와 같이 수정할것:

     (1) "armed services" 를 "armed forces" 로 수정. (1, 1(a), 1(b), 4 및 5(e)(ii) 항)

     (2) "execution of his official duties" 를 "performance of his official duties" 로 수정. (1(a) 항)

     (3) "in the execution of its official duty" 를 "for official purposes" 로 수정. (1(b) 항)

     (4) "Counter-measures" 를 "counter-claims" 로 수정. (2(a) 항)

   나. 문제점:

   다. 한국측 입장: 미국측의 제안을 수락.

2. 공무집행중 기타 정부재산(군대 재산은 상호 포기함)에 대한 손해배상 규정의 적용지역 (2(a) 항).

   가. 미국측 제안:

     한·미 양국군대는 한국영토내에 뿐만 아니라 외국 영토와 공해상에도 합동으로 주류하고 있으므로, 2항의 적용지역을 한국영토내로 극한할것이 아니라 한국영토 밖에서 일어나는 사건도 적용토록 하는 것이 상호 유리할것임. 따라서 한국안의 "대한민국 내에 위치한"이라는 귀절을 삭제하므로써 세계전역을 본항의 적용지역으로 할것.

0147

나. 본 쟁점 :

(1) 이미 합의된 본협정의 서문에는 주한미국군대의
지위를 규제하는 협정으로 명시되어 있음.

(2) 2항의 절차로 볼때 원칙적으로 한국인 중재인
을 통하여 한국내에 있는 양국정부 재산의 배상
문제를 해결하게 되어 있어, 미국측은 이런
절차에 따라 미국내에 혹은 제3국에 위치한
양국정부 소유의 재산에 대한 손해배상문제를
해결한다기 보다는, 본항에 규정되어있는 $1,400
이하의 손해의 포기 혹은 양국정부의 배상금
분담에 관한 원칙을 준용하려는데 그 저의가
있는것으로 보이며, 한국영토 박ㄱ에서 일어나는
사건에 대한 실제상의 해결은 본항에 있는
" unless the two Governments agree otherwise, ··· "
라는 귀절을 이용하여 별도의 방법에 따라
해결하지 않을수 없을 것임.

다. 한국측 입장 :

본 규정을 그대로 외국에서나 공해상에서 일어나는
손해에 적용하기에는 현실에 맞지 않는 점이 있으나,

(1) 미국측이 제안한 상호 이익을 위하여 적용범위를
확대한다는 원칙에는 비록 우리나라의 정부재산이
외국영토나 공해상에 극소수 밖에 없다 할지라도
반대할 이유가 희박하며,

(2) 현실에 맞지않을 때에는 당연히 호혜원칙에
입각한 본항의 해결절차에 준하는 별도의 절차
를 만들수 있을 것이므로,

미국측의 제안을 수락한다.

3. 공무집행중 기타 정부재산에 대한 손해에 있어 양국
정부의 상호 포기 금액의 한계 및 적용환률 (2(f) 항)

가. 미국측 제안 :

한국측이 제안한 $800 혹은 W104,000 이하의 손해는
상호포기하며 환률의 상당한 변회가 있을때에는

0148

양국정부가 다시 조정한다"는 규정은 포기금액의
한거가 적으며, 환률에 대한 규정이 모호하므로 그
내용을 "＄1,400 이하의 손해는 상호 포기하며, 이에
해당하는 "원"화는 외환통제 조항의 환률에 적용
한다"로 수정할것.

나. 문제점:

다. 한국측 입장 : 미국측의 제안을 수락.

4. 공무집행중 정부재산 및 제3자에 대한 손해배상금의
양국정부 분담률 (5 (e)(i) 항)

가. 미국측 제안 :

한국측의 "미국책임시의 분담률을 한국15 퍼센트
미국 85퍼센트"는 다른 나라에서 분담하는 표준금액
과 같이 "한국 25퍼센트, 미국 75퍼센트"로 수정할것.

나. 문제점:

다. 한국측 입장 : 미국측 제안을 수락.

5. 공무집행중 정부재산 및 제3자에 대한 손해배상금의
한국정부에 대한 판상 (5(e)(iii) 항)

가. 미국측 제안 :

한국측은 "양국정부간의 분담 안 "에만 합의할
것을 주장하고 있으나, 미국측이 지적한바와 같이
일본에서는 실제에 있어"배상책임"과 "배상금액"
에도 합의를 하고 있으며, 미국측이 인정하지 않은
청구에 대하여는 배상금이 지불된 예가 지금까지
없다. 이런 방법은 청구사건을 해결하기 전에
양측이 모두 배상책임과 배상금의 타당성을 각각
결정한 후에 상호 합의에 도달토록 하는 것인바,
미국측은 이 제도가 양측의 요구를 충족시켜주는
좋은 제도로 생각하고 있으며, 이런 내용을 협정
문에 확실히 규정하여야 될것으로 생각되어,
한국안을 " ... 배상책임, 금액 및 비율에 의한
분담안이 합중국에 의하여 인정된 각 사건에
관하여 ... "로 수정할것.

0149

나. 문제점 :

(1) 미국안을 수락하면 5 (b)및 (c) 항에 의거 "한국
　　정부가 배상금을 지불할수 있으며, 이 지불은
　　양 당사국을 구속하며 최종적인 것이라는"
　　귀절이 사실상 무의미하게 된다. 따라서,

　(가) 한국정부 당국에서 한국법에 의거 단독으로
　　　청구를 심사하여 해결한다 하여도 그 판상은
　　　미국이 인정하는 범위내에서만 받게 될것이며,

　(나) 미국측의 주장대로 사전에 합의하여 청구를
　　　해결한다하여도, 피해자가 민사재판을 제기할
　　　경우에는 배상책임과 배상금액에 대한 사전
　　　합의도 불가능 할것인바,

　(다) 상기와 같이 피해자가 민사재판을 제기할
　　　경우, 재판의 판결에도 미국측은 구속을
　　　받지 않고 오직 그들이 인정하는 청구에
　　　대하여만 한국정부에 배상금을 판상하여 주는
　　　결과를 초래하여 5(e) (i) 및 (ii) 항의 분담
　　　규정과는 사실상 관계없이 한국정부는 부당
　　　하게 많은 배상금을 부담하지 않을수 없을
　　　것이다.

(2) 또한 2항의 기타 정부재산에 대한 손해에 대한
　　양국정부간의 청산방법도 5 (e) (i), (ii) 및 (iii)
　　에 의거하게 되어 있으므로, 중재인이 결정한
　　배상금도 사실상은 미국측이 안정하는 한도
　　내에서만 그 효력을 갖게 될것이다.

(3) 이상과 같은 애로가 있다하여 피해자의 민사
　　재판권을 박탈하므로써 "비율빈", "리비아"
　　및 "에치오피아"의 경우와 같이 국민의 정당
　　한 법익을 침해 당하게 할수도 없을 것이다.

다. 한국측 입장 :
　이러한 문제점을 고려할때 미국측의 제안을 그대로
　수락할수는 없을 것이며, 미국측이 주장하는 상호

합의의 원칙을 일부 수락하되 피해자의 권리를
보호하는 동시에 한국정부의 부담을 최소한으로
축소하기 위하여 아래와 같은 합의의사록을 채택
하도록 대안을 제시한다.

합의의사록

"본조제5항에 해당되는 청구에 관하여는 대한
민국 당국이 해결하기 전에 손해배상의 책임과 그
손해에 사정할 배상금에 관하여 대한민국과 합중국의
당국이 상호 합의하여야 한다. 그러나 청구자가
제기할수 있는 고소의 결과로 대한민국의 권위있는
재판소에 의한 그 사건에 대한 어떠한 판결도 본
협정의 당사국에 대하여 구속력을 가지며 또한
최종적인 것이다."

AGREED MINUTE

"Regarding the claims falling under the provisions
of paragraph five of this Article, the authorities
of the Republic of Korea and the United States shall
seek mutual agreement as to the liability for damages
and compensation to be awarded ~~whereupon~~ prior to the
settlement by the authorities of the Republic of Korea.
However, any adjudication of the case by a competent
court of the Republic of Korea as a result of a suit
which may be instituted by the claimant shall be
binding and conclusive upon the Parties of this
Agreement."

6. 한국인 고용원의 공무집행중에 행한 행위에 대한
   민사재판 불복 (-5 (f) 항)
   가. 미국측 치안 :
   (1) 본항에 이미 한국인 고용원의 공무집행중의
       행위에 대하여도 미국정부의 책임이 있게 규정
       되어 있으므로 이규정과 모순되지 않게하고,
   (2) 일단 이규정에 의하여 해결된 문제와 관련하여
       한국인이 재차 민사재판을 받지 않도록 한국

한·미국 간의 상호방위조약 제4조에 의한 시설과 구역 및 한국에서의 미국군대의 지위에 관한 협정(SOFA)
전59권. 1966.7.9 서울에서 서명 : 1967.2.9 발효(조약 232호) (V.30 실무교섭회의, 제77-80차, 1965.5월) 421

인을 보오하기 위하여,

한국측이 제안한 "합중국 군대구성원 및
고용원(한국국민 혹은 통상적으로 한국내에
거주하는 사람을 제외한)은 공무집행중에 발생
하는 사항에 대하여 한국내에서 그들에게 대하여
내려진 판결의 집행을 위한 모든 조치에 복하지
않는다"를 "합중국 군대구성원 및 고용원
(한국국민 혹은 통상적으로 한국내에 거주하는
사람을 포함한)은 ···"으로 수정할것.

나. 문제점 :

다. 한국측 입장 : 미국측의 제안을 수락.

7. 미군 구성원 및 고용원의 민사재판으로 부터의 면제
한계 (9 (a) 항)

가. 미국측 제안 :

미군구성원 및 고용원이 한국의 민사재판에 불복하는
경우를,

(1) 공무집행중에 일어나는 사건과,

(2) 충분히 만족한 배상금을 지불한 경우,

로 명백히 규정에 기술할것.

나. 문제점 :

다. 한국측입장 : 미국측의 제안을 수락.

8. 미군시설내에 있는 사유동산의 강제집행문제 (9 (b) 항)

가. 미국측 제안 :

미군시설내에 있는 사유동산을 재판의 판결에 의하여
강제집행을 하여야 할 경우를 위하여,
한국측은 "한국법정의 요청에 의하여 미국당국은
이를 차압하여 한국당국에 인도하여야 한다"로
제안하고 있으나, 미국의 법규는 개인재산에 대한
군대 지휘관의 권한을 제한하고 있으므로, "미국
당국은 한국당국에 대하여 가능한 모든 원조를
제공한다"는 보장을 주는 내용으로 수정할것.

0152

나. 문제점 :

다. 한국측 입장 : 미국측의 제안을 수락.

9. 증거수집에 관한 한·미간의 협조 (9 (c) 항)

가. 미국측 제안 :

한국측의 제안은 " … 본조의 규정에 의한 청구의 공평한 심리와 처리를 위하여 증거수집에 한·미 당국은 협력한다 " 로 되어 있으나,

이는 개개의 청구사건에 대하여 심리 (hearing) 를 한다는 의미를 갖고 있으므로, 미국당국이 증거 수집에 협력하려는 의도에는 전연 변함이 없으나 한국측이 모든 청구사건에 대하여 심리를 하도록 제안하고 있지는 않는 이상 " … 청구의 공평한 처리를 위하여 … " 로 수정할것을 제안한다.

미국측의 이채안은 청구사건이 심리를 통하여 해결 되거나 혹은 기타의 절차를 통하여 해결되거나에 불문하고 청구의 공평한 처리를 위하여 증거수집에 상호 협조하는 것을 규정함으로서 한국측의 요구를 충족시키는 동시에 오해의 가능성을 제거하려는 것이다.

나. 문제점 :

다. 한국측 입장 : 미국측의 제안을 수락.

10. KATUSA 와 KSC 의 민사청구건 조항에 있어서의 지위 (한국안 : 합의의사록 3, 미국안 : 12항)

가. 미국측 제안 :

청구권 조항을 위하여 KATUSA 는 미국군대 구성원 으로 간주하며, KSC 는 한국군의 고용원으로 간주 하여야 하며,

이는 현재의 관행과 방침을 표시한 것으로서 그들도 청구사건을 발생시키고 있는 이상 이규정에 포함 하여야 한다.

한·미국 간의 상호방위조약 제4조에 의한 시설과 구역 및 한국에서의 미국군대의 지위에 관한 협정(SOFA)
전59권. 1966.7.9 서울에서 서명 : 1967.2.9 발효(조약 232호) (V.30 실무교섭회의, 제77-80차, 1965.5월)

나. 문제점 :

(1) 한국정부 (법무부 송무과) 는 KATUSA 의 행위로
인한 손해배상을 한 경우는 있어도, KSC 의
행위로 인한 사건에 대하여는 지금까지 전연
배상한 예가 없다.

(2) KSC 는 현재 미국군대의 지시에 의하여 미국군대
를 위한 일을 하고 있으며 미국군대가 급료를
지불하고 있을 뿐만 아니라 미국당국이 직접
고용 및 해고를 하고 있으므로 민사청구건 조항
을 위하여는 미국군대의 고용원과 하등의 차이가
있을수 없다.

다. 한국측 입장 :

현재 한국안의 합의의사록의 내용과 동일하게 KSC
는 미국군대의 고용원이라는 내용의 대안을 아래와
같이 제안한다 :

Paragraph 12

"For the purpose of this Article, members of the
Korean Augmentation to the United States Army (KATUSA)
and members of the Korean Service Corps (KSC) shall
be considered respectively as members and employees
of the United States armed forces."

11. 청구건 조항에서 취급될 청구건의 발생시기 (미국안 : 13항)

가. 미국측 제안 :

미국측은 "본조의 규정은 이협정이 효력을 발생하기
전에 일어난 여하한 청구건에도 적용되지 않는다"
라는 규정을 한국안에 추가할것을 제안함.

나. 문제점 :

미국측의 제안은 다른 나라의 경우와 같이 협정
발효 이전에 일어난 청구사건에 관하여는 아무런
규정이 없어, 실제에 있어서는 현재의 일방적인
주한미군 소청사무소를 통하여 해결하게 되겠지만,
협정문으로서는 모호한 점이 있다.

0154

다. 한국측 입장 :

미국측의 제안을 수락하는 동시에, 협정발효전에 일어난 청구권의 해결 책임은 미국당국에 있다는 내용을 협정 문에 명시하기 위하여 아래와 같이 대안을 제안한다 :

제 13 항

"본조의 규정은 이협정이 효력을 발생하기 전에 일어난 여하한 청구권에도 적용되지 않는다. 그러한 청구권은 합중국 당국이 취급하고 해결하여야 한다."

"Paragraph 13:

"The provisions of this Article shall not apply to any claims which arose before the entry into force of this Agreement. Such claims shall be processed and settled by the authorities of the United States."

⑫ 민사청구권 조항의 발효시기 (합의의사록)

가. 미국측 제안 :

본조 5,6,7 및 8항의 규정은, 서울특별시내의 사고로 부터 발생하는 청구권은 이협정이 발효한 날로부터 6개월 후에 효력을 갖게하며, 기타 지역은 한국당국의 사건 처리의 효율성을 감안하여 합동위원회의 결의를 통하여 점차적으로 효력을 갖도록 한다.

나. 문제점 :

기타 지역에 대한 발효시기는 합동위원회의 결의를 거쳐야 하므로 사실상, 미국측은 그들이 원하는 시기 까지 상기조항의 적용을 연기할수 있어 민사청구권조항 이 유명무실하게 될우려가 있다.

다. 한국측 입장 :

상기 문제점에서 지적한바와 같은 곤란한 점이 있으나, 이보다 더욱 근본적인 문제인 5 (e) (iii) 항, 배상책임 및 배상금의 합의문제와 한국측 합의의사록3항, KSC 문제에 대한 우리측안을 수락할것을 조건으로 미국측 제안을 수락한다.

0155

보통문서로 재분류(1966. 12. 31.)

법 무 부

법무법 722.2 — 19 (2 — 4072) 1965.5.18.

수신 외무부장관

제목 주둔군 지위협정중 민사청구권 조항에 관한 미국측 수정안에 대한 당부의견

주둔군 지위협정중 민사청구권 조항에 관한 미국측 수정안에 대하여 당부의 의견을 별첨과 같이 송부합니다.

유첨 의견서 1부. 끝

일반 문서로 재분류 (1966 . 12 . 31 .)

담당	과장	국장	차관	장관	5월 일 공람	美州課

법무부 장관 민

접수 No. 085 1965. 5. 19 외무부

196 년 월 일 예고문에 의거 일반문서로 재분류됨

1967, 1, 5 에 예고문에 의거 일반문서로 재분류됨

0156

민사청구권 조항
미국측 수정안에 대한 당부 의견

1. 미국측안.
   2항 (a) 중 "대한민국내에 위치한"을 삭제한다.
   └ 당부의견.
   미국측 제안을 수락한다.

2. 미국측안.
   2항 (f)를 다음과 같이 수정한다.
   "각 당사국은 미화 1,400불미만의 청구건 또는 청구
   건이 접수되었을 당시의 제__조에 대한 합의 의사
   록에 규정된 환률에 따라 동 미화에 해당하는 한화
   에 미달하는 금액의 청구건은 이를 포기한다."
   └ 당부의견.
   미국측 제안을 수락한다.

3. 미국측안.
   5항 (e) (ⅰ)를 다음과 같이 수정한다.
   "미합중국이 책임이 있는 경우에는 합의되고 재판에
   의하여 결정된 금액은 대한민국이 25%, 미합중국
   이 75% 부담하는 비율로 분담한다."
   └ 당부의견.
   미국측안을 수락할수 없고 대한민국이 15% 미합중
   국이 85% (한국측 원안)을 주장한다.

4. 미국측안.
   5항 (e) (ⅲ)을 다음과 같이 수정한다.
   "책임, 금액 및 비률에 기초를 ~~~~ 분담안의 미합중국

한·미국 간의 상호방위조약 제4조에 의한 시설과 구역 및 한국에서의 미국군대의 지위에 관한 협정(SOFA)
전59권. 1966.7.9 서울에서 서명 : 1967.2.9 발효(조약 232호) (V.30 실무교섭회의, 제77-80차, 1965.5월) 427

에 의하여 승인된 각 사건에 관하여 대한민국이 6개
월의 기간내에 지불한 금액의 명시서를 지불요청서와
함께 매 6개월마다 미합중국 당국에 송부한다. 지불
은 가급적 조속히 원화로서 행하여야 한다."

√ 당부의견.

미국측안을 수락할수 없으며 대안으로서 아래와 같은
합의의사록을 채택한다.

"본 조 제5항에 해당되는 청구에 관하여는 대한민국
당국이 해결하기 전에 손해배상의 책임과 그 손해에
사정할 배상금에 관하여 대한민국과 미합중국의 당국
이 상호 협의하여야 한다. 그러나 청구자가 제기할수
있는 소의 결과로 대한민국의 관할재판소에 의한 그
사건에 대한 어떠한 판결도 본 협정의 당사국에 대
하여 구속력을 가지며 또한 최종적인 것이다."

5. 미국측안.

5항 (f) ~~원~~ 중 "제외한다."를 "포함한다."로 수정한
다.

√ 당부의견.

미국측 제안을 수락한다.

6. 미묵측안.

9항 (a)를 다음과 같이 수정한다.

"미합중국은 대한민국 법원의 민사재판권에 관하여 미
합중국 군대구성원 또는 피용자에 대한 대한민국 법
원의 재판권으로부터의 면제를 주장할 수 없다. 단
공무수행으로 인하여 발생한 ~~사건에~~ 관하여 그들에게
내려진 판결을 ~~대한민~~ ~~~~ 집행하기 위한 절차에

0158

관한 경우 또는 청구에 대한 지불이 완전히 곤난 경
우는 예외로 한다."

당부의견.

<u>미국측 제안을 수락한다.</u>

7. 미국측안.

9항 (b)를 다음과 같이 수정한다.

"대한민국 법률에 의하여 강제집행을 행할 사유동산(
미합중국 군대가 사용하는 동산을 제외한다)이 미합중
국 군대가 사용하는 시설 및 지역내에 있는 경우에는
미합중국당국은 대한민국법원의 요청에 따라서 그 재산
이 대한민국당국에 인도되는것을 확인하기 위하여 그 권
한 내에서 모든 협조를 제공한다"

당부의견.

<u>미국측제안을 수락한다.</u>

8. 미국측안.

9항 (C)를 다음과같이 수정한다

"대한민국당국과 미합중국당국은 본조의 규정에 따라서
청구의 공정한 처리를 위한 증거의 입수에 관하여
협력한다".

당부의견.

<u>미국측 제안을 수락한다.</u>

9. 미국측안.

12항을 다음과같이 신설한다.

"본조의 목적을 위하여 미합중국군대에 파견된 한국군
(KATUSA)은 미합중국군대의 구성원으로 간주하며 한
국인노무근무단 (KSC)의 구성원은 대한민국군대의

0159

피용자로 간주한다"

✓ 당부의견.

12항을 다음과같이한다.

"본조의 목적을 위하여 미합중국군대에 파견된 한국군(KATUSA)및 한국인노무근무단 (KSC)의 구성원은 각각 미합중국군대 구성원 및 피용자로 간주한다"

10. 미국측안.

13항을 다음과같이 신설한다.

"본조의 제규정은 본협정의 효력발생일 이전에 발생한 청구에 대하여는 적용되지 아니한다"

✓ 당부의견.

미측안에 대하여 다음의 대안을 채택한다.

"본조의 제규정은 본협정의 효력발생일 이전에 발생한 청구에 대하여는 적용되지 아니한다 그와같은 청구는 미합중국 당국이 수리하고 해결하여야한다"

11. 미국측안.

용어를 다음과같이 수정한다.

1. "Armed services" 를 "Armed forces"로
2. "execution of his official duties" 를 "performance of his official duties" 로
3. "in the execution of its official duty" 를 "for official purpose" 를
4. "counter-measures" 를 "counter-claims"를

당부의견.

미측제안을 수락한다.

미국측안.

0160

12. 미국측안.

합의의사록 A 1 . 본조5항 6항 7항및 8항의 각규
정은 서울특별시내의 사고로부터 발생하는 청구에 관
하여는 본협정의 시행일로부터 6개월후에 효력을 발
생한다.

√ 당부의견.

미측제안을 수락한다.

13. 미국측안.

합의의사록 A 2 . 5항 6항 7항및 8항의 각규정은
합동위원회가 결정하고 한정하는 대한민국의 기타지역
에도 연차적용한다.

√ 당부의견

미측안에 대하여 다음의 대안을 채택한다

"대한민국의 기타지역에서 사고로 부터발생하는 청구에
관하여는 본조5항 6항 7항및 8항의 각규정은 본협
정시행일로 부터 12개월후에 효력을 발생한다 그러나
대한민국당국이 12개월내에 전항에 규정된 책임을 부담
할 준비가 되어 있지 아니할 경우에는 대한민국 당국
은 미합중국의 책임의 연장을 위하여 준비에 소요되는
부가 기간을 합동위원회에 통고할 수 있다"

14. 미국측안.

합의의사록 B . 5항 6항 7항및 8항의 각규정이
정하여진 지역에서 시행될때까지

1. 미합중국은 미합중국군대 구성원 또는 피용자가
공무수행중에 행한 작위 또는 부작위 또는 미합중국
군대가 법률상 책임을 지게되는 기타의 작위 부작위
또는 사고로 부터 발생하고 양국정부외의 제3자에게

0161

대한민국내에서 손해를 끼친 청구건 (계약상의 청구 건은 제외)을 처리하고 해결한다.

2. 미합중국당국은 미합중국군대 구성원 또는 피용자 에대한 그외의 비계약상의 청구를 받아들여야하며 그 에 대하여 당해 미합중국당국이 정한 금액의 위자료 지불을 제의 할 수 있다.

3. 각당사국은 각기 자국군대구성원 또는 피용자가 공무수행중에 있는가의 여부및 자국군대가 소유하는 재산을 그 군대가 공적목적을 위하여 사용하는 가의 여부를 결정할 권리를 가진다.

√당부의견.

미측제안을 수락한다.

15. 미측제안.

합의의사록 C . . 2항 (d) 의 목적을 위하여 5항 (e) 의 규정은 본협정효력발생일로 부터 대한민국 전역을 통하여 시행된다..

√당부의견.

미측제안을 수락한다.

0162

勞務條項 會議

1. 日時 : 1965. 5. 27. 15:00~16:00

2. 場所 : 保社部長官室

3. 參席者 :

   保社部 側 : 保社部長官.

   勞動廳長

   勞動廳次長

   勞政局長

   外務部 側 : 文次官

   張歐美局長

   美州課 金甲洙

次官 — 취지 說明
局長   爭議.
勞動方 — 20
合同 — 50
    P 30   比율   _Rusk_   合同 — 判例
         合同에 回附된 분쟁의 起草.

長官 〔勞動方 — 0
      合同委 — 20〕 ~~長官에 建議~~

KSC — Setting is different

         exclude
잠정계약지 ────── ①참동위에서 合同 ②現在의 것 인정
  〈1. 民事와 勞動.   其他의것 要求(건의)
  〈2. 한국에서 만수있는 만큼

0164

~2

434 주한미군지위협정(SOFA) 서명 및 발효 11

LABOR ARTICLE

(Underlining indicates modifications from Korean
draft of the Labor Article tabled at 69th session)

1. In this Article the expression:

(a) "employer" refers to the United States Armed Forces
(including non-appropriated fund activities) *and such persons referred
to in the first paragraph of article — as may be determined by the Joint
Committee.*
(b) "employee" refers to any civilian (other than a
member of the civilian component of the United States
except a member of the Korean Service Corps.
Armed Forces) employed by an employer. Such civilian
personnel shall be nationals of the Republic of Korea.

2. Employers may recruit, employ and administer their
personnel. Recruitment services of the Government of the
Republic of Korea shall be utilized to the maximum extent
practicable. In case employers accomplish direct recruitment of employees, The United States Armed Forces shall
provide such relevant information as may be required for
labor administration to the Office of Labor Affairs of the
Republic of Korea.

3. To the extent not inconsistent with the provisions of
this Article or except as may otherwise be mutually agreed,
the conditions of employment and work, such as those relating
to wages and supplementary payments, the conditions for the
protection and welfare of employees, compensations, and the
rights of employees, concerning labor relations shall
conform with those laid down by the labor legislation of
the Republic of Korea.

4. (a) With regard to any dispute between employers and
any employees or labor unions which cannot be settled through
the use of existing procedures of the United States Armed
Forces, settlement shall be accomplished in the following
manner:

0165

(1) The dispute shall be referred to the Office of Labor Affairs of the Republic of Korea for conciliation.

(2) In the event that the dispute is not settled by the procedures described in (a) above ~~within twenty (20 days~~, the dispute shall be referred to the Joint Committee, which may refer the matter to the Labor sub-Committee or to a specially-designated Committee, for further conciliation efforts.

(3) In the event that the dispute is not settled by the procedures outlined above, the Joint Committee will resolve the dispute. The decisions of the Joint Committee shall be binding.

(4) Neither employee organizations nor employees shall engage in any practice disruptive of normal work *during the period of conciliation by the Office of Labor Affairs mentioned in (1) above and* requirements unless a period of ~~seventy (70) days has~~ elapsed without settlement after the dispute is referred to the ~~Office of Labor Affairs~~ *Joint Committee* mentioned in (7) above.

(5) Failure of any employee organization or employee to abide by the decision of the Joint Committee on any dispute, or engaging in practices disruptive of normal work requirements in violation of the provisions laid down in (4) above, shall be considered cause for the depriviation of the rights and protection accorded by the relevant labor legislation of the Republic of Korea.

(b) The right concerning strike shall be accorded to employees except those whose exercise of the right prohibited by the Joint Committee.

0166

5. In the event of a national emergency, such as war, hostilities or situations where war or hostilities is imminent, the application of this Article shall be limited in accordance with the emergency measures taken by the Government of the Republic of Korea, and, in addition, the following arrangements will be made:

(a) Should the Government of the Republic of Korea adopt measures allocating labor, the United States Armed Forces shall be accorded allocation privileges no less favorable than those enjoyed by the Armed Forces of the Republic of korea.

(b) Employees who have acquired skills essential to the mission of the United States Armed Forces will, upon request of the United States Armed Forces and through mutual agreement, be deferred from Republic of Korea military service or other compulsory services. The United States Armed Forces shall in advance furnish to the Government of the Republic of Korea lists of those employees deemed necessary.

6. Members of the civilian component of the United States Armed Forces shall not be subject to Korean laws or regulations with respect to their terms and conditions of employment.

AGREED MINUTES

1. The undertaking of the United States to conform to the labor legislation of the Republic of Korea does not imply any waiver by the United States Government of its immunities under international law.

2. It is understood that the Government of the Republic of Korea shall be reimbursed for direct costs incurred in providing assistance pursuant to Paragraph 2.

한·미국 간의 상호방위조약 제4조에 의한 시설과 구역 및 한국에서의 미국군대의 지위에 관한 협정(SOFA)
전59권. 1966.7.9 서울에서 서명 : 1967.2.9 발효(조약 232호) (V.30 실무교섭회의, 제77-80차, 1965.5월) 437

3.   Employers will withhold from the pay of their employees, and pay over to the Government of the Republic of Korea withholdings required by the income tax legislation of the Republic of Korea.

4.   In case where it is impossible for employers to conform to the labor legislations of the Republic of Korea applicable under Paragraph 3 on account of the military requirements of the United States Armed Forces, the matter shall be referred, in advance, to the Joint Committee for mutual agreement. The Government of the Republic of Korea will give due consideration to the military requirements of the United States Armed Forces.

political

ideological

SOFA NEGOTIATIONS

Agenda for ~~the 80th Session~~

14 : 00   May 28, 1965.

1. Continuation of Discussions on:

  b a. Criminal Jurisdiction Article

  c b. Labor Article   (U. S.) 베출

  a c. Claims Article

2. Other Business

3. Agenda and Date of the Next Meeting

4. Press Release

0169

ARTICLE XXV   LABOR

(Underling indicates modifications from Korean draft tabled at 79th session)

1. In this Article the expression:

√(a) "employer" refers to the United States Armed Forces (including non-appropriated fund activities) and such persons referred to in the first paragraph of Article (XVIII) as may be determined by the Joint Committee.

√(b) "employee" refers to any civilian (other than a member of the civilian component) employed by an employer. Such civilian personnel shall be nationals of the Republic of Korea.

√2. Employers may recruit, employ and administer their personnel. Recruitment services of the Government of the Republic of Korea shall be utilized to the maximum extent practicable. In case employers accomplish direct recruitment of employees, employers shall provide such relevant information as may be required for labor administration to the Office of Labor Affairs of the Republic of Korea.

3. To the extent not inconsistent with the provisions of this Article or except as may otherwise be mutually agreed, the conditions of employment and work, such as those relating to wages and supplementary payments, the conditions for the protection and welfare of employees, compensations, and the rights of employees, concerning labor relations shall conform with those laid down by the labor legislation of the Republic of Korea.

√ 4. √(a) In consideration of provision for collective action in labor legislation of the Republic of Korea, any dispute between employers and employees or employee organizations, which cannot be settled through ~~grievance or~~ labor relations procedures established by the United States armed forces in accordance with the provisions ~~set forth in paragraph~~ applicable under this Article shall be settled as follows:

(1) The dispute shall be referred to the Office of Labor Affairs of the Republic of Korea for conciliation.

(2) In the event that the dispute is not settled

by the procedure described in (1) above, the matter shall *within twenty (20) days,* be referred to the Joint Committee, which may refer the matter to *the Labor Sub-Committee or to* a special committee (designated) ~~by the Joint Committee~~ for further conciliation efforts.

(3) In the event that the dispute is not settled by the procedure outlined above, the Joint Committee will resolve the dispute, assuring that expeditious procedures are followed. The decisions of the Joint Committee shall be binding.

(4) Neither employee organizations nor employees shall engage in any practice disruptive of normal work requirements ~~during the period of conciliation by the Office of Labor Affairs mentioned in (1) above, and~~ unless a period of seventy (70) days has elapsed after the dispute is referred to the ~~Joint Committee stipulated~~ *Office of Labor Affairs mentioned* in (1) above.

(5) Failure of any employee organization or employee to abide by the decision of the Joint Committee, or engaging in practice disruptive of normal work requirements in violation of the provisions laid down in (4) above, shall be considered cause for the depriviation of the rights and protection accorded by the relevant labor legislation of the Republic of Korea.

(b) The Joint Committee, taking into consideration of the role of the employees of the United States armed forces in the defense of the Republic of Korea, shall determine those categories of essential employees who shall not exercise the right concerning strike in the event a labor dispute is not resolved by the foregoing procedures. In the event an agreement cannot be reached on this question in the Joint Committee, it may be subject of discussions through diplomatic channel between the two Governments.

(c) In the event of a national emergency, such as war, hostilities, or situations where war or hostilities is imminent, the application of this Article will be limited in accordance with emergency measures taken by the Government

0171

of the Republic of Korea in consultation with the appropriate
authorities of the United States Government.

5. Should the Republic of Korea adopt measures allocating
labor, the United States Armed Forces shall be accorded
allocation privileges no less than favorable than those
enjoyed by the Armed Forces of the Republic of Korea.

(b) In the event of a national emergency, such as
war, hostilities, or situations where war or hostilities
is imminent, employees who have acquired skills essential
to the mission of the United States Armed Forces *except those eligible for conscription,* shall, upon
request of the United States Armed Forces and through mutual
agreement, be deferred from Republic of Korea military service or other compulsory services. The United States Armed
Forces shall furnish in advance to the Republic of Korea
lists of those employees deemed essential.

6. Members of the civilian component shall not be subject
to Korean laws or regulations with respect to their terms
and condition of employment.

AGREED MINUTES

1. It is understood that the Government of the Republic
of Korea shall be reimbursed for direct costs incurred in
providing assistance requested pursuant to paragraph 2.

2. The undertaking of the United States Government to
conform to the labor legislation does not imply any waiver
by the United States Government of its immunities under
international law.

3. Employers will withhold from the pay of their employees,
and pay over to the Government of the Republic of Korea withholdings required by the income tax legislation of the Republic of Korea.

4. In case where it is impossible for employers to conform to the provisions of labor
legislation of the Republic of Korea applicable under this
Article on account of the military requirements of the United
States Armed Forces, the matter shall be referred, in advance,

30-28

0172

to the Joint Committee for mutual agreement. The Government of the Republic of Korea will give due consideration to the military requirements of the United States Armed Forces.

5. A Union or other employee group shall be recognized unless its objectives are inimical to the common interests of the Republic of Korea and the United States. The decision as to whether the objectives of such groups are inimical or not inimical shall be made ~~by~~ *by the Joint Committee* ~~on mutual agreement between the two Governments.~~ Memberships or non-membership in such groups shall not be factor in employment or other actions affecting employees.

한·미국 간의 상호방위조약 제4조에 의한 시설과 구역 및 한국에서의 미국군대의 지위에 관한 협정(SOFA) 전59권. 1966.7.9 서울에서 서명 : 1967.2.9 발효(조약 232호) (V.30 실무교섭회의, 제77-80차, 1965.5월) 443

<u>LABOR ARTICLE</u>

(Underlining indicates modifications from the
Korean draft tabled at 79th session)

1. In this Article the expression:

(a) "employer" refers to the United States Armed Forces
(including non-appropriated fund activities) <u>and such persons</u>
<u>referred to in the first paragraph of Article (XVIII) as may be</u>
<u>present in the Republic of Korea at the time of coming into</u>
<u>force of this Agreement and as may be determined thereafter by</u>
<u>the Joint Committee.</u>

(b) "employee" refers to any civilian (other than a member
of the civilian component) employed by an employer. Such civilian
personnel shall be nationals of the Republic of Korea.

2. Employers may recruit, employ and administer their personnel.
Recruitment services of the Government of the Republic of Korea
<u>shall be utilized insofar as is practicable.</u> In case employers
accomplish direct recruitment of employees, employers shall provide
such relevant information as may be required for labor administration
to the Office of Labor Affairs of the Republic of Korea.

3. To the extent not inconsistent with the provisions of this
Article or except as may otherwise be mutually agreed, the conditions of employment and work, such as those relating to wages and
supplementary payments, the conditions for the protection and
welfare of employees, compensations, and the rights of employees,
concerning labor relations shall conform with those laid down by
the labor legislation of the Republic of Korea.

4. (a) <u>In consideration of provision for collective action</u>
<u>in labor legislation of the Republic of Korea, any dispute between</u>
<u>employers or any employee organization, which cannot be settled</u>
<u>through labor relations procedures established by the United</u>
<u>States armed forces in accordance with the provisions applicable</u>
<u>under this Article, shall be settled as follows:</u>

(1) The dispute shall be referred to the Office of Labor
Affairs of the Republic of Korea for conciliation.

0174

(2) In the event that the dispute is not settled by the procedures described in (1) above within twenty (20)days, the dispute shall be referred to the Joint Committee, which may refer the matter to the Labor Sub-Committee or to a specially-designated committee, for further conciliation efforts.

(3) In the event that the dispute is not settled by the procedures outlined above, the Joint will resolve the dispute, assuring that expeditious procedures are followed. The decision of the Joint Committee shall be binding.

(4) Neither employee organizations nor employees shall engage in any practice disruptive of normal work requirements unless a period of seventy (70) days elapsed after the dispute is referred to the Office of Labor Affairs mentioned in (1) above.

(5) Failure of any employee organization or employee to abide by the decision of the Joint Committee, or engaging in practice disruptive of normal work requirements in violation of the provisions laid down in (4) above, shall be considered cause for the depriviation of the rights and protection accorded by the relevant labor legislation of the Republic of Korea.

(b) The Joint Committee, taking into consideration of the role of theemployees of the United States armed forces in the defense of the Republic of Korea and pertinent provisions of legislation of the Republic of Korea, shall determine those categories of essential employees who shall not exercise the right concerning strike in the event a labor dispute is not resolved by the foregoing procedures. In the event an agreement cannot be reached on this question in the Joint Committee, it may be subject of discussions through diplomatic channel between the two Governments.

(c) In the event of a national emergency, such as war, hostilities, or situations where war or hostilities are imminent, the application of this Article shall be limited in accordance with emergency measures taken by the Government of the Republic of Korea in consultation with the appropriate authorities of the United States Government.

5. (a) Sould the Republic of Korea adopt measures allocating labor, the United States Armed Forces shall be accorded allocation privilege no less favorable than those enjoyed by the Armed Forces of the Republic of Korea.

(b) In the event of a national emergency, such as war, hostilities, or situations where war or hostilities are imminent, employees who have acquired skills essential to the mission of the United States/, Armed Forces except those eligible for conscription, shall, upon request of the United States Armed Forces and through mutual agreement, be deferred from Republic of Korea military service or other compulsory services. The United States Armed Forces shall furnish in advance to the Republic of Korea lists of those employees deemed essential.

6. Members of the civilian component shall not be subject to Korean laws or regulations with respect to their terms and conditions of employment.

AGREED MINUTES

1. It is understood that the Government of the Republic of Korea shall be reimbursed for direct costs incurred in providing assistance pursuant to paragraph 2.

2. The undertaking of the United States Government to conform to the labor legislation of the Republic of Korea does not imply any waiver by the United States Government of its immunities under international law.

3. Employers will withhold from the pay of their employees, and pay over to the Government of the Republic of Korea withholdings required by the income tax legislation of the Republic of Korea.

4. In case where it is impossible for employers to conform to the labor legislation of the Republic of Korea applicable under paragraph 3 on account of the military requirements of the United States Armed Forces, the matter shall be referred, in advance whenever possible, to the Joint Committee for mutual agreement. The Government of the Republic of Korea will give due consideration to the military requirements of the United States Armed Forces.

0176

5. A union or other employee group shall be recognized unless its objectives are inimical to the common interests of the United States and the Republic of Korea. ~~(The decision as to whether the objectives of such groups are inimical or not shall be made by the Joint Committee.)~~ Memberships or non-memberships in such groups shall not be factor in employment or other actions affecting employees.

36-26   0177

한·미국 간의 상호방위조약 제4조에 의한 시설과 구역 및 한국에서의 미국군대의 지위에 관한 협정(SOFA) 전59권. 1966.7.9 서울에서 서명 : 1967.2.9 발효(조약 232호) (V.30 실무교섭회의, 제77-80차, 1965.5월) 447

기 안 지

기 안 자	미주과 이 근 팔	전 화 번 호		공 보	필 요	불 필 요
	과 장 ✓	국 장	차 관	장 관		
협 조 자 서 명					보 존 년 한	
기 안 년 월 일	1965. 6. 12.	시 행 년월일		통 제 관	정 서	기 장
분 류 기 호 문 서 번 호	외구미 722. 2—					
경 수 참 조	대 통 령 참조: 비서실장 국 무 총 리 참조: 비서실장 법무부장관 및 보건사회부장관			발신	장	관
제 목	제 80 차 주둔군지위협정 체결 교섭 실무자회의 결과 보고					

1965 년 5 월 28 일 하오 2 시 부터 동 4 시 40 분 까지
외무부 제 1 회의실에서 개최된 제 80 차 주둔군지위협정 체결
교섭실무자회의에서 토의된 형사재판관할권, 민사청구권, 노무조달
협정의 발효 및 유효기간 등에 관한 회의내용을 별첨과 같이
보고합니다.

유 첨: 제 80 차 주둔군지위협정 체결 교섭실무
보고서 1 부. 끝.

보통군서류 재분류(1966. 12. 31)

발 송
No. 105-7
★ 1965. 6. 14 ★
외 무 부

기 안 지

기 안 자	미주과 이근팔	전 화 번 호		공 보	필 요	불필요

	과 장	국 장	차 관	장 관		
	(서명)			(서명)		

협 조 자 서 명		보 존 년 한	
기 안 년 월 일	1965. 6. 12.	시 행 년월인	통 제 관	정 서	기 장
분 류 기 호 문 서 번 호	의구미 722.2 —				

경 수 참 조	유 신 참 조	법무부장관, 참조: 검찰국장 및 법무국장 보건사회부장관, 참조: 노동청장	발 신	장 관

제 목	제 80 차 주둔군지위협정 체결 교섭실무자회의 개최

1965 년 5 월 28 일 하오 2 시 부터 동 4 시 40 분 까지 외무부
제 1 회의실에서 개최된 제 80 차 주둔군지위협정 체결 교섭 실무자
회의에서 토의된 형사재판관할권, 민사청구권, 노무조달, 협정의
발효 및 유효기간등에 관한 회의내용을 별첨과 같이 알리오니
참고하시기 바랍니다.

유 첨: 제 80 차 주둔군지위협정 체결 교섭 실무자회의
보고서 사본. 1부. 끝.

발송
N. 10
★ 1965. 6. 14 ★
외무부

제 80 차

한·미간 주둔군지위 협정 체결 교섭 실무자회의

보 고 서

1. 일시: 1965년 5월 28일 하오 2시 부터 동 4시 40분 까지

2. 장소: 외무부 제1 회의실

3. 토의 사항:

미측은 협정의 서문과 30개 조항에 관한 전 조문을 우리측에 수교
하고 협정의 유효기간 및 발효 사항에 관한 2개 조항이 금번 처음으로 제출
되었음을 밝히고 양국 대통령이 확부 회담시 본 협정의 중요 원칙에 이미
합의한 바에 따라 현안인 협정이 단시일내에 타결되기를 바란다고 말하고
다음과 같이 미측의 입장을 설명하였다.

가. 형사재판 관할권

(1) 제1차 관할권의 포기

(가) 한국측이 제77차 회의시 미측 포기 조항 제1항 서두에 "미국이
요청하면" 이라는 문구를 삽입하여 개개 특정사건이 발생할때
마다 미측이 관할권의 포기를 요청하여야 한다는 것은 미측이
제의한 포기조항이 협정 발효와 동시에 일괄적으로 포기할것을
주안으로 하는 원칙에 위배되는 것이며 따라서 미측은 한국측의
제안을 수락할수 없다.

(나) 한국측이 제4항 말미에 "포기의 철회는 본 합의 의사록 제3항에
규정된 포기의 철회를 위한 통고가 그러한 통고 발행후 21일
이내에 대한민국 정부에 의하여 취소되지 않는한 최종적이며,
확정적 이어야 한다" 는 것을 신설 삽입할것을 제의한데 대하여
미측은 동 규정은 미측의 제안 내용의 반복에 지나지 않음으로
불필요한 중복일 뿐더러 한정된 기간내에 해결되지 않을수도
있을것임으로 본문에 추가하는 것은 수락할수 없으나, 한국측의
요구를 받아 들여 양해 사항으로 다음과 같이 기록에 남길
용의가 있다.:

0180

65-5-08

/

0181

"포기의 철회는 본 합의 의사록 제3항에 규정된 포기의
철회를 위한 통고가 대한민국 정부에 의하여 취소되지 않는한
최종적이며 확정적이여야 한다."

(다) 한국이 포기한 사건과 공무집행중 법죄로서 대한민국 또는 그
국민에 대하여 범해진 법죄에 관한 재판의 장소 및 정부대표의
참석에 관한 한국측 제안은 미측이 독일 형태의 포기 조항을
제안하기 전에 양측이 합의를 한것이나 미측이 새로운 포기조항을
제안함으로써 사정이 판이하게 되었으며 따라서 한국측 제안은
수락할수 없다. 미측의 금번 제안은 독일 보충협정 제26조와
동일한 내용이다.

(2) 공무집행중 법죄

 (가) 공무 집행 증명서의 발행권자에 관하여 우리측이 "공무집행
증명서는 반드시 미군 법무관의 의견을 들은후에 발행되어야
하며 미군당국의 증명서 발행기관은 장성급으로 하여야 한다"
라는 양해사항을 기록에 남길것을 제의한데 대하여 미측은 우리측
양해사항을 수락하면서 지휘책임은 장군에게 있지만 실제 필요에
따라 그의 직무를 선임 부타장교에게 위임해야 할 경우가
있음으로 "또는 그가 지정하는 자"를 추가해야 한다고 말하였다.

 (나) 한국측이 합의 의사록에 규정할 것을 요구하고 있는 공무의 정의
는 미측으로서는 양해사항으로 의의록에 남기는 것으로서
충분한 것으로 본다.

(3) 피의자의 재판전 신병구금

 (가) 우리측이 제??차 회의에서 제안한 수정안을 전적으로 수락함
으로써 피의자의 재판전 신병 구금에 관하여 완전 합의에 도달
하였다.

(4) 피의자의 권리

 (가) 한국의 군법재판을 받지 않을 권리(합의 의사록 제 9 (a)항)
한국 당국의 관할권 행사 기관을 "대한민국 민사당국"으로 하는
조건하에 "미군인, 군속 및 가족은 대한민국 군법죄의에 회부

0182

65-5-25   기호 113항

0183

되지 아니한다"는 것을 양해 사항으로 수락한다.

(나) 미국정부 대표와 접견하는 권리 (합의 의사록 제9 (g)항)

한국측의 미국정부 대표의 결석시의 피의자의 진술은 유죄의
증거로 할수 없다"는 미측 초안 부분을 삭제할것을 주장하였
는바, 미측은 미국정부 대표는 미군관계 모든 소송절차에 참여할
의무가 있으며 이 규정은 피의자가 고문 기타 강제적인 방법으로
진술을 강요 당하지 않도록 보장하기 위하여서 절대로 필요함
으로 미측은 한국측 삭제 주장을 수락할수 없다.

(다) 피고의 상소권(합의의사록 제9항의 제2 (a)세항)

미측은 피고의 상소권에 관하여 애매한 점을 제거하기 위하여
다음과 같은 규정을 양해 사항으로 회의록에 남길것을 제안
하였다:

    "대한민국 법원의 상소제도에 의거 피고는 상급법원에
의한 새로운 발견의 근거로서의 새로운 증거 또는 증인을 포함한
증거의 재검증을 요청할수 있다."

(라) 불리의 변경의 금지에 관한 권리 (합의의사록 제9항의 제2 (d)
세항) 및 검사의 상소권의 제한 (합의 의사록 제9항의 제4세항)

미측이 제안한 "원심 판결의 형보다 중한 형을 선고 받지 아니하는
권리"에 대하여 한국측이 "피고인이 상소한 사건과 피고인을
위하여 상소한 사건에 있어서는 원심 판결보다 중한 형을 선고
받지 아니하는 권리"를 대안으로 제시한바 있으며 또한 검사의
상소권에 관하여 미측은 "법률의 착오의 경우를 제외하고 검찰
로 부터 상소 당하지 아니하는 권리"를 주장하고 있는바, 한국
측의 대안 및 삭제요구는 미국의 소송제도의 원칙에 대한 위배
이며, 미국정부와 시민의 법관념과 상반되는 것임으로 한국측
주장은 수락할수 없다.

(마) 심판 불출두 권리 (합의 의사록 제9항의 제2 (j)세항)

미측의 "육체적 또는 정신적으로 부적당한 경우의 심판불출두권리"

0184

65-5-50

65-5-15   미ㅁ113-6

한·미국 간의 상호방위조약 제4조에 의한 시설과 구역 및 한국에서의 미국군대의 지위에 관한 협정(SOFA)
전59권. 1966.7.9 서울에서 서명 : 1967.2.9 발효(조약 232호) (V.30 실무교섭회의, 제77-80차, 1965.5월)   455

4

에 대하여 한국측은 이 권리의 남용을 염려하여 삭제를 주장

하고 있으나 합동위원회에서 양국이 이 문제의 실지 운영상의

결정을 위하여 상방이 만족할 만한 절차를 마련할수 있을것

으로 믿으며 피고의 재판 불출두 권리는 피고의 본질적인 권리

임으로 한국측 제안은 수락할수 없다.

(바) 위법 부당한 방법으로 수집된 증거의 능력(합의의사록 제9항의
   제3 세항)

한국측이 "고문, 폭행, 협박, 기망 또는 신체구속의 부당한

장기화 기타의 방법으로 임의로 진술한 것이 아니라고 의심할

만한 이유가 있는 자백, 자인, 기타 진술은 유죄의 증거로 할수

없다" 라는 제안에 대하여 미측은 미국헌법에 의하여

"위법 부당한 방법 또는 불합리적인 수색 압수등에 의하여

입수된 물적 증거는 모든 미국 법원에서 증거로 채택할수 없게

되어 있으므로 한국측 제안을 다음과 같이 수정할것을 제의

하였다.:

"고문 폭행, 협박, 기망 또는 신체구속의 부당한 장기화

기타의 방법으로 임의로 진술한것이 아니라고 의심할만한 이유가

있는 자백, 자인, 기타 진술과 고문 폭행, 협박, 기망 또는

영장없는 불합리한 수사 및 압수의 결과로 수집된 물적 증거는

유죄의 증거로 할수 없다."

(5) 미국의 관할권 행사 기관

미측은 미국의 관할권 행사기관을 "미군당국"으로 하자는 한국측

주장에 동의하며 따라서 전 조항에 걸쳐 다음과 같은 부분에서 수정

될것이다.: 본문의 1 (a)항, 2(a)항, 3(a)항, 4항, 5(a)항,

5(b)항, 5(c)항, 6(a)항, 6(b)항, 7(a)항, 8항, 11항 및

합의 의사록의 제9(b)항의 제1 및 제2세항, 제3(a)항의 제1세항,

제6항의 제1 및 제3세항, 제9항 및 제10(a)및 10(b)항.

0186

한·미국 간의 상호방위조약 제4조에 의한 시설과 구역 및 한국에서의 미국군대의 지위에 관한 협정(SOFA)
전59권. 1966.7.9 서울에서 서명 : 1967.2.9 발효(조약 232호) (V.30 실무교섭회의, 제77-80차, 1965.5월) 457

나. 민사 청구권 조항

미국측은 78차 회의에서 우리측이 제안한 수정안에 대하여 요지 아래와
같은 회답을 하였다.

(1) 공무 집행중 정부 재산 및 제3자에 대한 손해의 경우 양국정부의
분담율은 국제적인 표준 비율인 25%-75%로 하여야 할것이며, 따라서
한국이 제안하는 15%-85% 비율은 수락할수 없다.

(2) 공무 집행중 제3자에 대한 손해의 경우로서 한국정부가 해결하는 때
에는 한.미 양 당사국이 사전에 배상 책임과 배상금액에 관하여 합의
하여야 한다는 원칙을 한국측이 제안하는 바와 같이 별도의 합의 의사록
으로 규정할 필요가 없으며, 미국측이 76차 회의시에 제안한 5(e)
(iii)항의 규정으로서 충분할것이다.

(3) K.S.C.는 미군의 고용원이 아니다 한국군의 고용원으로 간주하여야
할것이나 KSC 의 지위가 별도 협정으로 확정될때 까지는 이를
조문상에 언급하지 않고, "KSC 는 본조의 규정을 적용하지 않으며,
" KSC 의 지위는 별도의 교섭을 통하여 결정한다"는 양해사항을
채택하여야 한다.

(4) 한국측이 제안한 제13항에 "그러한 청구는 미군당국이 처리 해결한다"
다는 귀절을 추가하는데 합의 한다.

(5) 한국측은 본조 제5, 6, 7, 및 8항의 규정의 적용 시기를 협정 발효
12개월 후로 주장하고 있으나, 이는 그때까지 한국정부 당국이
상기 규정을 운영할수 있는 준비가 될수 있는지도 불확실하며, 또한
그 이전에도 준비가 완료되면 한국정부가 동 규정상의 임무를 수행
할수 있을 것이므로 한국측 제안은 부적합한 것으로서 미국측은 수락
할수 없다.

0188

65-5-15   가도113-b

0189

6

다. 노무조항

미국측은 대통령 방미시 한미간에 합의된 파업권의 인정과 70 일간의 분쟁 해결 절차에 관한 원측에 입각하여 수정안을 제출하였음. 수정된 부분의 내용은 다음과 같다.

(1) 분쟁 해결절차

분쟁은 노동청, 합동위 분과 위원회, 합동위원회 순으로 회부 조정 한다. 이경우 제3단계인 합동위원회에 회부된후 70 일이 경과하지 않는한 고용인은 정상 업무 방해 행위를 하지 못한다.

(2) 단체 행동권의 행사

합동위원회는 미군의 방위 임무와 한국법의 관계 조항을 참작하여 단체 행동권을 행사하지 못할 긴요한 고용인의 범위를 결정한다.

(3) 비상 조치

전쟁등 비상시 본 조항의 적용은 미군당국과 협의하에 한국정부가 취하는 비상조치에 따라 제한한다.

(4) 노동조합의 승인

노동조합은 그 목적이 미국의 이익에 배반되지 않는한 승인된다.

이상의 안에 대한 제안 설명에 대하여 우리측은 미측 제안 제1항은 제3단계인 합동위원회에 회부된때 부터 기산 한다는 것은 제2단계 도 사실상 합동 위원회임에 감하여 모순점이 있음을 지적하였다.

라. 협정의 유효기간

미측은 본협정이 한미 상호 방위 조약이 존속하는한 유효하다는 것을 제의 하였다.

마. 협정의 비준과 발효

미측은 한국정부가 국회의 비준과 기타 입법 및 예산조치를 위하고 미측 에 통고한후 4개월후에 발효 할것과 본협정 체결로 소위 "대전협정"을 무효로 할것을 제안 하였다.

0190 →

65-5-15

외 교 113-6

0191

우리측은 상기 제안에 대하여 이를 검토 한후 차기 회의에서
한국측의 입장을 밝히기로 하였다.

4. 기타 사항

　가. 차기회의 일시: 1965년 6월 7일　하오 4시

끝.

0192

한·미국 간의 상호방위조약 제4조에 의한 시설과 구역 및 한국에서의 미국군대의 지위에 관한 협정(SOFA)
전59권. 1966.7.9 서울에서 서명 : 1967.2.9 발효(조약 232호) (V.30 실무교섭회의, 제77-80차, 1965.5월) 463

STATUS OF FORCES NEGOTIATIONS: 80th Meeting

SUBJECTS: 1. Claims Article

                                      2. Criminal Jurisdiction Article

                                      3. Labor Article

                                      4. Duration of Agreement

                                      5. Ratification of Agreement

PLACE: Ministry of Foreign Affairs

DATE: May 28, 1965

PARTICIPANTS:
  Republic of Korea   United States

CHANG Sang-mum   Benjamin A. Fleck
CHU Mun-ki   Brig. Gen. Carroll H. Dunn, USA
HO Sung-chung   Col. Allan G. Pixton, USA
YI Nam-ki   Capt. George Hagerman, USN
Hur Hyong-koo   Col Kenneth C. Crawford, USA
Col KIM Won-kil   Frank R. LaMacchia
Maj YI Ke-hun, ROKA   Robert A. Kinney
KIM Ki-cho   Goodwin Shapiro
HWANG Yong-chae   Maj Alton Harvey, USA
KIM Tong-hui   David Y. C. Lee (Interpreter)
PAK Won-chol
YI Kun-pal (Interpreter)   G. W. Flowers, Observer

0164

1. Mr. Fleck opened the 80th meeting by stating that the US negotiators would like to table and distribute at this time the full text of the US draft of the US-ROK Status of Forces Agreement, including the Preamble and 30 articles. Article numbers had been tentatively assigned for the mutual convenience of the two sides in the negotiations, but of course are subject to change as agreed. He noted that this full text includes the US draft of the Articles on the Duration and Ratification of the Agreement, the last two Articles which were being tabled for the first time at this session.

2. Then Mr. Fleck stated that the leaders of the two Governments, at their recent conferences in Washington, had reached agreement in principle on the major outstanding issues of this Agreement. Therefore, the US negotiators proposed that consideration of the over-all agreement be expedited and that the minor differences remaining in several articles be resolved soon. Thereby, it is hoped that the expectations of the President of the Republic of Korea, who was reported to have predicted on May 23rd at Cape Kennedy that the SOFA would be concluded in two or three weeks, will be fulfilled.

3. Mr. Fleck indicated that the US negotiators, in addition to tabling the final two articles, also was submitting modifications of the text of the US drafts of the Criminal Jurisdiction, Labor, and Claims Articles. The US drafts of these key articles had been substantially modified in recent weeks, in response to Korean desires, thereby enabling the leaders of the two Governments to reach agreement in principle on the major unresolved issues. Since the US negotiators had made the major concessions necessary to reach accord on the major unresolved issues, they hoped that the ROK negotiators would now respond in kind and accept the revised US draft of the agreement as a whole, as is now being tabled at this meeting.

0195

CLAIMS ARTICLE

4. Mr. Fleck pointed out that, at the 76th meeting, the US Government *had* made a major concession by accepting the Korean draft of the Claims Article subject to certain important modifications. At the 79th meeting, the Korean negotiators *had* proposed certain changes which *would* now be briefly discussed. *(75.)* With reference to the proposed percentages of distribution contained in Paragraph 5(e) (i), *Mr. Fleck said* the US negotiators can see no reason to vary the standard 25% - 75% distribution that has been accepted by almost all other countries.

5. Regarding paragraph 5(e) (iii), ~~Mr. Fleck stated that~~ the US side is unable to accept the Korean proposal, *which* ~~it~~ would only require the parties to "seek mutual agreement." The United States regards the U.S. language requiring mutual agreement on liability, amount and proposed distribution as essential. There is no necessity for restating in *an* ~~the~~ agreed minute that decisions of Korean courts will be binding *since* this is already provided for in para *5ph* 5 (c). The United States recognizes that if a claimant rejects the settlement and takes his case to court, the decision of a competent tribunal of the Republic of Korea would be binding. The ~~Korean~~ *ROK* proposed changes are unnecessary and unacceptable.

6. Regarding Para *graph* 12, Mr. Fleck pointed out *that* the Korean negotiators contended that KSC personnel should be considered employees of the United States; also, that the Republic of Korea does not assume responsibility for claims generated by these individuals. The US position has always been that KSC personnel are not considered US employees and that the US does not assume responsibility for claims caused by their actions. The status of KSC personnel

2

0196

is now being negotiated in separate discussions. Therefore, ~~this is~~ deleted _the US negotiators had_

the last clause of Paragraph 12. In view of the separate discussions which are

taking place, it is appropriate that there be an understanding in the Joint

Agreed Summary that:

"This article is not applicable to claims generated by KSC

personnel. The status of the KSC members will be determined

by other negotiations between the United States and the

Republic of Korea."

By this means, neither the United States nor the Korean position is changed.
The entire question is left for future determination.

arising

7. With reference to Paragraph 13, _(Mr. Fleck stated that)_ the US negotiators accept the new second

sentence proposed by the Korean negotiators. This sentence pertains to claims

prior to the effective date of the SOFA and states: "Such claims shall be

processed and settled by the authorities of the United States."

8. Regarding Paragraph 42 of the Agreed Minute, Mr. Fleck stated that the US

negotiators have carefully considered the Korean proposal that ROK claims

settlement authority be automatically extended throughout Korea twelve months

after the effective date of the Agreement. The twelve-month period may be

sufficiently long to adapt the system throughout Korea. However, this is not

certain.

3

0197

한·미국 간의 상호방위조약 제4조에 의한 시설과 구역 및 한국에서의 미국군대의 지위에 관한 협정(SOFA)
전59권. 1966.7.9 서울에서 서명 : 1967.2.9 발효(조약 232호) (V.30 실무교섭회의, 제77-80차, 1965.5월) 467

Twelve months may not be long enough for the Korean Claims Service to make
preparations to take over these functions. Mr. Fleck emphasized that the US
draft provides the necessary flexibility to enable the transfer to take place
in an efficient manner. The US negotiators do not see any reason to eliminate
this flexibility by incorporating language ~~including language~~ providing for a
specific time frame.

9. The United States, *negotiators, Mr. Fleck said, had* made a major concession in accepting the Korean
draft as the basis of negotiations and ~~has~~ *had* made further concessions ~~today~~ *at this meeting*.
Mr. Fleck urged the Korean negotiators to consider carefully and to accept
these ~~reasonable~~ US proposals.

10. Mr. Chang thanked Mr. Fleck for his clear explanation and for preparing the notebook containing the full text of the US draft of the ~~US-ROK~~ SOFA.
Mr. Chang also stated he wanted to share the honor he recently had in Washington,
D. C. He ~~was~~ *had been* present when the leaders of ~~the~~ *the* two governments, in a spirit of
cooperation and understanding, ~~agreed on a solution to~~ *had reached agreement on* two major problems in the
Criminal Jurisdiction and Labor Articles. Mr. Chang expressed the hope *that* the SOFA
negotiators in Seoul could proceed in this same cooperative spirit and complete
the negotiations in a short time. He emphasized the need to concentrate the
negotiations on major issues, and not to ~~(haggle over)~~ *dwell on* minor points. He urged both
sides to tackle the problem in a spirit of mutual concession and pave the way for
early conclusion of the Agreement. Mr. Chang indicated he felt progress was being
made toward resolution of the problems in the Claims Article. The Korean negotiators
would study the US statement and the new proposals and respond at the next negotiating session next week.

11. Mr. Fleck thanked Mr. Chang for his comments on his recent trip to the

4

0198

United States, and for ~~whatever~~ part he _had_ played _(in Washington)_ in helping to reach agreement in principle on several important issues. He ~~expressed the belief~~ _stated_ that the US ~~authorities~~ _negotiators_ fully share the feelings of the Korean ~~authorities~~ _negotiators_ that a SOFA must be concluded as soon as possible. It was specifically for the purpose of expediting conclusion of this Agreement that the US negotiators ~~are tabling~~ _had tabled_ the full US draft ~~of the SOFA~~ at this meeting. He expressed the hope that the Agreement could be concluded ~~within two weeks, or maybe even in one week,~~ _speedily_ on the basis of the _U.S._ draft ~~of the entire SOFA~~ tabled at this meeting.

5

0199

CRIMINAL JURISDICTION ARTICLE

12. Mr. Fleck stated that the proposals of the Korean negotiators regarding waiver, pretrial custody and duty certificates, presented at the 77th negotiating session, and those regarding trial safeguards, presented at the 70th negotiating session, ~~have~~ *had* been given careful consideration. The US side ~~remarked~~ *had* attempted to be responsive to the desires of the Korean negotiators to the maximum extent possible. At the same time, ~~we believe~~ *believed to be* this draft is consistent with essential requirements of the United States. *Mr. Fleck said he would comment on the remaining* ~~The following comments are made regarding outstanding points.~~ *unresolved issues.*

13. Agreed Minute re Para*graph* 3(b). ~~Waiver:~~

With reference to the proposal of the Korean negotiators to insert the words "at the request of the United States" at the beginning of paragraph 1, the US negotiators *had* stated at the time it was proposed that this was unacceptable. The Korean negotiators are well aware of the US position. This would completely change the waiver formula as tabled by the US, and would be inconsistent with the remaining paragraphs of ~~that~~ *the* Agreed Minute. The so-called German formula provides for a general waiver at the time the agreement becomes effective. ~~It~~ It does not provide for individual requests for waiver in each case. *(Mr. Fleck stated that)* the inclusion of the phrase cannot be accepted and ~~we understand that you are~~ *that the U.S. negotiators understood that the Korean negotiators were* prepared to withdraw this proposal.

14. With reference to the ~~Kor~~ *Korean* proposal for an additional sentence to be inserted at the end of paragraph 4, the right of final determination by the Government of the Republic of Korea is affirmatively established in the US draft and ~~we~~ *the U.S. negotiators* see no reason for duplicating this language, *(Mr. Fleck continued. The U.S. negotiators)* ~~we~~ believe that the 21-day time limitation would be an unnecessary restriction. Although ~~we~~ *they* expect

6

0200

that the consultations referred to would normally be concluded within this time, such might not always be the case. However, even though ~~we~~ *they* do not believe it necessary, ~~it~~ *they* are prepared to generally accede to the desires of the Korean negotiators. ~~We propose to do this~~ by including an understanding in the Joint Agreed Summary. This understanding would read as follows:

"Recall of waiver shall be final and conclusive unless the statement for recall referred to in paragraph 3 of this minute is withdrawn by the Government of the Republic of Korea."

1̶4̶. 15. The next matter to be considered *Mr. Fleck noted, was* ~~is~~ Paragraph 6 of the Agreed Minute. This pertains to the place where trials for offenses committed against Korean interests take place. As ~~was~~ *had been* pointed out in the 77th meeting, ~~the~~ previous *U.S.* agreement to hold these trials in the Republic of Korea, unless mutually agreed otherwise, was directly related to the waiver formula ~~we~~ *(which the U.S. negotiators)* were proposing at that time. ~~We have~~ *They had* now offered the German waiver formula. Para 6̶ *6th* is identical to Article 26 of the German Agreement. These two provisions were designed to operate together. In addition, as ~~we have~~ *had been* stated, cases of the types referred to in Para 6̶ *6th* are extremely rare. ~~We~~ *(The U.S. negotiators)* do not expect them to present any problem. However, even though rare, such cases may arise and trial elsewhere may be required. For these reasons, ~~we deem~~ *(is deemed)* it necessary to retain paragraph 6.

16. <u>Agreed Minute re Para 3(a): (Duty Certificates)</u>

Mr. Fleck stated that the US negotiators ~~accept~~ *accepted* the modifications pertaining to duty certificates proposed by the ROK negotiators at the 77th negotiating sessions, with the following modifications:

a. ~~We agree~~ *They agreed* to inclusion ~~for~~ *of an* understanding in the Agreed Joint Summary, stating:

7

0201

"A certificate shall be issued only upon the advice of a Staff Judge Advocate, and the competent authority issuing the duty certificate shall be a General Grade Officer or his designee." (Mr. Fleck continued,) The Korean negotiators are well aware that a general officer must, of necessity, delegate many of his functions to his senior subordinates. The U.S. language requires that the responsibility remain at general officer level and only allows delegation of authority to act. ~~believe this will result in a more satisfactory procedure.~~

b. They accepted ~~We accept~~ substitution of the word "shall" for the word "may" in the second paragraph of Agreed Minute Re Paragraph 3(a) "shall be made the subject of review." They also accepted ~~accept~~ the modification of the first understanding proposed by the Korean negotiators.

c. With regard to the US definition of "official duty," the Korean negotiators originally had proposed and the United States had already agreed to, inclusion of this as an understanding in the Joint Agreed Summary. The United States negotiators are still willing to include this definition in the Agreed Joint Summary. However they cannot accept the proposal of the Korean negotiators that it be included in the Agreed Minute, Mr. Fleck said.

17. ←———— Paragraph 5: Pretrial Custody

Mr. Fleck stated that the United States negotiators accepted all modifications proposed by the Korean negotiators at the 77th Session relating to pretrial custody. Therefore, ~~their its assumed~~ the two sides had reached full agreement on paragraph 5.

8

18. Trial Safeguards.

With reference to the trial safeguards contained in Paragraph 9 and its related Agreed Minutes, Mr. Fleck emphasized that the Korean negotiators are well aware of the importance which the US Government attaches to these guarantees. The acceptance by the Korean negotiators at the 70th Negotiating Session of the principle of enumerating the trial safeguards had been a major step toward resolution of the differences on this important matter. At that session, the Korean negotiators proposed modification of some of the listed safeguards. These proposals had been given careful consideration in a maximum attempt to be receptive to the Korean desires. At the same time, the United States has certain essential needs that must be fulfilled. The United States negotiators would like to discuss each of the Korean proposals in detail.

a. Agreed Minute Re Paragraph 9a: Mr. Fleck said the U.S. negotiators agree that the original second sentence of this Agreed Minute was related to the use of the word "civil" in paragraph 1(b) of the text. They had carefully studied the Korean negotiators' proposal to delete both of these items and substitute an understanding in the Agreed Joint Summary. The U.S. negotiators believed that agreement had been reached on the principle that US personnel should not be subject to the jurisdiction of Korean military tribunals. What the negotiators had been discussing was where this principle should be stated. As indicated in the tabled U.S. draft, the U.S. negotiators are willing to delete the original second sentence of Agreed Minute Re Paragraph 9(a) in return for acceptance by the Korean negotiators of the word "civil" in paragraph 1(b).

9

0203

b. _Agreed Minute Re Paragraph 9(g)_: At the 70th Session, the Korean negotiators _had_ expressed disagreement with that portion of the Agreed Minute rendering inadmissible as evidence any statement taken from an accused in the absence of a United States representative. The Korean negotiators _had_ _contended_ ~~noted~~ that their proposed language for the 3rd unnumbered paragraph of Agreed Minute Re Paragraph 9, pertaining to the inadmissibility of statements obtained by illegal means, should render unnecessary this portion of the Agreed Minute. ~~Further, the ROK negotiators agreed that at at his discretion the United States representative might elect not to appear. We have~~ _The negotiators had_ previously discussed this provision in detail. The US representative has an affirmative duty to be present at these sessions. He will be available at all times and the United States authorities will insure that he fulfills this duty. _[The U.S. negotiators]_ ~~We~~ believe this provision is absolutely necessary to insure that no confession is obtained by coercion or other improper means. The United States Government is firmly committed to the principle embodied in this provision and we cannot agree to its deletion.

c. _Agreed Minute re Paragraph 9, subparagraph (a) of the Second Unnumbered Paragraph_: _Mr. Fisk noted that_ this provision guarantees the accused the right to appeal a conviction. It is ~~our~~ _the_ understanding _[of the U.S. negotiators]_ that the appellate procedure of the Korean Court allows the accused to request a review of the evidence used in the trial court. It is also ~~our~~ _their_ understanding that the appellate court may examine new evidence or witnesses and make new findings of fact on either its own motion or that of the accused. In order to prevent any possible confusion, ~~we~~ _they_ therefore propose insertion of the following

10

understanding in the Agreed Joint Summary:

"Under the appellate procedure of the Courts of the Republic of Korea the accused may request a re-examination of the evidence, including new evidence and witnesses, as a basis for new findings of fact by the appellate court."

They believe this is entirely consistent with Korean appellate procedure.

[redacted]

d. <u>Agreed Minute Re Paragraph 9, subparagraph (d) of the Second Unnumbered Paragraph and the 4th Unnumbered Para</u>. Mr. Fleck recalled that the Korean negotiators had proposed the deletion of the fourth paragraph and the adoption of an alternative subparagraph (d). The U.S. negotiators were aware of the fact that Article 361 of the Code of Criminal Procedure allows appeals by the prosecution based upon errors of law. They were also aware that increasing a sentence on appeal is a part of Korean law. At the 61st Session, they had pointed out that this was not only contrary to American judicial practice, but also to the fundamental understanding of justice held by the US Government and US personnel. Like the Korean negotiators, the U.S. negotiators must have an agreement that is acceptable to our government and people. An appeal by the prosecution, based upon mistake of fact or the increase of a sentence on appeal, would be viewed by the American people <u>as a miscarriage of justice</u>. The US negotiators deem these limitations essential safeguards which must be retained. They cannot, therefore, agree to alteration of subparagraph (d) or the deletion of unnumbered paragraph (4).

e. <u>Agreed Minute Re Paragraph 9, Subparagraph (j) of the Second</u>

<u>Paragraph</u>: With regard to this provision prohibiting trial of the accused

if physically or mentally unfit, *Mr. Fleck said the U.S. negotiators* ~~we~~ believe ~~our~~ *their* position is adequately clear.

The Korean negotiators seem to fear that this will be subject to abuse by the

accused if the final determination as his fitness is not left to the court.

This provision gives a firm right to postponement of trial if ~~X~~ the accused

is physically or mentally unfit. The Joint Committee is the proper place to

develop mutually ~~satisfactory~~ procedures for ~~making this~~ determination. The

right of postponement in event of mental or physical unfitness is a substantive

safeguard deemed absolutely essential by the United States.

f. <u>Agreed Minute re Paragraph 9, Third Unnumbered Paragraph</u>:

Mr. Fleck ~~stated~~ *recalled* that, at the 70th session, the Korean negotiators *had* proposed a

revision of the paragraph ~~of this Minute~~ which would omit the term "real

evidence". The United States cannot agree to ~~m~~ omission of the term "real

evidence" or of a guarantee that it will not be used if obtained illegally.

The use of evidence obtained by unreasonable search and seizure or by illegal

or improper means is inadmissable under the US Constitution in all courts of

the United States. The United States cannot consent to the use of evidence

obtained by this manner against any US citizen tried in a Korean Court under

this agreement. The United States negotiators believe that the provision in

our draft is quite suitable. In response to the proposals of the Korean

negotiators, however, *they were* ~~we are~~ prepared to accept the Korean revision of this

paragraph subject to ~~the~~ modifications indicated in the *tabled* draft ~~you have before you~~.

The United States ~~again~~ negotiators wish it to be clearly understood that

12

this is an essential requirement and that under no circumstances will the United States agree to the use of illegally obtained evidence.

19. Mr. Fleck recalled that, at various times in previous negotiating sessions, the Korean negotiators ~~have~~ *had* expressed a desire that the word "military" be inserted before the word "authorities" when referring to US military officials throughout the US draft. *(He said) The US side accepts this proposal* ~~and has inserted the word~~ "authorities" throughout the draft of this article, as follows: *"military".*

1(a); 2(a); 3(a); 4; 5(a); 5(b); 5(c); 6(a); 6(b); 7(a); 8; 11; and in the following Agreed Minutes: No. 1 and No. 2 re paragraph 9(b); No. 1 re paragraph 3(a); No. 1 and No. 3 re paragraph 6; re paragraph 9; and re paragraph 10(a) and 10(b).

20. In summary, Mr. Fleck noted that the United States ~~has~~ *had* made major concessions throughout the Criminal Jurisdiction Article in an effort to hasten conclusion of this agreement. ~~A fair and complete article has now been prepared to you. We ask your careful consideration of~~ *The U.S. negotiators asked the Korean negotiators to carefully consider* these proposals, ~~and await your~~ *They awaited Korean* acceptance of this draft of the ~~important~~ Criminal Jurisdiction Article.

13

한·미국 간의 상호방위조약 제4조에 의한 시설과 구역 및 한국에서의 미국군대의 지위에 관한 협정(SOFA)
전59권. 1966.7.9 서울에서 서명 : 1967.2.9 발효(조약 232호) (V.30 실무교섭회의, 제77-80차, 1965.5월) 477

Labor Article

21. ~~Labor Article~~ Mr. Fleck stated that the US negotiators ~~are~~ *were* tabling a revised Labor Article, which incorporates ~~the proposal to reach a~~ compromise *language in keeping with the recent agreement* ~~on this Article, as recently agreed to~~ by the leaders of ~~our respective~~ *the two* governments in Washington. In this new draft, paragraph 4 ~~is~~ *has been* revised. The previous subparagraphs 4(a), 4(c), and 4(e), have been deleted, as suggested by the ROK authorities. A new subparagraph 4(a) (5) ~~is~~ *has been* included, incorporating the concept of the ~~ROK~~ *Korean* proposal made at the 79th negotiating session, and providing for a 70-day cooling-off after a labor dispute ~~is~~ *has been* referred to the Joint Committee. The new subparagraph 4(b) incorporates the substance of the ROK draft of subparagraph 4(b). It gives the Joint Committee the responsibility for determining those categories of essential employees who shall not exercise the right of further collective action in the event ~~of~~ *a* labor dispute is not resolved by the mediation procedures. A new sub-paragraph 4(c) incorporates the language previously tabled by the ~~ROK~~ *Korean negotiators* in Paragraph 5. It provides that in a national emergency, application of this article will be limited in accordance with emergency measures taken by the Govdrnment of the Republic of Korea. In connection with this new subparagraph, it is ~~our~~ *the* understanding *(of the U.S. negotiators)* that ~~it~~ was proposed by the ~~ROK~~ *Korean* negotiators in order to assist in our joint defense effort in case of national emergency. During such an emergency every resource must be utilized to meet the crisis. Therefore, it is ~~the~~ *the* understanding *(of the U.S. negotiators)* that the limitation of the Labor Article would be selective. In other words, those provisions which ~~may~~ *might* hamper US operations during such a national emergency would *be* suspended. At the same time those provisions which *would* further our joint defense efforts and would be of assistance would remain in effect. The substance of the previous subparagraph 4(b) ~~of~~ the US draft, which is an essential provision, ~~is~~ *has been* incorporated as a new Agreed

14

0208

478 주한미군지위협정(SOFA) 서명 및 발효 11

Minute No. 5 in this draft.

22. Mr. Fleck stated that this revised draft incorporates the ~~ROK~~ Korean proposal to exclude the Korean Service Corps from coverage of the Labor Article. The KSC personnel are to be covered by a separate agreement. Therefore, the revised US draft on this subject merely affirms that ~~the KSC~~ they are not covered by the Article. The U.S. negotiators ~~We~~ agree to delete Agreed Minute No. 1, on the basis that ~~xxx~~ a separate agreement for the KSC will be negotiated. This deletion of Agreed Minute No. 1 is made with the understanding that, pending conclusion of a separate agreement, KSC personnel will continue to be made available by the ROK Government as at present. In other words, the 1960 US-Korean agreement will remain in effect until it is superceded by a new agreement, separate from the SOFA.

23. In tabling this revised US draft, (Mr. Fleck continued) the US negotiators believe they have met the Korean requirements on the key point of difference in ~~the~~ two drafts. In making this concession, ~~we~~ they would like to reiterate that ~~neither~~ U.S. armed forces are ~~maintain the position that~~ the ~~USFK are~~ here solely for the defense of Korea. ~~their~~ ~~our~~ Korean employees are vital to the joint US-ROK defense mission. As the U.S. negotiators had ~~have~~ explained, (the U.S. armed forces) ~~we~~ are relying more and more on ~~our~~ their Korean employees in semi-skilled and skilled occupations. Many of these employees are engaged in work which is essential to the combat readiness of both the US and Korean armed forces. Therefore, the U.S. negotiators were ~~we are~~ making these important concessions with the understanding the Korean negotiators would: ~~that you will~~ accept the remainder of the US draft of the Labor Article, and that ~~~~ in future the Joint Committee, when considering the role of the ~~US~~ Korean employees of the US armed forces under subparagraph 4(b), will ~~will~~ take into full consideration the importance of ~~USFK~~ the U.S. armed forces' Korean employees in the defense of their homeland and the special status of these employees.

15

24. Mr. Chang thanked Mr. Fleck for his presentation and indicated that the Korean negotiators would respond at the next negotiating session. The Korean negotiators asked questions about the meaning of Para 4 (a) (5) of the Labor Article, especially whether the reference therein should not be to subparagraph (2) rather than to subparagraph (3). Mr. Fleck explained that reference of a dispute to the special committee, provided for in subparagraph (2), was not intended to be compulsory or automatic. Under the provisions of the US draft, if the Joint Committee decides to refer the dispute to the special committee and the special committee having failed to resolve the dispute, then returns the dispute to the Joint Committee, the 70-day period would begin when the special committee returns the dispute to the Joint Committee. However, if the Joint Committee should decide not to refer the dispute to a special committee, the 70-day period would begin from the date the dispute was referred to the Joint Committee by the Office of Labor Affairs. The Korean negotiators expressed the opinion that the subparagraph (5) appeared to be faultily drafted, since it does not clearly provide for procedure explained by the US negotiators.

0210

25. Mr. Fleck tabled the U.S. drafts of articles on duration and ratification of the agreement. He explained that the Article on the Duration of the Agreement provides that this agreement shall remain in force while the Mutual Defense Treaty between the the US and the ROK remains in force, unless terminated earlier by agreement between the two Governments. This is standard language for such articles in US status-of-forces agreements.

26. In the Article on the Ratification of the Agreement, Mr. Fleck explained that paragraph one provides that this agreement shall enter into force four months after the date of a written notification from the Government of the Republic of Korea that it has approved the agreement and has taken the legislative and budgetary action necessary to give effect to its provisions. In specifying "legislative and budgetary action", the U.S. Government also expects any other necessary implementing action (~~e.g. Administrative Regulations~~) that will have been taken by the ROK Government authorities. The US Government would further expect to inform the ROK Government and be informed by the ROK authorities on a continuing basis of progress in the implementation (including exchange of texts of implementing materials) so that consistent and coordinated action by both sides would be assured. Mr. Fleck emphasized that, in the period between the notification of ROKG approval of the agreement and its entry into force, both Governments will have time to make further preparations for orderly and effective implementation of the Agreement. ROK and US authorities can utilize this period to organize the Joint Committee and its Sub-Committees, and to take other measures to insure smooth implementation of the Agreement.

27. The second paragraph of the US draft provides for termination of the Taejon Agreement for US armed forces, subject to the paragraph in the Criminal

17

Jurisdiction Article which provides that the Taejon Agreement will cover offenses which occur before entry into force of ~~the agreement.~~ *the SOFA.*

28. Mr. Fleck expressed the belief that the ROK negotiators, after study of these two drafts, ~~will~~ *would* find them acceptable. Mr. Fleck stated that, in addition to the five articles he *had* ~~has~~ discussed thus far in this meeting, there *remained* ~~are~~ several other articles *on* ~~in~~ which full agreement has not been formalized. Remaining differences in these articles are believed to be minor, and Mr. Fleck urged ROK acceptance of the US ~~positions in~~ *drafts of* these articles, which previously *had* ~~have~~ been fully explained, ~~at the negotiating sessions.~~ Having thus presented the over-all US position on remaining issues, Mr. Fleck concluded that the US negotiators look*ed* forward confidently to early conclusion of the Agreement. Mr. Chang thanked Mr. Fleck for his comprehensive presentation of the US position and indicated the Korean negotiators would respond on all unresolved issues ~~next week.~~ *at the next meeting.*

18

0212

PROPOSED OPENING STATEMENT - 28 MAY 1965

1. The US negotiators would like to table and distribute at this time the full text of the US draft of the US-ROK Status of Forces Agreement. This text includes the Preamble and 30 articles. Article numbers are tentatively assigned for our mutual convenience in the negotiations, but of course are subject to change as agreed. This full text of the SOFA includes the US drafts of the Articles on the Duration and Ratification of the Agreement, the last two SOFA Articles which we would like to table at this session.

2. The leaders of our respective Governments, at their recent conferences in Washington, reached agreement in principle on the major outstanding issues of this agreement. Therefore, we propose that the US-ROK negotiators expedite consideration of the over-all agreement, speedily ~~leading up~~ resolving the minor differences remaining in several articles. We would thereby hope to be able to fulfill the expectations of the President of the Republic of Korea, who on May 23rd at Cape Kennedy predicted that the US-ROK SOFA would be concluded in two or three weeks.

3. At this session the US negotiators, in addition to tabling the final two articles, also is submitting modifications of the text of the US drafts of the Criminal Jurisdiction, Labor, and Claims Articles. The US drafts of these key articles have been substantially modified in recent weeks, in response to Korean desires, thereby enabling the leaders of our two Governments to reach agreement in principle on the major unresolved issues. ~~Since the US side has made the major concessions ~~x~~ necessary~~ to reach this accord on the major unresolved issues, we/~~know~~ hope the ROK negotiators will now respond in kind and accept the revised US draft of the agreement as a whole, as we are tabling it today.

0213

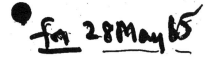

CLAIMS ARTICLE

At the 76th meeting the United States made a major concession by accepting the Korean draft of the Claims Article subject to certain changes. At the 79th meeting the Korean negotiators accepted the revised US position with certain changes which will now be briefly discussed.

With reference to the proposed percentages of distribution Para 5(e) (i) the US negotiators can see no reason to vary the standard 25% - 75% distribution that has been accepted by ▮▮▮▮▮ other countries.

Regarding paragraph 5(e) (iii), the United States is unable to accept the Korean proposal. It only requires that the parties "shall seek mutual agreement." The United States regards as essential this provision requiring mutual agreement on liability, amount and proposed distribution. Additionally, there is no necessity for restating in the agreed minute that decisions of Korean courts will be binding. This is already provided for in para 5 (c). The United States recognizes that if a claimant rejects the settlement and takes his case to court, the decision of a competent tribunal of the Republic of Korea would be binding. [The Korean proposed changes are unnecessary and unacceptable.]

Regarding Para 12, the Korean negotiators stated that KSC personnel should be considered employees of the United States and that the Republic of Korea does not assume responsibility for claims generated by these individuals. The US position has always been that KSC personnel would not be considered US employees and that the US would not assume responsibility for claims caused by their action. The status of KSC personnel is now being negotiated with the Republic of Korea. Therefore the US agrees to delete the last clause of Para 12 that pertains to KSC personnel and leave

0214

determination of their status to other negotiations. It is appropriate

that there be an understanding in the Joint Agreed Summary that:

"This article is not applicable to claims generated by KSC

personnel. ~~The status of the~~ ~~KSC members~~ will be

for liability for claim generated by KSC personnel.

determined by other negotiations between the United States and

the Republic of Korea."

By this means, neither the United States nor the Korean positions are

changed, but rather the entire questions is left for future determination.

With reference to Para 12, the US negotiators are pleased to accept

the new second sentence proposed by the Korean negotiators. (Pertains

to claims prior to the effective date and states: "Such claims shall be

processed and settled by the authorities of the United States.")

Regarding Para A2 of the Agreed Minute, the US negotiators have

carefully considered the Korean proposal that *ROK* claims settlement authority be

automatically extended throughout Korea twelve months after the effective

date of the Agreement. We agree that the twelve-month period may be suf-

ficiently long to adapt the system throughout Korea. However, this is not *certain.*

The United States made a major concession in basically accepting

the Korean draft and has made further concessions today. We ask the Korean

negotiators to accept these reasonable US proposals, and thereby enable the

US-ROK negotiators to reach full agreement on the Claims Article.

0215

Proposed Talking Paper

Criminal Jurisdiction Article

The proposals of the Korean negotiators regarding waiver, pretrial custody and duty certificates presented at the 77th negotiating session and those regarding trial safeguards presented at the 70th negotiating session have been given careful consideration. We have attempted to be responsive to the desires of the Korean negotiators to the maximum extent possible, consistent with essential requirements of the United States. We believe we have met the Korean negotiators' requirements and that with our response today a speedy conclusion to these negotiations is in order.

I. Agreed Minute re Para 3(b) Waiver:

With reference to the proposal of the Korean negotiators to insert the words "at the request of the United States" at the beginning of paragraph 1, we stated at the time it was proposed that this was unacceptable. The Korean negotiators are well aware of the US position. This completely changes the waiver formula as tabled by the US and is inconsistent with the remaining paragraphs of that Agreed Minute. The German formula provides for a general waiver at the time the agreement becomes effective -- not for individual requests for waiver in each case. The inclusion of the ROK proposed phrase cannot be accepted.

2. With reference to the additional sentence proposed for insertion at the end of paragraph 4, the right of final determination by the government of the Republic of Korea is affirmatively established in the US draft and we see no reason for duplicating this established right. Further, the 21-day

0216

time limitation is an unnecessary and unacceptable restriction. Although we expect that the consultations would normally be concluded within this time, such may not always be the case. However, even though we do not believe it necessary, we are prepared to generally accede to the desires of the Korean negotiators by including the following understanding in the Joint Agreed Summary:

"Recall of waiver shall be final and conclusive unless the statement for recall referred to in para 3 of this minute is withdrawn by the government of the Republic of Korea."

3. The next matter to be considered is Paragraph 6 of the Agreed Minute pertaining to the place of trial for offenses committed against Korean interests. As we pointed out in the 77th session, our previously tabled commitment to hold these trials in the Republic of Korea, unless mutually agreed otherwise, was directly related to the US waiver proposal then tabled. We have now offered the so-called German waiver formula and para 6 is identical to Article 26 of the German Agreement. These two provisions were designed to operate together. In addition, as we have stated, cases of this type are extremely rare and we do not expect it to present any problem. However, even though rare, cases such as this may arise and trial elsewhere may be required. For these reasons, we deem it necessary to retain paragraph 6 of the Agreed Minute.

Agreed Minute re Para 3(a): (Duty Certificates)

1. The US negotiators are now prepared to agree to the modifications pertaining to duty certificates proposed by the ROK negotiators at the 77th negotiating session subject to acceptance by the Korean negotiators of several changes.

2. We propose that the understanding state: "A duty certificate shall be issued only upon the advice of a Staff Judge Advocate, and the competent authority issuing the duty certificate shall be a General Grade Officer" be amended by adding "or his designee." The Korean negotiators are well aware that a general officer must, of necessity, delegate many acts to be done by his senior subordinates. Our proposed modification requires that the responsibility remain at general officer level and only allows delegation of authority to act. We believe this will result in a more satisfactory procedure.

3. We are prepared to accept substitution of the word "shall" for the word "may" in the second paragraph of Agreed Minute re paragraph 3(a)

3

한·미국 간의 상호방위조약 제4조에 의한 시설과 구역 및 한국에서의 미국군대의 지위에 관한 협정(SOFA) 전59권. 1966.7.9 서울에서 서명 : 1967.2.9 발효(조약 232호) (V.30 실무교섭회의, 제77-80차, 1965.5월)   487

/"shall be made the subject of review"7. We are also prepared to accept the modification of the first understanding proposed by the Korean negotiators /Note: Understanding will be: a. "The certificate will be conclusive unless modification is agreed upon. The United States authorities shall give due consideration to any objection which may be raised by the Chief Prosecutor of the Republic of Korea."7

4. With regard to the US definition of "official duty," the United States has already agreed to inclusion of this as an understanding in the Agreed Summary. The United States negotiators are still willing to agree to this, the original ROK proposal, that the US Army definition be an agreed (understanding in the Joint Summary)

However, we cannot accept the proposal of the Korean negotiators that it be included in the Agreed Minute.

Paragraph 5: Pretrial Custody

The United States negotiators are pleased to accept all modifications proposed by the Korean negotiators at the 77th Session relating to Pre-Trial Custody.

TRIAL SAFEGUARDS

1. With reference to the trial safeguards contained in Paragraph 9 and its related Agreed Minute, the Korean negotiators are well aware of the importance which we attach to these guarantees. The acceptance by the Korean negotiators at the 70th Negotiating Session of the principle of enumeration of the trial safeguards was a major step toward resolution of the differences on this important matter. At that session the Korean negotiators proposed modification of certain listed safeguards. These proposals have been given careful consideration in a maximum attempt to be receptive to the Korean desires. At the same time the United States has certain essential needs that must be fulfilled. The United States negotiators will now respond in detail to each of the Korean proposals.

2. Agreed Minute Re Paragraph 9a: We agree that the second sentence of this Agreed Minute is related to the use of the word "civil" in paragraph 1(b) of the text. We have carefully studied the Korean negotiators' proposal to delete both of these items and substitute an understanding in the Agreed Joint Summary. It is believed that there is agreement on the principle that US personnel should not be subject to the jurisdiction of Korean military tribunals with the difference being only the question of where this should be stated. The United States is now prepared to delete the second sentence of Agreed Minute Re Paragraph 9(a) in return for acceptance by the Korean negotiators of the word "civil" in paragraph 1(b).

-0218

3. <u>Agreed Minute Re Paragraph 9(g)</u>: At the 70th Session the Korean negotiators expressed disagreement with that pprtion of the Agreed Minute rendering inadmissible as evidence any statement taken from an accused in the absence of a United States representative. The Korean negotiators noted that their proposed subparagraph of Agreed Minute Re Paragraph 9 pertaining to the inadmissibility of statements obtained by illegal means should render this unnecessary. Further, that at his discretion the United States representative might elect not to appear. We have previously discussed this provision in detail. The representative has an affirmative duty to be present at these sessions. He will be available at all times and the United States will insure that he fulfills this duty. We believe this provision is absolutely necessary to insure that no confession is obtained by coercion or other improper means. The United States is firmly committed to the principle embodied in this provision and we cannot agree to its deletion.

4. <u>Agreed Minute re Paragraph 9, subparagraph (a) of the Second Paragraph</u>: This provision guarantees the accused the right to appeal a conviction. It is our understanding that the appellate procedure of the Korean Court allows the accused to request a review of the evidence used in the trial court. It is also our understanding that the appellate court may examine new evidence or witnesses and make new findings of fact on either its own motion or that of the accused. In order to prevent any possible confusion, we therefore propose insertion of the following understanding in the Joint Agreed Summary:

"Under the appellate procedure of the Courts of the Republic of Korea the accused may request a re-examination of the evidence, including new evidence and witnesses, as a basis for new findings of fact by the appellate court."

We believe this is entirely consistent with Korean appellate procedure.

0219

5. Agreed Minute Re Paragraph 9, subparagraph (d) of the Second Paragraph of the Fourth Paragraph: The Korean negotiators proposed the deletion of the fourth paragraph and an alternative subparagraph (e). We appreciate the fact that Article 361 of the Code of Criminal Procedure allows appeals by the prosecution based upon errors of law and that increasing of the sentence on appeal is a part of Korean law. At the 61st Session we pointed out that this was not only contrary to the American practice, but also to the fundamental understanding of justice as held by US personnel. We, like the Korean negotiators, must have an agreement that this is acceptable to [the United States] government and the people. We point out that the possibility of an appeal by the prosecution, based upon mistake of fact or the increase of a sentence on appeal, would be viewed by the American people as a miscarriage of justice. The US negotiators deem these limitations essential safeguards which must be retained.

6. Agreed Minute Re Paragraph 9, Subparagraph (e) of the Second Paragraph: With regard to this provision prohibiting trial of the accused if physically or mentally unfit, we believe our position is adequately clear. The Korean negotiators seem to fear that this will be subject to abuse by the accused if the final determination as to fitness is not left to the court. The US provision gives a firm right to postponement of trial if the accused is physically or mentally unfit. The Joint Committee is the proper place to develop a mutually satisfactory means of making this determination. The right of postponement in event of mental or physical unfitness is a substantive safeguard deemed absolutely essential by the United States.

0220

7. <u>Agreed Minute re Paragraph 9, Third Paragraph</u>: At the 70th session the Korean negotiators proposed a revision of this paragraph. As the Korean negotiators pointed out, their revision omitted the term "real evidence" /note: They stated that the fact that real evidence has been obtained illegally does not necessarily affect its admissibility as valid evidence in support of guilt./ The United States can not agree to omission of the term "real evidence" and a guarantee that it will not be used if obtained illegally. The use of evidence obtained by unreasonable search and seizure or by illegal or improper means is inadmissable under the US Constitution in all courts of the United States. The United States can not consent to the use of evidence obtained by this manner against any US citizen tried in a Korean Court under this agreement. The United States negotiators believe that the provision in our draft is most suitable. However, in response to the proposals of the Korean negotiators we are prepared to accept the Korean revision of this paragraph subject to modification as ~~follows:~~ See included in this Tabled draft.

The United States negotiators wish to clearly establish that this is an essential requirement and under no circumstances will the United States agree to the use of this illegally obtained evidence.

8. <u>Insertion of "Military" before "Authorities" In U.S. Draft</u>. At various times in previous negotiating sessions, the Korean negotiators have expressed a desire that the word "military" be inserted before the word "authorities" when referring to US military officials throughout the US draft. The United States negotiators now agree to this and the word "military" has been inserted before the word "authorities" in the following paragraphs of the US draft:

1(a); 2(a); 3(a); 4; 5(a); 5(b); 5(c); 6(a); 6(b); 7(a); 8; 11; and in the following Agreed Minutes: No. 1 and No. 2 re paragraph 9(b); No. 1 re paragraph 3(a); No. 1 and No. 3 re paragraph 6; re paragraph 9; and re paragraph 10(a) and 10(b).

CONCLUSION

The United States has made major concessions throughout the Criminal Jurisdiction Article in an effort to hasten conclusion of this agreement. ~~Session.~~ A fair and complete article has now been presented to you. We ask for serious consideration of these proposals and hope speedy agreement can be achieved.

0221

2. <u>Proposed Presentation.</u> The US negotiators are tabling a revised <u>Labor</u>
Labor Article, which incorporates the proposal to reach a compromise on this
Article, as resently agreed to by the leaders of our respective governments
in Washington. In this new draft, the US paragraph 4 is revised to delete
the previous subparagraphs 4(a), 4(c), and 4(e), as suggested by the ROK
authorities.

3. A new subparagraph 4(a) (5) is included, incorporating the concept
of the ROK proposal made at the 79th negotiating session, and providing for
a 70-day cooling-off after a labor dispute is referred to the Joint Committee.
It also incorporates in the new US draft subparagraph 4 (b) the substance of
the ROK draft of subparagraph 4(b), giving the Joint Committee the responsibility
for determining those categories of essential employees who shall not exercise
the right of further collective action in the event a labor dispute is not
resolved by the mediation procedures. A new US subparagraph 4 (c) incorporates
the language previously tabled by the ROK in Paragraph 5, which provides that
in a national emergency, application of this article will be limited in accordance with emergency measures taken by the Government of the Republic of Korea.
In connection with this new subparagraph, it is our understanding that it was
proposed by the ROK negotiators in order to assist in our joint defense effort
in case of national emergency, when every resource must be utilized to meet
the/~~crisis~~ crises. Therefore, it is our understanding that the limitation of the
Labor Article would be selective.

0222

The substance of the previous US subparagraph 4 (b), which is an essential part of the US draft, is incorporated as a new Agreed Minute #5.

These provisions which may hamper US operations during such a national emergency would be suspended, while those provisions which further our operations and are of assistance in our joint defense efforts, would remain in effect.

3. Our revised draft of the Labor Article accepts the ROK proposal made at the _____ negotiating session to exclude the Korean Service Corps from coverage of the Labor Article, covered by a separate agreement. Therefore, the revised US draft on this subject merely affirms that the KSC are not covered by the Article. We agree to delete Agreed Minute No. 1, on the basis that a separate agreement for the KSC will be negotiated. This deletion of Agreed Minute No. 1 is made with the understanding that, pending negotiation of a separate agreement. KSC personnel will continue to be made available as at present. In other words, the 1960 US-ROK agreement will remain in effect until it is superceded by a new agreement.

We believe the US side, in tabling this revised US draft, have met the Korean requirements on the key point of difference in our two drafts. In making this concession, we would like to reiterate that we maintain the position that the USFK is here solely for the defense of Korea that our Korean employees are vital to the joint US-ROK defense mission. As we have explained, we are relying more and more on our Korean employees in semi-skilled and skilled occupations. Many of these employees are engaged in work which is essential to the combat readiness of both the US and ROK armed forces. Therefore, we are making these important concessions with the understanding that the ROK Government will: (1) accept the balance of the US position on the Labor Article, and (2) in future the Joint Committee, when considering the role of the US Korean employees of the US armed forces under subparagraph 4 (b) will take into full consideration the facts incorporated by the US negotiators in the Joint Agreed Summary regarding the importance of USFK's Korean employees in the defense of their home land and their special status.

0223

Tabling U.S. Drafts of Articles on Duration and Ratification of Agreement

1. The US negotiators at this time would like to table the US drafts of the last two Articles of the US-ROK SOFA.

2. The Article on the Duration of the Agreement provides that this agreement shall remain in force while the Mutual Defense Treaty between the US and ROK remains in force, unless terminated earlier by agreement between the two Governments. This is standard language for such articles in US status of forces agreements.

3. In the Article on the Ratification of the Agreement, paragraph one provides that this agreement shall enter into force four months after the date of a written notification from the Government of the Republic of Korea that it has approved the agreement and has taken the legislative and budgetary action necessary to give effect to its provisions. In the period between the notification of ROK approval of the agreement and its entry into force, both Governments will have time to make preparations for orderly and effective implementation of the Agreement. ROK and US authorities can utilize this period to organize the Joint Committee and its Sub-Committees, and to take other measures to insure smooth implementation of the Agreement. The second paragraph of the US draft provides for termination of Taejon Agreement for US armed forces, subject to the paragraph in the Criminal Jurisdiction Article which provides that the Taejon Agreement to cover offenses which occur before entry into force of new agreement.

4. We believe the ROK negotiators, after study of these two drafts, will find them acceptable.

0224

<u>JOINT SUMMARY RECORD OF THE 80TH SESSION</u>

1. Time and Place: 2:00-4:40 P.M., May 28, 1965 at the
    Foreign Ministry's Conference Room
    (No.1)

2. Attendance:

    ROK Side:

    Mr. Chang, Sang Moon   Director
                               European and American Affairs
                               Bureau
                               Ministry of Foreign Affairs

    Mr. Huh, Suhg Joon   Director
                               Labor Administration Bureau
                               Office of Labor Affairs

    Mr. Hur, Hyong Koo   Chief
                               Prosecutors Section
                               Ministry of Justice

    Mr. Lee, Nam Ki   Chief
                               America Section
                               Ministry of Foreign Affairs

    Mr. Kim, Dong Hwi   Chief
                               Treaty Section
                               Ministry of Foreign Affairs

    Mr. Choo, Moon Ki   Chief
                               Legal Affairs Section
                               Ministry of Justice

    Col. Kim, Won Kil   Chief
                               Military Affairs Section
                               Ministry of National Defense

    Maj. Lee, Kye Hoon   Military Affairs Section
                               Ministry of National Defense

    Mr. Kim, Kee Joe   3rd Secretary
                               Ministry of Foreign Affairs

    Mr. Lee, Keun Pal   3rd Secretary
    (Interpreter)   Ministry of Foreign Affairs

    Mr. Hwang, Young Jae   3rd Secretary
                               Ministry of Foreign Affairs

    Mr. Park, Won Chul   3rd Secretary
                               Ministry of Foreign Affairs

    U.S. Side:

    Mr. Benjamin A. Fleck   First Secretary
                               American Embassy

0225

마 문 113-6

0226

Brig. Gen. Carroll H. Dunn	Deputy Chief of Staff 8th U.S. Army
Col. Allan G. Pixton	Deputy Chief of Staff 8th U.S. Army
Capt. George Hagerman	Assistant Chief of Staff USN/K
Col. Kenneth C. Crawford	Staff Judge Advocate 8th U.S. Army
Mr. Frank R. LaMacchia	First Secretary American Embassy
Mr. Robert A. Kinney	J-5 8th U.S. Army
Mr. Goodwin Shapiro	Second Secretary American Embassy
Maj. Alton H. Harvey	Staff Judge Advocate's Office 8th U.S. Army
Mr. David Y.C. Lee (Interpreter)	Second Secretary American Embassy
Mr. G.W. Flower (Observer)	8th U.S. Army

1. Mr. Fleck opened the 80th meeting by stating that the US negotiators would like to table and distribute at this time the full text of the US draft of the US-ROK Status of Forces Agreement, including the Preamble and 30 articles. Article numbers had been tentatively assigned for the mutual convenience of the two sides in the negotiations, but of course are subject to change as agreed. He noted that this full text includes the US draft of the Articles on the Duration and Ratification of the Agreement, the last two Articles which were being tabled for the first first time at this session.

2. Then Mr. Fleck stated that the leaders of the two Governments, at their recent conferences in Washington, had reached agreement in principle on the major outstanding issues of this Agreement. Therefore, the US negotiators proposed that consideration of the over-all agreement be expedited and that minor differences remaining in several

0227

미문1136

0228

articles be resolved soon. Thereby, it is hoped that the expectations of the President of the Republic of Korea, who was reported to have predicted on May 23rd at Cape Kennedy that the SOFA would be concluded in two or three weeks, will be fulfilled.

3. Mr. Fleck indicated that the US negotiators, in addition to tabling the final two articles, also was submitting modifications of the text of the US drafts of the Criminal Jurisdiction, Labor, and Claims Articles. The US drafts of these key articles had been substantially modified in recent weeks, in response to Korean desires, thereby enabling the leaders of the two Governments to reach agreement in principle on the major unresolved issues. Since the US negotiators had made the major concessions necessary to reach accord on the major unresolved issues, they hoped that the ROK negotiators would now respond in kind and accept the revised US draft of the agreement as a whole being tabled at this meeting.

Claims Article

4. Mr. Fleck pointed out that, at the 76th meeting, the US Government had made a major concession by accepting the Korean draft of the Claims Article subject to certain important modifications. At the 79th meeting, the Korean negotiators had proposed certain changes which would now be briefly discussed.

5. With reference to the proposed percentages of distribution contained in Paragraph 5(e)(i), Mr. Fleck said, the US negotiators can see no reason to vary the standard 25% - 75% distribution that has been accepted by almost all other countries. Regarding paragraph 5(e)(iii), the US side is unable to accept the Korean proposal, which would only require the parties to "seek mutual agreement." The United States regards the U.S. language requiring

0229

여운 113-b

0230

mutual agreement on liability, amount and proposed
distribution as essential. There is no necessity for
restating in an agreed minute that decisions of Korean
courts will be binding since this is already provided for
in paragraph 5(c). The United States recognizes that if a
claimant rejects the settlement and takes his case to
court, the decision of a competent tribunal of the
Republic of Korea would be binding. The proposed ROK
changes are unnecessary and unacceptable.

6. Regarding Paragraph 12, Mr. Fleck pointed out
that the Korean negotiators contended that KSC personnel
should be considered employees of the United States; also,
that the Republic of Korea does not assume responsibility
for claims generated by these individuals. The US position
has always been that KSC personnel are not considered US
employees and that the US does not assume responsibility
for claims caused by their actions. The status of KSC
personnel is now being negotiated in separate discussions.
Therefore, the US negotiators had deleted the last clause
of Paragraph 12. In view of the separate discussions which
are taking place, it is appropriate that there be an
understanding in the Joint Agreed Summary that:

"This article is not applicable to claims
generated by KSC personnel. The status of the KSC
members will be determined by other negotiations
between the United States and the Republic of Korea."
By this means, neither the United States nor the Korean
position is changed. The entire question is left for
future determination.

0231

마 ㄷ 113-6

0232

7. With reference to Paragraph 13, Mr. Fleck stated that the US negotiators accept the new second sentence proposed by the Korean negotiators. This sentence pertains to claims arising prior to the effective date of the SOFA and states: "Such claims shall be processed and settled by the authorities of the United States."

8. Regarding Paragraph A2 of the Agreed Minute, Mr. Fleck stated that the US negotiators have carefully considered the Korean proposal that ROK claims settlement authority be automatically extended throughout Korea twelve months after the effective date of the Agreement. The twelve-month period may be sufficiently long to adapt the system throughout Korea. However, this is not certain. Twelve months may not be long enough for the Korean Claims Service to make preparations to take over these functions. Mr. Fleck emphasized that the US draft provides the necessary flexibility to enable the transfer to take place in an efficient manner. The US negotiators do not see any reason to eliminate this flexibility by incorporating language providing for a specific time frame.

9. The United States negotiators, Mr. Fleck said, had made a major concession in accepting the Korean draft as the basis of negotiations and had made further concessions at this meeting. Mr. Fleck urged the Korean negotiators to consider carefully and to accept these US proposals.

10. Mr. Chang thanked Mr. Fleck for his clear explanation and for preparing the notebooks containing the full text of the US draft of the SOFA. Mr. Chang also stated he wanted to share the honor he recently had in Washington, D.C. He had been present when the leaders of the two

한·미국 간의 상호방위조약 제4조에 의한 시설과 구역 및 한국에서의 미국군대의 지위에 관한 협정(SOFA)
전59권. 1966.7.9 서울에서 서명 : 1967.2.9 발효(조약 232호) (V.30 실무교섭회의, 제77-80차, 1965.5월) 503

메모 113-b

0234

governments, in a spirit of cooperation and understanding, had reached agreement on two major problems in the Criminal Jurisdiction and Labor Articles. Mr. Chang expressed the hope that the SOFA negotiators in Seoul could proceed in this same cooperative spirit and complete the negotiations in a short time. He emphasized the need to concentrate the negotiations on major issues, and not to dwell on minor points. He urged both sides to tackle the problem in a spirit of mutual concession and pave the way for early conclusion of the Agreement. Mr. Chang indicated he felt progress was being made toward resolution of the problems in the Claims Article. The Korean negotiators would study the US statement and the new proposals and respond at the next negotiating session neat week.

11. Mr. Fleck thanked Mr. Chang for his comments on his recent trip to the United States, and for the part he had played in Washington in helping to reach agreement in principle on several important issues. He stated that the US negotiators fully share the feelings of the Korean negotiators that a SOFA must be concluded as soon as possible. It was specifically for the purpose of expediting conclusion of this Agreement that the US negotiators had tabled the full US draft at this meeting. He expressed the hope that the Agreement could be concluded speedily on the basis of the U.S. draft tabled at this meeting.

Criminal Jurisdiction Article

12. Mr. Fleck stated that the proposals of the Korean negotiators regarding waiver, pretrial custody and duty certificates, presented at the 77th negotiating session, and those regarding trial safeguards, presented at the 70th negotiating session, had been given careful consideration. The US side had attempted to be responsive to the

0235

미문 1136

0236

desires of the Korean negotiators to the maximum extent
possible. At the same time, this draft is believed to be
consistent with essential requirements of the United
States. Mr. Fleck said he would comment on the remaining
unresolved issues.

13. <u>Agreed Minute Re Paragraph 3(b)</u>:

With reference to the proposal of the Korean
negotiators to insert the words "at the request of the
United States" at the beginning of paragraph 1, the
US negotiators had stated at the time it was proposed that
this was unacceptable. The Korean negotiators are well
aware of the US position. This would completely change the
waiver formula as tabled by the US, and would be inconsistent
with the remaining paragraphs of the Agreed Minute. The
so-called German formula provides for a general waiver at
the time the agreement becomes effective. It does not
provide for individual requests for waiver in each case.
Mr. Fleck stated that the inclusion of the phrase cannot
be accepted and that the U.S. negotiators understand
that the Korean negotiators were prepared to withdraw
this proposal.

14. With reference to the Korean proposal for an
additional sentence to be inserted at the end of paragraph
4, the right of final determination by the Government of
the Republic of Korea is affirmatively established in the
US draft and the US negotiators see no reason for duplicating
this language, Mr. Fleck continued. The US negotiators
believe that the 21-day time limitation would be an unnecessary restriction. Although they expect that the
consultations referred to would normally be concluded
within this time, such might not always be the case.

0237 ⊢---→

마.문113

0238

However, even though they do not believe it necessary, they are prepared to generally accede to the desires of the Korean negotiators, by including an understanding in the Joint Agreed Summary. This understanding would read as follows:

"Recall of waiver shall be final and conclusive unless the statement for recall referred to in paragraph 3 of this minute is withdrawn by the Government of the Republic of Korea."

15. The next matter to be considered, Mr. Fleck noted, was Paragraph 6 of the Agreed Minute. This pertains to the place where trials for offenses committed against Korean interests take place. As had been pointed out in the 77th meeting, the previous U.S. agreement to hold these trials in the Republic of Korea, unless mutually agreed otherwise, was directly related to the waiver formula which the U.S. negotiators were proposing at that time. They had now offered the German waiver formula. Paragraph 6 is identical to Article 26 of the German Agreement. These two provisions were designed to operate together. In addition, as had been stated, cases of the types referred to in Paragraph 6 are extremely rare. The U.S. negotiators do not expect them to present any problem. However, even though rare, such cases may arise and trial elsewhere may be required. For these reasons, it is deemed necessary to retain paragraph 6.

16. Agreed Minute Re Paragraph 3(a): (Duty Certificates)

Mr. Fleck stated that the US negotiators accepted the modifications pertaining to duty certificates proposed by the ROK negotiators at the 77th negotiating session, with the following modifications:

0239

가 문 113-6

0240

a. They agreed to inclusion of an understanding in the Agreed Joint Summary stating:

"A certificate shall be issued only upon the advice of a Staff Judge Advocate, and the competent authority issuing the duty certificate shall be a General Grade Officer or his designee." The Korean negotiators are well aware, Mr. Fleck continued, that a general officer must, of necessity, delegate many of his functions to his senior subordinates. The US language requires that the responsibility remain at general officer level and only allows delegation of authority to act.

b. They accepted substitution of the word "shall" for the word "may" in the second paragraph of Agreed Minute Re Paragraph 3(a) "shall be made the subject of review." They also accepted the modification of the first understanding proposed by the Korean negotiators.

c. With regard to the US definition of "official duty," the Korean negotiators originally had proposed and the United States had already agreed to, inclusion of this as an understanding in the Joint Agreed Summary. The United States negotiators are still willing to include this definition in the Agreed Joint Summary. However they cannot accept the proposal of the Korean negotiators that it be included in the Agreed Minute, Mr. Fleck said.

17. <u>Paragraph 5: Pretrial Custody</u>

Mr. Fleck stated that the United States negotiators accepted all modifications proposed by the Korean negotiators at the 77th Session relating to pretrial custody. Therefore, the two sides had reached full agreement on paragraph 5.

0241

마은 113-6

0242

18. <u>Trial Safeguards</u>

With reference to the trial safeguards contained
in Paragraph 9 and its related Agreed Minutes, Mr. Fleck
emphasized that the Korean negotiators are well aware of
the importance which the US Government attaches to these
guarantees. The acceptance by the Korean negotiators at
the 70th Negotiating Session of the principle of enumerating
the trial safeguards had been a major step toward resolution
of the differences on this important matter. At that
session, the Korean negotiators proposed modification of
some of the listed safeguards. These proposals had been
given careful consideration in a maximum attempt to be
receptive to the Korean desires. At the same time, the
United States has certain essential needs that must be
fulfilled. The United States negotiators would like to
discuss each of the Korean proposals in detail.

a. <u>Agreed Minute Re Paragraph 9a</u>: Mr. Fleck said
the US negotiators agree that the original second sentence
of this Agreed Minute was related to the use of the word
"civil" in paragraph 1(b) of the text. They had carefully
studied the Korean negotiators' proposal to delete both of
these items and substitute an understanding in the Agreed
Joint Summary. The U.S. negotiators believed that agreement had been reached on the principle that US personnel
should not be subject to the jurisdiction of Korean military
tribunals. What the negotiators had been discussing was
where this principle should be stated. As indicated in
the tabled U.S. draft, the U.S. negotiators are willing
to delete the original second sentence of Agreed Minute
Re Paragraph 9(a) in return for acceptance by the Korean
negotiators of the word "civil" in paragraph 1(b).

0243

b. <u>Agreed Minute Re Paragraph 9(g)</u>: At the
70th Session, the Korean negotiators had expressed disagreement with that portion of the Agreed Minute rendering
inadmissible as evidence any statement taken from an accused
in the absence of a United States representative. The
Korean negotiators had contended that their proposed
language for the 3rd unnumbered paragraph of Agreed Minute
Re Paragraph 9, pertaining to the inadmissibility of statements obtained by illegal means, should render unnecessary
this portion of the Agreed Minute. The negotiators had previously discussed this provision in detail. The US
representative has an affirmative duty to be present at
these sessions. He will be available at all times and the
United States authorities will insure that he fulfills
this duty. The U.S. negotiators believe this provision
is absolutely necessary to insure that no confession is
obtained by coercion or other improper means. The United
States Government is firmly committed to the principle
embodied in this provision and we cannot agree to its
deletion.

c. <u>Agreed Minute re Paragraph 9, subparagraph (a)</u>
<u>of the Second Unnumbered Paragraph</u>: Mr. Fleck noted that
this provision guarantees the accused the right to
appeal a conviction. It is the understanding of the US
negotiators that the appellate procedure of the Korean
Courts allows the accused to request a review of the
evidence used in the trial court. It is also their
understanding that the appellate court may examine new
evidence or witnesses and make new findings of fact on
either its own motion or that of the accused. In order to
prevent any possible confusion, they therefore proposed the
insertion of the following understanding in the Agreed
Joint Summary:

0245

마 모 113-6

0246

"Under the appellate procedure of the Courts of
the Republic of Korea the accused may request a re-
examination of the evidende, including new evidence
and witnesses, as a basis for new findings of
fact by the appellate court."

They believe this is entirely consistent with Korean
appellate procedure.

     d. <u>Agreed Minute Re Paragraph 9, subparagraph (d)</u>
<u>of the Second Unumbered Paragraph and, the 4th Unnumbered</u>
<u>Paragraph</u>: Mr. Fleck recalled that the Korean negotiators
had proposed the deletion of the fourth paragraph and the
adoption of an alternative subparagraph (d). The U.S.
negotiators were aware of the fact that Article 361 of
the Code of Criminal Procedure allows appeals by the
prosecution based upon errors of law. They were also
aware that increasing a sentence on appeal is a part of
Korean law. At the 61st Session, they had pointed out
that this was contrary not only to American judicial
practice, but also to the fundamental understanding of
justice held by the US Government and US personnel. Like
the Korean negotiators, the U.S. negotiators must have an
agreement that is acceptable to our government and people.
An appeal by the prosecution, based upon mistake of fact or
the increase of a sentence on appeal, would be viewed by
the American people as a miscarriage of justice. The US
negotiators deem these limitations essential safeguards
which must be retained. They cannot, therefore, agree
to alteration of subparagraph (d) or the deletion of
unnumbered paragraph (4).

0247

한·미국 간의 상호방위조약 제4조에 의한 시설과 구역 및 한국에서의 미국군대의 지위에 관한 협정(SOFA)
전59권. 1966.7.9 서울에서 서명 : 1967.2.9 발효(조약 232호) (V.30 실무교섭회의, 제77-80차, 1965.5월) 517

e. <u>Agreed Minute Re Paragraph 9, Subparagraph (j)</u>
<u>of the Second Paragraph</u>: With regard to this provision
prohibiting trial of the accused if physically or mentally
unfit, Mr. Fleck said the U.S. negotiators believe their
position is adequately clear. The Korean negotiators seem
to fear that this will be subject to abuse by the accused
if the final determination as his fitness is not left to
the court. This provision gives firm right to postponement
of trial <u>if</u> the accused is physically or mentally unfit.
The Joint Committee is the proper place to develop mutually
satisfactory procedures for making this determination.
The right of postponement in event of mental or physical
unfitness is a substantive safeguard deemed absolutely
essential by the United States.

f. <u>Agreed Minute Re Paragraph 9, Third Unnumbered</u>
<u>Paragraph</u>: Mr. Fleck recalled that, at the 70th session
the Korean negotiators had proposed a revision of the
paragraph which would omit the term "real evidence".
The United States cannot agree to omission of the term
"real evidence" or of a guarantee that it will not be used
if obtained illegally. The use of evidence obtained by
unreasonable search and seizure or by illegal or improper
means is inadmissable under the US Constitution in all
courts of the United States. The United States cannot
consent to the use of evidence obtained by this manner
against any US citizen tried in a Korean Court under
this agreement. The United States negotiators believe that
the provision in our draft is quite suitable. In response
to the proposals of the Korean negotiators, however, they
were prepared to accept the Korean revision of this
paragraph subject to the modifications indicated in the
tabled draft. The United States negotiators wish it to be
clearly understood that this is an essential requirement

0249

마므113-6

0250

and that under no circumstances will the United States agree to the use of illegally obtained evidence.

19. Mr. Fleck recalled that, at various times in previous negotiating sessions, the Korean negotiators had expressed a desire that the word "military" be inserted before the word "authorities" when referring to US military officials throughout the US draft. He said the US side accepts this proposal and has inserted the word "military.es" throughout the draft of this article, as follows:

1(a); 2(a); 3(a); 4; 5(a); 5(b); 5(c); 6(a); 6(b); 7(a); 8; 11; and in the following Agreed Minutes: No.1 and No. 2 re paragraph 9(b); No.1 re paragraph 3(a); No. 1 and No. 3 re paragraph 6; re paragraph 9; and re paragraph 10(a) and 10(b).

20. In summary, Mr. Fleck noted that the United States had made major concessions throughout the Criminal Jurisdiction Article in an effort to hasten conclusion of this agreement. The U.S. negotiators asked the Korean negotiators to carefully consider these proposals. They awaited Korean acceptance of this draft of the Criminal Jurisdiction Article.

Labor Article

21. Mr. Fleck stated that the US negotiators were tabling a revised Labor Article, which incorporates compromise language in keeping with the recent agreement by the leaders of the two governments in Washington. In this new draft, paragraph 4 has been revised. The previous subparagraphs 4(a), 4(c), and 4(e), have been deleted, as suggested by the ROK authorities. A new subparagraph 4(a) (5) has been included, incorporating the concept of the Korean proposal made at the 79th negotiating session, and providing for a 70-day cooling-off after a labor dispute has been referred

0251

0252

to the Joint Committee. The new subparagraph 4(b)
incorporates the substance of the ROK draft of subparagraph
4(b). It gives the Joint Committee the responsibility for
determining those categories of essential employees who
shall not exercise the right of further collective action
in the event a labor dispute is not resolved by the
mediation procedures. A new subparagraph 4(c) incorporates
the language previously tabled by the Korean negotiators
in Paragraph 5. It provides that in a national emergency,
application of this article will be limited in accordance
with emergency measures taken by the Government of the
Republic of Korea. In connection with this new subparagraph,
it is the understanding of the U.S. negotiators that it was
proposed by the Korean negotiators in order to assist in
our joint defense effort in case of national emergency.
During such an emergency every resource must be utilized
to meet the crisis. Therefore, it is the understanding
of the US.negotiators that the limitation of the Labor
Article would be selective. In other words, those provisions
which might hamper US operations during such a national
emergency would be suspended. At the same time those
provisions which would further our joint defense efforts
and would be of assistance would remain in effect. The
substance of the previous subparagraph 4(b) of the US draft,
which is an essential provision, had been incorporated as
a new Agreed Minute No. 5 in this draft.

22. Mr. Fleck stated that this revised draft incorporates the Korean proposal to exclude the Korean Service
Corps from coverage of the Labor Article. The KSC personnel

0253

마.로 113-6

0254

are to be covered by a separate agreement. Therefore, the revised US draft on this subject merely affirms that they are not covered by the Article. The U.S. negotiators agree to delete Agreed Minute No.1, on the basis that a separate agreement for the KSC will be negotiated. This deletion of Agreed Minute No.1 is made with the understanding that, pending conclusion of a separate agreement, KSC personnel will continue to be made available by the ROK Government as at present. In other words, the 1960 US-Korean agreement will remain in effect until it is superceded by a new agreement, separate from the SOFA.

23. In tabling this revised US draft, Mr. Fleck continued, the US negotiators believe they have met the Korean requirements on the key point of difference in the two drafts. In making this concession, they would like to reiterate that the U.S. armed forces are here solely for the defense of Korea. Their Korean employees are vital to the joint US-ROK defense mission. As the U.S. negotiators had explained, the U.S. armed forces are relying more and more on their Korean employees in semi-skilled and skilled occupations. Many of these employees are engaged in work which is essential to the combat readiness of both the US and Korean armed forces. Therefore, the U.S. negotiators were making these important concessions with the understanding the Korean negotiators would accept the remainder of the US draft of the Labor Article, and that in future the Joint Committee, when considering the role of the Korean employees of the US armed forces under subparagraph 4(b), will take into full consideration the importance of the U.S. armed forces Korean employees in the defense of their homeland and the special status of these employees.

0255

0256

24. Mr. Chang thanked Mr. Fleck for his presentation and indicated that the Korean negotiators would respond at the next negotiating session. The Korean negotiators asked questions about the meaning of Para 4 (a) (5) of the Labor Article, especially whether the reference therein should not be to subparagraph (2) rather than to subparagraph (3). Mr. Fleck explained that reference of a dispute to the special committee, provided for in subparagraph (2), was not intended to be compulsory or automatic. Under the provisions of the US draft, if the Joint Committee decides to refer the dispute to the special committee and the special committee having failed to resolve the dispute, then returns the dispute to the Joint Committee, the 70-day period would begin when the special committee returns the dispute to the Joint Committee. However, if the Joint Committee should decide not to refer the dispute to a special committee, the 70-day peridd would begin from the date the dispute was referred to the Joint Committee by the Office of Labor Affairs. The Korean negotiators expressed the opinion that subparagraph (5) appeared to be faultily drafted, since it does not clearly provide for procedure explained by the US negotiators.

Articles on Duration and Ratification of Agreement.

25. Mr. Fleck tabled the U.S. drafts of articles on duration and ratification of the agreement. He explained that the article on the Duration of the Agreement provides that this agreement shall remain in force while the Mutual Defense Treaty between the US and the ROK remains in force, unless terminated earlier by agreement between the two Governments. This is standard language for such articles in US status-of-forces agreements.

0258

26. In the article on the Ratification of the Agreement,
Mr. Fleck explained that paragraph one provides that this
agreement shall enter into force four months after the date
of a written notification from the Government of the
Republic of Korea that it has approved the agreement and
has taken the legislative and budgetary action necessary
to give effect to its provisions. In specifying "legislative
and budgetary action", the U.S. Government also expects that
any other necessary implementing action will have been
taken by the ROK Government authorities. The US Government
would further expect to inform the ROK Government and be
informed by the ROK authorities on a continuing basis of
progress in the implementation (including exchange of texts
of implementing materials) so that consistent and coordinated
action by both sides would be assured. Mr. Fleck emphasized
that, in the period between the notification of ROKG approval
of the agreement and its entry into force, both Governments
will have time to make further preparations for orderly
and effective implementation of the Agreement. ROK and US
authorities can utilize this period to organize the Joint
Committee and its Sub-Committees, and to take other measures
to insure smooth implementation of the Agreement.

27. The second paragraph of the US draft provides
for termination of the Taejon Agreement for US armed forces,
subject to the paragraph in the Criminal Jurisdiction Article
which provides that the Taejon Agreement will cover offenses
which occur before entry into force of the SOFA.

28. Mr. Fleck expressed the belief that the ROK negotiators,
after study of these two drafts, would find them acceptable.
Mr. Fleck stated that, in addition to the five articles he
had discussed thus far in this meeting, there remained

0259

미ㆍ호113-ㅎ

0260

several other articles on which full agreement has not been formalized. Remaining differences in these articles are believed to be minor, and Mr. Fleck urged ROK acceptance of the US drafts of these articles, which previously had been fully explained. Having thus presented the over-all US position on remaining issues, Mr. Fleck concluded that the US negotiators looked forward confidently to early conclusion of the Agreement. Mr. Chang thanked Mr. Fleck for his comprehensive presentation of the US position and indicated the Korean negotiators would respond on all unresolved issues at the next meeting.

한·미국 간의 상호방위조약 제4조에 의한 시설과 구역 및 한국에서의 미국군대의 지위에 관한 협정(SOFA)
전59권. 1966.7.9 서울에서 서명 : 1967.2.9 발효(조약 232호) (V.30 실무교섭회의, 제77-80차, 1965.5월) 531

대령 113-6 (2너)

0262

외교문서 비밀해제: 주한미군지위협정(SOFA) 11
주한미군지위협정(SOFA) 서명 및 발효 11

초판인쇄 2024년 03월 15일
초판발행 2024년 03월 15일

지은이 한국학술정보(주)
펴낸이 채종준
펴낸곳 한국학술정보(주)
주 소 경기도 파주시 회동길 230(문발동)
전 화 031-908-3181(대표)
팩 스 031-908-3189
홈페이지 http://ebook.kstudy.com
E-mail 출판사업부 publish@kstudy.com
등 록 제일산-115호(2000. 6. 19)

ISBN   979-11-7217-022-6 94340
       979-11-7217-011-0 94340 (set)